Library of
Davidson College

Protection,
Growth and Trade

Protection, Growth and Trade
Essays in International Economics

W. MAX CORDEN

Basil Blackwell

© W. Max Corden, 1985

First published 1985

Basil Blackwell Ltd
108 Cowley Road, Oxford OX4 1JF, UK

Basil Blackwell Inc.
432 Park Avenue South, Suite 1505,
New York, NY 10016, USA

All rights reserved. Except for the quotation of short passages for the purposes of criticism and review, no part of this publication may be reproduced, stored in a retrieval system, or transmitted, in any form or by any means, electronic, mechanical, photocopying, recording or otherwise, without the prior permission of the publisher.

Except in the United States of America, this book is sold subject to the condition that it shall not, by way of trade or otherwise, be lent, re-sold, hired out, or otherwise circulated without the publisher's prior consent in any form of binding or cover other than that in which it is published and without a similar condition including this condition being imposed on the subsequent purchaser.

British Library Cataloguing in Publication Data

Corden, W. M.
   Protection, growth and trade : essays in
   international economics.
   1. Commerce
   I. Title
   382'.01   HF1008

ISBN 0–631–14529–X

Library of Congress Cataloging in Publication Data

Corden, W. M. (Warner Max)
   Protection, growth, and trade.

   Bibliography: p.
   Includes index.
   1. Commercial policy–Addresses, essays, lectures.
2. Free trade and protection–Protection–Addresses, essays, lectures. I. Title.
HF1411.C5956   1985   382'.3   85-6194
ISBN 0-631-14529-X

Typeset in Great Britain by
Photo·graphics, Honiton, Devon, England.
Printed in Great Britain by
TJ Press, Padstow

Contents

Preface		vii
Introduction		ix
PART I	NORMATIVE THEORY OF PROTECTION	1
1	The Calculation of the Cost of Protection	3
	Further Notes: The Cost of Protection Revisited	19
2	Tariffs, Subsidies and the Terms of Trade	29
	Further Notes: Tariffs versus Subsidies	37
3	Monopoly, Tariffs and Subsidies	46
	Further Notes: Monopoly and Economies of Scale	54
4	Economies of Scale and Customs Union Theory	58
5	A Tariff that Worsens the Terms of Trade (*with Fred H. Gruen*)	69
6	Urban Unemployment, Intersectoral Capital Mobility and Development Policy (*with Ronald F. Findlay*)	73
PART II	EFFECTIVE PROTECTION	95
7	The Structure of a Tariff System and the Effective Protective Rate	97
8	Effective Protective Rates in the General Equilibrium Model: A Geometric Note	118
9	The Substitution Problem in the Theory of Effective Protection	125
10	Effective Protection Revisited	141
PART III	MULTINATIONALS AND TRADE THEORY	155
11	International Trade Theory and the Multinational Enterprise	157
12	The Enclave Approach	178

PART IV GROWTH AND TRADE   185

13 Economic Expansion and International Trade: A Geometric Approach   187
    Further Notes: The Effects of Growth on Trade   192
14 The Effects of Trade on the Rate of Growth   198
    Further Notes: The Effects of Trade on the Rate of Growth   220
15 Booming Sector and De-Industrialization in a Small Open Economy   225
    (*with J. Peter Neary*)
16 Booming Sector and Dutch Disease Economics: Survey and Consolidation   246

PART V PROTECTION, THE EXCHANGE RATE AND MACROECONOMIC POLICY   269

17 Exchange Rate Protection   271
18 Relationships between Macroeconomic and Industrial Policies   288
19 Protection and the Real Exchange Rate   302
20 Real Wage Rigidity, Devaluation and Import Restrictions   311

Author Index   327

Subject Index   330

Preface

In this book I have collected together, a number of my papers in the trade theory field written over a period of twenty-eight years. To five of the essays I have added quite substantial 'Further Notes' which contain some of my subsequent thoughts and which deal with the relevant literature that followed the original articles. In addition I have written three new essays (essays 10, 19 and 20) especially for this book. I have abbreviated several of the papers to exclude material that seemed relatively less important, and have done some editing in practically all cases.

Readers familiar with my work will not be surprised to find that many of the essays deal with the theory of protection in one way or another; but there are also four essays on growth and trade, and four that are concerned with protection and macroeconomic considerations. Essays 11 and 16 are to a considerable extent surveys, but also aim to make some original contributions. I have not included four substantial surveys of aspects of trade theory and related fields published in 1965, 1975 and 1984, nor some papers that were subsequently incorporated in *Trade Policy and Economic Welfare*.[1]

Is there a unifying theme? Obviously this book does not have a unity in the way in which my two earlier books in the area, *The Theory of Protection* and *Trade Policy and Economic Welfare*, have. I have worked on matters that seemed important at the time and sought to clarify the issues or fill gaps in the established literature. The unity is mostly in the

---

1. The four surveys are *Recent Developments in the Theory of International Trade*, Special Papers in International Economics No. 7, International Finance Section, Princeton University, 1965; 'The Costs and Consequences of Protection; A Survey of Empirical Work' in Peter Kenen (ed.), *International Trade and Finance: Frontiers for Research*, Cambridge University Press, 1975; 'The Normative Theory of International Trade', in R. W. Jones and P. B. Kenen (eds.), *Handbook of International Economics: Volume 1*, Amsterdam: North-Holland, 1984; and 'Harry Johnson's Contributions to International Trade Theory', *Journal of Political Economy*, 92, August 1984.

method – the use of simple verbal exposition combined with numerous diagrams, preferably simple ones. Occasionally I have departed from simplicity – notably in essays 9 and 14 – but here I would claim that others who have written on those subjects have been more complicated. Mostly, the virtues and the faults of these essays follow from the aim of isolating a few factors, concentrating on them, and getting the *main* message across. There are clearly dangers in over-simplification and in a failure to specify models fully mathematically. These are particular dangers in my work, and I can only post up a *caveat emptor* notice here.

My first indebtedness is to James Meade, who was my supervisor at the London School of Economics, and whose ideas and writings influenced the three papers (essays 1, 2 and 13) written while I was a graduate student. Harry Johnson provided moral support over a long period and greatly influenced essay 7, as well as, less directly, many of the other essays. John Black read several of the articles before they were published, including the new essays 19 and 20, and had a particular influence on essay 14. I have always been fortunate in having many good friends who have been willing to read articles in draft and save me from bad errors or lack of clarity, and they are listed in footnotes at the beginning of each essay. I am grateful to my co-authors of Essays 5, 6 and 15, Fred Gruen, Ronald Findlay and Peter Neary, both for the pleasures of collaboration and for permission to republish our joint creations. I am grateful to Carol Kavanagh for helping me with the collating and editing of this volume, and especially making up systematic bibliographies. Finally, my greatest debt is owed to my wife, Dorothy, who has encouraged me and protected me from non-optimal disturbances over the whole period during which these essays were originally published, right up to now when they have their rebirth.

Acknowledgements

The publisher and author wish to acknowledge permission to reprint from the various holders of copyright, namely Economic Society of Australia (essay 1), the London School of Economics and Political Science (essays 2, 3 and 6), The University of Chicago (essays 4 and 7), North-Holland Publishing Company (essays 5, 9 and 14), Oxford University Press (essays 8, 13 and 16), Cambridge University Press (section III of essay 10), George Allen and Unwin (essays 11 and 12), the Royal Economic Society (essay 15), Ballinger Publishing Company (essay 17), and the Trade Policy Research Centre (essay 18).

Introduction

Part I: Normative Theory of Protection

The measurement of the welfare costs or benefits of protection is the subject of essay 1. This is a fundamental topic in trade theory and this essay treats it in a simple way, first in partial equilibrium and then in general equilibrium, distinguishing the production cost and the consumption cost of protection. The implication is either that a non-optimal protection policy is being followed for unspecified reasons, or that the costs calculated are elements in a benefit-cost calculation, to be set off against various benefits, such as long-term gains, a desirable sectoral income redistribution, and so on. The lengthy Further Notes that follow extend the analysis to allow (in the partial equilibrium model) for distortions elsewhere in the economy and (in the general equilibrium model) for generalization to a multi-good model, in the latter case seeking to explain ideas that originated in a well-known 1960 article by Harry Johnson.

Essay 2 also deals with a fundamental topic, namely the choice between a tariff and a subsidy to achieve a given protection objective. It is assumed that the aim is to maximize national welfare in the Pareto-efficiency sense and, very important, that the financing of a subsidy does not lead to any distortions. This assumption is still frequently made in the 'subsidy-biased' theory of domestic distortions that is so popular. The Further Notes remove this assumption. Essay 2 also presents an apparent paradox: an increase in protection may require a reduction in the tariff when terms of trade effects are taken into account, and the Further Notes show this to be an example of a two-instruments two-targets problem. This essay was one of the early papers in the 'domestic distortions' literature, but ignored the collection costs of various taxes as well as subsidy disbursement costs, both of which may, in some countries, strengthen the relative case for tariffs – given that there is to be any intervention at all.

Essay 3 is more specialized and, until recently, was out of the mainstream. It also compares a subsidy with a tariff, but this time there is a domestic firm (industry) which has a potential monopoly position and is subject to economies of scale. The distinction is made between the marginal and the structural optimum; a tariff is shown never to lead to an (Pareto-efficiency) improvement, while a subsidy may do so. Perhaps the principal limitation of this paper is that it ignores income distribution effects – only then can one suggest that a monopoly be subsidized! But the paper may be of interest because of the recent revival of interest in economies of scale and monopoly in the open economy; it foreshadows some ideas now being developed in general equilibrium models.

Essay 4 is a contribution to the theory of customs unions. Building on essay 3, it introduces economies of scale into customs union theory, something which had not been done systematically before. While essays 2 and 3 are concerned with policy optimization subject to constraints of some kind or other, essay 4, like essay 1, analyses the effects of given non-optimal policies, comparing the non-optimal customs union situation with the non-optimal (with tariff) pre-union situation. Its contribution is to introduce two new effects of the formation of a customs union, namely the cost reduction effect and the trade suppression effect, these having to be added to the usual trade creation and trade diversion effects.

Essay 5 is a short piece written with Fed Gruen which is primarily positive economics. The example it produces of a tariff that causes the output of a non-protected industry to expand, and so (possibly) the terms of trade to worsen, shows what one can achieve with a three-sector model, and how simple presumptions have to be modified when more than two sectors are allowed for. This turns out to be relevant for the issues discussed in essay 10.

Finally, essay 6 analyses the Harris–Todaro model, first with the assumption that the only factor that is mobile between the two industries is labour (the specific factors model), and then, that both labour and capital are mobile. This essay, written with Ronald Findlay, sits a little uneasily in this part of the book, since most of it is positive economics, and much of it has nothing very much to do with trade. But it uses the techniques of trade theory, and the last part of the essay compares various possible policies, such as subsidizing one sector or another, or imposing a tariff. Thus it takes up themes of earlier essays. Again, it has to be remembered that the distortionary effects of taxes that finance the subsidies, as well as collection costs, must be taken into account, matters discussed more fully in *Trade Policy and Economic Welfare*.

Part II: Effective Protection

Essays 7, 8 and 9 represent my principal contributions to the positive theory of effective protection (apart from a number of matters developed in *The Theory of Protection*, mostly in connection with non-tradables and the real exchange rate). Essay 7 has been my most widely read article and generated a large literature. These three essays cover the essentials of the positive theory, as I see it, and I thought it might be convenient to have them compactly available, even though they were all incorporated in *The Theory of Protection*.

A lengthy new essay 10, entitled 'Effective protection revisited', reviews two of the principal issues first raised in essay 7 – namely the conclusions that can be drawn from a scale of effective rates, and the 'substitution problem'. It argues that a 1975 article by Jones provides a rigorous basis for some crucial passages that appeared in essay 7 concerning the first of the two issues.

Part III: Multinationals and Trade Theory

Essay 11 is concerned with a topic that is very fashionable though not, on the whole, among people who are comfortable with the technicalities of trade theory. In fact, I wrote it to build a bridge between two 'worlds'. The essay is concerned with (what are now called) the transnationals. It aims to show that trade theory is very useful for analysing the positive and normative implications of multinationals. It contains a good deal of surveying of trade theory, but its principal feature is a systematic analysis of the elements that go into the location decisions of multinationals using some of the results of trade theory.

Essay 12 expounds the 'enclave approach' to analysing the normative effects of a multinational on a host country. It is an expanded version of a short discussion, originally incorporated in essay 11, which I have extracted in order to bring attention to it. It is quite simple, but it seems to me that it provides a useful framework for analysing issues that are very frequently discussed, but not necessarily in rigorous terms.

Part IV: Growth and Trade

Essay 13 presents a comparative static taxonomy of the effects of an economic expansion, whether through factor accumulation or technical progress, on the terms and volume of trade. It makes one particular point, namely that expansion of one factor only, when the import-competing industry is intensive in that factor, leads to an 'ultra-biased' expansion which will improve the terms of trade. This goes against earlier intuition, which had suggested that an economic expansion would tend to worsen a country's terms of trade. This short essay, and the theories underlying it, including the Rybczynski theorem, are extensions of Heckscher–Ohlin analysis.

The Further Notes summarize some of the subsequent work in this field and supplement the exposition. This body of theory, primarily associated with Hicks and Johnson, provides a neat framework for analysing many issues, for example, the effects of differential and biased growth in a 'two-country' world on the terms of trade, the two countries possibly representing exporters of manufactures on the one hand and exporters of primary products on the other.

Essay 14 is considerably more complicated. It uses a two-stage production structure to show how the opening-up of trade may affect the rate of growth of a small economy. It is designed to bring out clearly four distinct effects. It leaves out of account many other ways in which trade may affect growth (some of which are discussed in *Trade Policy and Economic Welfare*, chapters 9 to 12), and concerns itself only with those related to capital accumulation. The essay draws on standard neo-classical growth theory, and so goes well beyond comparative statics. The Further Notes discuss the implications of removing three simplifying assumptions. The analysis is wholly positive, and it is stressed that policies that may raise the rate of growth (such as opening or closing trade, or changing the degree of protection) are not necessarily beneficial.

Essay 15, written with Peter Neary, analyses the sectoral output and income distribution effects of a boom in one tradable sector of an economy. It was written to clarify the 'deindustrialization' and 'Dutch disease' discussions that took place in Britain and elsewhere as the result of the expansion of an oil sector.

Essentially, essay 15 is a development of the body of literature to which essay 13 contributed. In essay 13 there are just two sectors, while in essay 15 there are three – two tradable sectors, one booming and the other 'lagging', and a non-tradable sector. Much emphasis is put on the change in the real exchange rate, which is the relative price of non-tradables to tradables. By contrast with essay 13, the concern is not with effects on the volume and terms of trade but rather with the pattern of output and with factoral income distribution. But essay 15 follows directly from the type of analysis represented by essay 13. It is comparative static, and the exogenous change is sector-biased growth (possibly through a change in the world price rather than a production function shift), which was one case analysed in that earlier literature.

There has been a boom in 'booming sector' and 'Dutch disease' economics, and the lengthy essay 16, first published in 1984, surveys the resultant literature, as well as carrying the analysis of essay 15 forward by introducing endogenous migration, endogenous terms of trade effects, and various dynamic and other considerations. It also contains a discussion of protectionist proposals that result from sectoral booms. Thus this essay is wide-ranging. An appendix considers the specific case of Britain: did the oil price rise and the development of North Sea oil give rise to a Dutch disease problem in Britain?

Part V: Protection, the Exchange Rate and Macroeconomic Policy

The essays in this part deal with the region where the theory of protection and macroeconomics overlap. The first two essays were published in 1980

Introduction

and 1981 respectively, while I have written the last two especially for this volume. Most of the earlier essays in this volume (with the principal exception of essay 16) assumed current account balance, as is characteristic of much of trade theory. In these four essays the current account becomes a variable, possibly endogenous. Much emphasis is also put on the real exchange rate (which has already made its appearances in essays 7 and 15), and on the effects of various policies on real wages, the special assumption of real wage rigidity being central to essay 20.

Essay 17 introduces the concept of exchange rate protection, and can be regarded as an extension of the theory of protection, one which had not found a place in earlier literature, including my own books. There is some overlap between this essay and essays 15 and 16, since it analyses some policy proposals that have been made in countries presumed to be suffering from Dutch disease problems. Essay 15 was positive economics, and parts of essay 17 are a normative supplement. It has to be emphasized that exchange rate protection refers to the *real* exchange rate – policies that alter the nominal exchange rate possibly affecting the real rate in the same direction – and it refers to protection of the whole tradable sector (both exportables and importables) relative to non-tradables.

Essay 18 is an overview chapter showing the relationships between macroeconomic and industrial policies. This is a topic which was very popular during the world recession that began in 1980, due to the revival of protectionist attitudes caused to some extent by the recession as well as by changing patterns of world trade. In some countries this revival of protectionism was in the guise of 'industrial policy'.

The essay points out that two arms of a government can be at cross-purposes. Much stress is put on the effects of both kinds of policies – i.e. macroeconomic policy and industrial policy – on employment and on real wages. Exchange rate policy and trade protection are just parts of the whole story, and there is a close link between essay 17 and this essay.

Essay 19 sorts out systematically the relationship between the real exchange rate and ordinary protection. It picks up themes from essays 7, 17 and 18 and from *The Theory of Protection*.

Finally, essay 20 was inspired by the advocacy of wide-ranging protection by a group of Cambridge (UK) economists in 1975 and later. I had contributed to several papers on this subject, and many other 'orthodox' economists have analysed and refuted the somewhat unclear arguments coming out of a great centre of learning. But at the heart of the Cambridge argument were some good insights, in particular the assumption of real wage rigidity – which is more reasonable as a first approximation than the usual assumption of real wage flexibility (and which was central to the Brigden committee's model referred to in essay 1).

In this essay, on which I worked on and off for several years, I have analysed in detail the Cambridge argument and various modified versions of it, making ample use of diagrams. Because of the real wage rigidity assumption, the analysis may have an interest which should outlive the influence of the Cambridge Economic Policy Group. It might also be noted that in an earlier version I assumed a Heckscher–Ohlin production structure (with two factors mobile between exportables and importables), but this part of the analysis has now been banished to an appendix. In this essay, as in so many others, I have found the specific factors model the most appropriate.

Part I
Normative Theory of Protection

1
The Calculation of the Cost of Protection*

1 The Brigden Report and the Measurement of Excess Cost

The report on the Australian tariff produced in 1929 by a committee of economists headed by Professor Brigden[1] made two original contributions to economic thought and method. First, it developed a peculiarly Australian case for protection based on a distribution of income argument. Secondly, it attempted a thorough and detailed measurement of the 'excess cost' of protection. It is this second aspect of the report which will be discussed in this essay.

The committee's calculations were exceedingly complex and involved many bold approximations. But the object here is not to consider the practical statistical techniques or the reasonableness of the various approximations but rather the fundamental principles of the whole exercise.

To the Brigden committee the 'excess cost' of the tariff was the excess of the market value of the protected output over the cost of equivalent imports.[2] Protected output was that output which would cease if the tariff were removed, while the exchange rate, wages in real terms and other factor prices in money terms remained constant.

Two questions must then be answered. First, given that the volume of protected output is known, can the difference between the market value of protected output and the cost of equivalent imports be regarded as the excess cost of protection, and if it cannot, is it likely to overstate or to understate the true 'excess cost'? Secondly, how should the volume of protected output – the output which would not survive under free trade –

---

* *The Economic Record*, 33 (64), May 1957, 29–51. Substantially abbreviated: a lengthy discussion of some special features of the Brigden report has been excluded, as have also the analyses of the Gifford and Reddaway models. I am indebted to Professor J. E. Meade, Professor H. G. Johnson, Mrs. M. F. W. Hemming, Mr. R. G. Lipsey, Mr. A. Maizels and Mr. T. M. Rybczynski.
1. Brigden et al. (1929).
2. This method of determining the excess cost is also recommended in United Nations (1955, p. 67).

be determined, and is the Brigden committee's method likely to yield an overstatement or an understatement of it?

After pointing out some of the assumptions of the Brigden report, in the remainder of this essay a slightly different – but more useful – model will be employed to examine the Brigden method critically and to resolve the problem of how the 'excess cost' could be assessed in any future investigation. The Brigden report is unique as a full-scale statistical study of the effects of tariffs. Other investigators have tried only to measure the height of tariff levels.[3] Hence the theorists of international trade have rarely applied themselves to this particular problem, although it can in fact be handled with the usual techniques of international trade theory.[4]

In the 1930s the Brigden committee's methods gave rise to considerable discussion. The argument of the present paper is indebted to the valuable reviews by Viner (1929) and Loveday (1930), and to later articles by Gifford (1934) and Reddaway (1937). But Viner and Loveday, while highly critical of the committee's methods, did not attempt to define the extent or direction of the error to which these methods might give rise and the formal models constructed by Gifford and Reddaway did not pose precisely the same problem as that dealt with in this paper.

Turning to the special features of the Brigden method, one was the assumption that real wages would be the same under free trade as under protection, and that a move to free trade would reduce employment. The choice of the first assumption can be explained by the wage indexation that was prevalent in Australia at the time, while the second implied (without proof) that the abolition of the tariff would lower the marginal product of a given supply of labour. The necessary formal proof was supplied subsequently in a celebrated article by Stolper and Samuelson (1941), which proved that, subject to certain simplified conditions which might apply to Australia – notably that the import-competing industries are labour intensive and the export industries land intensive – a tariff would raise the marginal product and hence the real wage of fully-employed labour. The Brigden report also assumed a zero elasticity of substitution between goods, so that the rise in the relative home market prices of protected goods caused by the tariff would not have a significant effect on the pattern

---

3. See League of Nations (1927), Loveday (1929), Liepmann (1938), Crawford (1934). A recent index of the height of the Australian tariff has been constructed by Carmody (1952).
4. There is a discussion of the problem in Viner (1951, ch. 11). He defines as the burden of long-run protection what will be described here as the production cost. He also makes allowance for the distribution of income and terms of trade effects. He does not seem to regard this burden as directly measurable.

 On the basis of the detailed calculations of Blagburn (1950) it would be possible to work out the production cost of protecting British agriculture. His method is similar to the type of calculation to be suggested in this essay. A note by Robinson and Marris (1950) draws attention to Blagburn's neglect of the terms of trade effect.

of consumption. In this way the consumption or demand effect of the tariff was neglected, a neglect which was criticized by Viner and Loveday. Finally, it assumed that not only would the removal of the tariff create unemployment and a balance of payments deficit, but no further measures to restore employment and external balance would be taken. The implication was that those wage-earners who would be unemployed under free trade would not have migrated to Australia in the first place.

II Assumptions of an Alternative Model; Production, Consumption and Terms of Trade Effects

Some of the assumptions of the Brigden report can be considered neither realistic nor particularly convenient for analysis. Therefore an alternative model will now be constructed to provide a basis for determining what the excess cost consists of, in what direction the cost as calculated by the Brigden committee diverges from it, and how, finally, it ought to be calculated.

Assume then that real wages do not necessarily remain constant, but rather that they are adjusted so as to ensure full employment. Thus, if the tariff is removed, either money wages and other money factor prices fall until full employment and balance of payments equilibrium are again restored, or the exchange rate depreciates while money factor prices remain constant. Assume that in the calculation of the cost the effects of the tariff on the internal distribution of income can be disregarded. Thus the concern is only with the average real income of the population as a whole, a population which is given. Assume also that the elasticity of substitution between goods is not zero, so that changes in relative prices do affect the demand pattern. Finally, we assume that the customs revenue is replaced by direct taxes.[5]

These assumptions distinguish the model which follows from the model of the Brigden report. In addition, it will be assumed, in common with the Brigden committee, that in the calculation of the cost the effects of the tariff on the welfare of future generations, as well as its innumerable non-economic effects, can be disregarded.

A first need is to be quite clear not only what at every point one is assuming, but also what one is trying to measure. Broadly the object must be to compare the welfare derived from a situation of completely free trade with that derived from the existing protective situation. The excess cost of

---

5. If full employment and balance of payments equilibrium are maintained, and provided there is no change in private savings and investment, the government surplus or deficit needs to remain constant. Therefore a decrease in customs revenue would have to be exactly balanced by an increase in other revenue or by a decrease in government expenditure.

protection is the extent to which welfare under free trade exceeds welfare under protection.[6]

However, this excess cost will be very different according to which of the innumerable effects of a tariff one takes into account. If, for example, the calculation disregards twenty effects and measures only the net excess cost due to the remaining three, then in policy considerations the excess cost so calculated must be weighed against the net benefit or loss due to the neglected twenty effects. In our model, for example, no account will be taken of any benefits which future generations might derive from the encouragement of infant industries or from the diversification of the economy to provide against future declines in export prices. Yet the purpose of the tariff may be primarily as an investment and an insurance, and the present cost as calculated on the basis of the model must then be weighed against these future expected benefits.

Similarly, our model will disregard any effects of the tariff on the internal distribution of income.[7] Yet to achieve an internal redistribution may be one of the primary objects of the tariff, an object which could of course be achieved by other methods. The cost of the tariff as calculated – which is then the cost of achieving redistribution by tariff – should in this case be weighed against the costs of alternative methods of redistributing incomes.

In the same way the tariff may be designed primarily to maintain full employment and balance of payments equilibrium – something which *could* always be attained by internal financial policy combined with exchange rate adjustments. These alternatives have their own costs – such as the cost arising from speculative capital movements encouraged by exchange rate variations – and if they are neglected in the calculation they should be weighed against the cost. Alternatively it may of course be assumed, on the lines of the Brigden report, that the unemployment and balance of payments deficit following upon a removal of the tariff are allowed to persist. In this case the cost of the tariff would have to be weighed against the cost of unemployment and of running into external debt.

---

6. An alternative formulation of the problem is to measure not the cost of the tariff but the cost of the excess tariff. Welfare may be maximized not under free trade but under some positive or optimal tariff level. If the tariff exceeds this level the cost of the excess tariff will be greater than the cost of the tariff as a whole. Indeed, welfare under protection could be greater than under free trade and yet the tariff may be above the optimum so that there is an 'excess cost'. When this criterion is used the central problem clearly is to reconstruct not the free trade but the optimal situation.
7. Either of two assumptions can eliminate the distribution of income effect. One can assume that everyone in the community holds the same share in each of the factors of production. Thus every wage-earner would also be a part-time farmer as well as a company shareholder! Alternatively, one can assume that a compensation mechanism automatically offsets any redistributive effects of a tariff. When internal relative prices change due to protection, as they will when protection is achieved by tariff, it must also be assumed that, at the margin, everybody has the same preferences. These assumptions still permit a change in the ratios of real factor prices.

It follows that the cost of protection, if calculated subject to our assumptions, should be regarded as providing only part of the picture. Against it should be balanced the costs of alternative ways of achieving a redistribution of income, a balance of payments equilibrium, the encouragement of infant industries, and so on.

The aim of this discussion of the assumptions is to isolate three principal effects of a protective tariff. First, the tariff affects the allocation of resources within Australia. Resources have shifted out of export and other industries into the protected industries. This is the essence of the protective effect. Secondly, the tariff affects the patterns of consumption by raising the relative prices to consumers of imported and import-competing products. Thirdly, the tariff affects the terms of trade. These three effects will be described as the production, the consumption and the terms of trade effects. These are the only effects which will be taken into account in the following analysis.

The terms of trade effect can be divided into its two components, the effect on export prices and the effect on import prices. In the case of Australia and similar countries it is the effect on export prices which is by far the most important, and it may be reasonable, at least as a first approximation, to neglect the effect on import prices. It will therefore be assumed here that Australia cannot affect the prices of her imports and that the whole of the terms effect operates through export prices. This assumption does not affect the main lines of the argument though it simplifies the exposition.

The procedure will be as follows. The following section is devoted to considering the cost of protecting a small individual industry, an industry so small and so unimportant, both to the economy as a whole and to other industries, that any indirect effects of its protection on employment, the balance of payments, the demand for other products or the costs of other industries can be neglected. Thereafter it will be converted into a large and significant industry or group of industries; hence these indirect effects must then be introduced. It will also be shown how the volume of output which would not survive under free trade, and which is therefore truly protected, turns out to be overstated when the indirect effects are not taken into account. From page 12, the volume of protected output will be taken as given and it will be shown how the indirect repercussions affect the calculation of the excess cost of any given protected output. In fact the first section will use a partial equilibrium model and the final section a general equilibrium one.

III Partial Equilibrium Model; Producers' and Consumers' Surpluses

We begin then with a partial equilibrium model making assumptions appropriate to such models. It enables some useful conclusions to be

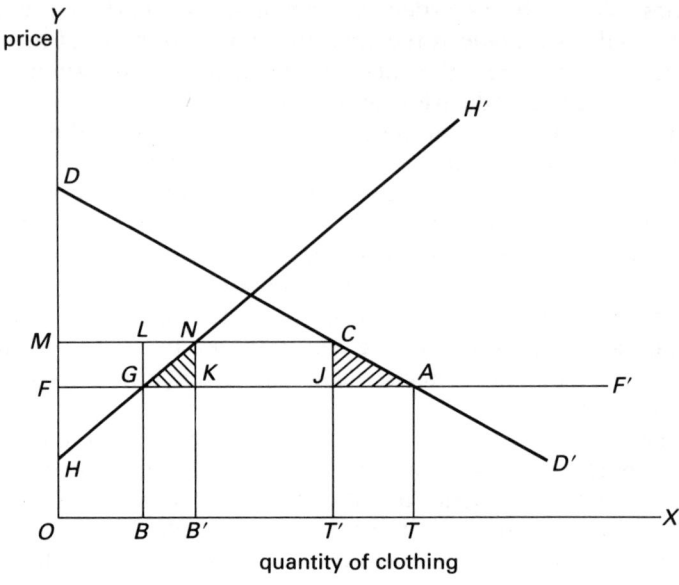

Figure 1.1

reached with the old-fashioned concepts of producers' and consumers' surpluses.

In figure 1.1, along the X axis is measured the quantity of the particular protected product, say clothing, and along the Y axis, costs and prices. DD' is the home demand curve for the product and HH' the home supply curve. These curves assume that everything else in the economy – notably factor prices, prices of other goods, and money incomes – are constant. FF' is the foreign supply curve, on the assumption that Australia cannot influence world prices of clothing. Since the demand for exports will not enter this partial equilibrium picture, this assumption means that there is no terms of trade effect in the model.

In the absence of protection the price will be OF and total home consumption OT, of which OB is home produced and BT imported. If a tariff FM/OF is imposed, home production rises to OB', home consumption falls to OT' and imports fall to $B'T'$.

Now the stage is set for some geometrical juggling. The rise in the home price due to the tariff has caused a loss in consumers' surplus of $MCAF$. This represents a loss incurred by the consumers of clothing.[8] Part of this

---

8. The consumers' surplus obtained from a purchase of OT of clothing at a price OF is the whole area under the demand curve up to A, i.e. $DATO$, minus the cost $OFAT$. It is thus DAF. Similarly the consumers' surplus obtained from a purchse of OT' at a

loss goes in customs revenue *NCJK* and can therefore be subtracted from the community loss. Another part is producers' surplus *FMNG* and represents a redistribution of income from consumers to producers of clothing.[9] This leaves the two triangles *NKG* and *CJA*. Now the total cost of producing the extra output *BB'* is *BB'NG*. If the same quantity had been imported it would have cost only *BB'KG*. The difference *NKG* is what we shall call the production cost – the cost of choosing to produce the protected output at home rather than importing it. The remaining triangle *CJA* represents the consumption cost – the cost due to distorting the consumption pattern by unduly raising the price of clothing to consumers. It follows then that in this sort of model, the cost of protection has two parts – *NKG* and *CJA*. If the elasticity of demand for clothing were zero the rise in the price would not affect the quantity consumed and there would be no consumption cost.

The Brigden committee regarded as the excess cost of protection the difference between the home market value of the protected output and the cost of equivalent imports. In the diagram the amount of protected output is *BB'*. If the Brigden method is then applied to this output the cost of protection turns out to be the area *LNKG*. It can be seen that it overstates the production cost by *GLN*, and how it compares with the total cost depends on whether *GLN* is greater or less than *CJA*.

It will have been noted that a rising supply curve has been assumed in the diagram. It is only because of this assumption that the Brigden cost is found to be greater than the actual production cost. It may be far more

---

price *OM* is *DCM*. The difference between the two consumers' surpluses, and hence the direct loss to the consumers from the rise in price due to the tariff, is *MCAF*. The main assumption involved in this concept is that the marginal utility of money is constant. Thus it assumes that the amount which consumers spend on clothing does not significantly affect their real income. The general argument is that the area under the demand curve indicates what consumers are willing to pay for the product, and hence what satisfaction they derive from it, while the price multiplied by the quantity indicates what they actually have to pay.

The limitations of this approach must be stressed. First, it requires the demand curve to be defined as a 'constant utility' curve. Secondly, it neglects all cross effects on other goods. Not only must it be assumed that the particular product does not enter significantly into the costs of other products, but, as Professor H. G. Johnson pointed out to me, all cross effects through demand must be neglected. Thus the demand for other goods may rise or fall as a result of the tariff and this can modify or increase the loss in surplus. If the demand curve for the product is of unit elasticity there would be no *net* move into or out of other goods, so then one might perhaps argue that this effect would be negligible.

9. The producers' surplus obtained from selling a quantity of output *OB* at a price *OF* is the total sales revenue *FGBO* minus the area under the supply curve – the total cost *HGBO*. It is thus *HGF*. Similarly the producers' surplus obtained from selling *OB'* at price *OM* is *HNM*, so that the increase in output from *OB* to *OB'* at the higher price yields producers the additional surplus of *FMNG*. This concept rests on the assumption that the supply curve indicates the marginal cost of production at various outputs.

realistic to assume constant or even falling costs in the sort of industries which Australia protects, and undoubtedly this was the committee's implied assumption.

If constant costs operate over the whole range of the home supply curve and the tariff were just sufficient to enable the protected industry to cover its costs, the home supply curve would coincide with the horizontal line *MC*. Protection would put an end to imports and the production cost would be equal to *MCJF*. This would be the cost as calculated by the Brigden committee. It would fall short of the total cost by the consumption cost *CJA*. Exactly the same applies if costs are falling. Protection would put an end to imports and the Brigden method would correctly yield the production cost, provided the price is equal not to the *marginal* but to the *average* cost of home production. Another possibility is that constant costs operate up to a certain output, say *OB'*, and then costs start rising. In this case the supply curve would be *MNH'*, the protected output would be *OB'* and again the production cost would be equal to the Brigden committee's excess cost *MNKF*. In this case imports would continue under protection.

The conclusion which emerges so far is that in so far as home prices reflect the average cost of the protected output the Brigden committee's method yields the partial equilibrium production cost of protection. But in so far as rising costs operate in the protected industries it is likely to overstate the production cost, though in doing so it may make up for the neglect of the consumption cost.

IV Indirect Repercussions; Effects on Costs of Other Industries and on Balance of Payments Equilibrium

Now we come to the indirect repercussions which arise if our clothing industry is sufficiently large or if a number of industries, perhaps individually small but collectively large, are protected. These indirect repercussions are of two types; both affect the volume of output which can be regarded as truly protected.

The first indirect repercussions arise when materials or semi-finished goods are being protected. A tariff upon the import of materials has an effect similar to that of an indirect tax on materials. Such an indirect tax raises the costs of the material-using industries, including perhaps import-competing (protected or non-protected) and export industries. From their point of view it has the same effect as a rise in money factor prices. It is an effect similar to an appreciation of the exchange rate. It will lower the volume of exports and raise the volume and value of imports. Thus it is possible that some import-competing output needs protection only because its materials are being protected. This indirect effect of the protection of materials is therefore likely to worsen the balance of payments, although the direct effect will improve it.[10] The greater the importance of the protected materials in export and import-competing production and the more important the revenue (as distinct from the protective) effect of the tariff on materials, the more likely it becomes that the indirect effect of the protection of materials offsets or even outweighs the direct effect.

This effect provides a certain stabilizing mechanism and if the tariff were removed, full employment and balance of payments equilibrium *might* be restored without any change in money factor prices or the exchange rate. But while likely to have some effect, it is unlikely to go all the way, and one can expect that unless money factor prices or the exchange rate alter, the removal of the tariff would leave the country with unemployment and a balance of payments deficit. It follows then that a further adjustment is needed. The Brigden committee failed to pursue the effects which such an adjustment is likely to have.

Equilibrium could be restored either by money factor prices falling or by the exchange rate depreciating. The volume of exports will then expand, the value rising if the foreign elasticity of demand is greater than unity and falling if it is less.[11] Both the volume and value of imports will fall, import-competing industries expanding. If the foreign elasticity of demand for exports is greater than unity this adjustment will certainly improve the balance of payments, while if it is less it may still do so provided the elasticity of supply of exports is low enough. What is important to note here is that some of the previously protected industries may become

10. The indirect effect will worsen the balance of payments in those circumstances in which an appreciation of the exchange rate would do so, i.e. when the home and foreign elasticities of demand and supply are such that the foreign exchange market is stable.
11. It is characteristic of much discussion about the Australian economy that the elasticity of supply of exports, or at least of the main exports, is assumed to be very low or zero. Thus it is argued that agricultural and pastoral industries would not be able to absorb the labour set free by a removal of the tariff. This is not the place to discuss the realism of this assumption, though it is certainly very relevant to any discussion of tariff policy. It should only be stressed here that for the purpose of determining what would have happened if in the first place the tariff had not been imposed, or if it were permanently removed, it is the long-term reactions which matter. And if sufficient time is allowed – time enough for new investment to find its way into rural industries and to mature – it is by no means certain, on the basis of recent experience, that this elasticity is so low.

However, if the extreme case where the elasticity of supply of exports is zero does apply, then the depreciation following upon the removal of the tariff would have no effect on the volume or value of exports. The depreciation would have to continue until all the displaced labour and capital were again employed in the import-competing industries and imports were restored to their original level. If the tariff had been uniform *ad valorem* on all imports, the final result would be a complete restoration of the tariff situation, and it would be correct to say that the tariff imposes no cost. But, of course, if the tariff had discriminated as between imports, there would still be some excess cost due to the over-import of some goods relative to others.

economical again; so even in the absence of any protection of materials or semi-finished goods, some industries, which appear to be protected when indirect repercussions are not taken into account, would in fact survive under free trade.[12]

This factor increases the difficulty of determining which industries are really protected. By not adequately taking it into account – or, to be fairer, by basing its analysis on slightly different assumptions – the committee overstated the volume of protected output.

The conclusion which emerges so far, on the basis of a partial equilibrium analysis combined with an allowance for indirect effects, is the following. First, the committee has understated the cost by neglecting the consumption effect. Second, it has overstated the cost in so far as protected industries are subject to diminishing returns (i.e. in so far as the supply curve rises) so that the average cost of protected output is less than its price. Thirdly, due to a partial neglect of indirect effects it has overstated the cost by an overstatement of the amount of output which can be regarded as truly protected.

V General Equilibrium Model

Effect on Exports

Although some indirect effects have now been taken into account the whole story has not yet been told. For, so far, all effects on the export industries have been neglected. It has been pointed out that the indirect repercussions and adjustments will stimulate the volume of exports, but the further implications of this have yet to be pursued.

What in fact has been assumed in the partial equilibrium analysis is that the true social cost involved in shifting resources out of the import-competing industries into the export industries (and so paying for the extra imports) is given by the average cost of imports. This is an assumption which cannot in fact be maintained.

It assumes that the quantity of imports which can be obtained via the foreign market per unit of factor input in the export industries remains

12. Surprising as it might seem on first thought, under certain not unreasonable assumptions, a tariff would lead to a balance of payments deficit. It need only be assumed first that the tariff does create an excess cost and thus a fall in real income for someone, and secondly, that money wages and other factor prices are adjusted so that the real incomes of factors as a whole (disregarding distribution of income considerations) remain constant. Then the whole of the excess cost can only be borne by external borrowing or a call on the external reserves – in other words by a balance of payments deficit.

In this sort of model, which may describe quite realistically some short-run situations, the fall in imports due to import replacement by protected industry would be less than the fall in exports due to the movement of factors out of export into protected industry.

Calculation of cost of protection

constant irrespective of the amount of export output. It neglects the effects of increased export output on average returns in the export industries. The export industries are subject to diminishing returns for two reasons. First, there are diminishing physical returns due to limited supplies of natural resources; and, secondly, there are diminishing value returns due to the adverse effects of increased sales on overseas prices. The first is one part of our production effect, and the second is our terms of trade effect.

These effects on the export industries cannot, however, be handled in the framework of a partial equilibrium model. Therefore a general equilibrium analysis must now be used, enabling a confirmation and extension of the arguments used so far.

It will now be assumed that the volumes of protected and free trade output are known, that in both the free trade and the protection situation the value of exports is equal to the value of imports, and that full employment is maintained. Hence, it is a 'real' model where equilibrating adjustments of the exchange rate or of money factor prices are assumed to take place automatically.

Finally, to avoid cluttering up the diagram with too many complications, the terms of trade effect will at first be neglected and only the general equilibrium *production* and *consumption* effects of protection will be illustrated. It will thus be assumed very provisionally that Australia's export prices would be unaffected by the supplies which Australia places on the world market.

The Production Effect

Suppose then that we know that under free trade Australia would produce 100 units of wheat and 20 units of clothing. The effect of protection is to transfer labour and capital out of the wheat industry into the clothing industry so that finally 80 units of wheat and 24 units of clothing are produced. Thus the total cost of the protected output of 4 units of clothing is 20 units of wheat. If the labour and capital which are used under protection to produce 4 units of clothing were instead employed in wheat production and if the 20 extra units of wheat were then used to buy clothing in the foreign market at the given terms of trade – say 1 unit of wheat for 1 unit of clothing – it would be possible to obtain 20 units of clothing. Therefore the cost of producing 4 extra units of clothing at home rather than using the resources to produce extra wheat with which to buy the clothing abroad is 16 units of clothing (or of wheat). It is the difference between the average cost of producing the 4 units of clothing at home (namely an average cost of 5 units of wheat) and the foreign price of clothing (namely 1 unit of wheat), multiplied by the volume of protected clothing output. In fact the community has suffered the equivalent of an income loss of 16 units of clothing (or 16 units of wheat).

This can be fairly regarded as the production cost of protection. Needless to say, benefits, utility or cost cannot really be measured. All one can say is that the act of protection causes the community the same loss as would some other act – such as a given decrease in its income. Hence the community is indifferent between these two losses. But since it is likely to have a clearer conception of the loss in utility which would result from a given fall in income than from the act of protection, to state the cost in terms of an income loss will give a better indication of the 'cost' of protection.

The argument is illustrated in figure 1.2 where clothing is measured along the OY axis and wheat along the OX axis. AB is Australia's home transformation curve showing the various combinations of wheat and clothing which could be produced with a given supply of fully-employed labour. An important feature of this curve is that it is drawn concave to the origin; the marginal rate of transformation between wheat and clothing is assumed to diminish. The full significance of this assumption will be discussed below. For the moment it is sufficient to note that it is through the concavity of this curve that diminishing physical returns in both wheat and clothing, or in either of the industries alone, are put into the diagram.

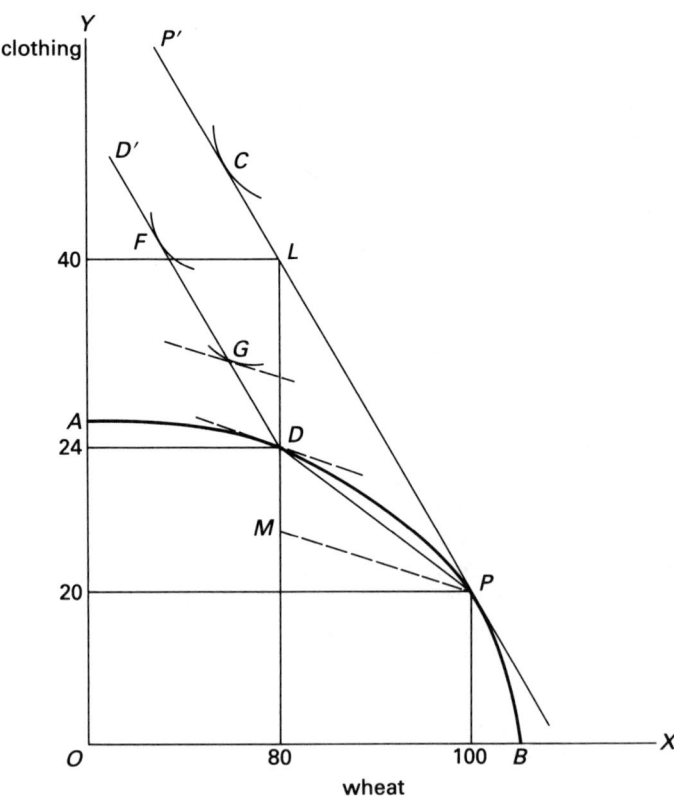

Figure 1.2

Calculation of cost of protection

It is assumed that the quadrant XOY contains a map of community indifference curves,[13] that the value of exports is equal to the value of imports and that the given foreign price ratio or terms of trade is represented by the slope of the line PP'. This line is in fact the foreign offer curve which shows, with the origin at P, the quantity of clothing which the rest of the world is prepared to exchange for any given quantity of wheat. In free trade competitive equilibrium (assuming no external economies or diseconomies) the combination of wheat and clothing produced is represented by the production point P, where the marginal rate of transformation is equal to the given price ratio, and the combination consumed by the consumption point C, where PP' is tangential to an indifference curve, and where therefore the marginal rate of substitution is equal to the price ratio. The difference between production and consumption gives exports and imports.

Now suppose a tariff is imposed, raising the relative price of clothing in the home market so that the new home price ratio is represented by the slope of the line PM. The tariff rate is then given by the ratio of the slope of PM to the slope of PP'. With these altered home prices production will shift to D, where the marginal rate of transformation is equal to the new home price ratio. This is the production effect of the tariff. With production at D and the same terms of trade and hence foreign offer curve as before, the country can trade along DD' (parallel to PP') and reach a consumption point anywhere on this line. With the home price ratio equal to the slope of PM, consumers will in fact choose to trade up to G, where DD' is intersected by a community indifference curve having this slope. Thus the consumption point is G and exports and imports are given by the horizontal and vertical distances between D and G.

Distinction between Production and Consumption Effect

Now we come to the really important distinction between the production and the consumption effect which it is the point of this diagram to illustrate.

Imagine for the moment that the shift of production from P to D is achieved not by a tariff but by some other way which does not affect prices facing consumers. Thus, the home and the foreign price ratio continue to be the same. It could, for example, be assumed that the protection is brought about by a subsidy to the clothing industry, and that this subsidy is financed either by poll taxes or – provided it is also assumed that taxes do not affect the incentive to produce – by an income tax.

---

13. One hesitates even to mention so doubtful a tool of analysis as a 'community indifference curve', which seems to be becoming somewhat discredited. See, for example, Samuelson (1956). But it might be noted that many of the objections to this tool rest upon distribution of income considerations which have been assumed away here, and that it is possible to avoid the concept and yet arrive at the same conclusions by the use of a somewhat clumsy verbal terminology.

With this assumption, and with production at D, the new consumption equilibrium would be at F, where a community indifference curve is tangential to the foreign trade line DD', and where thus the marginal rate of substitution continues to be equal to the foreign (and home) price ratio. Now the cost of moving from C to F is the production cost of protection. It is due to the shift in production from P to D. It is the same as the cost of a fall in income equal (in terms of clothing) to LD, the vertical distance between PP' and DD'. LD is equal to the difference between the foreign price ratio (the slope of LP) and the average rate of transformation between D and P (the slope of DP) multiplied by the volume of protected clothing output or wheat output foregone (depending on whether prices and transformation rates are expressed in terms of wheat or clothing).

The tariff divorces the home price ratio from the foreign price ratio and hence shifts the consumption equilibrium to G. This further shift from F to G is due then to the change in home prices brought about by the protection. Clearly the indifference curve at G represents a lower level of satisfaction than the curve at F. The real income loss represented by the movement from C to G has two components – first the shift from C to F (the production effect) and second the shift from F to G (the consumption effect). With two price ratios in the picture, the measurement of this loss would then involve the familiar index number problem.

The tariff is in fact the equivalent of an indirect tax on clothing which is used partly to finance a subsidy to the home clothing industry and partly to provide revenue to the government, revenue which enables the remission of other taxes. The consumption cost reflects the burden of this indirect tax in distorting choices between the protected good (clothing) and other goods.[14]

The Brigden Method

The Brigden committee's method of measuring the cost by taking the difference between the foreign and the home price can be represented on the diagram. It is given simply (in terms of clothing) by ML, the difference between the slopes of PM and PL, multiplied by the volume of protected output. ML overstates the production cost by DM, this being the difference between the home price and the average rate of transformation of the protected output multiplied by the volume of protected output (or wheat output foregone).

Now it is worth examining more closely the reasons why the Brigden method overstates the production cost. Clearly it depends on the fact that the marginal rate of transformation between P and D is assumed to diminish. This can have two distinct causes. There may be diminishing

---

14. Strictly speaking, this indirect tax distorts choices between clothing on the one hand and *all* other goods, including leisure, on the other. In other words, part of the consumption cost is a disincentive effect.

returns in the clothing industry; and there may be diminishing returns in the wheat industry. The marginal rate of transformation diminishes if there are diminishing returns in both industries or diminishing returns in one and constant or only slightly increasing returns in the other. Diminishing returns in the clothing industry have already been allowed for in the partial equilibrium analysis, but now it can be seen that even if there were constant returns in the clothing industry – not an unreasonable assumption – diminishing returns in the export industries would still lead the Brigden method into overstating the production cost.

There is an alternative way of stating this argument which avoids the use of the concept of 'diminishing returns' and is more in conformity with the sort of models used in international trade theory.

Suppose that there are constant returns to scale in both protected and export industries so that, for example, a 10 per cent increase in the input of all the factors (including land) causes a 10 per cent increase in an industry's output. Then the average rate of transformation between the industries will be constant if the relative importance of the different factors of production is the same in both industries. But if the 'factor intensities' differ, so that, for example, land is more important in the export industries and labour in the protected industries, then a transfer of factors from export to protected industries would tend to raise real wages and lower real rents and so cause costs in the protected industries to rise and in the export industries to fall. The Brigden method neglects this change in factor prices which would accompany a transfer of resources.

The Terms of Trade Effect

It would be possible to construct a more complicated diagram which illustrated not only the production and the consumption effect but also the terms of trade effect.[15] But it may be sufficient here to introduce the terms of trade effect by verbal reasoning.

The terms of trade effect of the tariff lessens the excess cost imposed both by the production and the consumption effect. Indeed, it is well known from the theory of the optimal tariff[16] that the terms of trade might improve sufficiently for the tariff to impose not a cost but a gain, and that if the tariff is not too high there is bound to be a gain. What is particularly important to note in this connection is that if the elasticity of demand for exports is less than unity, so that a reduced volume of exports would bring in a greater total export income, the degree of trade restriction is definitely below the optimum, although it may indeed be below the optimum even if this condition is not fulfilled. In this case the removal of the tariff

15. PP' (and DD') would then not be a straight line but a curve rising from right to left at a diminishing rate and, when the elasticity of demand for exports becomes less than unity, turning downwards from right to left.
16. See Kaldor (1940) and Scitovsky (1942–3). For a derivation of the optimum tariff formula and a list of other references see also Johnson (1951–2).

unsubstituted by other forms of trade restriction would inflict a cost and not a gain.

When the terms of trade effect is taken into account, foreign prices of imports and exports no more measure the average cost of additional imports or income from exports than home prices measure average costs of home production when there are diminishing physical returns. With a terms of trade effect on the export side the average price obtainable in the foreign market for an increased export output will be below the price ruling before the increase in exports. Similarly, if there were any terms of trade effect on the import side (something which is assumed away here), the average cost of the imports which would replace the protected output would be greater than the existing price of imports. Thus, as pointed out earlier, the export industries are subject to diminishing returns both because the average physical product falls as output rises and because the average price obtainable for a given unit of product declines. The terms of trade effect provides then a further reason why the Brigden method overstates the cost of protection.

Summary

It is now possible to sum up. The tariff has three effects – the production, the consumption and the terms of trade effect – of which the production and the terms of trade effects can be conveniently divided into an export and an import component, and the import component of the terms of trade effect can be neglected. The partial equilibrium approach takes into account only the consumption effect and the import (or protected industry) component of the production effect. The general equilibrium approach adds the terms of trade effect and the export side of the production effect.

Table 1.1 lists these effects. A plus (+) sign in the last column indicates that due to that particular effect the Brigden method overstates the cost of protecting a given volume of output, and a minus (−) sign that it

TABLE 1.1 THE EFFECTS OF A TARIFF

	Partial Effects	Consumption Effect		−
General Effects		Production Effect	Import (protected industry)	?
			Export Industry	+
		Terms of Trade Effect		+
		Volume Effect		+

understates it. The question mark opposite the production effect on the import side indicates that it is not certain whether on the whole protected industries are subject to constant returns, in which case there would be no overstatement or understatement, or to diminishing returns, in which case there should be a plus (+) sign. The last line allows for the Brigden committee's overstatement of the actual volume of protected output, due to its failure to allow for the equilibrating adjustments needed to maintain full employment and balance of payments equilibrium.

Table 1.1 thus shows that if the Brigden committee's method is used, the consumption effect will lead to an understatement of the cost of protection, while the various indirect effects which are neglected in a partial equilibrium approach will lead to an overstatement.

Further Notes: The Cost of Protection Revisited

Essay 1, originally published in lengthier form in 1957, has turned out to be the beginning of a large literature, both theoretical and empirical. Of course it had its precursors. Apart from the references given in that essay, one must add that the method of showing the gains from trade (and implicitly the cost of protection) by use of the Marshallian consumers' and producers' surpluses goes back a long way, probably to Barone (1913), and was for many years used, or referred to, by textbook writers, for example Haberler (1936). My paper applied both this method and the techniques of two-sector trade theory directly to analysing the measurement problem, incidentally giving each of the deadweight triangles their name.

Johnson (1960) tidied up the analysis (including a demonstration that the two-sector general equilibrium story can be geometrically represented by demand and supply curves) but then substantially carried it forward to the multi-commodity multi-tariff case. I shall discuss this extension at length below.

Since then there have been cost-of-protection calculations for particular industries, as well as some comprehensive calculations for the United States. The empirical studies up to 1973 are surveyed in Corden (1975). The outstanding study is that by Magee (1972) for the United States. While partial equilibrium calculations continue, more recently there has been a boom in general equilibrium calculations. This work was pioneered by Evans (1972) and has involved either programming models or some kind of computed general equilibrium system. Here one might particularly note de Melo (1978). There is a survey of the more recent empirical work in this general area given by Krueger (1984).

Some of my thoughts about the theory and practical problems of cost of protection calculations are given in Corden (1974, 1975, 1984). In the following notes I have tried to sort out a few ideas more systematically, primarily trying to show to what extent the simple analysis of essay 1 can be extended, and to what extent it must be qualified. While I have drawn on these earlier discussions, it is only in preparing these notes that I have finally come to understand a central feature of the Johnson (1960) approach.

Import Quotas and Rent Seeking

The partial equilibrium approach of essay 1 can be generalized or broadened in a number of ways to make it more useful.

First of all, it can be applied to import quotas. There is then the possibility that a monopoly in an import-competing industry has the opportunity, for the first time, to exploit its monopoly power, and the costs of that could be taken into account.[17] But here let us consider the simpler case where competition in the local industry remains but quota licences which have a market value of *KNCJ* in figure 1.1 (equal to the tariff revenue) are obtainable by means of luck, various allocation procedures and 'rent-seeking'. The latter involves a resource cost of obtaining the licences and could be included in the cost of protection. At the limit it could be equal to *KNCJ*, so that the cost of protection becomes *KNCJ* plus the production cost and the consumption cost.

Economies of Scale

Secondly, we could allow for internal economies of scale in the local industry. This is represented in figure 1.3 where *OF* is the free trade world

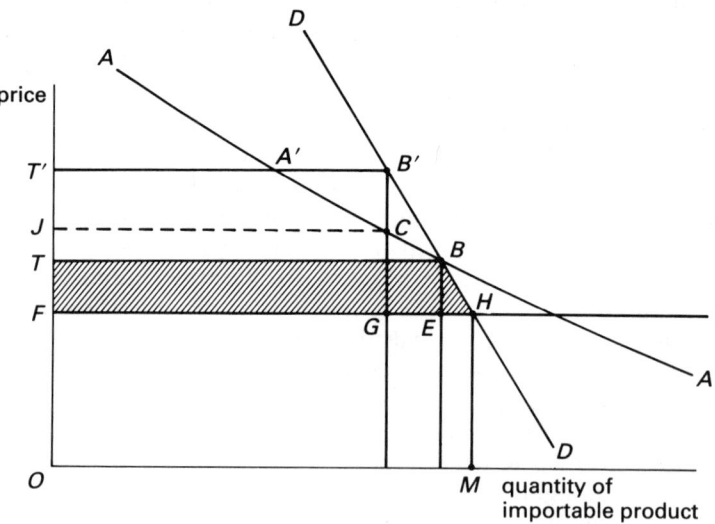

Figure 1.3

---

17. See Corden (1971, ch. 9).

price, AA is the average cost curve (including normal profits) of a single domestic producer and DD is the domestic demand curve. In the absence of a tariff or quota, imports are OM and there is no domestic production. A tariff of TF (or marginally above it) will cause domestic production to begin. The cost of protection will be $FTBE$ (production cost) plus EBH (consumption cost). The two areas are shaded. Assume then that there is a further rise in the tariff, to FT', and that local producer(s) price up to this level, so that demand moves to B'.

There are now two possibilities, at least as limiting cases. One is that a single producer remains, scale of output falls and the producer makes monopoly profits, which are not costs from a national point of view. The consumers then lose $TT'B'B$ as a result of this rise in the tariff (additional to the previous loss), but some part of this consumer loss goes in monopoly profits $JT'B'C$. Another possibility is that fragmentation of production is generated by the rise in the tariff above its initial 'made-to-measure' level of FT.[18] More firms (or perhaps just one extra firm) enter to absorb the monopoly profits, and so scale per firm falls and thus the average cost rises until the excess profits are eliminated. In that limiting case average costs at total output $T'B'$ would be OT', with each individual firm being at A' on its individual cost curve. The total cost of protection as a result of the imposition of a tariff FT' is then $FT'B'G$ (production cost) plus $GB'H$ (consumption cost).

Assumptions of the Partial Equilibrium Approach

A central question is what assumptions underlie the partial equilibrium approach. The most important assumption is that only the effects of a tariff (or other protective device) on a particular product or industry are being considered. If one is calculating the cost of protection of a number of industries, using this method, and then adding them up, the assumption is that demands and supplies of these various products or industries are not very directly related.

Another assumption which has been frequently stressed, and is noted in a footnote in essay 1, is that the demand curve must be a 'constant utility' one, that is it must reflect only substitution effects (movement along an indifference curve) so that the income elasticity of demand for the good concerned needs to be zero.[19] Since elasticity figures have such high margins of error and are often just guesses, and since income effects would

---

18. Fragmentation of production caused by protection has been stressed in an extensive Canadian literature, and is analysed rigorously in Corden (1974, pp. 210–15) where there are references to this literature. Most recently Harris (1984) has incorporated this effect in a general equilibrium analysis of the welfare gain from a move to US–Canadian free trade.
19. See Johnson (1960) and Leamer and Stern (1970, ch. 8) for careful analyses which bring out this point.

not be very large when just one or a few industries are being considered, this is probably not a serious problem. The next two considerations are more important.

All significant repercussions of a tariff being raised or lowered should, in principle, be reflected in the demand and supply curves. One would not expect the real exchange to be significantly depreciated as a result of a very small industry having its tariff removed. But the industry could be large enough for *some* effect on the real exchange rate to result, which would then affect the final demand and supply equilibria. So any likely exchange rate repercussion should be taken into account. A partial equilibrium approach does not necessarily imply ignoring such repercussions. It might also be noted that the approach in essay 1 made certain implicit monetary assumptions which meant that a nominal depreciation also led to a real depreciation. It could be assumed either that nominal income or the nominal price of non-tradables are held constant.

Distortions Elsewhere: a Crucial Issue

We come now to a major issue ignored in the partial equilibrium analysis of essay 1. A crucial assumption was that there were no distortions elsewhere in the economy. In the small country case, tariffs or quotas elsewhere in the economy would all be distortions, but there can be other distortions, whether in the product, labour or capital markets. These can be taken as given, but they must be incorporated in the analysis. Thus a tariff for the particular industry concerned may be offsetting of distortions elsewhere, in which case there could be a gain from this tariff, and the cost of protection could be negative. It is important to realize that these sorts of considerations *can* be incorporated in a partial equilibrium analysis. In fact, they *must* be if such analysis is to have any value. If they are, the case for an essentially partial equilibrium approach is greatly strengthened. Here it might be observed that partial-equilibrium cost-of-protection analysis, when complicated for 'distortions elsewhere', comes very close to modern social cost-benefit analysis, perhaps the main difference being that the former is conceived of as an *ex-post* calculation and the latter as *ex-ante*.[20]

Let us now give some examples of how 'distortions elsewhere' may affect the partial equilibrium approach.

1) Some of the labour used in the protected industry may come out of an unemployment pool, the wage that the industry has to pay being above the social opportunity cost of labour. The curve tracing out the marginal social

---

20. The domestic resource cost (DRC) concept takes into account the various distortions, and is essentially the same as the approach proposed here (though DRCs refer to marginal rates, like effective rates of protection, rather than to amounts, like triangles, as in the cost of protection or cost-benefit approach). On all these methods, see Corden (1984) and Krueger (1984). Standard references on domestic resource cost are Krueger (1966) and Bruno (1972).

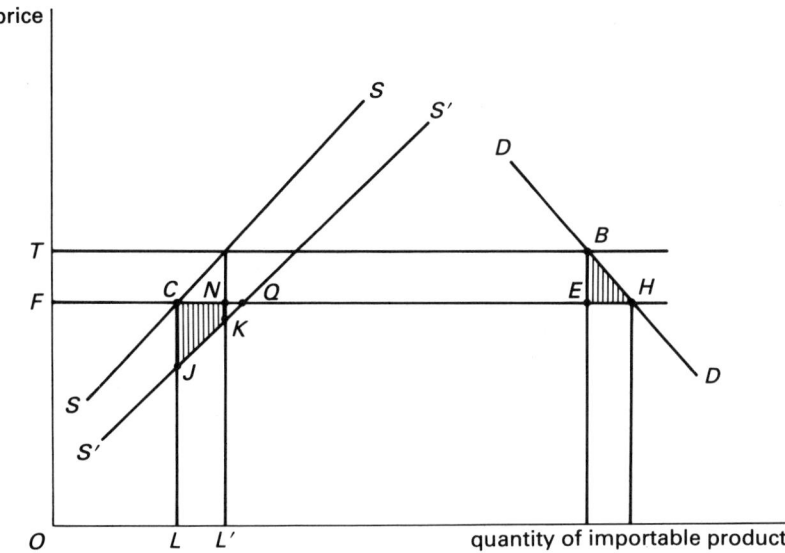

Figure 1.4

cost of production $S'S'$ will then be below the ordinary supply curve (marginal private cost), as in figure 1.4, and up to output FQ there will be a production gain (negative production cost). In the diagram the cost of protection of tariff FT is then EBH (consumption cost) less $CJKN$ (production gain), both being shaded. This could be positive or negative, and one particular level of the tariff will maximize the net gain. Of course, a tariff in this case is not first best.

2) There may be tariffs and export taxes elsewhere in the economy. If there are no other distortions, and no terms of trade effects (small country model), these will then tend to shift the private supply curve of the industry under consideration to the left and the demand curve to the right, this reflecting distortions created in the market of that industry as a result of distortions elsewhere. A tariff could then yield both a production gain and a consumption gain.

3) One special case is worth noting, at least as a reference point. It provides a lead into the general equilibrium discussion below. Suppose that all other industries could be aggregated into one, and that there is a uniform tariff plus export subsidy for these other industries. Put simply, suppose we have a two-sector model, consisting of 'our' industry and the 'other' industry, ours producing an importable and the other an exportable. Suppose that there is a given export subsidy for the other industry (and if there are many such 'other' industries, some of which are import competing, we must assume that these get a tariff at the same rate with nominal and effective rates all equal). Then a tariff on 'our' industry at that

same rate will exactly offset the distortion created. In other words, all protective rates will be equalized. Any tariff rate up to that level will yield a gain.

In figure 1.5 the tariff *FT* represents this offsetting tariff rate. In the absence of that tariff, but *with* protection elsewhere, domestic output is *OL* and demand *OH*. In the absence of protection elsewhere it would have been *OL'* and *OH'*. (This could be derived from the social supply and demand curves *S'S'* and *D'D'* or, alternatively, if one supposes that money income is held constant and all goods are traded, the exchange rate would have been depreciated in the alternative situation, and the social cost of imports would be *OT*, with the demand and supply curves unchanged.) The tariff *FT* brings domestic output and demand to the levels where they would have been with complete free trade, i.e. to *OL'* and *OH'*. The gain is the sum of areas 1 and 2. A further rise in the tariff would impose an incremental cost, so that tariff level *FT* maximizes the gain, given protection elsewhere. All this ignores rent-seeking costs, and also any 'fragmentation of production' effects when there are economies of scale.

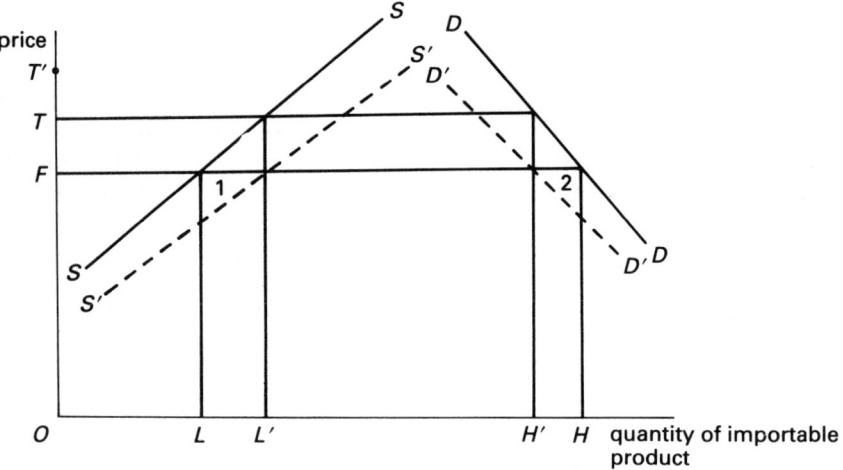

Figure 1.5

General Equilibrium with Many Goods and Tariffs

Let us now turn to general equilibrium. The matter is simplest to discuss when we adhere to a two-sector model as represented in the latter part of essay 1 and explored more fully by Johnson (1960). This model is quite straightforward and one thing only needs to be added. If there is an export tax or subsidy provided for the exportable (in the small country model), and a tariff for the importable, it is the difference between the rates of

Calculation of cost of protection

protection in the two industries that is relevant for the cost of protection. It has been stressed in the theory of effective protection and tariff structure that relative rates of protection, not absolute rates, matter for resource allocation effects, and this also applies to the welfare consequences.

Let us now move on to the most difficult problem, one not discussed in essay 1, but opened up by Johnson (1960), and subsequently dealt with explicitly or implicitly in several empirical exercises. In the real multi-product multi-industry world, suppose there is a complex set of tariffs and other protective devices, definitely non-uniform, whether in nominal or effective terms. What is the cost of protection of the whole system, i.e. what would be the aggregate gain from removing the whole set? This is a difficult problem to deal with rigorously, other than in the most abstract form. To narrow it down let us assume that there are no other distortions, apart from the various devices incorporated in the protection measures.

One question is how to handle terms of trade effects, that is the optimal tariff-export tax problem. Let us suppose (realistically for many countries) that there are potential terms of trade effects only on the export side. It is also necessary to assume that national monopoly power is not fully exploited by the country's own exporters (as it might be to some extent when differentiated products are being exported), and that foreign retaliation can be ignored. Non-imposition of optimal export taxes is then a form of distortion from the *national* welfare point of view.

One might then measure, as protective rates for various exportables, only the excess of actual rates of protection (which might be zero or negative) over the optimal rates – which would be negative when the optimal export tax is positive, and which would vary among exports, depending on estimated foreign elasticities of demand. The cost of protection for the whole system is then the cost of departing from the optimal situation, not the cost of departure from free trade. Removing protection should then be interpreted to mean the removal of all protective devices while imposing the optimal export tax structure. The latter may, of course, be very low or even zero, especially when the focus is on the long-run when the foreign elasticities of demand for the country's exports may be very high.

Coming to the main issue of calculating the cost of protection in a multi-product economy with non-uniform rates of protection, the central problem is to know what outputs and demand patterns would be if protection were abolished and free trade (plus optimal export taxes) were established. Short of rough guesses or estimates – which is all that may be possible in many countries – this problem can only be dealt with by computable general equilibrium models. This does not mean that such models necessarily give very precise or reliable results: everything depends on the precise details of the models and the data available. It is not difficult to fault in detail any model that has ever been constructed. One may have to concede that anything beyond the roughest estimates is not practicable.

The exchange rate aspect is just an incidental part of the exercise. If a general system of tariffs is removed and the exchange rate must then depreciate in order to restore external balance (while internal balance is maintained by aggregate demand policy), we can say that the exchange rate is part of the mechanism by which it is ensured that, when imports rise, finally exports rise as well. Some of the rise in exports may happen directly, without any change in the exchange rate – as resources move out of importables into exportables, and as costs of exportables fall – and some may be induced by a subsequent depreciation.

It is not sufficient to know the quantitative results of removing protection. This is only the first step. The next step is to get a welfare cost figure. One approach that has been used is to insert into the model some social utility functions (which usually have rather arbitrary properties), and use them to assess the social value of the package of goods and services consumed (strictly, *absorbed* by the economy, since investment also yields utility) with protection and with free trade. Another approach is that proposed by Johnson (1960) and is worth noting in some more detail. This proposal represented the principal development of my work in that part of his paper dealing specifically with the cost of protection.

Subject to certain assumptions which he carefully specified, Johnson suggested that the cost of protection was essentially *the sum* of all the separate costs as (apparently) defined in the partial equilibrium approach, that is (in the case of linearity) the sum of all the triangles. Let us just look at the production cost and ignore the consumption side. For each product the cost of protection is then the protected output multiplied by the rate of protection per unit (the Brigden cost) less the producer rent increase. This result looks deceptively simple, since one is apparently just adding up all the partial equilibrium measures. But this is not so. As Johnson pointed out but did not emphasize sufficiently, the output changes embody all general equilibrium repercussions. In other words, one needs the complete general equilibrium exercise before one can calculate the cost for each separate product. But there is a more important, and perhaps less obvious, point.

When a product has a positive tariff, but when its output under free trade would be greater than under protection (essentially because protection elsewhere is higher), then there is a gain from the tariff on that industry. Its own tariff has only helped to offset the anti-protection provided by tariffs elsewhere. The output change from free trade to protection has been negative, and the cost of protection of that industry has been negative. Using Johnson's method, all the triangles (or other areas) are added up algebraically, so that tariffs on particular products that protect industries which have declined as a result of the total system of protection reduce the cost of protection for the economy as a whole. If all industries obtained uniform effective protection (so that not only tariffs but also export subsidies made up the system), resources would not move at all, and the production cost of protection would be zero. A purely partial equilibrium calculation which just looked at one industry, with other tariffs constant, would not get this result.

References

Barone, E. 1913: *Principi di Economia Politica*. Rome: Athenaeum.
Blagburn, C. H. 1950: Import replacement by British agriculture. *The Economic Journal*, 60, 19–45.
Brigden, J. B. et al. 1929: *The Australian Tariff: An Economic Enquiry*. Melbourne: Melbourne University Press.
Bruno, M. 1972: Domestic resource costs and effective protection: clarification and synthesis. *Journal of Political Economy*, 80, 16–33.
Carmody, A. T. 1952: The level of the Australian tariff: a study in method. *Yorkshire Bulletin of Economic and Social Research*.
Corden, W. M. 1971: *The Theory of Protection*, Oxford: Oxford University Press.
─── 1975: The costs and consequences of protection: a survey of empirical work. In Peter B. Kenen (ed.), *International Trade and Finance*, New York: Cambridge University Press.
─── 1984: The normative theory of international trade. In R. W. Jones and P. B. Kenen (eds), *Handbook of International Economics: Volume 1*, Amsterdam: North-Holland.
Crawford, J. G. 1934: Tariff level indices. *The Economic Record*, 11, 213–21.
Evans, H. D. 1972: *A General Equilibrium Analysis of Protection*. Amsterdam: North-Holland.
Gifford, C. H. P. 1934: Protection and the price-level in Australia. *The Economic Record*, 10, 46–9.
Haberler, G. 1936: *The Theory of International Trade, With its Applications to Commercial Policy*, London: William Hodge.
Harris, R. 1984: Applied general equilibrium analysis of small open economies with scale economies and imperfect competition. *American Economic Review*, 74, 1016–32.
Johnson, H. G. 1951–2: Optimum welfare and maximum revenue tariffs. *Review of Economic Studies*, 19, 28–35.
─── 1960: The cost of protection and the scientific tariff. *Journal of Political Economy*, 68, 327–45.
Kaldor, N. 1940: A note on tariffs and the terms of trade. *Economica*, 7, 377–80.
Krueger, A. O. 1966: Some economic costs of exchange control: the Turkish case. *Journal of Political Economy*, 74, 466–80.
─── 1984: Trade policies in developing countries. In R. W. Jones and Peter B. Kenen (eds), *Handbook of International Economics: Volume 1*, Amsterdam: North-Holland.
League of Nations 1927: *Tariff Level Indices*, Geneva: League of Nations.
Leamer, E. E. and Stern, R. M. 1970: *Quantitative International Economics*. Boston: Allyn & Bacon.
Liepmann, H. 1938: *Tariff Levels and the Economic Unity of Europe*. London: Allen & Unwin.
Loveday, A. 1929: The measurement of tariff levels. *Journal of the Royal Statistical Society*. Reprinted in A. Loveday, 1931: *Britain and World Trade*, London: Longmans, Green & Co.
─── 1930: The Australian tariff: a criticism. *The Economic Record*, 6, 272–8.
Magee, S. P. 1972: The welfare effects of restrictions on U.S. trade. *Brookings Papers on Economic Activity*, 3, 645–707.
Melo, J. A. P. de 1978: Estimating the costs of protection: a general equilibrium approach. *The Quarterly Journal of Economics*, 92, 209–26.
Reddaway, W. B. 1937: Some effects of the Australian tariff. *The Economic Record*, 13, 22–30.

Robinson, E. A. G. and Marris, R. L. 1950: The use of home resources to save imports. *The Economic Journal*, 60, 177–81.
Samuelson, P. A. 1956: Social indifference curves. *The Quarterly Journal of Economics*, 70, 1–22.
Scitovsky, T. 1942–3: A reconsideration of the theory of tariffs. *Review of Economic Studies*, 10, 89–110.
Stolper, W. F. and Samuelson, P. A. 1941: Protection and real wages. *Review of Economic Studies*, 9, 58–72.
United Nations 1055: *Processes and Problems of Industrialisation in Under-developed Countries*. New York: United Nations.
Viner, J. 1929: The Australian tariff. *The Economic Record*, 5, 306–15.
——— 1951: *International Economics*. Glencoe, Illinois: The Free Press.

2
Tariffs, Subsidies and the Terms of Trade*

I Introduction

Is a tariff on imports or a direct subsidy to the import-competing industry a preferable method of protection? The discussion of this problem here will focus attention on two of the many considerations which affect the choice between tariff and subsidy as a protective device: (a) the relative effects of the two methods on the pattern of consumption, and (b) the effects on the terms of trade. In 'Constant Terms of Trade' it will be assumed that the country cannot affect its terms of trade. The core of the argument begins in 'The Optimal Tariff' where the terms of trade effect is introduced. The argument of this essay can be regarded as an extension of the theory of the optimum tariff.

The principal assumptions, to be maintained throughout, are:

1) Revenue derived by the government from a tariff is immediately returned to the community by a reduction in direct taxes, and the cost of subsidies is covered by an increase in direct taxes. Thus the government's fiscal position is assumed to remain unaffected by the choice of protective device.
2) The internal distribution of income is unaffected by any changes in the model, and the device of community indifference curves can be employed.
3) The elasticity of substitution between leisure and work is zero; so taxes have no disincentive effects.
4) Full employment is maintained by fiscal or other methods, and the balance of payments is kept in equilibrium by adjustments in internal prices or the exchange rate; it is a 'real' model.
5) There are no taxes or subsidies, other than those under discussion, and no monopolistic interferences with the adjustment of production or consumption.

* *Economica*, 24, Aug. 1957, 235–42. I am indebted to Mr J. Black, Mr R. G. Lipsey and Professor J. E. Meade.

6) Finally, there are only two products – wheat and clothing. Clothing is the product which is both imported and home produced and which is to be protected so that home production of it will increase. Some wheat output is home consumed and some exported. The marginal rate of transformation of wheat into clothing in home production is assumed to diminish. The assumption of a two-product model is required only for the sake of simple geometric exposition.

With these simple assumptions the difference between a tariff on clothing imports and a direct subsidy to the home clothing industry as a method of protection can be summed up as follows. With a tariff the price of clothing at home is higher than its price abroad, the difference being the tariff margin. But the price of clothing facing the consumer at home is the same as that facing the producer. In terms of the two-product model, the foreign price ratio (or terms of trade) diverges from the home price ratio, but the home price ratio is equal both to the marginal rate of transformation and the marginal rate of substitution at home. With a subsidy, on the other hand, the foreign price ratio is the same as the home price ratio – the price ratio facing home consumers. But the price of clothing facing the home producer is now greater than its price in the home (and the foreign) market. Thus the home price ratio is no longer equal to the marginal rate of transformation at home, though it is still equal to the marginal rate of substitution. To sum up, if

F = foreign price ratio

T = marginal rate of transformation (in home production)

S = marginal rate of substitution (in home consumption)

then

with a tariff $T=S$ but $F \neq T$ or S

with a subsidy $F=S$ but $T \neq S$ or F

II Constant Terms of Trade: Subsidy Preferable

Now assume provisionally that the country cannot affect its terms of trade. In these conditions it can be shown geometrically that a given degree of protection – a given shift of productive resources out of the wheat into the clothing industry – will involve a lesser fall in welfare when achieved by subsidy than when brought about by a tariff. The argument is the same, essentially, as the classical case against indirect taxation.[1]

---

1. See Joseph (1938–9). An explicit statement of the proposition of this section is given by Meade (1955, pp. 312–14). Meade shows that a tariff designed to redistribute

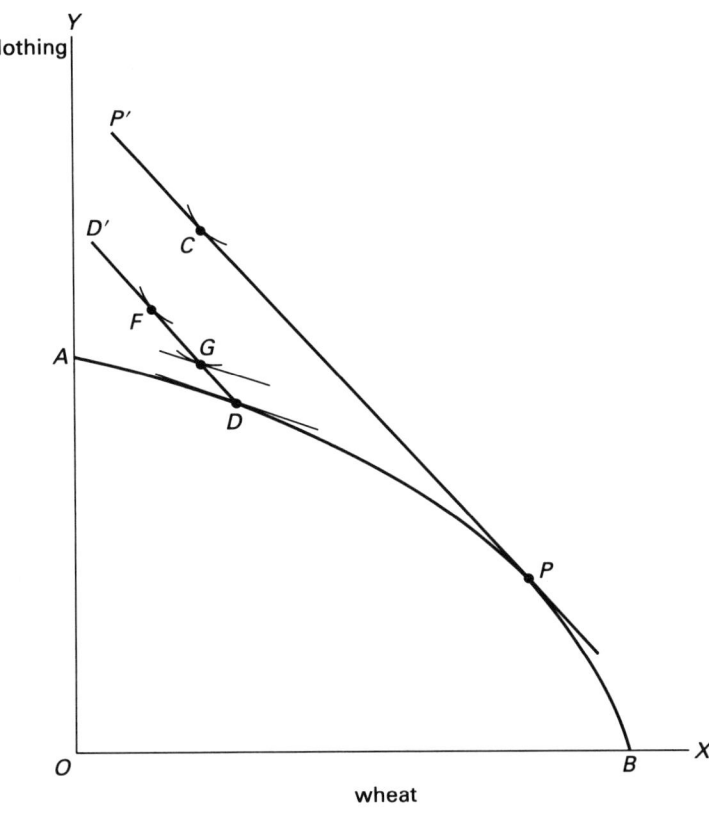

Figure 2.1

In figure 2.1 wheat is measured along the *OX* axis and clothing along the *OY* axis. *AB* is the home transformation curve showing the various combinations of clothing and wheat which could be produced with a given supply of fully-employed factors of production working a given number of hours. The quadrant *XOY* contains a map of community indifference curves having the usual characteristics of individual indifference curves.

> incomes interferes both with the 'optimisation of trade' (i.e. in the language of this essay, distorts the consumption pattern) and with the 'maximisation of production' (i.e. distorts the production pattern). On the other hand, a direct subsidy interferes only with production but not with trade. The present essay adds to the argument up to this point only by illustrating it diagrammatically.
>
> Meade's comparison is not extended to allow for terms of trade effects (though there is a hint in the footnote, p. 162). His later chapter 17 on the terms of trade argument for trade control does not explore the distinction between tariff and production subsidy.

The given foreign price ratio is represented by the slope of the line *PP'*. In free trade competitive equilibrium (assuming no external economies or diseconomies) the combination of clothing and wheat produced is represented by the production point *P* and the combination consumed by the consumption point *C*. The difference between production and consumption gives exports and imports.

The act of protection is to shift the production equilibrium to *D*. If this shift is attained by subsidy the internal price ratio will remain equal to the foreign price ratio and the new consumption equilibrium will be at *F*, where a community indifference curve is tangential to the foreign trade line *DD'* (parallel to *PP'*).

Now suppose that, instead of a subsidy, a tariff is used to shift production from *P* to *D*. Now the home price ratio and the foreign price ratio will be divorced; the home price ratio must alter sufficiently to equal the marginal rate of transformation at the new point of production *D*. The consumption equilibrium will therefore shift from *F* to *G*, where *DD'* is intersected by a community indifference curve having at the point of intersection the slope of the tangent at *D*.

Clearly the indifference curve at *G* represents a lower level of satisfaction than the curve at *F*. In this simple model the essence of the protective effect is indicated by the movement from the indifference curve through *C* to the indifference curve through *F*. The further movement from *F* to *G* represents the cost of protecting by tariff rather than by subsidy – the cost of distorting not only the production but also the consumption pattern.

III The Optimal Tariff

Now assume that the terms of trade are variable; the greater the volume of trade the worse the terms of trade. More specifically it will be assumed at this stage that the elasticity of the foreign offer curve is less than infinite but greater than unity, and that this elasticity is constant over the relevant range.[2]

In figure 2.2, *P* is again the production equilibrium under free trade, and *C* the consumption equilibrium. The free trade terms of trade are given by the slope of *PC* which is equal to the marginal rate of transformation at *P* and the marginal rate of substitution at *C*. *PP'* is the foreign offer curve with base at *P*; its curvature shows that the terms of trade deteriorate as the

---

2. The 'relevant range' includes what will be described below as the 'limited optimum' position. At this position the elasticity of the foreign offer curve must be greater than unity. This follows from the nature of the optimal tariff. If the elasticity were constant over the relevant range, it would then have to be greater than unity. But in this essay the elasticity is allowed to vary, so at points above the 'limited optimum' the offer curve elasticity could be less than unity. (The definition of the elasticity of the foreign offer curve implied here is in terms of the demand for exports as a function of the terms of trade. See footnote 4.)

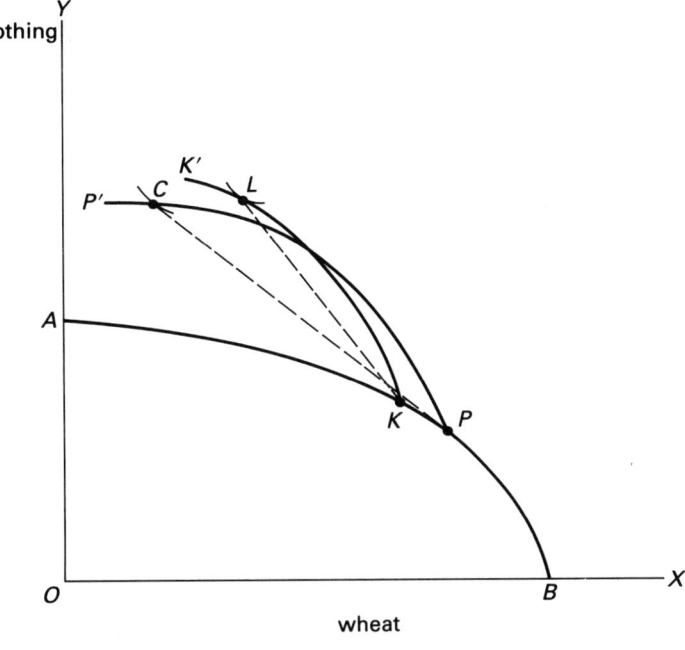

Figure 2.2

trading point moves up the offer curve, away from P. K is the production equilibrium and L the consumption equilibrium which would result from an optimal tariff.[3] The optimal tariff establishes the condition that the home price ratio is equal not to the foreign price ratio, as it would be under free trade, but to the slope of the tangent to the foreign offer curve at the trading point.[4] The foreign price ratio or terms of trade is indicated by the

---

3. See Kaldor (1940), Scitovsky (1942–3), de V. Graaff (1949–50) and other references cited therein, and Johnson (1951–2).
4. There are various ways of stating the optimal tariff formula, as shown by Johnson (1951–2). In terms of the elasticity of the foreign reciprocal demand for exports e – in fact literally the elasticity of the foreign offer curve – the optimal tariff rate $t=e-1$. But, as Johnson shows, from the reciprocal demand or foreign offer curve can be derived an ordinary demand curve expressing the demand for exports as a function of the exchange ratio between exports and imports (the 'barter terms of trade'). In terms of the foreign elasticity of demand for exports, defined as e'

$$t = \frac{1}{e'-1}$$

Similarly, in terms of the foreign elasticity of supply of imports e''

$$t = \frac{1}{e''}$$

slope of *KL*. This gives the average rate at which clothing can be exchanged into wheat on the foreign market at this particular volume of trade. The tangent to the foreign offer curve at *L*, on the other hand, indicates the marginal rate at which the two goods exchange on the foreign market. In the optimal situation this marginal rate of exchange is equal to the home price ratio and hence (in the absence of subsidies and taxes, and assuming perfect competition, and no external economies or diseconomies) to the marginal rate of transformation and substitution at home.

Geometrically the optimal position can be found as follows. Imagine the offer curve *PP'* (or *KK'*) to slide along *AB*, hence changing the production equilibrium. The axes of measurement of the offer curve remain parallel to the axes in figure 2.2. One can imagine an infinite number of positions for the curve, each position involving a different origin on *AB*. As the offer curve slides along *AB* it will trace out an 'envelope' (not drawn). This envelope shows the maximum consumption of clothing possible for any given consumption of wheat as the offer curve is moved along the transformation curve in the way described. Given *AB* and given the foreign offer curve, no consumption equilibrium can be above it. At some point a community indifference curve will be tangential to the envelope; this then represents the best consumption point which can be reached; it is in fact the point *L*. Thus the indifference curve at *L* is tangential both to the envelope and to the offer curve *KK'*. If the offer curve which is tangential to the indifference curve at *L* is followed down to *AB*, the point *K* is obtained indicating the production equilibrium resulting from an optimal tariff.[5]

IV Protection with Terms of Trade Effect

Now we come to the heart of the matter. Suppose that it is desired, say for strategic or other political reasons,[6] to protect the clothing industry sufficiently for the production point to move to the left of *K*. Let *M* (figure 2.3) represent this desired 'excess protection' production point. Possible

---

5. See Baldwin (1948). Baldwin developed the concept of this 'envelope', and indeed has been the first to make use of the technique of placing the foreign offer curve on top of the home transformation curve. He explores various properties of the envelope, and in particular proves 'that the slope of the offer curve where it is tangent to the envelope (or traces out part of the envelope) will always equal the slope of the transformation curve at the origin of the offer curve on the transformation curve'.
6. The reason for the protection could also be based on the infant-industry argument. This is not incompatible with the assumption of a diminishing marginal rate of transformation between the two products, since the infant-industry argument may be based not on decreasing opportunity costs at any given moment of time but on the expectation of falling costs over time. The loss of welfare resulting from the excess protection indicated by the analysis here should then be regarded as the static cost of protection against which the expected future benefits should be weighed.

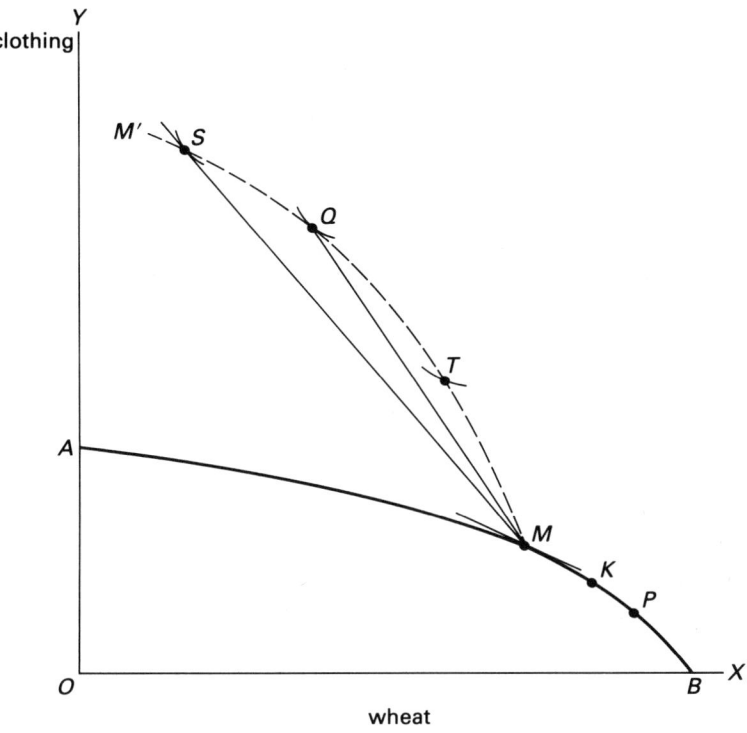

Figure 2.3

consumption equilibria are now on MM', the foreign offer curve with base at M.

If the protection were achieved solely by subsidy the consumption equilibrium would be at S. The foreign price ratio is given by MS and this will be equal to the home price ratio and hence to the marginal rate of substitution at S. But in order to obtain a production shift to M the price ratio facing home producers must be equal to the slope of the tangent at M – the marginal rate of transformation. The difference between the slope of this line and of MS gives the subsidy (and, expressed as a proportion of the slope of MS, it gives the subsidy rate).

If, on the other hand, the protection were achieved solely by tariff the consumption equilibrium would be at T. At this point a community indifference curve cuts MM' having the slope of the tangent at M. In other words the marginal rate of transformation at home is equal to the marginal rate of substitution at home, both being equal to the home price ratio. The difference between this home price ratio and the foreign price ratio (the slope of MT, not drawn) gives the tariff (and expressed as a proportion of the foreign price ratio, the tariff rate). It can be seen that now there is no presumption that a subsidy places the community on a higher indifference curve than a tariff.

In the absence of special conditions attached to the demand pattern, the transformation curve and the offer curve, it cannot be said whether the indifference curve through S is higher or lower than the curve through T, or whether indeed the same curve runs through both points.

Clearly the best consumption position is at Q where an indifference curve is tangential to MM'. This is the optimal position, in the limited sense that the production point M is taken as given. The slope of the tangent at Q indicates the home price ratio which would achieve this particular consumption equilbrium, given the foreign offer curve and the production point M. The difference between the slope of the tangent and the slope of MQ, the foreign price ratio, gives again the tariff. But the home price ratio brought about by this tariff will not in itself bring forth the production indicated by the production point M. The difference between the home price ratio and the marginal rate of transformation at M gives the subsidy required to supplement the tariff.

Therefore to obtain the limited optimum position Q a combination of tariff and subsidy is required. Now the significant feature is that the tariff rate required is in fact that given by the optimal tariff formula, a formula which always establishes the condition that the home price ratio is equal to the slope of the tangent to the foreign offer curve. To obtain the limited optimum Q, the optimal tariff should be imposed and any further protection required should be brought about by supplementing the tariff with a subsidy.[7]

Now consider the possibility that the elasticity of the offer curve changes with the volume of trade. The more probable case is where the elasticity of the foreign offer curve falls as the volume of trade rises.[8] In this case the optimal tariff rate falls as the degree of protection increases. So a surprising conclusion emerges from our argument. Suppose, to begin with that the optimal tariff is in operation. It is then desired to increase protection further. This should be done, as has been shown, by supplementing the optimal tariff with a subsidy. But the trade-restricting effect

---

7. If the degree of protection desired is *less* than that resulting from the optimal tariff alone, the optimal tariff should be supplemented by a *tax* on the clothing industry. One special case of this is when the free trade output, represented by the point P, is desired. Only in the special case when the degree of protection desired is K, is a tariff alone a satisfactory policy. In this case the points Q and T coincide. In no case will a subsidy alone (or a tax on the clothing industry, i.e. a negative subsidy) achieve the limited optimum. For, whatever the production point, S must always be above Q.
8. When a country is not able to extend the range of its export products, so that an increased volume of exports is brought about by greater sales of its existing exports rather than by widening the export range, there is possibly some presumption that the foreign elasticity of demand for its exports falls the greater the volume it places on the foreign market. Of course the elasticity of the offer curve depends also on the elasticity of supply of imports.

of this subsidy to the import-competing industry will now alter the optimal tariff rate itself. The tariff rate should actually be lowered! Therefore, at the same time as the direct subsidy to the clothing industry is raised, the tariff on clothing imports should fall. It should fall so as to modify, but not of course to offset completely, the effect of the subsidy on the volume and terms of trade.

V Qualifications

Finally it should be pointed out that the conclusions of this essay are subject to the same qualifications as the classical case against indirect taxation, a case which has been weakened (or even overthrown) by the introduction into the model of (a) a third good – leisure – which can be substituted for the taxed or the untaxed good, and (b) an existing network of taxes and other factors causing a divergence from the perfect competition optimum.[9]

Furthermore, no conclusions on the choice between tariffs and subsidies can clearly be drawn without taking into account the relative administrative and political advantages, the fiscal effects and the repercussions on the internal distribution of income.[10]

Further Notes: Tariffs Versus Subsidies

Introducing a New Distortion: Substitution Relative to Leisure

In the model of essay 2 a subsidy is financed by income tax, which is non-distorting because the elasticity of substitution between work and leisure is assumed to be zero. Implicitly it was also assumed that income tax can be levied equally on all kinds of income. Thus we have the contrast between a tariff, which is effectively a tax on consumption of clothing that finances a subsidy to clothing producers as well as allowing some reduction in income tax (to maintain fiscal balance), and an income tax that finances the same level of subsidy for clothing production. The tariff creates a by-product distortion (the consumption cost of protection) while the income tax does not.

Let us now allow for substitutability of leisure for work. How does that affect the story? To simplify the exposition a little (without altering any conclusions), let us assume that the tariff is prohibitive, thus raising no revenue. We are then comparing two ways of financing a given production subsidy, namely (a) by a tax on consumption of clothing only, this being

---

9. See Little (1951), Berry (1954), and the references cited in these two articles.
10. See Threlfell (1946), Browne (1946), de V. Graaff (1947), Brigden et al. (1929), Meade (1955).

what a tariff does, and (b) by a tax at an equal rate on consumption of clothing and of wheat, this being (in effect) an income tax.

In both cases leisure fails to be taxed. In both cases a distortion is imposed. With the tariff there is a distortion of clothing relative to wheat and leisure combined, and with the income tax there is a distortion of leisure relative to wheat and clothing combined. One cannot say in general which distortion cost would be greater. If clothing and leisure were complements, the distortion cost of the tariff might be less.

Has the basic argument of essay 2 then been destroyed? Fortunately, it has not. In essay 2 a tariff has been compared with a subsidy that is financed by income tax. But one can go further. Any given revenue can be raised in a minimum-distortion way. Except in special cases, this will be neither an income tax nor a tax solely on one commodity, such as clothing. It will be a system that will tax that commodity more which is relatively less substitutable, or more complementary, with leisure.[11] Say clothing is that commodity. First an income tax might be imposed to raise the required revenue. Then the rate of income tax might be reduced while some tax on clothing consumption alone is imposed. This will reduce the distortion relative to leisure and create a distortion for the first time between clothing and textiles. These two effects have to be traded off, but the minimum-distortion tax package will involve a non-uniform set of commodity taxes.

Given that it is desired to achieve a target output level of clothing, the optimal policy is to subsidize production of clothing to the extent desired, and then to finance the subsidy by a minimum-distortion tax package.[12] Provided the subsidy is financed in that way, a subsidy is still better than a tariff – other than in the special case where the minimum-distortion package would involve a tax on clothing only, in which case tariff and subsidy would have the same effect. Thus the argument that a subsidy is preferable to a tariff remains, provided the subsidy is assumed to be financed optimally.

Fixed Target versus Trading off the Protection Objective

The approach in essay 2 has been to assume a fixed target and then consider two ways of achieving it, one being costless (the subsidy) and the other imposing a by-product consumption distortion cost. Now we find that both methods impose a distortion cost, but that the cost of the tariff is always higher (except in one special case) provided the subsidy is financed in a minimum-distortion way. The next step is to allow for the possibility that the protection target is not fixed, but rather, that a marginal benefit (which can be valued) attaches to getting closer to it, the marginal protection benefit curve being negatively sloped.[13] The benefit from

11. This important proposition originated with Corlett and Hague (1953–4).
12. I follow here arguments developed by Corden (1974, ch. 3).
13. This refers to a benefit *perceived* by the policy makers. We do not pursue here the reasons for it, i.e. whether the desire to protect the clothing industry is justified or

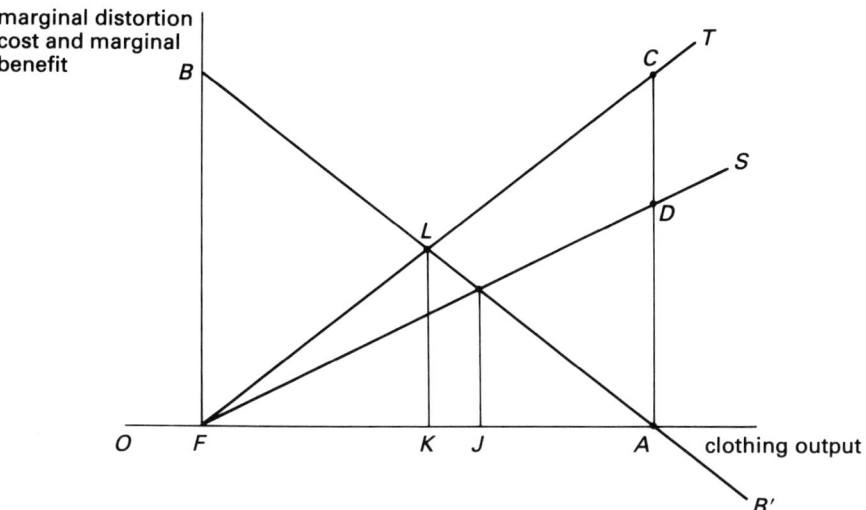

Figure 2.4

getting closer to the target can be traded off against the distortion costs. We have then a somewhat more general model.

This is presented in figure 2.4. We will only be considering the small country case here, so that a tariff must impose a cost. The horizontal axis shows the level of clothing production and the vertical axis shows both the marginal distortion cost and the marginal benefit from protection. Free trade clothing output is *OF* and target output is *OA*. The marginal protection benefit curve is *BAB'*. When the distortion cost of a subsidy is zero, first-best policy is to impose a subsidy that brings clothing output to *OA*. The total net benefit will then be *FBA*. The curve *FT* traces out the consumption distortion cost of a tariff. If a tariff were imposed so as to attain the same target output level a cost of *FCA* would be imposed. The theme of essay 2 has been that a tariff imposes this additional cost.

Now allow for leisure–work substitution and assume that a subsidy is financed by minimum-distortion taxes. Because of the leisure substitution effect, the curve *FT* is then likely to change, probably moving upwards. More important, we must now draw a new curve *FS* which traces out the marginal distortion cost of a subsidy, resulting from the taxes needed to

> not, but just *assume* a protectionist motive and then build a theory of rational policy making around it. Of course, the original premise – that there is a benefit from increased output of clothing at the expense of wheat – may not be rational. The general idea of trading off the 'non-economic' benefits from protection against the cost of protection stems from Johnson (1960, 1965), though the benefits need not be described as 'non-economic': they need only be ones that are not included in the normal measures of aggregate national product.

finance a subsidy. The distortion cost of the subsidy is *FDA*, which must still be lower than the distortion cost of the tariff.

However, we can go a little further. If a subsidy is used (as it should be if a first-best policy is pursued) and its cost is traded off against the benefit from protection, clothing output should only be brought as far as *OJ*. This would be the first-best policy: full achievement of the target should be foregone. If policy were constrained to the use of a tariff, output should only go as far as *OK*. If (unwisely) a tariff were used to achieve target *OA*, a net loss could actually result, since *LCA* could be greater than *FBL*.

Tariffs versus Subsidies with Terms of Trade Effects

Let us now look at the paradox at the end of essay 2. Because of the terms of trade effects, increased protection seems to be associated with a reduction in the tariff rate. It can be summed up neatly in figure 2.5. The vertical axis shows the tariff rate, and the horizontal axis the rate of subsidy for the import-competing product, clothing. *AA* shows all the combinations that yield a given amount of domestic clothing production. We assume that the subsidy is varied so as to attain the desired production (as indicated by the horizontal arrows). *TT* traces out the optimal tariff rate

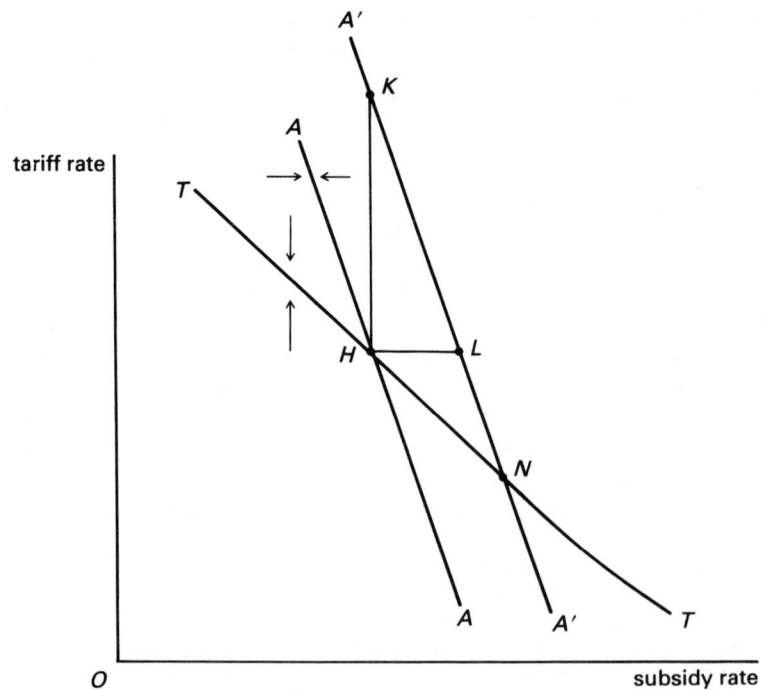

Figure 2.5

for various levels of subsidy. A movement down the curve leads to more clothing output, hence lower imports, and thus (by assumption) a higher elasticity of the foreign offer curve. This, in turn, means that the optimal tariff rate falls. The vertical arrows show that the tariff rate is targeted on attaining this optimal tariff rate. We thus have two instruments and two targets, and the assignment of instrument to target is stable.[14]

Suppose that the output target shifted from AA to $A'A'$. It could be attained by a rise in the tariff rate (from H to K), by a rise in the subsidy rate (to L) or some combination. Given the assignment, the movement will be to N, with a *fall* in the tariff rate, the rise in the subsidy being more than enough to compensate for the adverse output effect of the lower tariff. This (superficially) is the paradox. If, over the relevant range, the elasticity of the foreign offer curve *fell* as the volume of trade falls, so that the optimal tariff rose, the TT curve would slope upwards, and higher target production of clothing would then require some *rise* in the tariff.

Wider Applicability of Analysis

The propositions of essay 2 supplemented by the considerations introduced above are applicable more widely than might appear at first sight.

1) Quantitative import restrictions and voluntary export restraints (VERs) are now more important instruments of trade restriction in many countries than tariffs. Hence it should be noted that the principal argument of essay 2 is applicable to the comparison between these devices and subsidies. Quantitative restrictions reduce supplies of the restricted goods on the domestic market and VERs reduce supplies on the market of the importing country. In both cases this raises prices in these markets not only to producers but also to consumers, hence bringing about a by-product consumption distortion, which is the source of the inferiority of a trade restriction relative to the equivalent subsidy. Of course, there are further distinctions between various trade restrictions, the subject of an extensive literature.

2) The analysis is applicable to a model with many commodities and many tariffs and subsidies, subject to the complications discussed in the Further Notes to essay 1. Subsidies that are aimed to achieve specific objectives with regard to the pattern of production (such as offsetting given production distortions or achieving non-economic targets) are preferable to a regime of tariffs or of quantitative import restrictions. On the other hand, if there are non-optimal tariffs for product group X that have to be taken as given, then a second-best optimal structure for product group Y may include some tariffs. The point is that the tariffs on products X will

---

14. AA could not be flatter than TT. If it were, a rise in the subsidy when associated with the optimal tariff adjustment would lead to *lower* output of clothing. But it is the higher output of clothing resulting from the subsidy that causes the changed trade volume which brings about the fall in the optimal tariff rate.

have distorted the consumption pattern, and tariffs on products Y may then be offsetting.

3) Most goods traded in world markets are intermediate goods, not final products. Apart from their direct protective effect, tariffs on such goods have two effects.

First, if there is scope for substitution they create distortions in input use. Importable inputs with high tariffs will be used less relative to importable inputs with low tariffs, and use of all inputs on which there are tariffs or other trade restrictions will be reduced relative to exportable and non-traded inputs, and relative to primary factors. These substitution effects are by-product distortions equivalent to the consumption distortion created by a tariff in our simple model.

Secondly, tariffs on inputs raise the costs of the using industries and so reduce their effective protection (as discussed in essay 7). Now there are two possibilities. The first is that this is *not* offset by higher tariffs or by subsidies for the using industries. In that case a by-product production effect has been created which may or may not be distorting, depending on the relationship to the direct protection effect of the tariffs for the inputs and on the welfare function. The second possibility is that the effects of the tariffs on inputs are offset by other tariffs or export subsidies (when the using industries are export industries) being increased, so that effective protection for the using industries is not reduced. In that case prices to consumers of the final products will be raised, and the system of tariffs will have created the usual consumption distortion, but in this case through an indirect process. If the offsetting had been brought about with production subsidies no such distortion would have been created. Thus the case for the use of production subsidies in preference to tariffs remains.

Collection and Disbursement Costs

It is hardly reasonable to compare tariffs and subsidies without taking into account collection costs of tariffs and other taxes as well as subsidy disbursement costs. These have been left out of essay 2. We shall adhere to the small country model here.

Consider first the following simple case. (a) We have, as in essay 2, a two-product model, so that there can be only one tariff. (b) There are very high collection costs for taxes other than tariffs, e.g. for income tax, while the collection cost for the tariff is low or zero. Given the desire to increase domestic production of the import-competing product, it may then be optimal to do so with a tariff rather than a subsidy. The general principle might be thought of as follows. First a subsidy is provided. Then it is financed in a minimum-cost way. The costs of the financing have two parts, namely the by-product distortion costs already discussed and the collection costs. If the latter are very high for non-tariff taxes relative to the use of a tariff, it may then be optimal to finance the subsidy with a tariff. But in this two-product model there is only one possible tariff, namely the tariff on the product the domestic output of which is to be increased. It follows that protection can be directly by tariff.

Next, allow for a model with more than two imports. Again, suppose that collection costs for non-tariff taxes are very high. The optimal policy is then to subsidize the industry to be protected, and to finance the subsidy with a minimum-cost tax package. This package will take into account both by-product distortion costs and collection costs. It may well include tariffs, and possibly consist exclusively of tariffs (if the collection cost effect dominates the by-product distortion effect). But there is no presumption that it would consist solely of a tariff on the product the output of which was to be increased in the first place. For example, collection costs may be very low for tariffs or export taxes on products X, while product Y is to be protected. The optimal policy may then be to subsidize domestic production of product Y and finance the subsidy with tariffs or export taxes on products X. The basic principle remains that a subsidy to achieve a protection objective is first best, provided it is financed in a minimum-cost way.[15]

Finally, there are subsidy disbursement costs. Protecting directly with a tariff involves only one transaction. The revenue from the tariff can contribute to financing the public sector and so allow existing other taxes to be reduced. By contrast, protecting with a subsidy involves two transactions, namely the collection of the extra revenue, yielding the by-product distortion costs and the collection costs already discussed, and the disbursement cost of the subsidy. The latter may also be costly, and these costs could in theory be high enough to shift the balance in favour of the use of a tariff that directly protects the industry which it is desired to expand.

Political Economy: Transparency and Lobbying

The choice between a regime of tariffs and a regime of subsidies should also be influenced by political economy considerations. We now assume that free trade would actually be optimal from a social point of view, so that a regime should be favoured if it leads to relatively less protection.

It has usually been argued that subsidies are more transparent than tariffs. The cost to consumers of tariffs are not clearly visible while a subsidy has to be financed by tax revenue, must appear in the budget, and hence is clearly visible. Indeed, it may have to be approved every year. 'For this very reason – the obscurantist aspect of tariffs and quotas – free-trade minded economists preferred subsidies to tariffs long before the theory of domestic distortions was developed.[16] Since the raising of explicit taxes – as distinct from taxing consumers indirectly through tariffs or

---

15. When there are significant collection costs for trade taxes there is a qualification to this argument set out by Corden (1974, p. 46).
16. Corden (1974, p. 56), where this argument is more fully developed.

import quotas – is politically difficult, pressure groups demanding subsidies are more likely to be resisted than those demanding tariffs or quotas. On the other hand, these very pressure groups will prefer the non-transparent tariffs or quotas just because they do not want the community to realize that an income transfer is taking place. This helps to explain why tariffs and import restrictions are so widely used as protective devices. The regime choice has been influenced more by the pressure groups than by detached considerations of the social interest.

More recently stress has been laid on the non-transparent nature of many subsidies, notably those that operate through tax concessions (tax expenditures), or through various special arrangements, such as grants for labour training, regional employment subsidies, and the covering of losses of state enterprises. Thus the transparency criterion does not unambiguously lead to a preference for a subsidy regime, though the traditional argument, on the basis of which economists have preferred subsidies to tariffs or quotas while protectionist interests have preferred the latter to subsidies, still seems powerful.

Another political economy consideration has recently been introduced by Rodrik (1984). The argument is that in a regime of tariffs there is likely to be less lobbying than in a regime of subsidies. The reason is that a tariff usually provides protection for a number of firms, so that the lobbying activity has a public good element for any individual firm. The greater the number of firms producing a given product, the less lobbying for tariffs there is likely to be (or the more need there is for group organization) and the less likely it is that a tariff will be imposed. Assuming that we are in a situation where free trade is actually first best – or, at least where tariffs obtained by lobbying are always, on balance, distorting – an increase in the number of firms will reduce both the total costs of lobbying – which is a social cost – and the likelihood that a distorting tariff will be imposed.

By contrast, a subsidy is more likely to be firm-specific. If it is, then there is no public good element for the lobbying activities of a particular firm since it will be the only beneficiary from successful lobbying. Hence there is likely to be more lobbying than in the case of a tariff, and it is more likely that protection will be granted. It follows that, from this point of view, a tariff regime is preferable to a subsidy regime. Furthermore, the larger the number of firms that would potentially benefit from a tariff, the more important this consideration is. If there were only one firm this distinction between a tariff and a subsidy would disappear, and only the considerations discussed earlier would be relevant to the regime choice.

References

Baldwin, R. E. 1948: Equilibrium in international trade: a diagrammatic analysis. *The Quarterly Journal of Economics*, 62, 748–62.
Berry, D. 1954: Modern welfare analysis and the forms of income redistribution. In A. T. Peacock (ed.), *Income Redistribution and Social Policy*. London: Cape.
Brigden, J. B. *et al.* 1929: *The Australian Tariff: An Economic Enquiry*. Melbourne: Melbourne University Press.
Browne, G. W. B. 1946: A note on tariffs and subsidies. *South African Journal of Economics*, 14, 224–5.
Corden, W. M. 1974: *Trade Policy and Economic Welfare*. Oxford: Oxford University Press.
Corlett, W. J. and Hague, D. C. 1953–4: Complementarity and the excess burden of taxation. *Review of Economic Studies*, 21, 21–30.
Graaff, J. de V. 1947: A note on the relative merits of tariffs and subsidies. *South African Journal of Economics*, 15, 149–50.
―――― 1949–50: On optimum tariff structures. *Review of Economic Studies*, 17, 47–59.
Johnson, H. G. 1951–2: Optimum welfare and maximum revenue tariffs. *Review of Economic Studies*, 19, 28–35.
―――― 1960: The cost of protection and the scientific tariff. *Journal of Political Economy*, 68, 327–45.
―――― 1965: An economic theory of protectionism, tariff bargaining and the formation of customs unions. *Journal of Political Economy*, 73, 256–83.
Joseph, M. F. W. 1938–9: The excess burden of indirect taxation. *Review of Economic Studies*, 6, 226–31.
Kaldor, N. 1940: A note on tariffs and the terms of trade. *Economica*, 7, 377–80.
Little, I. M. D. 1951: Direct versus indirect taxes. *The Economic Journal*, 61, 577–84.
Meade, J. E. 1955: *Trade and Welfare*. Oxford: Oxford University Press.
Rodrik, D. 1984: Tariffs, subsidies, and welfare with endogenous policy. Discussion Papers in Economics, Woodrow Wilson School of Public and International Affairs, Princeton University.
Scitovsky, T. 1942–3: A reconsideration of the theory of tariffs. *Review of Economic Studies*, 10, 89–110.
Threlfell, R. L. 1946: The relative merits of tariffs and subsidies as methods of protection. *South African Journal of Economics*, 14, 117–31.

3
Monopoly, Tariffs and Subsidies*

International trade theory usually assumes perfect competition, this being one of the more glaring of its deficiencies. This essay is a limited attempt to explore some implications of assuming increasing returns and monopoly in an import-competing industry. The approach is subject to all the usual limitations of partial equilibrium analysis. Assumptions are chosen so as to make the model relevant to considering the effects of tariffs and subsidies in a 'young' industrializing economy which plays a relatively small part in world trade, such as Brazil or Australia.

I Monopoly in the Open Economy

In figure 3.1 the domestic demand curve for the product of the industry (firm) is DD' and the marginal revenue curve derived from it is MM'. The demand curve is assumed to trace out the private and social value of marginal units of product in money terms; the marginal utility of money is assumed constant. The average cost of domestic output is given by the curve AA' and the marginal cost by CC'. There are increasing returns to scale and factor prices are assumed constant. Hence the cost curves decline and they do not embody any element of producers' surplus. While average costs are assumed to be falling over the range of output under discussion here, it is not assumed that they would fall indefinitely; at some high level of output, average costs would stabilize or even rise. It is assumed that the use of the inputs does not generate any non-market externalities. In other words, the cost curves reflect both private and social costs. There are no distortions elsewhere in the economy. Normal profits are included in costs. The demand curve is assumed to cut the cost curve from above, so that stable equilibrium results. Income distribution effects on social welfare are ignored; appropriate compensation could be assumed.

If the economy were closed, and assuming profit maximization, output would be at OR, where marginal revenue equals marginal cost, and hence

* *Economica*, 34, Feb. 1967, 50–8. I am indebted to H. W. Arndt.

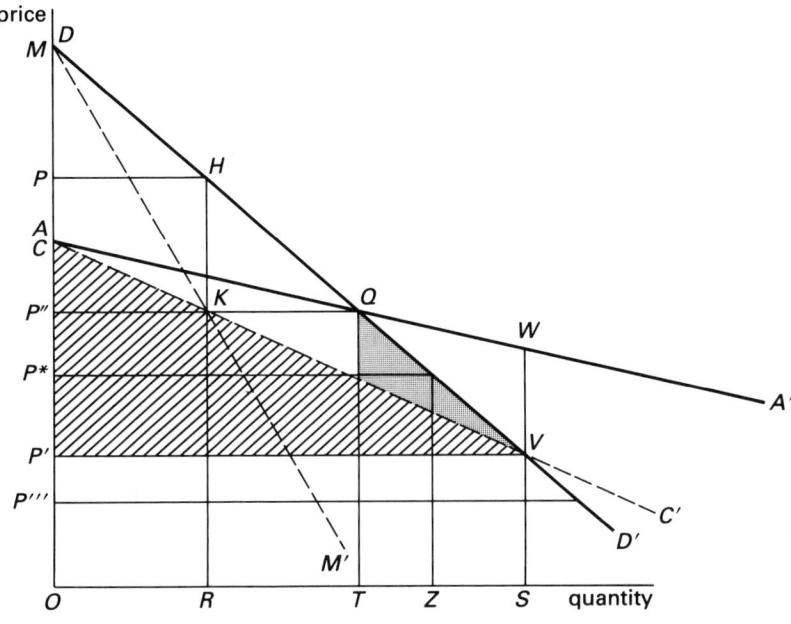

Figure 3.1

price would be OP. Monopoly profits would result. As is well known, given our assumptions the socially optimum output would be where price equals marginal cost, namely at OS with price of OP'. At this output a loss would be made since average cost is above price. We thus have the familiar contrast between the private equilibrium output OR and the social optimum OS.[1] One other output level is of interest. At output OT, with price OP'', price is equal to average cost, so that both monopoly profit and a loss are avoided. This output is above the profit maximization but below the socially optimum output.

Now open the economy. We assume that the product is importable and that the elasticity of the foreign supply of it is infinite. There is now a given import price of the product, the price of the identical product in the world market plus transport costs. The domestic price may be below it but cannot exceed it. We shall assume that when the domestic price is equal to the import price, customers purchase all available domestic output before buying imports; alternatively we might assume that the upper limit to the domestic price is set by the import price less a small margin designed to

1. This essay is a development of marginal-cost pricing theory, and is subject to all the qualifications and limitations of this theory. The present essay is written in the belief that the theory needs to be appropriately qualified rather than dismissed; it would be a useless exercise if the theory should be dismissed entirely, as Little (1957) seemed to suggest.

ensure that the domestic product is bought in preference to the identical imported product.

We also make the important assumption that there is no possibility of exporting the product. This is on the whole not an unrealistic assumption for the type of 'young' economy for which the model has been constructed. But why should it be possible to import the product but not to export it? The impossibility assumed is not a technical one but purely the result of assumed price and cost relationships. It will be assumed that transport costs and other obstacles to trade given as constraints to the country (such as the tariffs of other countries) establish a margin between the import price at the border (the cost-insurance-freight or c.i.f. import price) and the export price at the border (the free-on-board or the f.o.b. export price). The f.o.b. export price is assumed to be not only lower than minimum average costs but lower even than minimum marginal costs. Thus, whatever the volume of output, profitable exporting is impossible. Even if the price charged were equal to marginal costs (a case considered below), there would be no exports. Of course an export subsidy, a policy device not considered here, could make exporting possible and, more generally, the analysis could be extended to allow for the possibility of exporting.

If the given import price is at or above OP, the opening of the economy will make no difference to the output and price equilibrium. At OP the import price happens to coincide with the monopoly price; if the import price rises above this the domestic price will not follow it. If the given import price is below OP'' the domestic monopoly will find it impossible to avoid losses and will go out of business (or will not come into existence in the first place). If the import price is at or above OP'' but below OP the monopoly will stay in business, but output will be greater and price and monopoly profits lower than in the closed economy situation.[2] To sum up the three possibilities: the opening of the economy may (a) make no difference to this industry, (b) lead to the closing down of the industry, complete replacement of domestic output by imports and an expansion of demand as a result of the fall in the domestic price, or (c) lead to increased output by the industry and squeezing of its monopoly profits. A fourth possibility, that the industry commences to export, has been ruled out by assumption.

II The Social Optimum in the Open Economy

We know the social optimum in the closed economy: it is where the marginal cost of the domestic producer equals price. Now, what is the

2. With an import price such as OP, the marginal revenue curve facing the firm is the discontinuous curve $PHKM'$, and the monopolist will choose to produce at the point where it is intersected by CC'. If the import price is less than OP this point will be to the right of K.

social optimum in the open economy? There are really two issues, the structural and the marginal one. The structural question is whether the industry should or should not exist. We consider first the marginal question: what should the quantity of output or of imports be? If the industry exists, so that its own cost curve is the relevant one, the marginal optimum is clearly the closed-economy socially optimum output OS. If the industry did not exist, so that the foreign supply curve would be the relevant average and marginal cost curve, the socially optimum supply would be where DD' cuts the import price line.

The structural question is the more complex one. The first point is that with falling costs, the industry, if it exists, should supply the whole market; thus the choice is an all-or-nothing one between having the industry and having imports. For if the market were divided between imports and home production and the marginal cost of home production were above the import price, total cost of supplies could always be reduced by replacing home production by imports; while if the marginal cost of home production were equal to or less than the import price, the total cost of supplies could be reduced by replacing imports by home production.

If the import price were at OP'' and imports were allowed to supply the local market, the consumers' surplus (measuring the social gain) would be the triangle $P''QD$. But if domestic production replaced imports and satisfied the marginal condition (output at OS) the surplus would be greater. For with domestic output of OT and hence average costs of QT and equal to the average cost of the import alternative, the surplus would be the same as with the import alternative; but since domestic output would actually be at OS there would be an additional surplus, indicated in figure 3.1 by the small shaded triangle. Thus if the import price is at OP'' the social optimum requires the industry to exist and then to produce OS of output. This would of course also be true if the import price were above OP''.

If the import price were at OP' and imports supplied the whole market, imports would be OS, identical with the domestic producer's marginal social optimum. Consumers' surplus would be the triangle $P'VD$. But if there were domestic production of this amount the surplus would be only CVD (the area under the demand curve minus the area under the marginal cost curve), which is less than $P'VD$ by the large shaded triangle $P'VC$. The same point can be made in terms of average cost. At OS the average cost of imports is VS but the average cost of domestic output is WS; so, if there is domestic production, the surplus per unit of output falls short by WV of the surplus per unit of imports when the market is supplied by imports. Thus if the import price is at OP' the social optimum requires the whole market to be supplied by imports; the industry should not exist. This would also be true if the import price were below OP'.

It remains only to determine whether the industry should or should not exist when the import price is somewhere between OP'' and OP'. Imagine the import price gradually to fall from OP'' to OP'. One can think in terms of the two surpluses represented by the triangles coming together in size. Somewhere between OP'' and OP' is an import price OP^* at which there is social indifference whether or not the industry is established. At this price, imports (if there were any) would be OZ and we have the following equality: area under the CC' curve up to output OZ minus value of imports of OZ equals area under demand curve for output ZS minus area under CC' curve for output ZS. In other words, the excess cost of domestic production of OZ relative to the cost of the import alternative is just equal to the surplus from that amount of domestic production ZS which is in excess of the quantity of the import alternative. To define OP^* precisely one would have to specify the shapes of the demand and cost curves. If the import price were above OP^* the industry should exist and produce output OS. If the import price were below OP^* demand should be wholly satisfied by imports, the quantity imported being given by the demand curve and the import price.

Now the private and the social optima in the open economy can be related. There are three zones: (1) At the import price OP'' and above it the industry will exist and produce somewhere from OR to OT, and hence less than OS. The social optimum requires it to exist and produce OS. (2) Below the price OP'' and above OP^* the industry will be privately unprofitable. Yet socially it is required to exist and produce at OS. (3) Below the price OP^* the industry will be privately and socially unprofitable. Thus private and social benefit diverge marginally in (1) and structurally in (2), and do not diverge in (3). The next question is naturally what devices can ensure that the social optimum is attained when the economy is in zones (1) or (2).

III A Tariff

The effect of a tariff can readily be seen. Suppose the free-of-duty import price is OP''', that is somewhere below OP'' and hence at a level at which the firm could not exist without losses. If a tariff were imposed which raised the duty-paid price to OP'' the industry would come into existence but would make no monopoly profits; imports would cease completely. A further increase in the tariff would enable the firm to exploit some monopoly power; the price would rise and output decline. There could not, of course, be any more import replacement. If the tariff were high enough to raise the duty-paid import price to OP the firm would be fully able to exploit its monopoly position. Further increases in the tariff above that would have no effect. We can conclude that a certain level of tariff may be required to establish the industry. Increases above that, up to a limit, give it increasing monopoly power.

Can a tariff be of any help in bringing the social optimum closer? In zone (1) a tariff can only make matters worse. It raises the price which the monopolist can charge and thus (unless the price is at or above OP) causes output to be reduced and monopoly profits to be increased. So output actually moves away from the marginal social optimum. In zone (2) a tariff sufficient to raise the duty-paid import price to OP'' would bring the industry into existence and so appear to bring about the structural optimum. But it would not lead to a marginal optimum, since output would be OT instead of OS (and less than OT if the tariff were higher). Now establishment of the industry is structurally optimum only if the marginal optimum is fulfilled; in fact, with output of OT consumers' surplus would be $P''QD$ which is less than consumers' surplus when there are imports at an import price below OP''.[3] In zone (3), as in zone (2), a tariff will lead to the establishment of the industry if it is high enough to bring the duty-paid import price up to or above OP''. A tariff less than this has no effect. But in fact the industry should not be established, so that if the tariff has an effect it must be adverse.

We may conclude that in zones (1) and (2) a tariff will increase the existing divergence between private and social benefit, unless the price is already at or above OP, or is insufficient to bring it to OP'', in which two cases it would have no effect. In zone (3) it will bring about a divergence between private and social benefit where none existed before, unless, again, it is insufficient to bring the duty-paid import price to OP''. For the purpose in hand a tariff is therefore either bad or useless. This conclusion is not quite as obvious as might seem here. It is well known that to attain a social optimum with increasing returns in the closed economy a subsidy is required; it will be shown below that this may also be true in the open economy. Now, in some circumstances, especially in a competitive situation with a rising industry supply curve, a tariff has the same effect on domestic production as a unit subsidy to domestic producers. Tariffs and subsidies are correctly regarded as alternative protective devices. It might therefore be concluded that a monopolized industry with a falling cost curve should obtain a tariff to bring it to the optimum. But where the assumptions of the present model apply this is not so.

An import subsidy (or negative tariff) may be more appropriate. In zone (1) an import subsidy will squeeze monopoly profits and bring output closer to the optimum, provided the import price is above OP''. An import subsidy can reduce the domestic price to OP'' and thus eliminate monopoly profits and bring output to OT. This is not the optimum, but is closer to it. It should be noted that in zone (1) the import subsidy would be only a threat; since domestic output would continue to supply the whole market the subsidy would cost nothing and would in fact be a form of price control. An import subsidy sounds more unreal than it really is. Some countries

---

3. Drawing on a well-known analogy, given by Meade (1955, p. 119), without the tariff the economy is at the top of a small mountain peak. The tariff causes it to come down from that peak and climb towards the higher peak, but it fails to lead it to the top, and in fact leaves the economy at a lower altitude than when it was at the top of the smaller peak.

have overvalued exchange rates and low or zero tariffs on some imports. In relation to the equilibrium exchange rate at which the true cost of imports should be calculated, these particular imports are subsidized. And in certain cases tariffs are explicitly kept low to 'keep the local monopoly on its toes'.

The conclusion at this stage is that a tariff is likely to increase a gap between social and private benefit while an import subsidy may reduce it but cannot eliminate it. Thus taxes on trade are inadequate devices for coping with distortions brought about by monopoly and increasing returns. Put in this general way this is a conclusion which follows naturally from the theory of the second best.

IV Subsidies

In zones (1) and (2) the social optimum can be attained in either of two ways.[4] (a) The firm can be *ordered* to produce to output OS, and then be paid a lump-sum subsidy to cover the resultant loss. This is the familiar Lerner approach and is perhaps appropriate for public enterprises. (b) The monopoly can be *induced* to produce to OS by being given an appropriate subsidy per unit of output, this being possibly the appropriate method for private enterprise. In both cases to clear the market the domestic price will be OP' which will be below the import price.

The cost of the subsidy and the effect on monopoly profits of the order and the inducement method differ. This distinction is as relevant in the closed economy as in the open economy so that it is not specifically related to the international trade aspects of monopoly and increasing returns. But it can be explained here briefly with the aid of figure 3.2. With the order method the cost of the lump sum subsidy need only be sufficient to cover the gap between price and average cost at output OS. Per unit it averages VW and it is shown by the shaded area. With the inducement method the subsidy must be sufficient to shift the monopolist's marginal revenue curve upwards until it crosses the marginal cost curve at V. Including the subsidy in his revenue, the monopolist will then choose to produce the optimum output. The unit cost of the subsidy is then clearly UV, the vertical gap between the marginal and average revenue curves. Now UV must be greater than VW. For DD' is steeper than AA', so the elasticity of DD' at output OS is less than that of AA'; hence the gap between average revenue and marginal revenue must be greater than the gap between average cost and marginal cost. It follows that the unit inducement subsidy must be greater than the lump sum order subsidy. Furthermore, the minimum required lump sum subsidy will not create any monopoly profits. On the

---

4. The reader must be reminded that the social optimum is conceived of in very simple-minded terms here. It ignores income distribution effects as well as the administrative and distortion costs involved in financing subsidies.

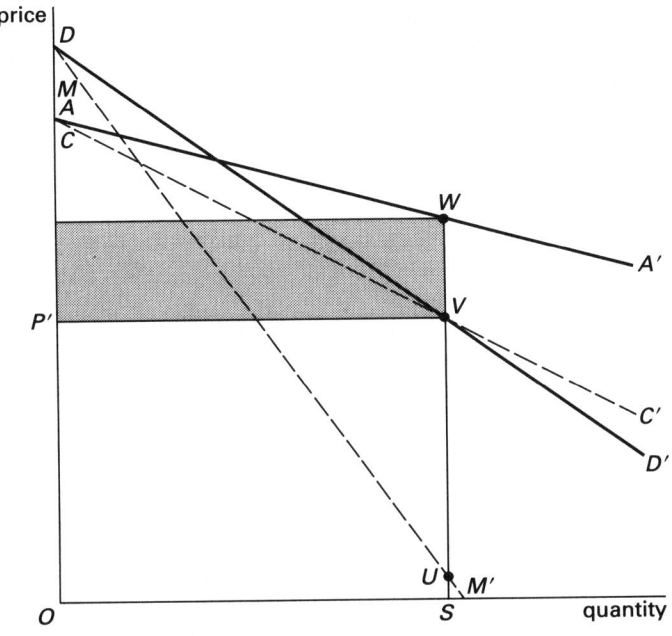

Figure 3.2

other hand, the inducement subsidy will actually increase monopoly profits above what they would be if the firm existed and followed its natural monopolistic bent. The point is simply that the subsidy shifts the firm's demand curve to the right so that, following a profit maximization policy both before and after, the firm's profits must increase. Thus the inducement method means that private monopolies are induced to produce a less monopolistic output by a method which actually increases their monopoly profits. It seems therefore a rather strange proposal. But this difficulty could in theory be overcome: the monopoly profits, or the addition to monopoly profits, could be eliminated by combining the unit subsidy with an appropriate lump sum tax which is charged irrespective of the volume of output.[5]

5. An alternative inducement approach (but no more realistic as a practical proposal than the two schemes described above) has been suggested to me by H. W. Arndt. The monopolist may be offered a conditional lump sum subsidy which would cover (a) his potential loss at output *OS*, (b) his existing monopoly profits, if any, and (c) an inducement margin sufficient to induce him to move from his existing monopoly output to *OS*. The payment of (a) and (b) at output *OS* leaves him as well off as before; (c) therefore may not need to be large. But the monopolist must agree to produce at *OS* if he wishes to obtain any part of the subsidy. The cost of this subsidy would be greater than the lump sum order subsidy (which avoids a loss but does not

Finally a warning must be given about the following conclusion which might be wrongly derived. The monopoly and the existence of increasing returns are domestic distortions which are correctly overcome by a domestic subsidy. Therefore, irrespective of the trade situation – that is, irrespective of where precisely the import price is – the social optimum can be obtained by consistently applying the subsidy. While this conclusion is true in zones (1) and (2) it is not necessarily true in zone (3). Suppose the economy were in zone (3), with the import price at OP' or above. With the appropriate order or inducement subsidy the firm will come into existence and produce at OS, selling the product at OP'. Since the world price is at OP' or above it will be able to sell its output. As we saw earlier, the social optimum requires the firm *not* to exist; imports should supply the whole market. Thus the result of the subsidy in this case is to attain a marginal optimum but not the structural optimum.[6] If, on the other hand, the economy were in the lower part of zone (3), with the price below OP', a subsidy which enables the firm to sell at OP' would not in fact allow the firm to survive (or bring it into existence). Thus the subsidy would have no effect; it would leave the economy at the social optimum which it would have attained in any case in the absence of a subsidy.

Further Notes: Monopoly and Economies of Scale

Bilateral Monopoly

In essay 3 a single government confronts a single firm. The government has available to it two instruments of policy, namely a tariff and a subsidy, while the firm's instrument is the ability to determine whether it should go into domestic production and how much it shall produce. In the case of the order subsidy there is, in fact, only one decision maker, namely the government, so that the possibility of bargaining is ruled out. But an interesting issue does arise in the case of the tariff and the inducement subsidy. It is clearly in the interests of the firm that it receives the maximum subsidy or tariff for any given output it produces. We have two agents in a potential bargaining situation: the objective of one is to bring output as close as possible to the social optimum, while that of the other is to maximize profits.

Consider the case where the social optimum requires the firm to go into domestic production. It may refuse to do so unless it receives a subsidy which is actually larger than that required for the social optimum. But if it does not go into production it would be worse off than if it had received the

> maintain monopoly profits) but probably less than the unit inducement subsidy (which may increase monopoly profits by something more than the inducement margin).

6. Without the subsidy the economy is at the top of the highest peak. The subsidy causes it to climb to the top of a lower peak.

lower required subsidy and gone into production. If we assume that the government's policy is a variable, we have then a prisoner's dilemma situation. In essay 3 it is implicitly assumed that the government is a Stackelberg leader: it knows the firm's potential reaction to various levels of subsidy, and then fixes the optimal subsidy. The firm knows that this subsidy level will not be changed, and so adapts to it in the expected way. Of course, it is also assumed that the government knows the firm's cost curve.[7]

Product Differentiation: Snape's Contribution

In the model of essay 3 the subsidy reduces the domestic price and leads to an increase in consumption. This increase in consumption is the source of welfare gain from the subsidy, and this gain may exceed the cost that results from domestic production replacing cheaper imports. A tariff, by contrast, cannot increase consumption. In fact, it will reduce it. Thus there can be no welfare gain resulting from a tariff. If a subsidy of any kind is ruled out, the optimal tariff will be zero. This outcome is different from the results one gets in the usual diminishing returns models, where the optimal tariff to remedy a domestic distortion is likely to be positive, even though the optimal subsidy would attain a higher level of welfare, so that the tariff is second best or worse.

A valuable development of the model of essay 3 has been provided by Snape (1977). He shows that, *in the presence of product differentiation*, the strong result that the second-best optimal tariff can never be positive disappears. Snape assumes that the domestic import-competing product is an imperfect substitute for the import, rather than the two being identical. We can then imagine that the domestic product (still subject to economies of scale) faces a downward-sloping demand curve which shifts to the right when a tariff is imposed on the import. There will again be a social loss from the replacement of imports by domestic production. But consumption of the home-produced product will now rise above zero, so there is now a source of gain: the excess of the pre-tariff demand curve for the domestic variety over the marginal costs of producing the extra output that results from the tariff. Thus a tariff *may* now lead to a net gain. Snape shows this both in partial equilibrium terms and in a three-product general equilibrium model.

Here it should be noted that the partial equilibrium presentation in essay 3 makes the exposition simple, but is not a serious limitation, as shown by Snape. It would be possible to tell the story of essay 3 in terms of a two-sector model (with an importable and an exportable) where home production of the importable is monopolized while there is perfect

---

7. A literature has recently developed on strategic behaviour in international trade and on the effects of tariffs in oligopolistic models. See Dixit (1983), Spencer and Brander (1983), and Grossman and Richardson (1984).

competition in the exportable industry. Snape's model, where the import is a different product from the import-competing product, requires three products.

Further Developments

Extensions of the approach of essay 3 to allow for the possibility of exporting are given by Basevi (1970) and Pursell and Snape (1973). They also show possible divergences between private and social optima.

More recently this whole subject of protection in the presence of economies of scale and monopoly has been revived, with a new interest in increasing returns, product differentiation and monopolistic competition in relation to the gains from trade and optimal trade policy. An extensive literature, though mostly not policy orientated, is surveyed by Helpman (1984) (see also Kierzkowski, 1984).

The most relevant paper is that of Markusen and Melvin (1984). They are concerned with the gains from trade, i.e. comparing no-trade with free trade, rather than optimal trade policy, and treat the matter thoroughly and in a unified manner in general equilibrium terms. They find that there are two elements to the problem of determining the gains from trade when there are increasing returns to scale: first non-fulfilment of the 'tangency conditions' (prices not being equal to marginal costs), and secondly, non-convexities (the 'convexity conditions'), that is problems caused by economies of scale. In effect, this is the same distinction as that made in essay 3 between the marginal optimum and the structural optimum.

References

Basevi, G. 1970: Domestic demand and ability to export. *Journal of Political Economy*, 78, 330–7.
Dixit, A. 1983: International trade policy for oligopolistic industries. *The Economic Journal*, 94 (Supplement), 1–16.
Grossman, G. M. and Richardson, J. D. 1984: *Strategic U.S. Trade Policy: A Survey of Issues and Early Analysis*, NBER Research Progress Report. Cambridge, Mass: National Bureau of Economic Research.
Helpman, E. 1984: Increasing returns, imperfect markets, and trade theory. In R. W. Jones and P. B. Kenen (eds), *Handbook of International Economics: Volume 1*, Amsterdam: North-Holland.
Kierzkowski, H. (ed.) 1984: *Monopolistic Competition and International Trade*. Oxford: Oxford University Press.
Little, I. M. D. 1957: *A Critique of Welfare Economics*, 2nd edn. Oxford: Oxford University Press.
Markusen, J. and Melvin, J. 1984: The gains-from-trade theorem with increasing returns to scale. In H. Kierzkowski (ed.), *Monopolistic Competition and International Trade*, Oxford: Oxford University Press.

Meade, J. E. 1955: *Trade and Welfare*. Oxford: Oxford University Press.
Pursell, G. and Snape, R. H. 1973: Economies of scale, price discrimination and exporting. *Journal of International Economics*, 3, 85–92.
Snape, R. H. 1977: Trade policy in the presence of economies of scale and product variety. *The Economic Record*, 53, 525–34.
Spencer, B. J. and Brander, J. A. 1983: International R&D rivalry and industrial strategy. *Review of Economic Studies*, 50, 707–22.

4
Economies of Scale and Customs Union Theory*

Orthodox customs union theory assumes constant or increasing costs for each industry and is frequently criticized for failing to allow for economies of scale. The aim of this essay is to incorporate economies of scale systematically in customs union theory. In particular, we want to see whether the familiar concepts of trade creation and trade diversion are still relevant.[1]

The approach will initially be partial equilibrium and static, this being also the way in which the principal propositions of established customs union theory were originally expounded. The economies of scale will be assumed to be internal to firms, so that the traditional assumption of perfect competition cannot be maintained. A crucial simplification will be the assumption that the countries forming the union face given prices from the outside world, economy-of-scale effects in the outside world as a result of the formation of the union being insignificant. We shall assume three countries, countries A and B, which form the union, and country C, representing the rest of the world.

I Simple Model: Two New Effects Introduced

We begin with a single homogeneous product which is produced in country C and is at least capable of being produced in the two union countries. There is a single actual or potential producer in each of the union countries. He has a declining average cost curve which indicates private and social average costs. He is assumed to pay constant prices for his factors of production whatever the scale of output, so that there are no

---
* *Journal of Political Economy*, March/April 1972, 80, pp. 465–75.
1. Viner (1950, pp. 45–6) gives a substantial discussion of economies of scale, but this has not been followed up in the literature. Some of his conclusions differ from those in the present essay, possibly because his (unspecified) assumptions differ. See also Johnson (1962, p. 59).

factor rents. The average cost curve is assumed to include normal profits. Each union country faces a given c.i.f. import and f.o.b. export price set by country C; because of transport costs and C's tariff, the export price is below the import price. It is convenient, though not essential, to assume that the two countries face the same import and export prices for the product. The average cost curve in each country is assumed to reach its minimum at a level above the export price, so that exporting the product to country C is ruled out. We also assume that, because of their tariffs and their relatively high costs, neither country initially exports to the other.[2]

We must now introduce tariffs. We have a choice of two simple assumptions. (1) We could assume that the two countries have the same tariff rate on the product before the union is formed. This is not a very realistic assumption, but it is implicit in much of orthodox customs union theory and means that one can focus on the effects of the freeing of trade within the union and need not be concerned with the establishment of a common external tariff, since such a tariff already exists. Since we want to define precisely what has to be added to orthodox theory when economies of scale are introduced, we should explore this case. (2) Alternatively, we could assume that tariff rates are 'made to measure' at levels designed to make the tariff-inclusive import price just equal to average costs, including normal profits, hence avoiding any excess profits. If there is no domestic production, there will be no tariff. This may be a more realistic assumption, and we consider it in the next section. But we begin with assumption (1).

Subject to a qualification to be considered below, in each country the domestic price is determined by the cost of imports from C plus the given tariff on imports from C. At this price there is a given quantity of domestic demand, and at this quantity there will be an average cost of actual or potential production. If this average cost is less than the domestic price, there will be domestic production and no imports; and if the average cost of the potential domestic producer exceeds the domestic price at that quantity, there will be imports and no domestic production.[3] The qualification is that the price of imports from C, including tariff, sets only an upper limit to the price a domestic producer can charge. It might pay a profit-maximizing producer to charge less. But we assume at this stage that he maximizes profits by charging right up to the 'import-preventing' price.

The same analysis applies once the customs union is formed, provided we assume no transport costs within the union. Either the union demand will be supplied wholly by imports from C, or there will be a single domestic producer within the union. In the latter case he might price below the price set by imports from C, but we shall assume at this stage that he

---

2. The requirements for this condition emerge precisely from the diagram in the appendix.
3. See Corden (1967). The present essay is essentially an extension of the analysis of this earlier paper to customs union theory.

prices up to the limit price. This has the important implication that the prices facing consumers are not affected by the establishment of the union: hence (a) the total market for the product in each country remains unchanged and (b) there are no welfare effects on consumers. This assumption will be removed in the next section.

Now we come to the main analysis, which can be very brief. Initially there may be production of the product in both countries, in one only, or in neither. We consider each of these three cases briefly.

Intitial Production in Both Countries

When the union is formed, one of the two producers, say country A's, will capture the whole union market, the other going out of business. Hence the average costs of country A's producer fall. Total costs of producing the product in the union thus decline because of specialization. This effect can be decomposed into two parts.

1) Country B's expensive domestic production is replaced by imports from A which are cheaper to produce; hence there has, in a sense, been a movement to a cheaper source of supply through the opening up of trade between A and B, and hence an orthodox trade-creation effect. But it must be remembered that the domestic price in B is assumed to be given at this stage. So none of the gain will go to B; it will all go to excess profits in A, and indeed B may lose, since its expelled producer may have earned excess profits.

2) Country A obtains its domestic supplies at lower cost of production. This can be called the cost-reduction effect. While it is a consequence of the creation of trade with B, it is not an orthodox trade-creation effect, since it is the result not of a movement to a cheaper source of supply but rather of the cheapening of an existing source of supply. Country A's consumers will gain nothing (because they face the same price as before), and the whole gain will go in profits to the producer.

Initial Production in Country A Only

There are two possibilities now. The most likely is that country A's producer captures the whole union market.[4] The effects can again be decomposed: (a) Country B replaces imports from C with imports from A. The latter are dearer than imports from C, since otherwise A would not have needed the formation of the union to break into B's market. Hence B loses from trade diversion, a dearer source of imports replacing a cheaper source of imports. The trade diversion loss to B will be equal to the loss of tariff revenue on imports from C. For the union as a whole the trade diversion loss may be less, since A's producer may earn some excess profits on imports to B. (b) As in our earlier example, A obtains its own product

---

4. See the appendix for a geometric exposition of this case. This case is also expounded geometrically by Johnson (1962, p. 59) and is described by Viner (1950, pp. 45–6).

at lower cost now, so that there is a cost-reduction effect equal to the extra profits earned on sales at home.

The other possibility – production reversal – seems less likely. When the union is formed, production in B may start, and B's producer may drive A's producer out of business and capture the whole union market. His costs will be less than A's were before the union was formed, so that this time there is a trade-creation gain through A obtaining its needs from a cheaper source (though this gain will go wholly to B), while B loses through the replacement of cheap imports from C with somewhat dearer domestic production. The costs of its newly established producer when he is supplying the whole union market must be greater than the cost of imports from C, for otherwise he could have become established even before the union was formed. When imports from C are replaced by domestic production, there is a trade-suppression effect.[5] It is akin to the trade-diversion effect, since a dearer source replaces a cheaper source, but this time the dearer source is a newly established domestic producer, not the partner country.

Initial Production in Neither Country

When the union is established, production in, say, country A may begin for the first time, since its average costs may now fall below the given domestic price. They will still be above the costs of imports from C, excluding duty, for otherwise A could have broken into B's market even without the union and so obtained the benefits of the combined market. In this case there is a trade-suppression effect for A (more expensive domestic production replaces cheaper imports from C) and a trade-diversion effect for B (more expensive imports from the partner replace cheaper imports from C). In both countries the whole loss is reflected in the loss of tariff revenue; this revenue loss will exceed the combined real income loss if the new producer earns excess profits.

Our conclusion is that the trade-creation and trade-diversion concepts are still relevant but that they must be supplemented by two other concepts, the 'cost-reduction effect' and the 'trade-suppression effect'. This is the main conclusion of this essay and remains even when some of the awkward or limiting assumptions are removed. Our examples suggest that the cost-reduction effect is likely to be the more important of the two.

II Made-to-Measure Tariff Making: Consumption Effects Introduced

The assumption that the tariffs in country A and country B are the same initially, so that a common external tariff already exists, and that domestic producers always price up to the tariff-inclusive price, has conveniently

---

5. The term comes from Viner (1950, p. 45).

eliminated any consumption effects but has led to the peculiar result in our first example that the trade creation gain through B getting its product from a cheaper source goes wholly to country A. It seems more sensible to assume that the purpose of tariffs is protection, not revenue, and that either a tariff will be high enough to bring domestic production into being (with imports wholly excluded) or it will not be imposed at all. Furthermore, we can now assume, as an interesting limiting case, that if a tariff is provided, it is just high enough to allow the domestic producer to cover his costs plus normal profits. These are the two components of what can be called made-to-measure tariff making.[6] Thus there are now no tariff revenues and no excess profits. All gains and losses will be borne by consumers. With this revised approach let us look at two of our cases.

Initial Production in Both Countries

The average costs of country A's producer when he supplies the whole union will be less than his costs when he supplied only his home market, and less than the costs of the former producer in B when he was supplying *his* own market. Thus the union domestic price can be less than the domestic price ruling initially in either country. Given made-to-measure tariff making, the common external tariff will thus be less than the two initial tariffs and consumers in both countries will gain from the establishment of the union. (a) In country B there is a familiar trade-creation gain having two components: the production effect results from the replacement of dearer domestic production by cheaper imports from A, and the consumption effect results from the increased consumption induced by the lower domestic price. (b) In country A there is a cost-reduction gain going to its consumers; this has also a production and a consumption component. The production effect is that the original amount of production sold domestically is now obtained at a lower price, while the consumption effect is that at the lower price an extra amount is purchased on which consumer's surplus is obtained.

The fact that the made-to-measure policy requires the common external tariff to be less than both initial tariffs suggests that made-to-measure tariff making may not be a wholly realistic assumption. In practice the result may be intermediate to that of this model and the previous one: the tariff may fall in at least one country, the gain going mainly or wholly to consumers there, while in the other country the gain goes in excess profits to the union producer (who may not belong to that country).

---

6. The term comes from Australia; the complicated structure of the Australian tariff system can be explained partly by an attempt to apply (not entirely consciously) the made-to-measure principle.

Initial Production in Country A Only

The made-to-measure model is applied quite easily to this case. Only one point need be noted here. If country B initially did not have domestic production, then its tariff will have been zero. If country A is to capture B's market – which A is assumed not to have captured before – this will result not from the freeing of trade within the union but from country B imposing a tariff – that is, from the establishment of the common external tariff at a positive level. The price to domestic consumers in B will then rise, and their losses can be divided into production- and consumption-effect components: the new, lower, amount consumed is now obtained at a higher cost than before, this being a shift to a dearer source of supply – the familiar trade-diversion effect – and in addition there is a loss in consumer's surplus on the reduced amount of consumption induced by the higher price. This latter consumption effect of trade diversion does not emerge in orthodox partial-equilibrium customs union theory.

We can conclude that our four effects – trade creation, trade diversion, cost reduction and trade suppression – each have a production and a consumption component. In a limiting case (the model of section I) the consumption components disappear. In another limiting case (the present section) all the gains and losses (whether from production or consumption effects) are borne by consumers. One can conceive of intermediate cases where there are some consumption effects and where some of the gains go in excess profits and some of the losses are borne by the government through loss of customs revenue. The extent of consumption effects and of excess profits depends on the extent to which the tariff system permits monopolists to exploit their position and whether they choose to do so. The distribution of gains and losses among government, producers and consumers is crucial, since it affects the distribution of the gains and losses between the partner countries.

III Oligopoly and Product Differentiation

We now depart from the assumption of a single producer in each country and in the union and allow for oligopoly and product differentiation.

Initial Production in Both Countries

Suppose that there are initially two producers in each country. It can no longer be assumed that the increased size of the market must lead to scale economies; if the two firms in each country did not amalgamate originally, or one of them did not attempt to out-compete the other, there is no strong reason to assume that amalgamation or competition would operate in the larger area. Of course, in the world of oligopoly anything is possible, but it is conceivable that the four producers all stay in business, dividing up the market of the union among them. They may do this by differentiating their products, and since there can now be four versions of each product available to each consumer instead of two, there will be a welfare gain; this is essentially a trade-creation effect. There need be no cost-reduction effect, since the increased trade in differentiated products need not necessarily be associated with increased output by any firm.

There may initially have been more than one firm in each country because the potentially dominant producer was reluctant to swallow up the weaker firms for fear of public hostility to monopoly, leading possibly to public intervention. When the customs union is established, it becomes possible to preserve the semblance of competition while eliminating all but one producer in each country; indeed, a government may urge the national firms to amalgamate so as to strengthen the competitive power of domestic production. The two remaining firms – one in each country – may not combine either because of fear of antimonopoly action or because of the difficulty of arranging amalgamations of firms across countries, combined with hostility to, or legislation against, takeovers by foreign firms. The reduction in the number of producers will then lead to a cost-reduction gain. In addition, trade across the borders may increase, or start for the first time, as a result of product differentiation. This may or may not represent a trade-creation gain. On the one hand, the number of firms the consumer can choose to purchase from is the same as before, so he may have no more choice in variety of product; but, on the other hand, he can now choose between products made in different countries.

Initial Production in Country A Only

There may be several producers in country A; when the union is formed, they all enter B's market, and there is the usual cost-reduction gain for A and trade-diversion loss for B. Two complications can be noted. (a) If the expansion of output by the various producers has brought them all closer to scales of output where average costs are at the minimum, the joint loss that they incur by failing to amalgamate is reduced; hence it becomes likelier that the oligopolistic situation will persist. (b) Some of the cost-reduction gains may be lost because producers in B may enter the field for the first time, since they now have a larger potential market available.

IV General Equilibrium

A really satisfactory general-equilibrium customs union model with economies of scale is difficult to produce. Some of the propositions of orthodox customs union theory have been expounded in terms of the two-good model, and this has led to results similar to those that emerge from the partial-equilibrium exposition. Models with more goods become rather

Economies of scale and customs union theory

complicated and tend to be expounded in a piecemeal way. There seems little point in developing the economies-of-scale argument in terms of a two-good model; it generally leads to the result that a country produces only one product, though no doubt many of the results produced so far in partial-equilibrium terms could be obtained. Here an alternative approach will be sketched out. It should be borne in mind that the aim is to isolate economy-of-scale effects.

There are many import-competing products; each product is produced, or potentially produced, in each country by only one firm. For each product the average cost curve is downward sloping up to a point, the curve turning upward eventually, so as to rule out exports of the product to country C. In addition, there is an export product with constant costs. There is a single mobile factor of production – labour – and its money wage is given. The cost curves for each product are thus independent of each other, since they depend only on the given money wage and the relevant production functions. In the initial situation each country has a made-to-measure tariff structure, leading to domestic production of some products and imports of others. Our partial-equilibrium analysis can now be applied directly. When the union is formed, production of some products will expand as the partner's market is taken over (cost reduction), production of others will cease as the domestic market is vacated for the partner (trade creation), and imports from C may cease because they are replaced either by imports from the partner (trade diversion) or by domestic production (trade suppression). All our four effects will happen at the same time.

Are there any general equilibrium complications? First, the demand curves for different products may shift because real income as a whole and income distribution may change, and because there are cross-elasticities. A fall in the price of one product would shift the demand curve for another product to the left. For any particular product the level of demand is crucial in determining either the tariff rate required to sustain a domestic industry or, alternatively, whether a domestic industry can be sustained with a given tariff rate. Furthermore, it determines the actual volume of output. Because of these demand relationships one cannot look at each product separately as if the general-equilibrium story were just made up of a set of separable partial-equilibrium stories. But it remains true that there are our four effects.

A second general-equilibrium complication is the need to maintain balance-of-payments equilibrium, which (with constant money wages) would be brought about through exchange-rate adjustment. In the first instance, with a given exchange rate, many of country A's industries might expand into B's market, while many of B's industries close down. Such a situation will then provoke appreciation of A's and depreciation of B's currency, and hence declines in the prices facing A's producers and increases in the prices facing B's producers (each in terms of their own currencies). This will then cause some of A's industries to go out of business and some of B's industries to revive again. In considering our

66 *Normative theory of protection*

effects in a general-equilibrium model, we should compare the initial preunion situation with the situation after the union is formed, each situation having its own equilibrium exchange rate.

V Dynamic Considerations

There is nothing essentially 'dynamic' about economies of scale. The whole of the analysis so far has been comparative static. But it is true that in a comparative-static model when there are economies of scale it is not possible to describe precisely the equilibrium that will be reached in a customs union. If initially our product is produced in both partner countries, we can say that when the union is formed one country might take over the whole market. But we cannot say which country it will be: that depends on dynamic considerations – on the nature of oligopolistic competition, the relative rates of gross investment in the two countries, and so on.[7] In the comparative-static model it is clear that, if only one firm survives, there will be trade-creation and cost-reduction effects, both of which represent gains to someone, but one cannot say which country will obtain the trade-creation and which the cost-reduction effect.

More generally, customs union theory may not tell us much about the reallocation of existing resources, owing to their immobility, but it can tell us something about the allocation and productivity of new investment. In the short run, capital is immobile and industries do not just 'take over' the whole market in another country or 'close down' as neatly as a comparative-static model might suggest. Assuming a 'putty-clay' model, the more gross investment there is in proportion to existing output, the more outputs will respond over a given period to price changes. Hence the effects described in this essay will take time, how much depending on the rate of gross investment.

Appendix

In figure 4.1, DD' is country A's demand curve for the product, and LL' is the horizontal sum of country A's and country B's demand curve. The c.i.f.

---

7. One might envisage a process of cutthroat competition to decide which of the two firms will survive. The firm that would have the relatively lower average costs if it supplied the union market on its own will have an advantage; this may depend on relative factor intensities, and so on. If 'learning by doing' counts for anything and provided it is related to output, one might expect (other things being equal) the firm that initially enjoyed the larger home market to have the lower costs after the union is formed, and so to survive. Relative financial resources to bear temporary losses are also relevant. During the process of 'sorting out', the union price may fall substantially, so that there may be a temporary income redistribution from producers to consumers.

Economies of scale and customs union theory

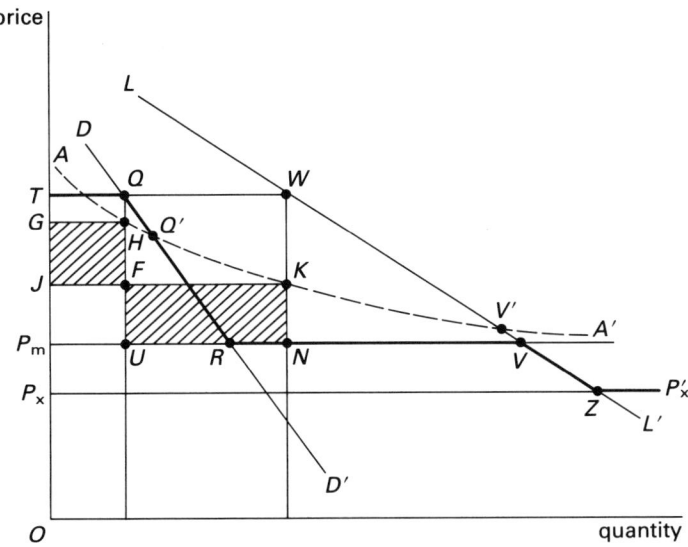

Figure 4.1

import price (when importing from C) is OP_m, and the f.o.b. export price (to C) is P_x. These prices are identical for countries A and B. We illustrate the argument of section I here. The given tariff is $P_m T$. Before the union is formed B has to pay this tariff on imports from A as well as from C, so that the combined demand curve facing A's producer is $TQRVZP'_x$. Once the union is formed, the demand curve facing him is $TWZP'_x$.

Curve AA' is country A's average-cost curve. If it cuts DD' below Q (as drawn) then there is domestic production in A before the union is formed; if it cuts DD' above Q, the whole amount of domestic consumption TQ will be imported (unless there are exports to B). If AA' cuts LL' above V (as drawn), there will be no exports to B in the absence of the union (unless there are exports to C) because B will find imports from C cheaper, while with the union production will depend on a positive common external tariff. If AA' cuts LL' below V there will be exports to B even in the absence of the union, and with the union production will not depend on a positive common tariff; furthermore, there will be production in A even if AA' happens to cut DD' above Q. If AA' cuts LL' above W (which it can do only if there is no production initially, AA' also cutting DD' above Q), then there will be no production even with the union. Provided the minimum-cost point on AA' is above $P_x P'_x$ (as drawn), there will no exports to C.

The diagram assumes (a) that even though B may have produced initially, it vacates production once the union is formed, and (b) that there are no transport costs within the union.

If (1) the producer prices right up to the import-preventing price OT and (2) B imported from C before the union, then the cost-reduction effect is $GHFJ$ and the trade-diversion effect for the union as a whole is $FKNU$ (both shaded). The loss of customs revenue to B, and hence the total loss to B, is $UQWN$, of which the trade-diversion effect $FKNU$ is a net loss to the union countries combined and $FQWK$ is a redistribution toward A's producer, who gains $FQWK$ plus the cost-reduction effect. From the point of view of B alone, one would describe the customs revenue loss $UQWN$ as the 'trade-diversion effect'.

If the made-to-measure system operated, the price to A's consumers before the union is formed would be given by the point Q', and the price to A's and B's consumers after the union is formed, by V'. Bearing this in mind, the diagram could be used to illustrate the various arguments of section II.

References

Corden, W. M. 1967: Monopoly, tariffs and subsidies: *Economica*, 34, 50–8. (Essay 3, this volume.)

Johnson, H. G. 1962: *Money, Trade and Economic Growth.*. London: Allen & Unwin.

Viner, J. 1950: *The Customs Union Issue*. New York: Carnegie Endowment for International Peace.

5
A Tariff that Worsens the Terms of Trade*

It is a familiar proposition that the imposition of some level of tariff can raise a country's real income by improving its terms of trade. This argument is usually demonstrated by means of a two-product, two-factor and two-country model.

In the past the terms of trade argument has been used on occasions as a justification for protecting manufacturing industry in Australia. This essay seeks to show that, once a second export product is explicitly allowed for in the analysis, a favourable terms of trade effect of protection is less likely. In fact we shall show that in a particular world with three products and three factors and certain factor-intensity conditions not unlike those of Australia, a tariff may worsen the terms of trade by leading to increased production of one of the export products.

I The Model

Suppose we have an economy A operating under free trade where one product, textiles, is imported and two products, wool and grain, are exported. Initially we shall suppose that A is a small country confronted with an infinitely elastic demand for its exports. This assumption will of course be removed later, since otherwise there could be no terms of trade effect.

There are three factors of production, land, labour and capital. We assume that the production of both wool and grain require land and labour but not capital, and that textile production uses capital and labour but not land. Capital is therefore a specific input for the textile industry, land is specific for the two agricultural industries, while labour is mobile between all three industries. We assume perfect competition throughout, perfect

---

* From I. A. McDougall and R. H. Snape (eds) 1970: *Studies in International Economics*, Monash Conference Papers, Amsterdam: North-Holland. Written jointly with Fred H. Gruen.

divisibility of all factors and that all production functions are linear and homogeneous. Finally, and this assumption is crucial, we assume that grain production is always more labour intensive than wool production. In other words, for any given ratio of the price of labour to the price of land the labour/land ratio is always higher in grain than in wool production.

II The Imposition of a Tariff

We shall now examine the effect of the imposition of a tariff on the imported good, textiles. This will have two effects: (a) on the allocation of productive resources within the economy, and (b) on the allocation of consumers' expenditures. We shall first examine the effect on the allocation of productive resources.

The imposition of a tariff will raise the domestic price of textiles. As a result textile production will become relatively more profitable and the value of the marginal product of labour and capital in textile production will increase. On the other hand, the marginal product of labour in wool and grain production has not altered. Some labour previously used in the production of wool and grain will therefore be attracted to textile production. The effect of protecting textile production will thus be to reduce the amount of labour which remains available for wool and grain production.

What will be the effect of a reduction in the supply of labour on the quantities of wool and grain? This question has in fact been answered by Rybczynski (1955). He shows that, in a two-factor, two-product model, if the quantity of one factor is increased with the quantity of the other remaining unchanged, the maintenance of the same factor–price ratio requires that there be an absolute expansion in the production of the commodity intensive in that factor and an absolute curtailment of production of the other commodity. In our model this means that if the quantity of labour available to agricultural industries is reduced while the quantity of land is fixed, and if the factor–price ratio is to stay unchanged, there must be an absolute reduction in the production of the labour-intensive good, grain, and an absolute increase in the production of the land-intensive good, wool. In this model, and at this stage of the argument, the factor–price ratio must stay unchanged, since, with constant returns to scale in both industries, there is a unique relation between the product–price ratio, which is given by the world prices of wool and grain, and the factor–price ratio. Hence the imposition of a tariff on textiles will increase the production of textiles *and of wool* and reduce the production of grain.

The effect of the imposition of a duty on textiles on consumers' expenditures will be to reduce consumption of textiles (since the local price has risen) and to increase the consumption of grain and wool.

If we look at the total effect of the duty on imports and exports of particular products, we obtain the following picture:

Tariff that worsens terms of trade 71

1) Imports of textiles will decline since local production of textiles increases whilst consumption declines.
2) Exports of grain will decline since local production declines whilst consumption increases.
3) The effect on exports of wool is uncertain. Both production and consumption will increase. Obviously if the increase in production exceeds the increase in consumption, exports of wool will increase and vice versa.

III The Terms of Trade Effect

We shall now drop the 'small country' assumption for wool exports and suppose that increased exports of wool would lead to a fall in the price of wool. We continue to assume that the country cannot affect the prices of grain and textiles. In the case of Australia there is some justification for this type of model.

The imposition of a duty on textiles may then lead to a deterioration of the country's terms of trade. The external prices of wheat and textiles have remained unchanged whilst the possible increase in wool exports would reduce local and world prices of wool and thus adversely affect the economy's terms of trade.

If our model were to present a valid and useful simplification of the real world, what policy should country A adopt in order to improve its terms of trade? Obviously the first-best policy would be to put an export tax on wool. Exactly the same result could be obtained by an appropriate export subsidy on grain combined with a tariff at the same rate on textiles. While a tariff on its own may worsen the terms of trade, this policy would be biased against wool, hence would reduce wool output and increase consumption of wool, and so would improve the terms of trade.[1] If the only available policy instrument is a tariff on textiles, the optimal tariff is zero. If taxes and subsidies on production and consumption of grain and textiles are feasible, then taxing production of textiles, subsidizing production of grain, and taxing consumption of textiles and of grain would all improve the terms of trade.

IV Effect on the Pattern of Exports

Apart from this demonstration of a possible perverse terms-of-trade effect of protection, the model can be used to examine some interesting effects of

---

1. These two sentences were not in the original article. The original article contained the following sentence, which I now believe to be wrong: 'Exactly the same result could be obtained by an appropriate export subsidy on grain combined with an import subsidy (negative tariff) at the same rate on textiles.'

protection on the allocation of resources between different export industries. In our example, with grain a closer subsitute on the side of production for textiles than is wool, wool production increased and grain production decreased; factors of production moving from grain to wool. We might replace grain with another product M which can be taken to represent actual or potential exportable manufactures. A tariff will then shift resources out of industries producing manufactured exports into wool. Alternatively we might let M represent the domestic value-added element in exports of a processed (refined) mineral, say steel, and replace wool with the crude mineral iron ore. Exports consist then of iron ore and steel, the latter being a package of iron ore and the value added element in steel. A tariff will then increase the crude content of exports and reduce the processing or value added element in total exports. In this model protection will thus encourage more minerals to be exported *before* being processed.[2]

References

Rybczynski, T. N. 1955: Factor endowment and relative commodity prices. *Economica*, 22, 336–41.
Suzuki, K. 1973: The deterioration of the terms of trade by a tariff. *Journal of International Economics*, 6, 173–182.

2. Another alternative is to assume that there is only one export, but there are two importables, on only one of which a tariff is imposed, this being the one that is complementary with the exportable. The basic story is then the same: a tariff may worsen the terms of trade. Suzuki (1973) has analysed this case and has provided general conditions (allowing also for effects on the demand side) under which a tariff may worsen the terms of trade.

6
Urban Unemployment, Intersectoral Capital Mobility and Development Policy*

A recent contribution by Harris and Todaro (1970) presents a simple but powerful explanation of urban unemployment in less-developed countries. Rural–urban migration is assumed to take place until there is equality between the actual rural wage and the *expected* urban wage, which is the actual wage times the probability of being employed. Unemployment is thus consistent with equilibrium in this model. Essential ingredients are an institutionally or parametrically determined minimum wage in manufacturing and a wage differential between the two sectors. (Some of the main ideas in this explanation were originated by Todaro (1969). They were developed independently by Wellisz (1968) and Harberger (1971). See also Frank (1968) and Stiglitz (1974).) The implications differ considerably from those of the orthodox wage differentials model on the basis of which familiar arguments for subsidizing labour in manufacturing or using a shadow wage below the actual wage have been developed (Hagen, 1958; Bhagwati and Ramaswami, 1963). In this orthodox model there is no urban unemployment and the wage differential, rather than the urban wage, is fixed.

Our objectives in this essay are to present (a) a simple geometric exposition of the Harris–Todaro model designed to make its principal implications readily accessible to the reader; (b) an extension of the model to permit capital mobility between the two sectors in response to any differential in the return on capital; (c) examination of the effects of economic expansion both in the original model and the model with perfect capital mobility; and (d) policy implications of the model in each of its two versions. Our main contribution is the introduction of capital mobility, but we also feel it desirable to bring out clearly some positive and normative implications of the original model of which the authors were obviously aware but which are left implicit or not very clear. A simplification which we introduce – letting commodity prices be externally determined – greatly helps in this respect.

* *Economica*, 43, Feb. 1975, pp. 59–78. Written jointly with Ronald F. Findlay.

74   *Normative theory of protection*

The first section deals with the model in its original form, for capital stocks specific to each sector. The next section extends the model to include capital mobility, while those following discuss policy implications and introduce some complications.

A limitation of the approach in this essay, as also of the Harris–Todaro article, is that it is comparative static. The phenomenon under discussion, namely migration and unemployment induced by job vacancies, is of course essentially dynamic. The model can be regarded either as representing the steady state equilibrium or as being an ingredient in a more complete dynamic model. But the limitation may not be so serious since a number of writers who have allowed for dynamic considerations (Lal, 1973; Stiglitz, 1974) have come up with results similar to this comparative static model.

I The Simple Harris–Todaro Model

The Model in Outline: a Geometric Exposition

The Harris–Todaro model assumes that the economy is divided into an urban manufacturing sector and a rural agricultural sector. The capital stocks in each sector are given, and there are neoclassical production functions for each of the two outputs, with labour and capital as the inputs in manufacturing, and labour, capital and land as the inputs in agriculture. Since capital and land are both perfectly immobile the production functions essentially have labour as the only input to be determined in each case. The total supply of labour is fixed, so that the central problem is to determine the allocation of labour between sectors.

The model as presented by its originators is a closed economy one, so that the terms of trade must be determined within the model. In the present essay it will be assumed instead that the economy is a 'small country' embedded in a world economy which determines relative prices of manufactures and agricultural commodities independently of local demand and supply. This assumption makes it possible to use a much simpler method of exposition than Harris and Todaro use (though allowance for terms of trade effects is unlikely to alter the main arguments).[1]

In figure 6.1 the total labour force is measured on the horizontal axis with O_a as the origin for labour employed in agriculture and O_m for manufacturing. MM' is the value-of-the-marginal-product curve for manu-

---

1. This assumption is also made by Stiglitz (1974), who uses a diagram somewhat similar to our figure 6.1. Independently the present authors and Stiglitz have arrived at some of the same conclusions, though Stiglitz' model does not have a parametric minimum wage; the urban wage is determined by labour turnover and its costs. The diagram (figure 6.1) is used by Corden (1974, pp. 144–54) for an analysis of the policy implications of the Harris–Todaro model in the presence of capital immobility.

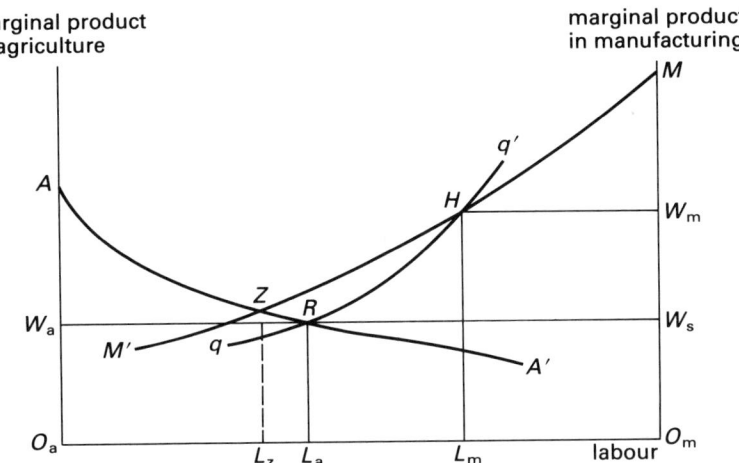

Figure 6.1 Allocation of labour between manufacturing ($L_m O_m$), *agriculture* ($O_a L_a$) *and urban unemployment* ($L_a L_m$), *with minimum wage* W_m *and capital stocks specific.* qq' *is the Harris–Todaro curve.*

facturing, measured at the externally given world prices. Similarly, AA' is the value-of-the-marginal-product curve of the agricultural sector, measured also at world prices. In the standard competitive model the intersection of the two curves at Z would determine employment levels in the two sectors and the uniform wage rate ZL_z. The wage rate in manufacturing is, however, fixed institutionally at a level of $O_m W_m$, which determines manufacturing employment at $O_m L_m$. In the orthodox wage-differentials literature – which does not allow for urban unemployment – the remainder of the labour force $O_a L_m$ would be employed in agriculture.

The Harris–Todaro argument is that rural–urban migration will bring the wage in agriculture – which is equal to the value of the marginal product in agriculture – into equality with the expected wage in manufacturing. The latter is a weighted average of the actual wage in manufacturing $O_m W_m$ and the zero wage of the urban unemployed, the weights being the actual numbers employed and unemployed respectively in the urban sector. The model therefore assumes a random turnover in the manufacturing labour force, with each member of the total urban labour force having an equal chance of being employed on any given day, as if jobs were allocated by lottery or a game of musical chairs. Furthermore, it assumes that there is no discount for risk – the risk of settling in the urban unemployment pool rather than into a factory job. It must be assumed that a subsistence income is available to the unemployed from their relatives, either in the country or the city. This fundamental Harris–Todaro assumption of how the expected urban wage is determined might be regarded as a limiting case, and in the section 'Complications' it will be varied in a number of ways.

The problem in figure 6.1 is then to determine the allocation of that part of the labour force which is not employed in manufacturing O_aL_m between the urban unemployed and the agricultural labour force. Draw a rectangular hyperbola qq' through the point H on MM' corresponding to the urban wage of O_mW_m. This rectangular hyperbola we shall also call the Harris–Todaro curve. It intersects AA' at R and gives a labour allocation represented by L_a. The distance O_aL_a is agricultural employment, O_aW_a is the agricultural wage and the distance L_aL_m is urban unemployment. The total urban labour force, consisting of those employed in manufacturing and the urban unemployed, is O_mL_a.

The rationale for the use of the rectangular hyperbola is provided by the equilibrium condition

$$W_a = \frac{L_m}{L_u} W_m \qquad (6.1)$$

where W_a and W_m are the two wage rates, and L_m and L_u are the employment in manufacturing and the total urban labour force respectively. From (6.1) it follows that

$$W_aL_u = W_mL_m \qquad (6.2)$$

This condition, and the requirement that wage rates equal marginal product in each sector, are met by the points H and R on the rectangular hyperbola and only by those points.

The Manufacturing Elasticity

In comparison with the standard competitive equilibrium at Z, the output of the manufacturing sector is reduced by the existence of a minimum wage above the competitive level of ZL_z since the higher wage leads to less employment with a fixed capital stock. But the output of the agricultural sector could be higher or lower. In figure 6.1, with the point Z to the left of the point R, it is higher.

The crucial consideration is the elasticity of the MM' curve (the proportional change in labour input in manufacturing divided by the proportional change in marginal product). We shall call this the manufacturing elasticity η_m. It will play an important role in the analysis in section II. It is evident from the diagram that when $\eta_m = 1$ over the relevant range, so that Z and R coincide, the output in agriculture will stay unchanged as a result of the existence of the minimum wage, when $\eta_m > 1$ (as drawn in figure 6.1), the agricultural output increases as a result of the minimum wage, and when $\eta_m < 1$ agricultural output falls. Unless the AA' curve is horizontal, the manufacturing elasticity will also determine whether the minimum wage in manufacturing causes the agricultural wage to stay unchanged ($\eta_m = 1$), to fall ($\eta_m > 1$) or to rise ($\eta_m < 1$).

Economic Expansion

The effects of an increase in the capital stock or technological progress in either sector can be readily handled by shifting out the relevant marginal productivity curve. With a fixed urban wage rate, shifting out the marginal productivity curve in manufacturing would raise the agricultural wage rate (unless AA' is horizontal), since the rectangular hyperbola qq' would be displaced leftwards, cutting AA' at a higher wage rate. The ratio of manufacturing employment to total urban labour force must therefore rise as a result (except when AA' is horizontal, when the ratio will stay constant). An outward shift in AA' for the same reasons would also raise the agricultural wage rate, since the new AA' curve would intersect the rectangular hyperbola at a higher point. Thus capital accumulation or technical progress would always reduce the unemployment ratio in the urban sector irrespective of the sector in which it takes place (except for the limiting case of AA' being horizontal).

II Inter-Sectoral Capital Mobility

The model of section I differs from the usual two-factor two-good neoclassical model not only with respect to the assumption made about the labour market but also in supposing the capital is specific to each sector. We shall now replace that specific capital stock assumption which is made in all the formal models (Harris and Todaro, 1970; Stiglitz, 1974; Bhagwati and Srinivasan, 1974) with the hypothesis of a fixed but intersectorally perfectly mobile total capital stock. Land in agriculture is ignored at first, but the consequences of introducing it are examined subsequently. We assume linear homogeneous production functions. We shall consistently assume that manufacturing is capital intensive relative to agriculture. This will be important for many of the particular results obtained but the techniques used here can, of course, also be used to analyse the opposite case where manufacturing is relatively labour intensive.

The Box Diagram Geometry

In figure 6.2 the dimensions of the Edgeworth–Bowley box show the total factor stock, origin O_m referring to manufacturing, origin O_a to agriculture, and the curve $O_m O_a$ tracing out points of tangency between manufacturing and agriculture isoquants.

One can imagine rays radiating out from O_m, one of them being $O_m R$. Each ray shows a particular capital–labour ratio in manufacturing. Given our constant returns to scale assumption, it also shows a particular marginal physical product of labour and similarly of capital. The steeper the ray the higher the capital–labour ratio, the higher the marginal physical product of labour and the lower the marginal physical product of capital.

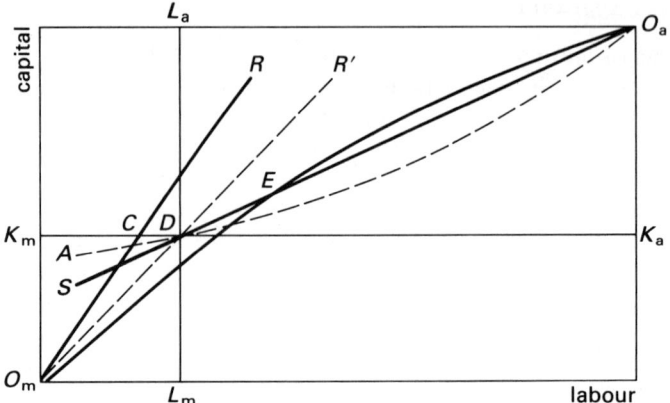

Figure 6.2 Allocation of labour between manufacturing (K_mC), *agriculture* (O_aL_a) *and urban unemployment* (CD), *with capital mobile.*

Given the prices of the products determined in the world market, each ray is also identified with a unique value of the marginal product and, given the marginal-product factor-pricing assumption, with a unique real wage and unique real capital rental. Let us assume that the ray O_mR yields that real wage which is the institutionally determined minimum one in the manufacturing sector. It will also yield a certain real capital rental. Given mobility of capital between sectors this rental must be the same in both sectors, and hence the capital–labour ratio in agriculture must be such as to yield this capital rental. Let us assume that the required capital–labour ratio in agriculture is shown by the ray O_aS.

If the two rays intersected on the contract curve then the minimum wage in manufacturing would be equal to the real wage yielded by the orthodox competitive solution. We assume here that the minimum wage is higher. The wage in agriculture along the ray O_aS must then be lower. Thus we have a wage differential. This gives rise to urban unemployment. From equation (6.1) this wage differential determines the unemployment ratio. This ratio is shown by the relationship between the rays O_mR and O_mR', O_mR showing the actual capital–labour ratio in manufacturing industry while O_mR' shows the capital–labour ratio in the urban sector, including the unemployed. With capital O_mK_m in manufacturing, urban unemployment would be CD.

These points, C and D, are actually the equilibrium points. The labour force in the urban sector is O_mL_m, of which CD is unemployed. The capital–labour ratio in manufacturing is given by O_mR, which goes through C, and this factor ratio yields the required minimum real wage. The labour force in agriculture is O_aL_a and the capital–labour ratio there is given by the ray O_aS, which goes through D and yields the required rental on capital equal to that in manufacturing.

Effects on Output Levels of Minimum Urban Wage

In section I we say that with no capital mobility the output of manufactures must be lower in the Harris–Todaro case as compared with what it would be in the standard competitive model, while the output of agriculture can rise or fall. Let us now see what happens to outputs when there is capital mobility. Our method of analysis will be as follows. First we ask what happens to the marginal products of capital in the two sectors, and hence the capital rentals, if capital did not move. Then we allow capital to move in response to intersectoral differences in rental created by the minimum wage, and analyse the consequences on outputs of this movement. There are three cases to consider, each associated with a particular manufacturing elasticity condition. We begin with the simplest case, where $\eta = 1$.

In figure 6.3 competitive equilibrium is represented by the point E. Capital in manufacturing is $O_m K'_m$ and in agriculture is $O_a K'_a$. The minimum wage is established, yielding the ray $O_m R$. If capital is immobile, employment in manufacturing then falls from $K'_m E$ to $K'_m C'$. The manufacturing elasticity tells us what happens to output in agriculture as a result of the minimum wage when capital is immobile. If this elasticity is unity, there is no movement of labour in or out of agriculture, and agricultural output stays constant at the point represented by E.

Next, imagine capital to become mobile. We can suppose that the movement of capital responds to a newly created differential in the return to capital after a time lag. In the manufacturing sector the capital–labour ratio has risen and so the capital rental has fallen, while in agriculture it has stayed constant. So capital moves out of manufacturing into agriculture until the marginal product of capital in agriculture falls to the same level to which it has been reduced in manufacturing by the minimum wage. This

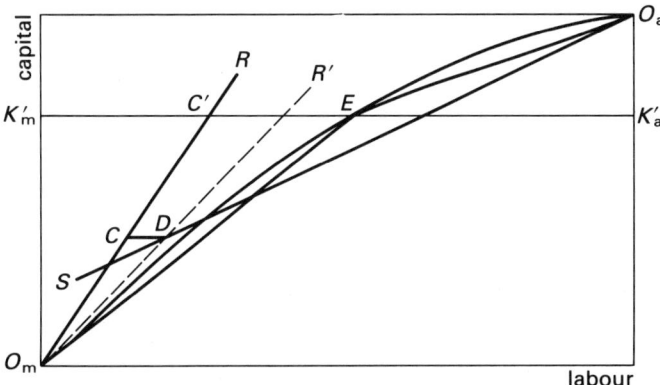

Figure 6.3 Effects of minimum wage on output levels, with capital mobile. Case where capital and labour move out of manufacturing.

lower marginal product of capital is associated with the higher capital–labour ratio in agriculture represented by the ray O_aS. At the same time the wage in agriculture must rise (since the capital–labour ratio is higher). With the given minimum wage in manufacturing and a higher wage in agriculture the unemployment ratio in the urban sector must fall. The new (higher) capital–labour ratio in the urban sector, created by the lower unemployment ratio, is shown by the ray OR'. The point D shows the allocation of labour and capital between the two sectors and the point C the factor allocation to manufacturing industry.

It can be seen that capital mobility has caused both capital and labour to move out of manufacturing and into agriculture. Manufacturing output has fallen to below the Harris–Todaro level which was already below what it would be in the standard model. Agricultural output, on the other hand, expands in the capital mobility case whereas compared with the standard competitive level, it was unchanged in the Harris–Todaro case.

A similar sort of analysis can be used to analyse the case of $\eta_m > 1$. In that case, with capital immobile, the establishment of the minimum wage causes labour to move *into* the agricultural sector and so causes agricultural output to rise. The increased labour input raises the marginal product of capital in that sector and so, once capital is allowed to be mobile, leads to a movement of capital from the urban sector into agriculture, as in the previous case. The agricultural wage rate rises, and so the urban unemployment ratio falls. The effects are the same as in the previous case. Introducing capital mobility compounds both the fall in manufacturing output and the rise in agricultural output that would take place in the Harris–Todaro model if a minimum manufacturing wage were established above the competitive equilibrium wage.

The case of $\eta_m < 1$ is slightly more complicated. This time, with capital specific, labour moves *out* of agriculture, and this lowers the marginal product of capital in agriculture. But the establishment of the minimum wage has also lowered the marginal product of capital in manufacturing. The direction of capital movement therefore depends on which sector experiences the greater decline in the marginal product of capital. If it is manufacturing, then output will fall in that sector to below its Harris–Todaro level and in agriculture will rise above it. Compared with the standard competitive case, the output of agriculture may rise or fall depending on whether the initial loss of labour to the urban sector is offset or not by the inflow of capital and the reverse flow of labour that it brings in its train.

If the marginal product of capital falls more in agriculture, then capital will move out of agriculture into manufacturing. The wage rate in agriculture will fall and the urban unemployment ratio will thus rise. By contrast with all the cases so far considered, capital mobility raises manufacturing output and lowers agricultural output in relation to the Harris–Todaro outcome. Bearing in mind that in the Harris–Todaro case the minimum wage causes manufacturing output to fall compared with the

Urban unemployment, capital mobility

standard competitive case, the question then arises whether the net result of capital mobility could be for manufacturing output actually to increase when a minimum wage is imposed, so reversing the sign of the Harris–Todaro effect.

Fixed Coefficients and a Paradox

Contrary to one's intuition it can be shown that such a paradoxical outcome is actually possible, on not too implausible assumptions. A sufficient condition is simply that there are fixed coefficients of production in both sectors with manufacturing being the relatively capital-intensive sector, as we have been assuming all along.

The economic reason for the paradox is rather simple. The higher urban wage does not reduce urban employment with the initial capital since no technical substitution is possible. The higher wage with initial full employment in the urban sector attracts rural labour. With fixed coefficients this means that some agricultural capital would be redundant, driving the rental to capital to zero in that sector. This induces capital movement as well as migration to the cities, which stops when the capital rental is equalized and the expected urban wage is equal to the agricultural wage. The additional urban capital and fixed coefficients imply that manufacturing output and employment must be higher.

Figure 6.4 illustrates the initial equilibrium of the competitive case and the new equilibrium, with a minimum wage and capital mobility. The initial equilibrium point is E. The fixed coefficients are indicated by the rays $O_m R''$ and $O_a S''$. In the new situation these rays must continue to indicate the factor ratios in the two industries. But with the minimum wage in manufacturing higher than the wage in the competitive case, there must be some urban unemployment. Thus the capital–labour ratio in the urban

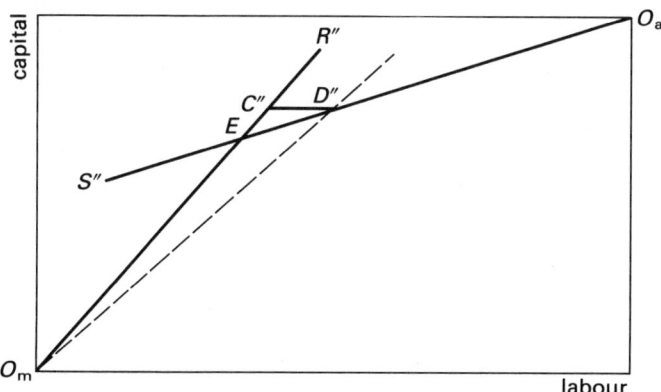

Figure 6.4 Effects of minimum wage with fixed coefficients. Output of manufacturing increases.

sector, as distinct from manufacturing industry, must fall. It is shown by the ray $O_m D''$. The new factor allocation between sectors is given by the point D'', factor input in manufacturing is shown by C'', and urban unemployment is $C''D''$. It can be seen that manufacturing output has increased and agricultural output decreased.

The paradox of higher manufacturing output and employment as a consequence of the urban minimum wage could still follow if some limited degree of technical substitution were possible but not enough to offset the effect of urban unemployment in lowering the ratio of capital to urban labour force. The exact extent of the substitution that is consistent with the paradox is not given here but should not be too difficult to ascertain by mathematical methods.

Economic Expansion

The effects of changes in the fixed factor supplies on output levels can easily be determined and results corresponding to the theorem of Rybczynski (1955) for the standard case derived. It must be remembered that economic expansion will leave relative factor prices and the urban unemployment *ratio* unchanged, since these depend only on relative product prices, the production functions and the urban wage rate, all of which are independent of overall factor endowments so long as both output levels are positive. Even though the production functions permit substitution the fixity of relative factor prices means that capital–labour ratios will not change in either sector.

In figure 6.5 the initial factor allocation between the sectors is shown by the point D, and urban unemployment is CD, the given capital–labour ratio in manufacturing being shown by the ray $O_m R$ and in agriculture by $O_a S$. Suppose that there is an increase in total capital, with the total labour supply unchanged. The O_a origin then shifts vertically upwards to O_a^*, this representing an expansion of the box. The ray $O_a^* S^*$ now determines factor allocation in agriculture, and the new allocation point is D^*. Urban unemployment expands to $C^* D^*$. Note that the urban unemployment ratio stays constant but, since manufacturing output has expanded, the absolute amount of urban unemployment has increased. It seems surprising that capital accumulation has led to an *increase* in urban unemployment. It follows from the assumption, perhaps not implausible, that manufacturing is relatively capital intensive.

A completely symmetrical paradox also follows. An increase in the labour force, with total capital stock constant, reduces manufacturing output and employment and raises agricultural output and employment. (In figure 6.5, O_a^* would be vertically below O_a and hence D^* below D.) Urban unemployment must therefore fall in proportion to the reduction in manufacturing output. Hence an increase in population or labour force participation *reduces* unemployment instead of raising it. Both this result and the previous one on capital accumulation follow from combining the

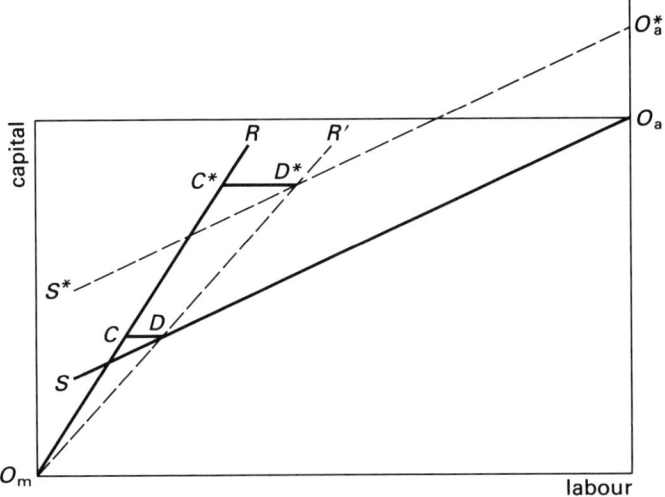

Figure 6.5 Effects on outputs of increase in capital stock. Unemployment expands from CD to C*D*.

Rybczynski theorem with the Harris–Todaro labour market equilibrium condition.

We now turn to the analysis of technical progress, restricted to once-over Hicks-neutral changes in either sector. We begin with technical progress in manufacturing.

Since the urban wage rate is fixed, the marginal product of labour in manufacturing must stay fixed. Because technical progress raises the marginal product of labour at the original capital–labour ratio, this ratio must fall until equality with the fixed urban wage rate is restored. The marginal product of capital in manufacturing is therefore raised, both as the result of the neutral technical change itself and because of the fall in the capital–labour ratio. Since perfect capital mobility requires the same marginal product of capital in agriculture, the capital–labour ratio must fall in that sector as well, thus reducing the equilibrium agricultural wage rate and raising the unemployment ratio in the urban sector. The various changes are shown in figure 6.6, the arrows showing the changes in factor ratios. The factor allocation between sectors shifts from D to D', and the allocation to manufacturing industry from C to C'. Manufacturing output and employment both increase, while the opposite effects take place in agriculture. Urban unemployment increases for two reasons – the rise in the unemployment ratio resulting from the wider wage differential and the expansion in the absolute level of manufacturing employment.

Similarly one can analyse the effects of technical change in agriculture. It can be shown that agricultural output and employment will expand while

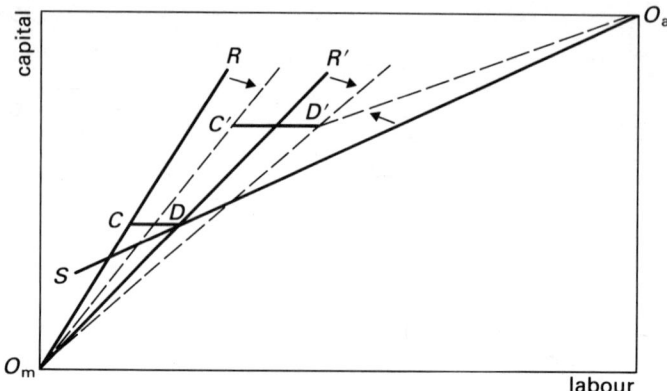

Figure 6.6 Neutral technical progress in manufacturing. Unemployment increases from CD to C'D'.

the opposite effects occur in manufacturing. Urban unemployment will decline both because of a fall in the unemployment ratio and the fall in manufacturing output.

Scarcity of Land in Agriculture

We shall now examine the consequences of removing the assumption that land is not a scarce factor in agriculture. Conditions in the manufacturing sector are of course unaffected by removing this assumption. The agricultural production function is now a function of three variables, one of which is in fixed supply. It is assumed to be separable, taking the form

$$Y_a = F\{O(K, N), L\}$$

where Y_a is agricultural output and K, N and L are respectively capital, labour and land.

We refer back to figure 6.2. The capital–labour ratio in manufacturing represented by the ray $O_m R$ makes the marginal product of labour in that sector equal to the fixed urban wage rate and thereby determines the marginal product of capital that must prevail in both sectors. The curve $O_a A$ is the locus of input combinations in agriculture that keep the marginal product of capital in that sector equal to the fixed return on capital in manufacturing. Since the marginal product of capital falls as we move along a given ray from O_a (owing to the fixed quantity of land) the capital–labour ratio must fall in agriculture to keep the marginal product of capital constant.

At the intersection of $O_a A$ with OR the wage rate in agriculture is below the urban level and unemployment is zero. As we move along $O_a A$ towards

O_a the wage rate in agriculture rises, both because of lower scale and a higher capital–labour ratio. The ratio of the urban labour force to manufacturing employment, measured by the horizontal distance between O_mR and O_aA, rises as we move towards O_a. At a point such as D the Harris–Todaro labour market equilibrium condition of the expected urban wage being equal to the agricultural wage is met.

The only difference in introducing land as a scarce factor in agriculture is therefore to replace a single ray from O_a, along which the rural marginal product of capital is equal to the fixed urban level, by a curve. But it could be shown that this serves to dampen the paradoxical effects of capital accumulation and labour force growth on unemployment obtained earlier. For example, labour force growth is no longer certain to lead to lower unemployment. Furthermore, the earlier results on technical progress will be modified by land scarcity.

III Policy Implications

We shall now examine the effects of some policy interventions, notably employment (wage) subsidies, assuming initially that subsidies can be financed by non-distorting taxes, and that there are no collection costs of taxes or disbursement cost of subsidies. (A fuller analysis of policy implications, but assuming capital *im*mobility, is given in Corden, 1974, pp. 144–54.) In practice countries make little use of such subsidies, but rather use various forms of indirect subsidization, including subsidization through trade policy, and we shall refer to these later in this section (p. 89). We shall ignore income distribution considerations, and so are concerned only with Pareto-efficiency.

Wage Subsidy in Manufacturing

It is a familiar conclusion of the orthodox wage-differentials model that the first-best policy (from a Pareto-efficiency point of view) is a wage subsidy in manufacturing. Since the minimum wage causes the manufacturing sector to pay a price for labour that exceeds its social opportunity cost, the remedy is to subsidize it and so bring the price down to this cost. In the Harris–Todaro model the matter is not so simple.

The effects of a wage subsidy in manufacturing on the assumption of specific capital are shown in figure 6.7. A subsidy of $H'Q$ per man will expand manufacturing output by $L_mL'_m$. The value of the extra manufacturing output is the shaded area L'_mQHL_m. One must then draw a new rectangular hyperbola through H' (in the space with origin O_m), and the intersection of this new curve with AA' will show the new equilibrium allocation of the remaining labour between the agricultural sector and the unemployment pool. Labour in agriculture declines by L'_aL_a. The value of agricultural output lost is the shaded area $L'_aR'RL_a$.

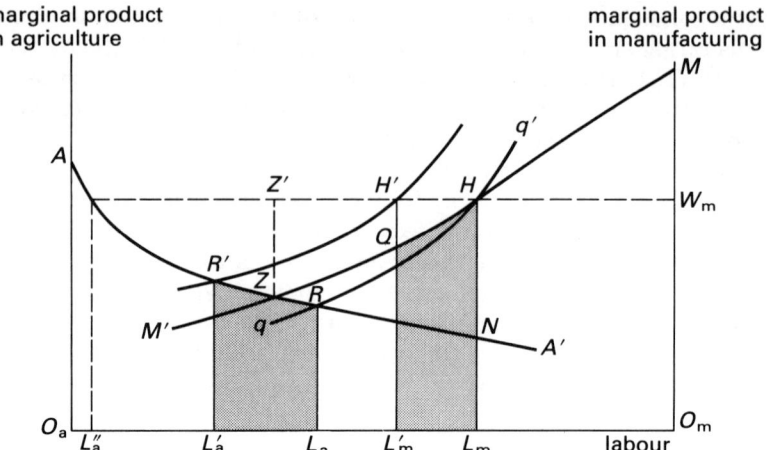

Figure 6.7 Effects of wage subsidy in manufacturing. Employment in manufacturing expands by $L'_m L_m$ and in agriculture contracts by $L'_m L_a$. Shaded areas represent changes in output values.

If one is interested in the effect on total output, one must compare the two shaded areas. It cannot be said in general whether total output will rise or fall or what will happen to the absolute size of the unemployment pool, though the urban unemployment *ratio* must decline. It is perfectly possible that total output might fall. It could be shown that a particular wage subsidy would restore full employment. But a lower wage subsidy, possibly a very low one, may maximize real output, given that such a wage subsidy in manufacturing is the only available instrument of policy. (Harris and Todaro (1970, appendix III) have provided precise conditions for the optimal wage subsidy for manufacturing. Bhagwati and Srinivasan (1974) show that the optimal subsidy must be positive.)

Let us now introduce capital mobility. The wage subsidy in manufacturing causes the marginal product of capital in manufacturing to rise (the ratio of labour to capital having increased). So capital moves out of agriculture into manufacturing until the marginal product of capital in agriculture has risen to the same level as that in manufacturing. But with a higher marginal product of capital in agriculture there must be a lower marginal product of labour and hence a lower wage; thus the wage differential is increased and the unemployment ratio rises.

The mobility of capital thus reinforces the output effects of the wage subsidy: output of manufacturing rises and in agriculture falls. But it causes the agricultural wage to fall and hence the unemployment ratio to rise, while in the absence of capital mobility the agricultural wage would have risen and the unemployment ratio declined. In general, one still cannot say whether there will be a net gain or loss in output from the subsidy.

Urban unemployment, capital mobility

When scarcity of land is introduced into agriculture it still follows that the manufacturing wage subsidy increases output and employment in that sector while reducing it in agriculture. The effect on the urban unemployment ratio is, however, uncertain, since the agricultural wage rate can now move in either direction because the reduction in the scale of agricultural output raises the wage at a given capital–labour ratio, while the fall in the capital–labour ratio reduces it.

Wage Subsidy in Agriculture

If employment in agriculture, rather than manufacturing, were subsidized, a gain would be certain as long as there is any urban unemployment and provided the minimum wage does not change as a result. A subsidy on the use of labour in agriculture would reduce the wage differential and hence bring some of the urban unemployed back to the land, reducing the unemployment pool. The opportunity cost of labour to agriculture would be zero. This could be represented in figure 6.7. A wage subsidy in agriculture of HN per man would expand agricultural employment from O_aL_a to O_aL_m, hence completely eliminating urban unemployment. The wage paid by employers in agriculture would be NL_m while the wage received by wage earners would be HL_m, equal to the urban minimum wage. The value of the extra agricultural output would be the area L_aRNL_m.

While in the absence of capital mobility a wage subsidy in agriculture leaves output of manufactures unchanged, capital mobility will bring about some fall in output of manufactures. Initially, before capital moves, the wage subsidy in agriculture will have raised the marginal product of capital in agriculture. So capital will move out of manufacturing into agriculture. It will do so until the marginal product of capital in agriculture has returned to where it was originally, namely equal to that in manufacturing (where the marginal products of capital and labour are fixed because the minimum wage is fixed).

The effect of capital mobility is thus to reinforce the expansion of the agricultural sector, but actually to cause manufacturing output to fall. In spite of the last effect it will *increase* the gain from an agricultural wage subsidy, so that it remains true that such a subsidy must yield a net gain. Making capital mobile so as to equate its marginal products in the two sectors must in itself yield a gain since it makes the allocation of capital more efficient. This gain is added to that which results from the subsidy in the specific-capital model.

It is possible to be precise about the rate of subsidy in agriculture required to attain full employment provided there are constant returns to scale. Since capital mobility will keep the marginal product of capital in agriculture constant at its pre-subsidy level, it must, with constant returns to scale, also keep the marginal product of labour constant. (The capital–labour ratio stays unchanged, and in figure 6.2 the movement is from D to the full employment point E.) Let the pre-subsidy wage rate in agriculture be W_a, the wage rate after a subsidy has been imposed sufficient to attain full employment W'_a, the constant marginal product of labour in agriculture m, while the rate of subsidy as a proportion of m is s. As before, W_m is the unchanged minimum wage in manufacturing. Then

$$m = W_a \text{ (wage equals marginal product of labour initially)} \quad (6.3)$$

$$m(1 + s) = W'_a \text{ (wage equals marginal product of labour plus subsidy at full employment)} \quad (6.4)$$

$$W'_a = W_m \text{ (wages in both sectors are equal at full employment)} \quad (6.5)$$

From (6.1), (6.3), (6.4) and (6.5)

$$s = \frac{L_u}{L_m} - 1 \quad (6.6)$$

The First-best Optimum

Thus it seems that it is labour in agriculture rather than in manufacturing that should be subsidized, since a subsidy in agriculture is certain to yield a gain while a subsidy in manufacturing may not do so. This preference for an agriculture subsidy is indeed justified if one has to choose between subsidizing labour in manufacturing and subsidizing labour in agriculture, and if one does not know the precise shapes of the curves. But it will not lead to a first-best result.

The first-best solution requires labour to be allocated such that (a) the values of the marginal products in manufacturing and agriculture are equal and (b) there is no unemployment. It is represented by the point Z in figure 6.7. When capital stocks are specific there is no need to worry about the marginal products of capital, and when there is perfect mobility of capital, returns will be equalized by the free market itself; hence we need only concern ourselves with the allocation of labour here.

As noted by Harris and Todaro, the first-best solution could be attained by a wage subsidy in manufacturing equal to the excess of the minimum manufacturing wage over the competitive equilibrium wage (namely ZZ' per man in figure 6.7), combined with a restriction of migration out of agriculture. Alternatively, in this simple model it could be attained by an equal wage subsidy for both industries of ZZ' per man (Bhagwati and Srinivasan, 1974; Corden, 1974). But such a uniform wage subsidy is a somewhat far-fetched proposal. To finance the subsidy one would ideally have to find some sectors of the community that are taxable either directly or indirectly (for example, through trade policy) without affecting supplies of the taxed factors as a result. If such factors do not exist, or the collection costs of taxes are significant, first-best tax-subsidy policy could not bring about the resource allocation that wage flexibility would have attained. Nevertheless, some wage subsidy in both sectors may still be better than nothing. In any case, when the subsidization of the *whole* labour force is under discussion one cannot ignore the financing problem. The implications of this are discussed in detail by Corden (1974, pp. 151–3). Harris and Todaro (1970, p. 132) show awareness of the financing problem, but theorists have generally tended to ignore it, for example, Bhagwati and Ramaswami (1963) and Bhagwati and Srinivasan (1974).

Output Subsidies and Tariffs

It does not seem very realistic to talk about labour subsidies in agriculture or industry. In practice governments influence resource allocation in many other ways which have somewhat similar effects. The main methods are the provision of public facilities below cost and trade policies. Subsidized public facilities are sometimes roughly equivalent to wage subsidies and in other circumstances closer to output subsidies. Inputs may also be taxed or subsidized, so indirectly taxing or subsidizing outputs of using industries. Let us look briefly at subsidies to outputs of the two sectors and then at tariffs.

When capital is specific a subsidy to agricultural output can have the same effect as a wage subsidy. But when capital is mobile an output subsidy will attract not only labour but also capital into agriculture, and so is inferior to the labour subsidy if initially there is no distortion in the usage of capital. But there may in fact be a distortion in the capital market, the cost of capital in manufacturing being lower than that in agriculture. This important consideration, ignored so far, becomes relevant at this point. Given that the capital market distortion cannot be eliminated at source, there is a case for subsidizing capital in agriculture or taxing it in manufacturing. An output subsidy in agriculture – or a combination of labour and capital subsidy – financed by a tax on capital in industry may then be preferable to a labour-subsidy alone. As for an output subsidy on *manufacturing*, this becomes even less desirable than a labour subsidy alone.

Next, consider tariffs on imports of manufactures. Familiar arguments against tariffs compared with employment subsidies are that they (a) create consumption distortions, (b) foster sales for the home market but not for export and so create a distortion within the manufacturing sector, and (c) draw capital into manufacturing out of agriculture, hence, like an output subsidy, creating or intensifying the misallocation of capital.

In the Harris–Todaro model there are two additional objections to tariffs. (1) Tariffs, like a wage subsidy in manufacturing, may fail to raise net output at world prices because the rise in manufacturing output may be offset by a greater fall in agricultural output owing to the extra urban unemployment created. (2) Tariffs are likely to raise the cost of living and the cost of inputs in the agricultural sector, in which case they are like subsidies to manufacturing financed by taxes on agriculture. This agricultural tax effect will increase the wage differential further, hence creating even more urban unemployment, and so increase the likelihood that the rise in manufacturing output is more than offset by a fall in agricultural output.

IV Complications

It is possible to make a number of amendments to the preceding analysis which move it considerably towards realism.

High Risk Aversion and Low Labour Turnover

Suppose that potential migrants into the urban sector in search of a job are risk-averse, that labour turnover is not perfect or continuous – so that the actually employed have a greater chance than the unemployed in getting a job – or that the unemployed cannot easily finance themselves at subsistence level or obtain assistance from relatives. All these conditions will obviously apply. The expected urban wage will then be closer to the zero wage of the unemployed than to the actual minimum wage, compared with the case of the pure Harris–Todaro model. Equation (6.1) should be rewritten as follows:

$$W_e = \alpha \frac{L_m}{L_u} W_m \qquad (6.7)$$

where W_e is the expected wage and α allows for risk aversion, non-random labour turnover and financing difficulties. In the Harris–Todaro model, with no risk aversion, with labour turnover random and with the unemployed assumed to be financed by the rural sector, α is unity, but in general it would be less than unity. (This possibility is briefly mentioned by Harris and Todaro (1970, footnote 7, p. 129), while Stiglitz (1974) allows for it systematically.)

In terms of figure 6.1, when $\alpha = 1$ the Harris–Todaro curve qq' is a rectangular hyperbola, but when $\alpha < 1$ it will be steeper. Thus the rectangular hyperbola represents only a limiting case. The steeper this Harris–Todaro curve the less urban unemployment is generated by a given minimum wage, the more people will remain in agriculture as a result, and the lower the agricultural wage will be.

In the limiting case of $\alpha = 0$ the expected wage is zero, either because jobs in the urban sector are not expected to become available to the unemployed or there is very high (infinite) risk aversion. The Harris–Todaro curve is then vertical. This is the case of the orthodox wage-differentials model, which turns out to be a special case of the Harris–

Todaro model. It should be noted that if the marginal product of labour in agriculture remains positive when $O_a L_m$ of labour is employed in that sector (figure 6.1) the equality between the agricultural wage W_a and the urban expected wage W_e will be broken; the agricultural wage must be equal to the agricultural marginal product at the limit, and hence above the expected wage.

Some of the policy conclusions of section III must be modified or elaborated once we allow for a variable α. The lower α the more likely is it that a given wage subsidy to manufacturing would yield a net gain in output. At the limit $\alpha = 0$ a gain is certain (apart from the financing complication). Furthermore, the lower α the less gain there is to be derived from a subsidy to labour in agriculture, though, as long as there is any urban unemployment, some gain can be obtained from at least a modest subsidy.

Another elaboration, similar to making α a parameter, is to allow for a part of the manufacturing labour force which is fully 'tenured' – with little or no labour turnover – while another part produces regular job vacancies. In that case one might exclude the first part completely from the model. The distance $O_m L_m$ in figure 6.1 would refer only to the second part. The distance $O_a L_m$ would refer to the whole national labour force excluding the part that is 'tenured' in manufacturing.

An Urban Services Sector

It is possible that there is a low-productivity urban services sector into which hopeful applicants for factory jobs move. Thus we might replace the zero productivity unemployment pool with a low-productivity services pool. This is very easily handled provided we can assume that marginal productivity and hence the wage rate in this services sector are constant, not varying with the number of people in it. Furthermore, the marginal product in services must be lower than the marginal products of manufacturing and agriculture at the competitive optimum (at Z).

The expected urban wage would then be a weighted average of the minimum wage in manufacturing and the services wage. In figure 6.1 one would draw the Harris–Todaro curve in the space with origin W_s if the constant marginal product in the services sector is $O_m W_s$. The analysis would have to be somewhat more elaborate if one ceased to assume a constant marginal product in the services sector, but rather allowed for an upward-sloping marginal cost curve and a downward-sloping demand curve, the latter perhaps depending on the size of the manufacturing sector.

Income sharing in Agriculture

The wage in agriculture may be equal to the average product in agriculture, not the marginal product. Furthermore, not only may the marginal product be below the average product and hence the agricultural wage, it might even be zero, the latter being the familiar surplus labour case. In figure 6.1 one might then draw an average product curve (not actually drawn) above AA'. Equilibrium would be attained at the point where the Harris–Todaro curve cuts this average product curve and hence would be at a higher level of agricultural output and lower level of urban unemployment.

There would be both income sharing in agriculture (the Lewis model) and *potential* income sharing in manufacturing (the Harris–Todaro model). The first, on its own, keeps too many people in the agricultural sector; the second, also on its own, draws too many people into the urban sector. Given the minimum wage situation that gives rise to the Harris–Todaro effect, income sharing in agriculture will thus have a beneficial effect in reducing urban unemployment and increasing aggregate output.

Most of the analysis in the first two sections would remain unaltered, but the policy analysis in the third would have to be amended. The likelihood of a gain from subsidizing labour in manufacturing will be greater (since the loss of agricultural output will be less, the agricultural marginal product being lower relative to that in manufacturing), and the extent of a gain from subsidizing labour in agriculture less. As long as the marginal product of labour in agriculture is positive and there remains some urban unemployment, the subsidization of agriculture must yield some gain, since labour will be moved out of a zero productivity pool into positive productivity employment. This conclusion must be amended if the labour would come out of the urban services sector; one must then compare marginal productivity in that sector with marginal productivity in agriculture. Furthermore, if there is surplus labour in agriculture (zero marginal product), there can be no gain from an agricultural subsidy; and, in that case, if the subsidy actually drew labour out of urban services rather than unemployment, there would be a loss.

References

Bhagwati, J. N. and Ramaswami, V. K. 1963: Domestic distortions, tariffs and the theory of optimum subsidy. *Journal of Political Economy*, 71, 44–50.

Bhagwati, J. N. and Srinivasan, T. N. 1974: On reanalysing the Harris–Todaro model: policy rankings in the case of sector-specific sticky wages. *American Economic Review*, 64, 502–8.

Corden, W. M. 1974: *Trade Policy and Economic Welfare*. Oxford: Oxford University Press.

Frank, C. R. Jr. 1968: Urban unemployment and economic growth in Africa. *Oxford Economic Papers*, 20, 250–74.

Hagen, E. 1958: An economic justification of protectionism. *The Quarterly Journal of Economics*, 72, 496–514.

Harberger, A. C. 1971: On measuring the social opportunity cost of labour. *International Labour Review*, 103, 559–79.

Harris, J. R. and Todaro, M. P. 1970: Migration, unemployment and development: a two-sector analysis. *American Economic Review*, 60, 126–42.

Lal, D. 1973: Disutility of effort, migration and the shadow wage-rate. *Oxford Economic Papers*, 25, 112–26.
Rybczynski, T. M. 1955: Factor endowment and relative commodity prices. *Economica*, 22, 336–41.
Stiglitz, J. E. 1974: Alternative theories of wage determination and unemployment in LDCs: the labour turnover model. *The Quarterly Journal of Economics*, 88, 194–227.
Todaro, M. P. 1969: A model of labour migration and urban unemployment in less developed countries. *American Economic Review*, 59, 138–48.
Wellisz, S. 1968: Dual economies, disguised unemployment and the unlimited supply of labour. *Economica*, 35, 22–51.

Part II
Effective Protection

7
The Structure of a Tariff System and the Effective Protective Rate*

The theory of tariff structure is concerned with the effects of tariffs and other trade taxes in a system with many traded goods. It allows for the vertical relationships between tariff rates derived from the input–output relationships between products, an aspect until recently completely neglected in the literature of international trade theory. Early contributions to the theory of tariff structure, developing the idea of the effective protective rate with respect to the policies of particular countries, have come from Barber (1955) for Canada, Humphrey (1962) for the United States, and Corden (1963) for Australia.[1] The exposition by Johnson (1965) is the fullest available so far and also explores many implications. Empirical contributions in which calculations of effective rates have been made on a large scale are given by Balassa (1965) and Basevi (1966).[2] The present essay builds on this earlier work. In particular, in the first section the general equilibrium implications of the effective-protective-rate concept are spelled out, its relation to equilibrating exchange-rate adjustment is shown, and non-traded goods are introduced explicitly into the model. The second section suggests a variety of applications and extensions of the concept. The effective protective rate is a new measure which has considerable possibilities for the study of systems of protection. I have attempted here to show what it means, how it can be used and how calculations of it must be interpreted when there is substitution between inputs.

It will be assumed in most of this paper that (a) the physical input–output coefficients are all fixed, (b) the elasticities of demand for all exports and

---

* *Journal of Political Economy*, 74, June 1966, pp. 221–37. I am indebted to H. W. Arndt and H. G. Johnson, and also to members of seminars at the London School of Economics, Oxford, MIT, Yale, Brookings, Chicago, Berkeley and Stanford.
1. Barber's article represents the pioneering contribution on this subject. It is perhaps not surprising that the main idea is discussed briefly by J. E. Meade (1955).
2. A recent Australian official committee has made some calculations of effective protective rates and has given the concept some prominence in Australia (Vernon et al., 1965).

supply of all imports are infinite, and (c) all tradable goods remain traded even after tariffs and other taxes and subsidies have been imposed, so that the internal price of each importable is given by the foreign price plus tariff. Throughout it will be assumed that (d) appropriate fiscal and monetary policies maintain total expenditure equal to full employment income and that (e) all tariffs and other trade taxes and subsidies are non-discriminatory as between countries of supply or demand. Assumption (a) is reconsidered on p. 112 and assumptions (b) and (c) on p. 116.

I The Basic Theory of Tariff Structure and Effective Protective Rates

The Effective Protective Rate

Ordinary nominal tariffs apply to commodities, but resources move as between economic activities. Therefore, to discover the resource-allocation effects of a tariff structure one must calculate the protective rate for each activity, that is, the effective protective rate. This is the main message of the new theory of tariff structures. The effective protective rate is the percentage increase in value added per unit in an economic activity which is made possible by the tariff structure relative to the situation in the absence of tariffs but with the same exchange rate. It depends not only on the tariff on the commodity produced by the activity but also on the input coefficients and the tariffs on the inputs.

Consider the simple case of an importable product j, which has only a single input, also an importable i. There are no taxes and subsidies affecting j and i other than the import tariffs. The formula for the effective protective rate for the activity producing j can be derived as follows:

Let

v_j = value added per unit of j in activity j in absence of tariffs;
v'_j = value added per unit of j in activity j made possible by the tariff structure;
g_j = effective protective rate for activity j;
p_j = price of a unit of j in absence of tariffs;
a_{ij} = share of i in cost of j in absence of tariffs;
t_j = tariff rate on j;
t_i = tariff rate on i.

Then

$$v_j = p_j(1 - a_{ij}) \tag{7.1}$$

$$v'_j = p_j[(1 + t_j) - a_{ij}(1 + t_i)] \tag{7.2}$$

$$g_j \equiv \frac{v'_j - v_j}{v_j} \tag{7.3}$$

From equations (7.1), (7.2), and (7.3),

$$g_j = \frac{t_j - a_{ij}t_i}{1 - a_{ij}} \tag{7.4}$$

This is the key formula, the implications of which can really be summarized as follows:

If $t_j = t_i$, then $g_j = t_j = t_i$

If $t_j > t_i$, then $g_j > t_j > t_i$

If $t_j < t_i$, then $g_j < t_j < t_i$

If $t_j < a_i t_i$, then $g_j < 0$

If $t_j = 0$, then $g_j = -t_i \dfrac{a_{ij}}{1 - a_{ij}}$

If $t_i = 0$, then $g_j = \dfrac{t_j}{1 - a_{ij}}$

$$\frac{\partial g_j}{\partial t_j} = \frac{1}{1 - a_{ij}}$$

$$\frac{\partial g_j}{\partial t_i} = -\frac{a_{ij}}{1 - a_{ij}}$$

$$\frac{\partial g_j}{\partial a_{ij}} = \frac{t_j - t_i}{(1 - a_{ij})^2}$$

Furthermore, equation (7.4) can be rewritten as

$$t_j = (1 - a_{ij})g_j + a_{ij}t_i \tag{7.4.1}$$

This means that the nominal rate on the final good is a weighted average of its own effective rate and the tariff rate on its input.

For many importable inputs into the jth product (inputs 1, 2,. . .,n), but with no exportable or non-traded inputs, it can similarly be shown that[3]

---

3. See Johnson (1965) and Basevi (1966).

$$g_j = \frac{t_j - \sum_{i=1}^{n} a_{ij} t_i}{1 - \sum_{i=1}^{n} a_{ij}} \qquad (7.4.2)$$

The implications are the same as above, except that in place of the single input tariff t_i it is necessary to write the weighted average of input tariffs

$$\frac{\sum_{i=1}^{n} a_{ij} t_i}{\sum_{i=1}^{n} a_{ij}}$$

It is important to note that the effective protective rate for a product is not influenced by tariffs on inputs into its inputs. One need go only one step downward in the input–output structure. For example, a tariff on raw cotton, while it reduces effective protection for spinning, has no effect on the effective rate for weaving. To the weavers only the cost of yarn matters, and that is determined by the given world yarn price plus tariff.

Introducing Exportables

So far we have been concerned with the effective protection for an importable where the only inputs are importables. It is easy to encompass the discussion to include exportables. We can calculate the effective protection for an importable where some or all inputs are exportables, or for an exportable where the inputs are importables or other exportables. It needs only to be remembered that an export subsidy raises the internal price of a product and is the equivalent of a tariff, while an export tax is the equivalent of an import subsidy. In equation (7.4.2), g_j could be defined as the effective protective rate for any traded good, and the values of i would include all inputs, whether importables or exportables. We continue to assume absence of non-traded inputs. Two examples can be given of how this method works. Suppose we have an exportable not subject to an export tax or subsidy. Its input is an importable paying a 10 per cent tariff. If the free-trade share of this input in the exportable's cost is 50 per cent, then effective protection for the exportable is negative, namely – 10 per cent. Alternatively, consider an importable which does not benefit from a tariff but which uses as an input an exportable paying a 25 per cent export tax (expressed as a percentage of the tax-free price). If the free-trade share of the exportable in the cost of the importable is 60 per cent, then the effective protection of the importable is 37.5 per cent.

Production and Consumption Taxes on Tradables

So far we have allowed only for taxes and subsidies on trade. But effective protective rates are also affected by taxes and subsidies on domestic production or on domestic consumption of tradable goods – in the case of importables, taxes and subsidies which apply either to domestically produced import-competing goods alone or uniformly to these and to equivalent imports. We are concerned here only with taxes and subsidies levied specifically on tradable goods. Consumption taxes on finished goods do not affect effective protective rates. Consumption taxes on inputs have the same effect as tariffs on inputs: they raise the costs of the inputs to the using industries and therefore reduce effective protective rates for users. A production tax on any product has the same effect as an import subsidy or an export tax for that product: it reduces its effective rate. A production tax on an input, while it reduces the protection for the input, has no effect on effective protection for the using industry. Thus in our formula, t_j should be redefined to represent the net effect of the tariff or export subsidy and any production tax on industry j, while t_i nets the tariff or export subsidy on input i with any consumption tax on it.

The Scale of Effective Rates

Assume that the effective protective rate for each activity producing a tradable product has been calculated, taking into account tariffs, export taxes, export and import subsidies, consumption taxes and production taxes. The next step is to order all these effective rates on a continuous scale through zero. The order is likely to be quite different from a similar scale based on nominal tariff rates and nominal export subsidies and taxes. It is quite possible that the nominal rates consist wholly of tariffs and export subsidies and hence are all *positive* nominal protective rates, and yet the scale of effective rates may include many negative rates. But whether a rate is positive or negative does not really matter for the present: all that matters is the order on the scale. The scale summarizes the total protective-rate structure. Assuming normal non-zero substitution elasticities in production, it tells us the *direction* in which this structure causes resources to be pulled as between activities producing traded goods. Domestic production will shift from low to high effective-protective-rate activities. Leaving aside for the moment a complication to be discussed below, namely, substitution between traded and non-traded goods, if four activities producing traded goods can be ordered along a scale A, B, C, D in ascending order of effective rates, we can say that output of A must fall and of D must rise and that resources will be pulled from A to B and from A and B to C; but without more precise information about production-substitution elasticities, we cannot say whether the outputs of B and C will rise or fall.

This is the production effect of the protective-rate structure and depends, thus, on the scale of effective rates and on production-substitution elasticities. In addition, the pattern of consumption will be affected by the protective-rate structure; consumption will shift from final goods with high nominal tariffs toward goods with low nominal tariffs. Thus the consumption effect still depends on the nominal tariffs of final goods as well as on consumption- (or expenditure-) substitution elasticities. Since fixed input coefficients and continued imports of all importables are assumed (assumptions (a) and (c) above), no consumption or usage effect results from tariffs on inputs.

The Exchange-rate Adjustment

Now introduce into the analysis a single and only non-traded good N. Assume that it is not an input into any tradable good, and no tradable good is an input into it. If the price of N remained constant, some resources would move from N into activities which obtain positive effective rates and toward N from activities with negative effective rates. Similarly, some consumption would be diverted toward N from products with positive nominal rates and in the reverse direction where nominal rates are negative (for example, export taxes). Assumption (d) was that aggregate expenditure is maintained equal to full employment income, so that this change in the production and expenditure patterns must lead to excess demand for or excess supply of N (internal imbalance) and a balance-of-payments surplus or deficit (external imbalance). To restore internal and external balance, a change in the price of N relative to the general internal price level of traded goods is then necessary. This could be brought about by flexible factor prices or by exchange-rate adjustment. If we assume a constant price of N, the exchange rate must alter; the function of exchange-rate adjustment in the model is to alter the price relationship between N and traded goods. This can clearly be generalized for the case where there are many non-traded goods; one must then hold constant not the price of each separate non-traded good but, rather, some kind of average price level. It should be noted that if the activities producing traded goods did not have significant production-substitution relationships with non-traded goods and if consumption-substitution relationships among traded and non-traded goods were also low, then the exchange-rate adjustment needed to maintain internal and external balance would also not be significant.

Suppose that in the first instance the protective-rate structure leads to balance-of-payments surplus and excess demand for non-traded goods as a whole.[4] Exchange-rate appreciation is then required to restore internal and

4. Even when the protective-rate structure consists wholly of positive nominal tariffs, it is not inevitable that excess demand for non-traded goods (and hence exchange-rate appreciation) results. For the tariff structure may have yielded some negative effective rates; these draw resources from tradables into non-tradables and create a tendency toward excess supply of non-tradables. But, unless consumption-

external balance. In relation to non-traded goods, the exchange-rate appreciation is the equivalent of a uniform *ad valorem* import subsidy (negative tariff) and export tax, applying to all tradables including, of course, tradable inputs. Thus it provides a uniform rate of negative effective protection for all tradables. This exchange-rate adjustment must be regarded as an integral part of the effect of a protective structure. If the appreciation were, for example, 20 per cent, all tradables with an effective rate of less than 20 per cent will, in a sense, have been taxed in relation to non-tradables, and only effective rates over 20 per cent mean protection in relation to non-tradables. If we subtract 20 per cent from all effective protective rates as previously calculated, we obtain a scale of net effective protective rates. Only when the net rate is positive is an activity protected relative to non-tradables. Clearly the exchange-rate adjustment implied by a protective structure must be estimated if the full effects of such a structure on resource allocation are to be understood.

Four Concepts of Protection

There emerge from this analysis four distinct concepts of when an industry is really protected.

First, there is the old-fashioned approach that an industry is protected if its nominal tariff is positive. But it is the message of this essay that, while the nominal tariff is relevant to the consumption effect, in itself it can tell us nothing about the production effect.

Second, there is the more sophisticated approach which emerges from the new theory of tariff structure that an industry is protected if its effective tariff is positive. It is true that, if the prices of non-traded goods are given and the exchange rate does not alter, any industry with a positive effective rate will tend to attract resources into it from non-traded goods and is thus protected relative to non-traded goods. But it clearly may not be protected relative to non-traded goods once exchange-rate adjustment is permitted.

Third, one might take into account the exchange-rate effects of a protective structure and consider an industry to be protected only when its *net* effective rate is positive, for only then is it protected relative to non-traded goods.

Fourth, one might argue that an activity is only truly protected if the net result of the protective structure combined with the appropriate exchange-rate adjustment is to raise value added in that activity. This is the concept of total protection. The direction of change in output or value added depends not only on protection relative to non-traded goods but also on protection relative to other traded goods. Even if we find that a particular

substitution elasticities are zero, positive nominal tariffs on final goods must lead at least to some shift in the demand pattern toward non-tradables. It is possible that the extra supply of non-tradables just happens to equal the extra demand, so that no exchange-rate adjustment is required.

tradable activity has a positive net protective rate and its production-substitution elasticity with the non-traded sector is positive so that there is a movement of resources into that activity from the non-traded sector, it does not follow that output of that activity must increase. For there may be substitution against it because some other tradable activities have higher effective rates. Whether an industry is protected in this fourth sense (that is, is *totally* protected) depends not only on substitution relative to non-tradables (the direction of which is indicated by the sign of the *net* rate) but also on substitution relative to other tradables (which is influenced by its position in the scale of effective rates).

Non-traded Inputs

So far it has been assumed that there are no non-traded inputs (for example, electricity or services) in traded goods. If there are, then the non-traded sector is affected in three ways by a protective structure, the first effect not having entered so far. First, positive total protection of traded goods leads to additional demand for non-traded inputs; those non-traded inputs intensive in the protected industries will rise in price relatively to the general price level in the non-traded sector. Second, positive nominal tariffs or export subsidies on finished traded goods will divert demand from these goods on to substitute non-traded goods. Third, primary factors will move from the non-traded sector in general into protected traded-goods industries (and also into industries producing those non-traded inputs which are indirectly protected).

Now the important question arises whether, to calculate effective protective rates of tradables, non-traded input should be treated in the same way as tradable inputs or whether they should be treated like primary factors. Balassa (1965) and Basevi (1966) treat a non-tradable input just like any tradable input with a zero tariff or export-tax subsidy. In defence it could be argued that the effective protective rate refers to the effect of the tariff structure on value added per unit in the industry under consideration; and to obtain value added all inputs, whether traded or non-traded, must be excluded. The alternative approach is to treat non-traded inputs in the same way as primary factors. Value added per unit in a tradable industry would then be defined as value added by primary factors plus value added by non-traded inputs. The intuitive defence is that protection for an activity producing a traded product represents not only protection for those primary factors intensive in that activity but also protection for those industries producing non-traded inputs in which that activity is intensive and thus, indirectly, protection for the primary factors intensive in these non-traded input industries. There appears, thus, to be a complete identity between primary factors and non-traded input industries.

To resolve the issue, one must ask what the purpose of the effective-protective-rate concept is. The answer is that it should shed light on the direction of the resource-allocation effects of a protective structure. If we have calculated that tradable industry X has 10 per cent effective protection and tradable industry Y has 20 per cent, we should be able to conclude that resources will be drawn from X to Y and into both from those non-traded industries where prices have stayed constant.

Consider a simple model so constructed as to isolate the first of our three effects of a protective structure on the non-traded sector and, thus, to focus on the essentials of the problem. Let there be three industries producing M (importables), X (exportables) and N (non-traded goods). There are two primary factors: L, which is an input into M and X but cannot be used in N; and L_m, which is an input specific to N. Both M and X are final consumption goods, while N is an input into M and X and is not consumed directly. All three production functions are constant returns to scale, and (departing from the fixed coefficient assumption) in M and X there is continuous substitutability between the two inputs L and N. Internal and external balance are maintained with a flexible exchange rate and appropriate monetary policy. Equilibrium can be represented in a familiar manner with a box diagram, the dimensions of which are the stock of L and the output of N (depending on the stock of L_m), and a production-possibility curve in a quadrant with axes showing outputs of M and X. In free trade, the price ratio between M and X is given, and from this can be deduced outputs of M and X and inputs of L and N into each industry. Now suppose that a 10 per cent nominal tariff is imposed on M and a 10 per cent export subsidy on X, so that the price ratio remains unchanged. Our simple model tells us that outputs and resource allocation also will not change. Now suppose that we use the first method in calculating the effective rates and so treat N as we would a traded input. Assume that M is L-intensive relative to X; therefore the share of value added (defined as the cost of L) in the price of M will be greater than in the price of X. Thus the nominal protective rates of 10 per cent would yield an effective rate for M less than that for X (in both cases greater than 10 per cent). We would then conclude wrongly that resources will move from M to X. On the other hand, if non-traded inputs were treated as primary factors, we would calculate both effective rates at 10 per cent (as there are no traded inputs). Since relative effective rates would not have changed, we would conclude correctly that resources will not move as between X and M. While this model is very simple, it seems to prove conclusively that non-traded inputs should ideally be treated like primary factors and not like traded inputs.

The essence of the distinction between traded and non-traded inputs stems from our assumptions (b) and (c) (infinite foreign-trade elasticities; trade in tradable products remains after protection). Thus a tradable input is in infinite supply to an industry, and the price of each individual traded good is given (apart from the effects of taxes and subsidies). If non-traded inputs were also in infinitely elastic supply, they could indeed be treated like traded inputs. But in the absence of unemployment and excess capacity a user industry can obtain extra non-traded inputs only at increased cost, and some part of the increment in the price of the final good on account of the tariff will not increase value added per unit but will raise the price of the input. The tariff protects not only those primary factors but also those non-traded inputs (and hence their factors) which are intensive in the using industries. But the effects on the primary factors and the non-traded inputs cannot be separated out. Unless there are two inputs only and one is in infinitely elastic supply so that its price does not rise when the price of the output rises, it is impossible to distinguish the effective protective rate for different inputs. For each product one can talk only about a single effective rate for all those inputs combined which are not in infinitely elastic supply to the industry.[5]

It was argued (p. 103) that if the net effective rate is positive an activity is protected relative to non-traded goods. This must now be qualified. It is protected relative to the non-traded sector as a whole, assuming that the average price level of non-traded goods stays constant. But it will not be protected relative to all non-traded goods, since the protective structure will have led to increases in the relative prices and so resource movements into those non-traded industries which produce inputs primarily for highly protected traded industries.

II Applications and Extensions of the New Concept

Escalation of the Tariff Structure

By translating a set of nominal rates into a set of effective rates, one can understand more clearly the general characteristics of a tariff structure and of changes in it. For example, a widely noted characteristic of the tariff structures of many countries is that nominal rates tend to be low or even zero for raw materials and to rise or 'escalate' with the degree of processing.[6] In an escalated structure, the nominal rate on made-up clothing is higher than that on cloth, the cloth rate is higher than the yarn rate, and at the bottom is the raw-cotton rate. Two distinct implications

---

5. If there are traded inputs in those non-traded goods which are themselves inputs in traded-goods industries, the matter becomes more complicated. Only that part of the value of the input which is value added by primary factors directly and indirectly (that is, via non-traded inputs into these non-traded inputs, and so on) should be treated like a primary factor and so included in value added in the protected industry. In other words, ideally one should go down the input–output structure until a traded input is reached; and, to obtain value added for our formula, all direct contributions by primary factors should be summed with all indirect contributions by primary factors through non-traded inputs. In the summation process, tradable inputs (even though they may actually be produced domestically) should be treated as leakages.
6. This is so well known that detailed substantiation is hardly needed. But see the papers by Balassa (1965) and Basevi (1966) cited earlier, and in particular Travis (1964). The subject is discussed thoroughly by Johnson (1965), but the distinction made in the present section of this essay under point (b) below is not made by him.

Structure of tariff system

follow. (a) Except for the basic material which has no other tradable product as an input, the effective rate is always higher than the nominal rate. This indeed is the attraction of escalated structures to protectionists: the degree of protection provided to industries is not so obvious. (b) It means low or zero protection for the raw material at the bottom of the chain. This is not significant when, as often, there is no potential domestic production of the material; but when there is, then an escalated structure biases trade in favour of raw materials against processed products. It is then correct to say that the escalated structures of the advanced countries encourage underdeveloped countries to export less processed products. If an advanced country replaced an escalated structure with a uniform tariff leading to the same value of imports, its production mix would include a higher proportion and its import mix a lower proportion of raw materials. On the other hand, when there is no potential production of raw materials in the advanced country, replacing the escalated structure with the uniform tariff would not raise the import of processed products. In that case, the criticism of the escalated structure is not a criticism of its effect on the pattern of protection but, rather, of the level of protection.

Effect of Reduction in Tariff on an Intermediate Good

Another application of the new concept concerns a country which offers to reduce the tariff on an intermediate good at international tariff negotiations and so appears to be making a 'concession' that will reduce protection and increase trade. In fact, the extra imports and lower domestic production of the intermediate good which may result must be set against the consequences of the higher effective rate for the user industry. A change in the nominal rate for an intermediate good alters at least two effective rates in opposite directions. On balance, total protected production may rise or fall, with trade moving in the opposite direction. This is clearest in the special case where the elasticity of supply of the intermediate good is zero, so that the only consequences of the tariff reduction result from the rise in the effective rate for the user industry.

Infant Industries Growing Up

The following example suggests that historians of commercial policies and of industrialization should calculate effective rates. In a normal process of industrial development by import replacement, a country starts with importing nearly finished products free of duty, carrying out final processing or assembly behind a tariff wall, and gradually moves backward into earlier productive stages, extending the tariff at the same time. The number of nominal tariffs increases, and no nominal tariff may ever be reduced. While the historian naturally reports a growth in the tariff, effective rates are falling and infant industries are growing up. In the first stage, for example, cotton cloth pays a duty of 40 per cent, while yarn enters duty free, the effective rate for weaving being (say) 100 per cent. In the second stage, the 40 per cent tariff is extended to yarn. So the effective rate for cloth now drops from 100 per cent to 40 per cent. Therefore, weaving has at least partially grown up. In the third stage, the effective rate for spinning might fall. It should be noted, incidentally, that an industry would be regarded as having 'grown up' in the sense of the fourth meaning of protection above (total protection) not when its effective rate falls to zero but, rather, when it falls to the level when a restoration of free trade in all goods associated with the appropriate exchange-rate adjustment would leave output in this industry unchanged.

Multiple Exchange Rates

Our concept and technique of analysis can be used to analyse multiple exchange-rate systems. The first step is arbitrarily to choose any rate, say the official or the free market rate, and define it as the 'base' rate. Then all rates charged on imports and paid on exports can be converted into nominal tariff rates, import subsidies, export taxes or export subsidies. For example, if the rate applying to capital-goods imports is 9 pesos to the dollar, and 10 pesos has been chosen as the base rate, then there is an import subsidy of 10 per cent. The set of nominal rates is next converted into a set of effective rates using the procedure already described. This set is then ordered so that it can be seen in which direction resources are pulled by the multiple rate system as between traded-goods producers. Next, from the set of effective rates and a similar set of nominal tariffs and consumption taxes and from guesses or estimates of elasticities, must be estimated the single exchange rate which would achieve the same balance-of-payments result as the multiple rate system.[7] Finally, the set of effective rates must be restated in relation to this equilibrium rate. If the resulting net effective rate is negative, the multiple system has exerted a pull of resources out of that activity into the non-traded sector; while if it is positive, it is likely to have attracted resources into it. Any rate can serve as a base to start the calculation off; the vital subsequent step is to estimate correctly the equilibrium rate in relation to which all the effective rates must finally be restated to yield the net effective rates.

Analysing the Effects of Foreign Tariffs

Let 'our' country be Canada and the 'foreign' country the United States. Assume that the US demand curves for Canadian exports and the US supply curves to Canada of US exports are all infinitely elastic. Now the tariffs and other taxes and subsidies imposed by the United States provide protection or 'antiprotection' for the industries of Canada, and their effect

---

7. The effects of the multiple exchange rate system on the capital account are ignored here. In fact, the method can readily embrace all current and capital account items.

on the allocation of resources in Canada can be analysed in the same manner as the effects of Canada's own tariffs and other taxes. For example, a US tariff on furniture lowers the demand curve facing Canadian exporters and has the same effect on the allocation of resources in Canada as a Canadian export tax on furniture. The concern here is only with resource-allocation effects. The fiscal effects obviously depend on which country taxes and subsidizes, and by assumption there are no terms-of-trade effects.

A scale of effective rates can then be constructed which represents the protection or antiprotection imposed by the US tax-subsidy structure on Canadian industry. The effects of this structure can be analysed alone, holding constant Canada's own structure; the effects of the Canadian structure could be analysed alone, this being the approach expounded in this essay so far; or the combined effects of the two structures could be analysed, constructing a scale of combined effective rates. In any particular case, the two components of a combined effective rate (say a Canadian export subsidy combined with a US import tariff) could cancel each other. The exchange-rate adjustment must again be taken into account. Even in the simple case when both the Canadian and the US tax-subsidy structures consist mainly of tariffs on finished goods, the required exchange-rate adjustment could go either way and would, in any case, be less than when the effects of one of the structures alone is considered.[8]

Labour as an Input

So far we have distinguished between traded inputs, assumed to be in infinitely elastic supply, and non-traded inputs plus the primary factors of production (labour, capital, etc.) where extra quantities are likely to come forth only at higher cost. The argument was that a tariff on a final good raises the returns per unit only to the non-traded inputs and primary factors and, therefore, should be related to the sum of their shares in total cost. If any non-traded input were in infinitely elastic supply, it could be grouped with the traded inputs (it would be counted among the values of i in equation (7.4.2)). The effective rate would then describe the degree of protection (percentage increment in returns per unit) to the primary factors and any remaining non-traded inputs.

Now this principle could also be applied to any primary factors which are in infinitely elastic supply. Suppose that there are no non-traded inputs but only traded inputs and three factors of production: labour, capital, and land. If labour were in infinitely elastic supply, it could be grouped with the traded inputs; and the effective rate would be calculated in relation to the

---

8. This may be a defence of those discussions of the effects of the Canadian tariff which set up as the alternative to the Canadian tariff, not unilateral free trade but rather world free trade or a free-trade area with the United States, and which ignore the exchange-rate adjustment. See Young (1957).

shares of capital and land, being then the effective protective rate for these two factors only. Alternatively, capital might be in infinitely elastic supply, in which case capital cost would be treated as just another input (another i in the equation); the result would be an effective rate of protection for labour and land. If labour and capital were in infinitely elastic supply, the effective rate to land would be calculated. To extend our previous method in this way, fixed physical input coefficients must be assumed for all those factors in infinitely elastic supply which are to be grouped with the tradable materials. Our earlier assumption of fixed input coefficients was necessary only for the tradable materials and not for other inputs or each primary factor separately.

The case where labour, or some types of labour, are in infinitely elastic supply may be relevant for some underdeveloped countries. While the cause is likely to be a given income or wage level in the subsistence hinterland, or perhaps in a neighbouring country which supplies immigrants, the given money wage facing the protected industry need not be at the same level as that in the hinterland, the margin between them being the equivalent of the difference between the f.o.b. and the c.i.f. price of an import. Now, when labour is treated as just another input, what is the equivalent of a tariff on the input? All such 'tariffs' will of course reduce the effective protection for the employing industries. One such 'tariff' is a payroll tax on the use of labour, another is any tax which raises costs of transport of immigrants or costs of transfer from the hinterland. If it is the real wage rather than the money wage which is fixed, then anything which raises labour's cost of living is like a tariff on this input. To give a very Ricardian example, a tariff on corn will raise money wages and reduce effective protection for labour-using weavers. In fact, corn is an input into labour, and labour is an input into cloth; we are back to the case where a tariff on a tradable input reduces effective protection for the using industry. If it is the real wage after tax which is fixed, then an income tax levied on labour employed in industry reduces effective protection. On the other hand, state provision of urban facilities which raise the real value of a given money wage spent in the city increases the effective protective rate for the employing industries.

Capital as an Input

All calculations which treat labour as an input yield, in fact, effective protective rates for capital (plus land and other factors). Similarly, a calculation which treats capital as an input yields the effective protective rates for labour (plus any other factors). This calculation has been made by Basevi (1966) for the US tariff.[9] But there are some conceptual problems

---

9. Apart from his actual statistical work, Basevi's highly original contribution is this concept of the effective protective rate for labour. He does not deal with the difficulties discussed here – that is, he ignores tariffs on capital goods and the possibility of non-traded capital goods.

Structure of tariff system

here which must be explored. In particular, how do tariffs on capital goods enter the calculation?

First of all, at this stage fixed physical capital–output ratios must be assumed just as fixed labour–output ratios were needed before. Now let b_k be the cost of a unit of physical capital per annum to the users, just as the wage rate is the cost of a unit of labour; it is the equivalent of the price of a tradable input. It is b_k which has to be constant, except when it is increased by tariffs or their equivalents. Since

$$b_k = (r + q) p_k \qquad (7.5)$$

where p_k is the price of capital goods, r is the rate of interest, and q is the annual rate of depreciation on capital, it follows that p_k, r and q must all be constant in response to changes in demand for capital from protected industries. Now q can be regarded as a fixed coefficient (dependent on the method of depreciation chosen), and r is constant if we assume (as Basevi does) that the interest rate is a given world market rate. But what about p_k? Extending our earlier analysis, this is given when the capital goods are tradables and is not given when they are non-tradables. Traded capital goods with annual cost per unit of b_{kt} must really be distinguished from non-traded capital goods with annual cost per unit of b_{kn} where

$$b_{kt} = (r + q_t) p_{kt} \qquad (7.5.1)$$

$$b_{kn} = (r + q_n) p_{kn} \qquad (7.5.2)$$

Only the annual service of tradable capital goods can be treated as an input, like tradable goods themselves, and only when it is legitimate to assume in addition a perfectly elastic supply of capital funds. The resulting effective rate will then be the protective rate for labour, for producers of non-tradables, whether capital goods or consumer goods, and for land. In equation (7.4.2) there is needed for the capital cost (referring only to tradable capital goods) an equivalent of the tariff on an input. This must incorporate the tariff on capital goods, any other taxes or subsidies affecting the total investment cost, such as investment allowances, and any taxes or other measures which alter the rate of interest. This equivalent is db_{kt}/b_{kt}. From (7.5.1), taking differentials

$$db_{kt} = rd\, p_{kt} + p_{kt}\, dr + q_t d\, p_{kt} \qquad (7.6)$$

From (7.6)

$$\frac{d\, b_{kt}}{b_{kt}} = \frac{r\, p_{kt}}{b_{kt}} \left[\frac{d\, r}{r} + t_k \left(1 + \frac{q_t}{r} \right) \right] \qquad (7.6.1)$$

where

$$t_k = \frac{d\,p_{kt}}{p_{kt}}$$

In (7.6.1) the percentage increase in the rate of interest resulting from the tax structure is dr/r, the tariff on capital goods minus any investment subsidies as a percentage of the capital cost is t_k and $r\,p_{kt}/b_{kt}$ is the share of interest charges in the capital cost.

Substitution

So far, fixed physical input ratios of material inputs to outputs have been assumed. Let us now allow for the possibility that changes in price relationships bring about substitution between material inputs and inputs of primary factors and that this substitution in turn causes changes in the input coefficients. So the tariff structure itself, through its effects on internal price relationships, may induce changes in input coefficients. Two questions then arise. The first concerns the nature of the thing which ideally we are trying to measure when we calculate an effective protective rate. The second question is to define the direction of the error, if any, which results on account of induced changes in input coefficients when certain practicable methods of calculation are used. Thus, first, we define the ideal measure and then we relate the results of measures which are practicable to the ideal.

The exposition will be in terms of a very simple model, though probably most of the conclusions would aply even when some of the constraints of the model are removed. We assume for each tradable product j a twice-differentiable linear homogeneous production function $j = f_j(i, y)$, where input i is a tradable material and input y a primary factor, with positive marginal products and a diminishing marginal rate of substitution. We assume competitive pricing. Both the material input i and the primary factor y can be regarded as bundles of inputs, but we must then assume fixed ratios between inputs within each bundle. We focus, in fact, on one particular substitution relationship, that between the material inputs and the primary factors. Prices are p_j, p_i and p_y, where p_j is a product price, p_y a factor price and p_i is both. The only changes in prices we consider are due to tariffs or similar taxes or subsidies. When p_j, p_i and p_y are defined as representing prices in the free-trade situation, then the tariff on the final product t_j is $d\,p_j/p_j$, and the tariff on the material t_i is $d\,p_i/p_i$. Since prices of inputs must be equal to the value of their marginal products, it follows that the marginal physical products of i and y are p_i/p_j and p_y/p_j respectively. We denote the physical ratio of material input i to output j in the free-trade situation as b (the input coefficient) and the physical ratio of material input i to primary factor input y in the free-trade situation as c (the factor ratio).

Therefore

$$a_{ij} = b \frac{p_i}{p_j} \qquad (7.7)$$

We must note here the well-known relationship between input substitution and input coefficients which holds when one assumes a given linear homogeneous production function with two inputs only and with continuous substitution between these inputs. The input coefficients (that is, the ratios of each input to output) depend only on the ratio between the inputs and must change when there is substitution between the inputs. In our model, the input coefficient is b, namely, the ratio of material input to output. This must rise whenever there is substitution away from y toward i, so that c rises. If c falls, b falls; and if c does not change, b does not change.

It was explained earlier that the calculation of effective rates is designed to indicate the direction in which resources will be pulled by the tariff structure. It should not incorporate the effects of these resource shifts. Therefore, the effective rate can no longer be the actual percentage rise in returns per unit to the primary factors (and non-traded inputs) resulting from the tariffs, since that depends partly on the substitution effects which have actually taken place. Thus, g_j cannot be defined as $d\,p_y/p_y$ in the present model. Rather, we want to know what the rise in the rate of return to a factor is before any resources move in response to this rise. Hence, the effective rate should be the percentage rise in the return to the primary factor which would result if there were no substitution between inputs and, hence, if there were no change in the input coefficient. It follows that the ideal calculation should use the input coefficient of the free-trade situation; the formula which we have been using remains the correct one and, with or without actual substitution, the coefficient to use is b and, in value terms, a_{ij}. The difficulty is that, while previously the physical input coefficients were the same in the protection as in the free-trade situation, when there is a possibility of substitution between inputs they may be different. So starting with the protection situation, we no longer know the input coefficient required for the formula. If, nevertheless, we use the coefficient of the protection situation, we need at least to know whether we will be understating or overstating the effective rate.

In the protection situation the information available consists of the two tariff rates t_j and t_i and the share of material input in total cost a'_{ij}

$$a'_{ij} = b' \frac{(p_i + d\,p_i)}{(p_j + d\,p_j)} \qquad (7.8)$$

where b' is the physical ratio of material input i to output j (the input coefficient) in the protection situation. Primes refer to the protection situation. Since $t_j = d\,p_j/p_j$ and $t_i = d\,p_i/p_i$, we have from (7.7) and (7.8)

$$a'_{ij} = \frac{(1 + t_i)\,a_{ij}}{(1 + t_j)\,w} \qquad (7.9)$$

where $w \equiv b/b'$ (that is, w is the ratio of the free trade to the protection physical input coefficients). We have

$$g_j = \frac{t_j - a_{ij}t_i}{1 - a_{ij}} \qquad (7.4)$$

Substituting (7.9) and (7.4), we have

$$g_j = \frac{t_j - a'_{ij}wt_i(1 + t_j)/(1 + t_i)}{1 - a'_{ij}w(1 + t_j)/(1 - t_i)} \qquad (7.10)$$

which may be rewritten as[10]

$$g_j = \frac{1 - a'_{ij}w}{1/(t_j + 1) - a'_{ij}w/(t_i + 1)} - 1 \qquad (7.10.1)$$

My calculations,[11] those of the Australian committee[12] and the calculations by Basevi (1966) of the US effective rates represent an application of this formula on the assumption that $w = 1$, that is, that the input coefficients in the free-trade and the protection situation are the same. They would be the same if there were a fixed ratio between inputs. Even when there are substitution possibilities, they will be the same if $t_j = t_i$, so that p_i/p_j does not change. For p_i/p_j is equal to the marginal physical product of i, which can stay constant in this model only if the input ratio also stays constant. If $t_j > t_i$, so that p_i/p_j falls, there will be substitution toward i ($c' > c$) so that the input coefficient rises ($b' > b$) and thus $w < 1$. If $t_j < t_i$, the substitution will be away from i, so that $w > 1$.

Now consider the effect of a change in w on g_j. From (7.10.1)

$$\frac{\partial g_j}{\partial w} = (t_j - t_i) \frac{a'_{ij}}{(t_j+1)(t_i+1)[1/(t_j+1) - a'_{ij}w/(t_i+1)]^2} \qquad (7.11)$$

It follows that $\partial g_j/\partial w > 0$ if $t_j > t_i$ and $\partial g_j/\partial w < 0$ if $t_j < t_i$.

Bringing all this together, we arrive at a rather surprising conclusion. Suppose that $t_j > t_i$, so that there is substitution toward i. A correct calculation of the effective rate requires then a value of $w < 1$. But the actual calculation which is made assumes that $w = 1$. Therefore, w has been overstated, and we must ask whether this leads to an understatement or overstatement of g_j. It can be seen from (7.11) that when $t_j > t_i$ $\partial g_j/\partial w > 0$, so that if w is too high g_j must also be too high. Therefore, by assuming

10. This is my original formula, see Corden (1963, p. 197).
11. Corden (1963, pp. 208–13).
12. Vernon et al. (1965, appendix L.4).

$w = 1$ (no substitution), the effective rate has been *overstated*. Next we do the same exercise for the case where $t_j < t_i$, so that there is substitution against i and $w > 1$. This time, by assuming that $w = 1$, we have understated it. But it has also been seen from (7.11) that when $t_j < t_i$, $\partial g_j/\partial w < 0$, so that if w is too low g_j is too high. In other words, by assuming that $w = 1$, the effective rate has again been *overstated*. We may conclude that calculations of effective rates which use the data of the protection situation will always tend to overstate the effective rates if there is any substitution from primary inputs toward material inputs or vice versa and, of course, unless other errors are offsetting.

Use of Foreign Input Coefficients

Instead of using the input coefficients in the protection situation of the country for which the effective rates are to be calculated, an alternative is to use the input coefficients of another country, the prices of which are not distorted to the same extent by tariffs. This method is used by Balassa.[13] Can one then generalize about the direction of the error?

If the production functions are the same in the country which supplies the coefficients (say the Netherlands) as in the country for which the effective rates are required (say Australia) and if price ratios in the Netherlands are the same as free-trade price ratios in Australia, then there will be no error. In fact, production functions do not even have to be the same; they may differ neutrally (in the Harrod, not Hicks, sense), so that the input coefficient b stays constant even though the factor ratio c varies. The assumption of similar production functions (or ones that differ only neutrally) is perhaps not unreasonable. But the existence of transport costs may cause the Netherlands price ratio to diverge from the free-trade Australian ratio. Suppose that the Netherlands is the exporting country and that her exports are not differentially priced; so her internal prices are identical with Australian f.o.b. import prices, excluding duty. The Australian internal free-trade price ratio, that is, the ratio of c.i.f. prices, will then differ from the Netherlands ratio if the percentages of transport costs differ between the material and the finished good. Let us work through the implications in a special, and not implausible, case. Suppose that the transport-cost percentage is higher for materials than for finished goods, so that p_i/p_j is lower in the Netherlands than it would be in free-trade Australia; that the elasticity of substitution in the production function is less than unity, so that a_{ij} is less in the Netherlands than in free-trade Australia; and that $t_j > t_i$, so that an understatement of a_{ij} understates the effective rate g_j. It follows that the use of Netherlands coefficients understates effective rates in Australia, the answer depending in fact on a

---

13. Balassa (1965), in making calculations for the United States, United Kingdom, EEC, Sweden and Japan has 'relied largely on the input–output tables for Belgium and the Netherlands'.

combination of three assumptions. Though each of these assumptions seems rather more reasonable than its alternative, it is clear that, in contrast to the previous case, there is no general presumption about the direction of error resulting from the method used.

Other Assumptions

In conclusion, attention should be drawn to assumptions (b) and (c), maintained throughout this essay. Removing assumption (c), namely, that all tradable goods continue to be traded even after tariffs and other taxes have been imposed, presents few difficulties in principle. Part of a tariff can now be redundant. As is well known, many tariff structures have redundant elements in them ('water in the tariff'), and it is these elements which trade negotiators are usually most ready to sacrifice. Since a redundant tariff has no effect of any kind other than as an insurance to protected industries against falls in import prices, all calculations should ideally be based only on the *utilized* parts of tariffs – an ideal which requires detailed price data and which may not always be practical. It should also be noted that, once imports of an input cease, further protection of the input requires the tariff on the final good to be increased (up to the point where imports of the final good cease). Thus, not only does the protection for the final product depend on both its own tariff and the tariffs on its inputs, but the protection of the inputs depends on their own tariffs and the tariff on the final good. Finally, removing assumption (b), namely, that the export-demand and import-supply elasticities are all infinite, presents considerable difficulties; and, when the elasticities for inputs are less than infinite, the effective-protective-rate concept strictly interpreted appears to break down. But perhaps if the elasticities are generally close to infinite, the calculation of effective rates and the derivation of various conclusions from the calculations are justified as reasonable approximations. The present author applied the concept in Australia, a country which, like most countries of the 'periphery', faces import-supply curves which are commonly accepted to be infinitely elastic. Some export-demand curves are no doubt less than infinitely elastic, but the exportable content in protected import-competing production is fairly unimportant. So, for Australia and similar countries, no difficulty arises.

References

Balassa, B. 1965: Tariff protection in industrial countries: an evaluation. *Journal of Political Economy*, 73, 573–94.

Barber, C. L. 1955: Canadian tariff policy. *Canadian Journal of Economics and Political Science*, 21, 513–30.

Basevi, G. 1966: The United States tariff structure: estimates of effective rates of protection of United States industries and industrial labor. *Review of Economics and Statistics*, 48, 147–60.

Corden, W. M. 1963: The tariff. In A. Hunter (ed.), *The Economics of Australian Industry*, Melbourne: Melbourne University Press.

Humphrey, D. D. 1962: *The United States and the Common Market*. New York: Praeger, 61–3.

Johnson, H. G. 1965: The theory of tariff structure with special reference to world trade and development. In *Trade and Development*, Geneva: Institut Universitaire des Hautes Etudes Internationales.

Meade, J. E. 1955: *Trade and Welfare*. Oxford: Oxford University Press.

Travis, W. P. 1964: *The Theory of Trade and Protection*. Cambridge, Mass: Harvard University Press.

Vernon, J. et al. 1965: *Report of the Committee of Economic Enquiry*. Canberra: Commonwealth of Australia.

Young, J. H. 1957: *Canadian Commercial Policy*. Ottawa: Royal Commission on Canada's Economic Prospects.

8
Effective Protective Rates in the General Equilibrium Model: A Geometric Note*

The purpose of this essay is to show how effective protective rates fit into the simple Heckscher–Ohlin general equilibrium model. By making very simple assumptions the richness of the theory of tariff structure as sketched out in essay 7 is lost, but more rigour and precision is given to a central element in this theory. The model is designed particularly to show that the simplifying assumption of fixed input–output coefficients does not exclude substitution between primary factors and so permits output patterns to change while maintaining full employment.

As is usual so far in the present stage of development of the theory of effective protection, we consider a small country which faces infinitely elastic import supply and export demand curves. We begin by describing its free-trade equilibrium.

There are two final products A and B, and two produced inputs M_a being the input into A and M_b the input into B. Thus we have a four-good model. There are fixed input–output coefficients; these coefficients apply to the input of M_a into A and of M_b into B. In addition we will shall invent two other products, namely V_a and V_b. These are the 'value added products' into A and B, the units being so defined that one unit of V_a is required, together with the appropriate M_a, to make one unit of A, and one unit of V_b, with the appropriate M_b, to make one unit of B. These 'value added products' or activities of A and of B represent the contributions of the primary factors to the outputs of A and of B. Finally we have two primary factors L and K, these being inputs into V_a and V_b. The stock of the primary factors is fixed. There is no domestic production of the produced inputs, M_a and M_b; they are all imported. It follows that consumption consists of A and B and production of V_a and V_b. The production functions of V_a and V_b are both constant returns to scale with continuous substitution between the inputs.

In figure 8.1 consider first the north-eastern quadrant. Quantities of A are shown along the vertical axis and of B along the horizontal. The quadrant shows consumption of these two goods and may be supposed to

* *Oxford Economic Papers*, 21 (2), July 1969, pp. 135–41.

Effective protective rates

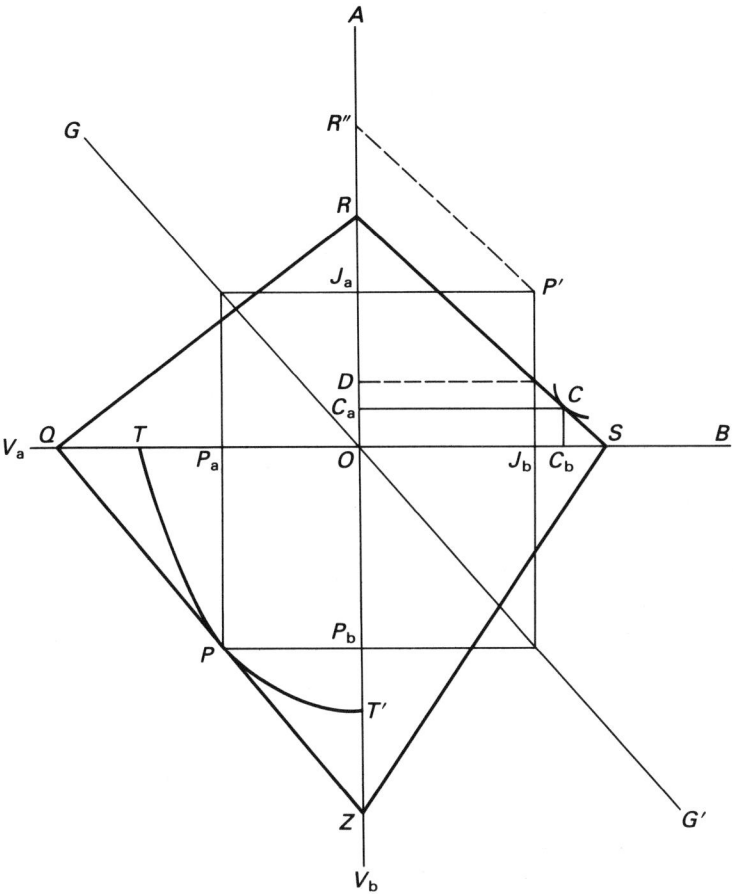

Figure 8.1

contain a map of community preference (or indifference) curves. Suppose that national income measured in terms of A (which will be taken as the *numéraire*) is OR and that the given price ratio between the two goods in the world market is given by the slope of RS. Consumption will then be at some point such as C. The slope of RS is a ratio between *nominal* prices, not effective prices. So we shall call it the nominal price ratio.

Next we come to the north-western quadrant. The vertical axis shows again quantities of A and the horizontal axis shows this time quantities of V_a. Now the price of V_a (pV_a) is determined as a residual by the price of A (pA) and the price of a unit of M_a (pM_a), defining units of M_a so that one unit of M_a is required for each unit of A. The price of M_a is of course also given in the world market. If $pM_a = \alpha pA$, then $pV_a = (1-\alpha)pA$, or

$pV_a/pA = (1 - \alpha)$. This price ratio is represented by the slope of RQ, the price of V_a being OR/OQ. Another name for the price of V_a could be the effective price of A as distinct from its nominal price. It is the price of *activity A* as distinct from *product A*.

Similarly we can obtain the price of V_b – that is the effective price of B – from the nominal price of B and the price of M_b, defining units of M_b and V_b again so that a unit of M_b and a unit of V_b are required to produce a unit of B. The southern part of the vertical axis shows quantities of V_b, and the price of V_b is assumed to be OS/OZ measured in terms of B or OR/OZ measured in terms of the *numéraire A*. Thus the slope of the line SZ gives the price ratio between the nominal and the effective price of B just as the slope of RQ gives such a price ratio for A.

Finally we link up the points Q and Z to obtain the ratio between the prices of V_a and V_b, namely the effective price ratio. This will determine the pattern of production just as the nominal price ratio has determined the pattern of consumption. But before looking at production more closely, let us pause for a moment. We have a quadrilateral $SRQZ$. The slope of SR gives the nominal price ratio, determined from outside by the world prices of A and B. The slope of RQ gives the ratio of the nominal to the effective price of A, determined by (a) the nominal price of A, (b) the nominal price of M_a, and (c) the choice of units of M_a and V_a, which depends in turn on the input–output coefficients in A. Similarly the slope of SZ gives the ratio of the nominal to the effective price of B. Finally, the slope of QZ is derived from these three price ratios, and is the effective price ratio. The latter can alter if any one of four prices (pA, pB, pM_a, pM_b) given from outside alters or if one or both of the two input coefficients change. One can experiment with changing shapes of the quadrilateral in response to exogenous changes in any of the prices or in the input coefficients.

The next step is to draw a production possibility curve for V_a and V_b, derived from the stocks of the primary factors L and K and the two production functions. Geometrically we may imagine an Edgeworth box with the stocks of L and K as the dimensions, points in the box representing possible primary factor allocations between V_a and V_b, optimal points being along the usual contract curve which traces out tangency points of the isoquants. To each point on the contract curve corresponds a point on the production possibility curve TT'. This curve is drawn as continuously concave to the origin, implying that there is substitution between the factors in each industry and that the factor intensities between V_a and V_b differ. Movements along TT' have familiar effects on relative and absolute factor prices, the direction of effect depending on which product is intensive in which factor (Stolper and Samuelson, 1941). The changes in relative factor prices will lead to appropriate factor substitutions in each industry. For example, if V_a is L-intensive relative to V_b a movement along the curve towards V_a will lead to a rise in the price of L relative to that of K, and to substitution of K for L in both activities V_a and V_b.

Assuming perfect competition and no externalities the production point is determined in the usual way by the tangency of the relevant price ratio – this time the effective price ratio – so that the point of production is P. It should be noted that the four given world prices and the two fixed input coefficients determine not just a single quadrilateral, but a map of such quadrilaterals, all with the same slopes. One of them will yield a tangency point with the production possibility curve, and so represent the level of income appropriate to free trade and full employment. It is this particular one which we have drawn as $SRQZ$.

We now know production P and income OR, both determined by the production possibility curve and the effective price ratio, and consumption C, determined by this income, by the nominal price ratio and by the community preference (indifference) map. It remains to show trade. Draw a 45° line GOG' through the north-western and south-eastern quadrants. By drawing a perpendicular and a horizontal from P to the axes we find that production of V_a is OP_a and of V_b is OP_b. Continuing these two lines to the 45° line and then drawing a horizontal to the A axis and a perpendicular to the B axis we obtain the outputs of A and B, namely OJ_a and OJ_b that must be associated with the outputs of V_a and V_b given originally by the point P. This follows from our assumption that one unit of V_a is required to make one unit of A and one unit of V_b to make one unit of B. The point P' in the north-eastern quadrant is the production point, showing outputs of A and B, and corresponds to P in the south-western quadrant. Drawing a horizontal and a perpendicular to the axes from C we find that consumption of A is OC_a and of B is OC_b. The differences between the production quantities and the consumption quantities yield exports of A of J_aC_a and imports of B of J_bC_b. At the given price ratio between A and B exports of A exceed imports of B, because exports of DC_a pay for imports of J_bC_b, leaving exports of J_aD. These are required to pay for imports of M_a and M_b. A little more geometry could show imports of M_a and M_b separately, each valued in terms of A, and it could be proven that these imports must sum to J_aD. Furthermore the gross value of output OR'' (derived by drawing $R''P'$ parallel to RS) must exceed the net value of output (equal to income) of OR by the value of imports of the two produced inputs, i.e. $R''R = J_aD$.

All this seems a little complicated, but is simply meant to show the relationship between the roles of the nominal and the effective price ratio, one helping to determine the pattern of consumption and the other the pattern of production. As pointed out above, it also emphasizes that the simplifying assumption of fixed input–output coefficients in the production functions of A and B does not exclude substitution between primary factors in the production functions of V_a and V_b. The crucial ingredient in the analysis is the concept of the 'value added product' which is really just the net output of the *activity* producing A or B.

The next step is to introduce tariffs, import subsidies, export subsidies and export taxes. All revenues are assumed to be redistributed and subsidies financed in non-distorting ways. The essential point is simple. Nominal protective rates on A and B will change the nominal price ratio facing domestic consumers and hence the pattern of consumption. These two nominal rates (tariff or import subsidy for B and export subsidy or tax for A), together with any tariffs on M_a and M_b, will change the two effective prices facing domestic producers, the extent of these changes for given nominal protective rate changes depending on the input coefficients. The proportional changes in the effective prices are the effective protective rates. They can be derived for each from the effective protective rate formula as given in essay 7. So we obtain the change in the effective price ratio facing producers and hence the change in the pattern of production.

It is important to stress that changes in price *ratios*, not absolute price changes, matter. If, for example, the rate of nominal tariff for B happened to be the same as the rate of export subsidy for A there would be no change in the pattern of consumption since the nominal protective rates would then be equal. Similarly the movement of resources will depend on *relative* effective rates. For example, as the result of a nominal tariff on B of 20 per cent combined with a tariff on M_b of 10 per cent and a free trade price ratio pM_b/pB of 50 per cent, the effective rate of B will be 30 per cent. If an export subsidy on A of 15 per cent is then combined with no tariff or import subsidy on M_b, and the free trade price ratio pM_a/pA is 75 per cent, the effective rate of A will be 60 per cent so that resources will move out of B into A even though the effective rate for B has been positive.

We shall now represent a new tariff-distorted equilibrium. It must be noted here that the new equilibrium must satisfy two requirements. First, domestic consumption and production must be determined by the tariff-distorted domestic nominal and effective prices. Secondly, trade must satisfy the given set of undistorted world prices since the value of exports must be equal to the value of imports at world prices. As this is quite clear from the familiar two-product geometry it need not be elaborated here. I proceed directly to describe the final situation.

In figure 8.2 the new tariff-distorted quadrilateral is given by $S^*R^*Q^*Z^*$. There is a map of such tariff-distorted quadrilaterals, $S^*R^*Q^*Z^*$ being the one which yields a tangency point P^* with the production possibility curve. So output is given by that point and the corresponding point $P^{*\prime}$ in the north-eastern quadrant. Now through P^* we draw an undistorted (free-trade) quadrilateral $S'R'Q'Z'$. This quadrilateral $S'R'Q'Z'$ belongs to the set of free-trade quadrilaterals to which $SRQZ$ in figure 8.1 also belongs, but $S'R'Q'Z'$ is *within* $SRQZ$. Comparing the slope of R^*S^* with that of $R'S'$, and the slope of Q^*Z^* with that of $Q'Z'$ we see that, as drawn, the nominal tariff on B must have been greater than the nominal export subsidy (if any) on A and the effective protective rate for B must have been greater than the effective rate for A. The nominal and/or effective rates for A could, of course, have been zero or negative; as pointed out above, in this model only changes in *relative* prices, not the *absolute* price changes, are relevant.

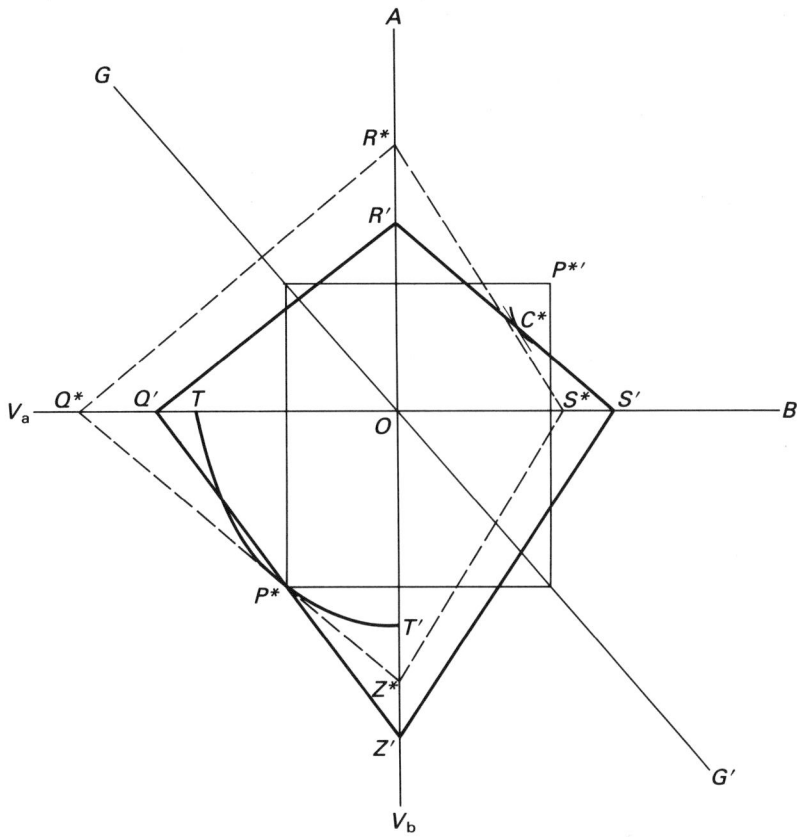

Figure 8.2

The new consumption point has to satisfy two conditions: First, it must be on the free-trade quadrilateral $S'R'Q'Z'$ – and hence must be on the line $R'S'$ – so as to satisfy the requirement that exports equal imports at free-trade prices. Secondly, since the consumption pattern is now determined by the tariff-distorted domestic nominal price ratio, it must be at a point on $R'S'$ where an indifference curve has the same slope as R^*S^*. The new consumption point is thus C^*. Relating this consumption point to the production point $P^{*'}$ we find that, as drawn, production of B is greater than consumption of B, so that B has turned from an import into an export; it must have obtained not just a tariff but also an export subsidy (unless an import subsidy was given for M_b). In addition, as in free trade, production of A is greater than consumption of A ($P^{*'}$ is above C^*), so that there are exports of A. Hence exports of A and of B now pay for imports of M_a and M_b. This was, of course, only one possible, and not a necessary, result.

One could go on to show the new export and import quantities, but this would only clutter up the diagram. The main point is made: in a model with two goods consumed and two goods produced it is possible to introduce some of the central ideas of the new theory of effective rates. But one must go on in two directions, first to allow substitution not just in the V_a and V_b production functions but also in the A and B production functions, and secondly to less elegant but more useful models with many goods produced and consumed.

Reference

Stolper, W. and Samuelson, P. A. 1941: Protection and real wages. *Review of Economic Studies*, 9, 58–73.

9
The Substitution Problem in the Theory of Effective Protection*

The simple theory of effective protection has been developed with the assumption of fixed coefficients between any particular good and its produced traded inputs. The purpose here is to remove this assumption and to consider the general equilibrium implications of doing so.[1]

One can imagine each product to be produced by produced inputs plus its 'value-added product', the latter in turn being produced by primary factors. As shown in essay 8, it is possible to have fixed coefficients between a good and its produced inputs and yet have normal substitution between primary factors in the 'value-added' production functions. The price of the value-added product is the effective price and the effective protective rate is the proportional increase in this price brought about by the structure of tariffs and other trade taxes and subsidies. The analysis here is meant to provide answers to two questions. The first is how substitution between produced inputs and the value-added product affects actual effective protection provided by a protective structure. The second question is what errors in measurement result from such substitution. In particular, if the input–output coefficients of the protection situation are used for measurements, will substitution cause the measured rates to exceed or fall short of the actual effective rates?

---

* *Journal of International Economics*, 1, Feb. 1971, pp. 37–57. Abbreviated: a section on substitution between different produced traded inputs has been excluded. I am indebted to John Black, Ronald Jones, Peter Lloyd and Richard Portes.

1. The substitution problem was first discussed in a partial equilibrium context by Corden (1966), now essay 7. The present essay is a revision of the relevant part of this earlier essay as well as an extension to general equilibrium. The following papers also touch on or deal with substitution and effective protection: Anderson and Naya (1969), Balassa (1971), Balassa et al. (1970), Ethier (1972), Finger (1969), Grubel and Lloyd (1971), Guisinger (1969), Humphrey and Tsukahara (1970), Jones (1971), Leith (1968, 1971), Ramaswami and Srinivasan (1968, 1970), Tan (1970), Travis (1968), Walker (1968).

Effective protection

It will be assumed here that there are no non-traded produced inputs into traded goods, that world prices of all traded goods are given and that the imposition of a protective structure does not end trade in any good that was traded under free trade.

I Substitution Between Primary Factors and Traded Inputs: The Model

We consider an industry producing an importable product j which is produced by two inputs i and v, where i is a produced importable input and v is the value-added product. There is a twice differentiable linear homogeneous production function with positive marginal products and a diminishing marginal rate of substitution. The prices of factors are equal to their marginal products. There is some difficulty about the concept of the 'value-added product' now. This will be dealt with in section V. For the moment let us think of v as a factor of production which has 'natural' units that can be produced in turn by varying combinations of primary factors.

In figure 9.1, input i is shown along the horizontal axis and input v along the vertical axis, the quadrant containing a map of j isoquants. Along any given ray through the origin the marginal physical products of i and of v are constant. In figure 9.2 the marginal physical product of i (μ_i) is shown along the horizontal and the marginal physical product of v (μ_v) along the

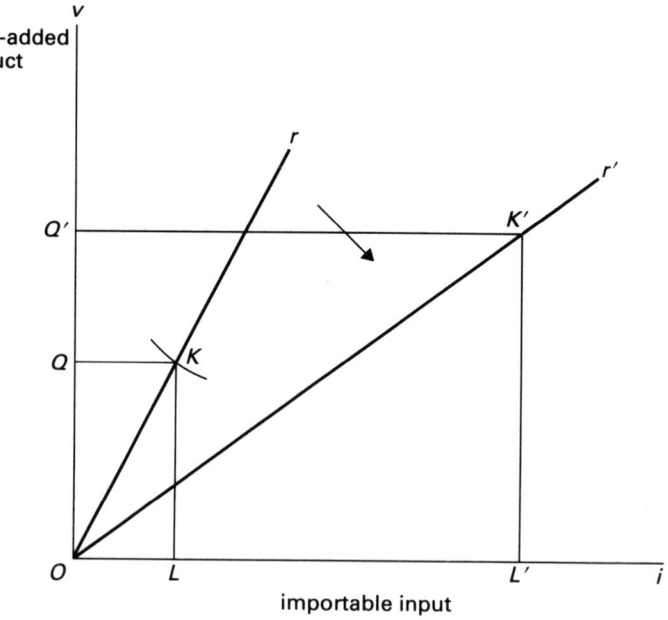

Figure 9.1

Substitution problem

vertical axis; the quadrant contains a curve FF', which shows the inverse relationship between the two marginal physical products. A flattening of the ray through the origin in figure 9.1 leads to a corresponding movement up the FF' curve. It can be simply shown that the slope of FF' at any point $(d\mu_v/d\mu_i)$ is equal to the negative of the factor ratio associated with that point. This result will turn out to be important later. By Euler's theorem

$$j = \mu_v v + \mu_i i \tag{9.1}$$

From the production function

$$dj = \mu_v \, dv + \mu_i \, di \tag{9.2}$$

From (9.1)

$$dj = v \, d\mu_v + \mu_v \, dv + i \, d\mu_i + \mu_i \, di \tag{9.1.1}$$

From (9.2) and (9.1.1)

$$\frac{d\mu_v}{d\mu_i} = -\frac{i}{v} \tag{9.3}$$

Next prices must be introduced into the model. The prices of j, i and v are p_j, p_i and p_v (the nominal price, the input price and the effective price). Given competitive pricing,

$$\mu_i = \frac{p_i}{p_j} \tag{9.4}$$

$$\mu_v = \frac{p_v}{p_j} \tag{9.5}$$

Before tariffs are imposed the prices p_j and p_i are given by the world market. Thus in the free trade situation p_i/p_j is determined, and hence μ_i is determined. In figure 9.2 we obtain thus a point G on the horizontal axis. This yields in turn an equilibrium point R on FF' and hence the marginal physical product of v, μ_v, namely OH. Furthermore, with the point R is associated a ray through the origin (and hence a factor ratio i/v) in figure 9.1. The final step is to show how the effective price p_v is derived. It is represented in figure 9.3 along the vertical axis, the horizontal axis showing quantities of v used by industry j. Now p_v can be obtained from figure 9.2 and the free trade values of p_j and p_i. For the ratio p_i/p_j gives us μ_i which in turn yields, via the curve FF', μ_v, which is equal to p_v/p_j. But since p_j is given, p_v follows. The resultant value for p_v is then inserted in figure 9.3. It is assumed to be OT. Nothing has so far been said, or need be said, about the quantities of v used by industry j.

Effective protection

Now let us introduce tariffs. The tariff t_j raises p_j ($t_j = \Delta p_j/p_j$) and the tariff t_i raises p_i ($t_i = \Delta p_i/p_i$). The question is how these tariffs affect p_v. The effective rate g_j is the proportional increase in the effective price. Suppose that t_j is greater than t_i. So p_i/p_j falls and hence μ_i falls; hence there is substitution from v to i. The fall in μ_i must be associated with a rise in μ_v. But a rise in μ_v must mean that $\Delta p_v/p_v$ is greater than $\Delta p_j/p_j$. It follows that in this case $g_j > t_j > t_i$. In figure 9.2 equilibrium moves from R to R' and in figure 9.1 from the ray Or to the ray Or'. The story could also be told for the case where t_j is less than t_i. This time μ_i would rise and μ_v would fall so that the movement would be to the right along FF' in figure 9.2. Since μ_v would fall, g_j would be less than t_j and therefore $g_j < t_j < t_i$. It would now be possible for g_j to be negative. These results are the same in kind as emerge from the familiar fixed coefficient formula for the effective rate. Assuming that the effective rate is positive, the effective price p_v will rise, such an increase being indicated by the movement from OT to OT' in figure 9.3.

What is the formula for the effective rate g_j when there is substitution? We shall consider the case where the movement in figure 9.2 has been from R to R'. Define

$$\Delta \mu_v / \Delta \mu_i = -\alpha \tag{9.6}$$

Thus α is the slope of the line RR' defined as a positive number.

From (9.4)

$$\Delta \mu_i = \left(\frac{\Delta p_i}{p_i} - \frac{\Delta p_j}{p_j} \right) \frac{p_i}{p_j + \Delta p_j} \tag{9.4.1}$$

From (9.5), similarly

$$\Delta \mu_v = \left(\frac{\Delta p_v}{p_v} - \frac{\Delta p_j}{p_j} \right) \frac{p_v}{p_j + \Delta p_j}. \tag{9.5.1}$$

From (9.4.1) and (9.5.1)

$$\frac{\Delta \mu_v}{\Delta \mu_i} = \frac{\left(\frac{\Delta p_v}{p_v} - \frac{\Delta p_j}{p_j} \right)}{\left(\frac{\Delta p_i}{p_i} - \frac{\Delta p_j}{p_j} \right)} \frac{p_v}{p_i} \tag{9.7}$$

From (9.6) and (9.7) and remembering that $\Delta p_v/p_v = g_j$; $\Delta p_j/p_j = t_j$; $\Delta p_i/p_i = t_i$

$$\alpha = -\left(\frac{g_j - t_j}{t_i - t_j} \right) \frac{p_v}{p_i} \tag{9.8}$$

Substitution problem

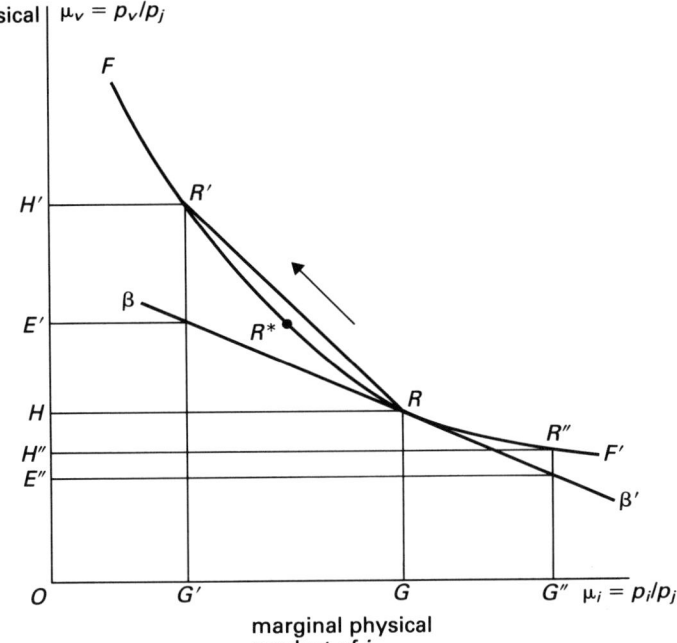

Figure 9.2

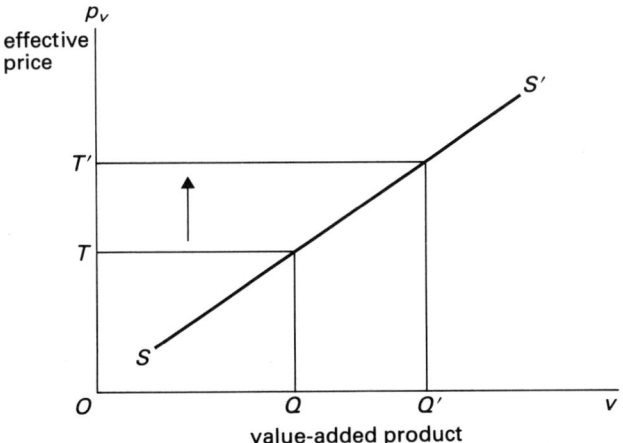

Figure 9.3

From (9.8)

$$g_j = t_j + \alpha \frac{p_i}{p_v} (t_j - t_i) \qquad (9.8.1)$$

Somewhere between R and R' on FF' is a point R^* where the tangent to FF' has the same slope as the straight line RR'. Let the factor ratio associated with this point be i^*/v^*. It follows from (9.3) and (9.6) that

$$\alpha = \frac{i^*}{v^*} \qquad (9.9)$$

Now define the share of materials in total cost at free trade prices, given this factor ratio, as a_{ij}^*:

$$a_{ij}^* = \frac{p_i (i^*/v^*)}{p_i (i^*/v^*) + p_v} \qquad (9.10)$$

From (9.9) and (9.10)

$$a_{ij}^* = \frac{p_i \alpha}{p_i \alpha + p_v} \qquad (9.11)$$

From (9.8.1) and (9.11)

$$g_j = \frac{t_j - a_{ij}^* t_i}{1 - a_{ij}^*} \qquad (9.12)$$

This is essentially the familiar formula for the effective rate. It differs only from the usual fixed coefficient formula in that a_{ij} has been replaced by a_{ij}^*. Both are input shares at free trade prices; but a_{ij}^* is derived from the input coefficient associated with R^*, which is *between* the free trade situation R and the protection situation R', while a_{ij} is derived from an input coefficient which is identical for the free trade and the protective situations.

The analysis which has been presented here is best thought of as an ingredient in a general equilibrium story. But let us for the moment see how it fits into the partial equilibrium analysis. It then becomes possible to close off the model. Draw a supply curve SS' for the value-added product in figure 9.3. Hence free trade output of this product is OQ. This output is inserted in figure 9.1, and is related to the ray Or appropriate to free trade, so obtaining the point K. The isoquant through K shows free trade output of j. If the tariff structure has raised the effective price to OT' (figure 9.3), output of the value-added product rises to OQ'. Inserting this in figure 9.1 and relating it to the ray Or' appropriate to the protection situation the point K' is obtained. It shows output of j and input i under protection.

One can get a little confused about this model and emerge with some pseudo-paradoxes. Note that in this case the physical ratio of value added to gross output, that is the ratio v/j, has declined (since it must fall when i/v rises) but nevertheless the effective price has increased (the effective rate is positive), and this increase has induced the absolute amount of v to increase. It is also possible for the physical ratio of value added to gross output to rise and the effective price to fall (the effective rate being negative), hence causing the absolute amount of v to decline. One apparent paradox emerges when one looks at what might happen to gross output. The effective rate might be positive, and yet gross output of j could decline. The increase in the effective price will have increased v, but a rise in v/j may have been sufficient to lower j. A necessary but not sufficient condition for this result is that t_i is greater than t_j but not so much greater that it makes the effective rate negative. In the special case where t_i exceeds t_j just sufficiently to make the effective rate zero, v will stay constant and v/j will rise, so that gross output j must fall. (Of course, in general equilibrium, with tariffs on other products, a zero effective rate does not necessarily mean a constant v.) The effective rate indicates the change in the price of the value-added product, and in this case correctly predicts output changes in the latter. The concept is concerned with resource movements into the relevant activity, not with gross output.

The other apparent paradox arises when the effective rate is defined inappropriately. When there is substitution it would be inappropriate to use the definition of essay 7: the 'percentage increase in value added per unit in an economic activity which is made possible by the tariff structure. . .' Let us call 'value added per unit' in this sense $\bar{v}$ so that

$$\bar{v} = \frac{vp_v}{j}$$

If one defined the effective rate in this inappropriate way it would be $\Delta\bar{v}/\bar{v}$. Now when there are fixed coefficients, so that v/j is constant, $\Delta\bar{v}/\bar{v}$ will be equal to $\Delta p_v/p_v$, which is the effective rate as defined in this article. Hence the definition creates no problems for the fixed coefficient case for which it was originally developed. They will also be equal if $t_j = t_i$ for then there is no substitution. But with substitution, v/j may rise or fall and hence $\Delta\bar{v}/\bar{v}$ may be greater or less than $\Delta p_v/p_v$. In the example illustrated in the diagrams here, where $t_j > t_i$, we find that v/j falls and $\Delta\bar{v}/\bar{v}$ is less than $\Delta p_v/p_v$.

II Substitution between Primary Factors and Traded Inputs: The Questions Answered

How does substitution between the value added product and the traded input affect the size of the effective rate provided by a given protective structure? We must thus compare a situation where there is no substitution with one where there is.

Suppose we start in free trade with a particular set of prices and an input coefficient i/j and factor ratio i/v. In figure 9.2 the starting point is R. The slope of the tangent at R, $\beta\beta'$, is given by the factor ratio. If the ratio were fixed then the relationship between p_v/p_j and p_i/p_j would be a straight line one, given by $\beta\beta'$. On the other hand, when the elasticity of substitution is positive the relationship is given by a curve such as FF'. The greater the convexity of FF' from below the higher the elasticity of substitution,[2] the line $\beta\beta'$ being the limiting case of zero elasticity. Bearing in mind equation (9.3) the curvature tells us that if μ_i falls below G the factor ratio i/v will rise above its free trade level while if μ_i rises above G the factor ratio will fall below its free trade level.

Now consider the effects of tariffs. If $t_j > t_i$, then p_i/p_j will fall to a point such as OG' in figure 9.2. If there were fixed coefficients, p_v/p_j would then rise to OE'. But with substitution it rises to OH'. For a given rise in p_j/p_i, as determined by t_j and t_i, the increase in p_v (the effective rate, g_j) is thus greater with substitution than without. The more convex from below the FF' curve the higher g_j would be. Exactly the same result ensues when $t_j > t_i$. This time the movement is to the right, to OG''. With fixed coefficients, p_v/p_j would fall to OE'' while with substitution it actually falls to OH''. A fall in the ratio p_v/p_j does not necessarily mean that the effective rate is negative. All it means is that $g_j < t_j$. Substitution causes the ratio to fall less and so leads to a higher effective rate g_j than with fixed coefficients. Thus substitution causes the effective rate to be higher relative to what it would be if there were fixed coefficients both when $t_j > t_i$ and when $t_j < t_i$. When $t_j < t_i$, it is also possible that the effective price falls; in that case substitution will cause the effective price to fall less.

The simple economic explanation of our result is that substitution increases the choices open to the j industry. The factor ratio of the free trade situation is still open to it, but in addition, in adjusting to the new tariff situation it can choose from other ratios. It can therefore increase its gain from a tariff t_j on its own product or reduce its losses from an input tariff t_i. These gains are measured by the effective rate; following maximization principles it can obtain a higher effective rate with substitution than without.

What error in measurement results from substitution between the value

---

2. The elasticity of substitution of the production function is the reciprocal of the 'elasticity of substitution' on the curve FF' at its corresponding point. We are comparing various FF' curves with different curvatures, but all tangential to $\beta\beta'$ at R, and hence all yielding the same marginal products for the two inputs at one particular input ratio. In terms of an isoquant map, the slopes of the isoquants are identical at one input ratio, but vary at all other input ratios. It can be shown that this must mean that the production functions differ not just in respect of their elasticities of substitution; in terms of the CES function the distribution parameters must differ.

added product and the traded input? Again we refer to figure 9.2, beginning, as usual, with the case where $t_j > t_i$, so that the movement is from R to R'. The correct calculation of the effective rate requires use of the factor ratio at the point R^* where FF' has the same slope as RR'; this point must be somewhere between R and R'. But if the data of the protection situation are used for making calculations the factor ratio appropriate to the point R' will be used. Now this ratio i/v will be higher than the ratio at R^*, so if it is used to approximate to the latter ratio, there will be an overstatement. As a result the input share at free trade prices a_{ij}^*, which is an ingredient in the effective rate formula, will be overstated. Referring to equation (9.12), if a_{ij}^* is overstated and $t_j > t_i$, then g_j will be overstated. Next suppose that $t_j < t_i$ so that the movement is to the right in figure 9.2, from R to R''. The correct effective rate calculation would require a factor ratio which is given by the slope of the tangent to a point on FF' somewhere between R and R'', the tangent having the same slope as the line RR''. But the factor ratio i/v of the protection situation R'' will be lower than this, so that the input share a_{ij}^* will be understated. Referring to the effective rate formula equation (9.12), if a_{ij}^* is understated and $t_j < t_i$, then g_j will again be overstated. Thus the use of the data of the protection situation will lead to an overstatement of the effective rate irrespective of whether the substitution is towards i or v. A similar analysis will lead to the conclusion that the use of the free trade factor ratio, as given by the slope of $\beta\beta'$, will always lead to an understatement of the effective rate.

We can thus sum up the answers to our two questions as follows. Substitution between the traded input and the value added product always raises the effective rate but if the data of the protection situation are used then the increase in the effective rate owing to substitution will be overstated. Furthermore, the greater the elasticity of substitution over the relevant range, the greater the overstatement. This complication does not arise when $t_j = t_i$ for then, though substitution may be technically possible, there will not actually be any substitution. If the effective rate is negative the conclusion must be interpreted as meaning that substitution causes the effective price to fall less than it would with fixed coefficients, but that the use of the data of the protection situation will lead to an understatement of its fall, and indeed may yield a measured rate that is positive.

III Negative Value Added and Substitution

Various writers have noted the phenomenon of 'negative value added'.[3] In the protection situation the value of inputs measured at world prices may

---

3. Early examples were given by Soligo and Stern (1965) and Basevi (1966). See also Lewis and Guisinger (1968), Tan (1970) and Guisinger (1969). An exposition is given by Corden (1971, pp. 51–5).

exceed the value of the final product, also measured at world prices. If the input coefficients are fixed it means that the effective price would be negative under free trade (in which case there would of course be no domestic output). How does the possibility of substitution affect the interpretation of this phenomenon? It remains true that value added at world prices can be negative in the protection situation. But it is no longer true that there would then necessarily be a negative effective price under free trade. If $t_j > t_i$ protection will have raised the factor ratio i/v, so that a restoration of free trade would lower the ratio, and with the lower free trade ratio the cost of the inputs may no longer exceed the value of the final product. Hence the high input coefficient under protection and so the high share of input costs may be the result of the substitution induced by the tariff structure. It should be added that if we assume a production function with continuous substitution between v and i where the marginal products are always positive, there cannot be a negative effective price in any situation; a fall in p_v will always be modified sufficiently to avoid p_v becoming negative.

These arguments can again be represented geometrically. We refer to figure 9.4 which is a version of the earlier figure 9.2, showing again the curve FF'. The free trade ratio p_i/p_j is given by OG and the free trade

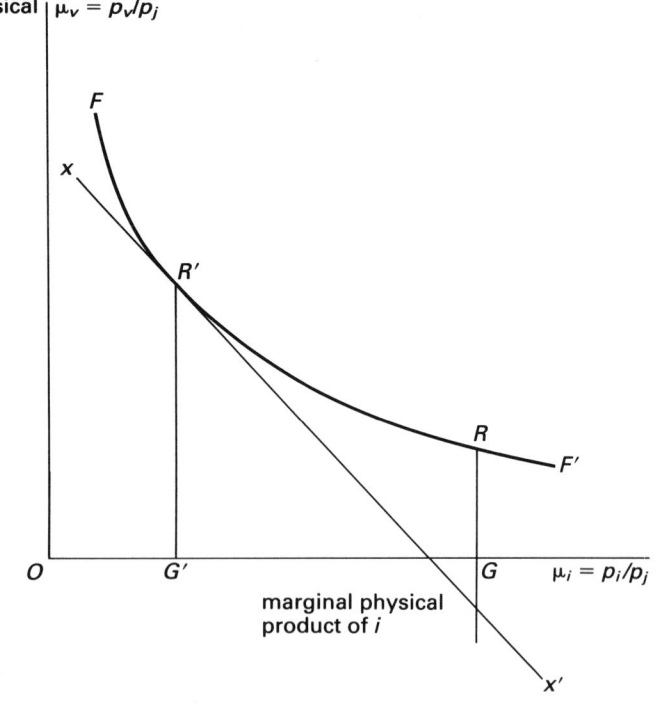

Figure 9.4

equilibrium is at the point R. We then suppose that a tariff t_j is imposed; for simplicity we can assume that $t_i = 0$ (though this is not essential to the argument). So p_i/p_j falls to OG' and the protection equilibrium is at R'. Next draw the tangent to R', namely xx'. Let it intersect the vertical through R below G, as drawn. Now suppose that we start in the protection situation and our data include the protection factor ratio represented by the slope xx'. Assuming this factor ratio to be constant we could then work back to the free trade situation by allowing t_j to be reduced to zero, so bringing us back to OG. This would lead to the result that p_v/p_j must be negative under free trade, as indicated by the intersection of xx' with the vertical through R. It is the result to which a calculation based on the protection factor ratio would lead. But in fact the ratio would change in the movement to free trade and p_v/p_j would be positive, namely GR. And it is also clear that if FF' never touches the horizontal axis (the marginal product of v is always positive) p_v must always be positive, whatever the ratio p_i/p_j.

IV Substitution and General Equilibrium

To present a coherent general equilibrium story we must at this stage continue to think of value added as having natural units. Each traded product has its value-added product and each value-added product has its price, the change in this price brought about by the protective structure being its effective protective rate. For each product this effective rate depends on the nominal tariff, on the tariffs on the relevant inputs and on the production function. In the fixed coefficient case the production function could be summed up by a single input–output coefficient while in the substitution case there is a schedule of these coefficients. This is the essential difference between the fixed coefficient and the substitution case. Thus, when there is substitution the effective rate embodies certain reactions of the industry to the protective structure. We can thus in principle obtain a scale of effective rates as in the fixed coefficient case, this scale helping to determine the flow of primary factors between the various industries. If we think of a model with only two value-added products, the substitution effect in each industry will influence the effective rate for each product, and primary factors will flow into the product with the higher effective rate.

Nevertheless there is a serious difficulty. If the data of the protection situation are used, effective rates will be overstated. It is quite possible that the errors differ in size so that the order of industries in the measured scale of effective rates will not be the same as the order in the scale of correct effective rates. In the two-product model the measured effective rate for A may be less than that for B but the substitution elasticity in A may be very low and in B very high, so that the true effective rate of A may be higher than the true rate of B. It follows that the protective structure will actually

136   *Effective protection*

have drawn resources from B into A and not the other way, as seemed to be suggested by the measured effective rates. We can conceive of one scale of measured effective rates and another of correct effective rates, the latter being generally below the former and possibly displaying industries in a different order.

Further research involving calculations with various plausible substitution elasticities and protective structures is needed to determine how important this consideration is.[4] Provisionally it can be suggested that the analysis of the effects of a protective structure be carried out with the use of measured effective rates but that some downward adjustments might be made in those cases where substitution effects are believed to be very important. Substitution may be important either because the elasticity of substitution is high or because the incentive to substitute is high owing to a large dispersion of the relevant tariffs.

V Biased Substitution Effects and the 'Value-added Product' Concept

Is the concept of the 'value-added product' useful or valid? Assume that we have a three-factor production function, product j being produced by one produced input i and by two primary factors L and K. The value-added product v is supposed to sum up the contribution of the two primary factors. But what is the unit of v? This indeed presents no problem when there are fixed coefficients between j and i. The unit of v is then the unit of the final product, v being simply the output of j less the input i. A higher price of j, owing to a tariff t_j, increases the amount available for the primary factor content in j, that is for v. No problem is presented by the fact that v itself can be produced in varying proportions of L to K. All those combinations of L and K which are just sufficient to produce one unit of j, when associated with the fixed amount of i, represent one unit of v.

The problem becomes more complicated with substitution. Since the v/j ratio changes when relative prices change we cannot define a unit of v in terms of units of j. What then is a unit of v, bearing in mind that it has no 'natural units'? Travis (1968) first drew attention to this question. A way of justifying the use of the value-added product concept, even when there is substitution, is needed.

We shall now make the following crucial assumptions. The ratio between

---

4. Grubel and Lloyd (1971) have made some calculations using CES production functions which suggest that, for plausible substitution elasticities, substitution effects may not make a great deal of difference. See also Leith (1968). Ramaswami and Srinivasan (1970) attach great importance to substitution effects. Travis (1964) has some evidence suggesting the importance of substitution effects. Balassa et al. (1970) have examined this and conclude that the substitution elasticity appears to be low.

the primary factors in industry j, that is the L/K ratio, will change only if the price ratio between L and K alters, and the ratio between the produced input i and the final good j, that is the input coefficient i/j, will alter only if the price ratio between these two alters. Hence the production function has the special separable form $J[V(K, L), i]$ where K and L are the amounts of the two primary factors, i is the amount of the produced input, and J and V are linear homogeneous functions of their respective arguments. Thus, suppose that the price ratio between L and K is in fact given from outside. Then a protective structure is imposed so that $t_j > t_i$. This will now lead to substitution of i for both L and K to the same extent, so that the L/K quantity ratio will not change provided the L/K price ratio does not change. We can define v in this case as a bundle of L and K containing the two factors in fixed proportions.

But this is not the whole story. Effective protection for j increases the demand of the industry for the two primary factors. Similarly effective protection for other industries affects the demands for L and K. All this can initially be thought of as happening at a constant L/K price ratio. But the net result will be for the demand for one factor to expand relatively to that for another, causing the L/K price ratio to change; hence there will be substitution in industry j between the two factors. How then can we talk about a bundle of primary factors in fixed proportions? We can handle this by holding constant now the prices of j and i, while allowing the L/K price ratio to change. Hence we can say that a unit of v is all those combinations of L and K that can produce a unit of j, together with the appropriate amount of i, given the ratio i/j established by the p_i/p_j price ratio.

Our special assumption means that the elasticity of substitution of i for L is the same as the elasticity of subsitution of i for K. The substitution effects are unbiased. The fictional concept of the value-added product, with the two-stage production function, is a convenient way of presenting our argument so as to yield the same result as would follow from making this assumption.

If we remove this assumption complications result. If the produced input is a much closer substitute for one primary factor than for another, and if the domestic price of the produced input alters then the technique of the value-added product, if crudely applied, could give a misleading result.

Consider an economy with two industries, A and B, each of which uses an imported input. B is the export industry. Suppose that A obtains positive effective protection, whether calculated at free trade or at protection coefficients, while effective protection for industry B is zero. In the *unbiased* case we would expect some quantities of both primary factors to move from B to A, though it is indeed possible that gross output of A falls for reasons explained earlier. But with respect to resource allocation effects there could be no paradox. Now allow for *biased* substitution effects, supposing that A's imported input is a much closer substitute for L

than for K. We can now display the possibility of a paradoxical result.[5] Conceivably resources (or, at least one of the primary factors) could move from A to B.

To narrow the problem down, assume that nominal protection for B and the tariff on its input are both zero. But the tariff on A's input is positive and its nominal tariff is sufficiently high for its effective rate to be positive. Also assume that A is labour intensive, the L/K ratio in A being greater than that in B. Now there are two forces at work affecting the resource movement. The first might be called the normal effect. For reasons that follow from the usual analysis, resources will tend to move from the industry with the zero effective rate to the one with the positive rate. But now there is a second effect, the bias effect. In our example it can be shown to pull in the opposite direction from the normal effect. The price of A's imported input has gone up because of the positive input tariff. Mainly labour will be substituted for this input since labour is a closer substitute for it than is capital. At a given ratio of the primary factor prices A will raise its L/K ratio. But this makes labour scarce relative to capital in the economy as a whole. So the size of the labour-intensive industry must contract and of the capital-intensive industry must expand. The effect is not unlike that of a labour-using bias in technical progress. Since A happens to be the labour-intensive industry in our example the bias effect thus creates a tendency for A to lose resources. Bearing in mind that the normal effect sets up the opposite tendency, on balance resources may move in either direction. When there is a positive tariff on A's input, the sign of the bias effect depends on whether the input is a closer substitute for K or for L and whether A is labour intensive or capital intensive. There are of course numerous possible combinations of cases one might consider.

The general conclusion is that even in a two-sector model the direction of resource pulls may depend not just on relative effective rates, but also on biases in substitution effects and on relative factor-intensities. One can no longer look at each product, with its tariff and production function, separately and build up a scale of adjusted effective rates which can form the basis for a general equilibrium analysis. The direction of resource movement depends also on relative factor intensities.

One question is whether biased substitution effects are important in practice. To obtain paradoxical results for given relative factor-intensities the biases must be of particular form and sufficiently large. Furthermore, input tariffs must be sufficiently high or changes in them significant. This consideration is important in a world of escalated tariff structures where

5. The possibility of a paradoxical result brought about by substitution in a general equilibrium model was first indicated by Ramaswami and Srinivasan (1968, 1970), who produced counter-examples. The exploration of biased substitution effects here was inspired by an attempt to explain their results. Jones (1971) has analysed biased substitution effects and gives a precise statement of necessary conditions for a paradoxical result.

input tariffs tend to be low relative to nominal tariffs on final goods or using industries. For practical work it may be reasonable to assume that substitution effects are not significantly biased, but in special cases, where input tariffs are high, substitution effects are believed to be large and biased, and relative factor intensities significantly different, some modifications to our simple analysis could be introduced.

References

Anderson, J. and Naya, S. 1969: Substitution and two concepts of effective rate of protection. *American Economic Review*, 59, 607–12.

Balassa, B. 1971: Effective protection in developing countries. In J. N. Bhagwati *et al.* (eds), *Trade, Balance of Payments and Growth: Essays in Honor of Charles P. Kindleberger*. Amsterdam: North-Holland.

Balassa, B., Guisinger, S. and Schydlowsky, D. 1970: The effective rates of protection and the question of labor protection in the United States: a comment. *Journal of Political Economy*, 78, 1150–62.

Basevi, G. 1966: The United States tariff structure: estimates of effective rates of protection of United States industries and industrial labor. *Review of Economics and Statistics*, 48, 147–60.

Corden, W. M. 1971: *The Theory of Protection*. Oxford: Oxford University Press.

Ethier, W. J. 1972: Input substitution and the concept of the effective rate of protection. *Journal of Political Economy*, 80, 34–47.

Finger, J. M. 1969: Substitution and the effective rate of protection. *Journal of Political Economy*, 77, 972–5.

Grubel, H. G. and Lloyd, P. J. 1971: Factor substitution and effective tariff rates. *Review of Economic Studies*, 38, 92–103.

Guisinger, S. E. 1969: Negative value added and the theory of effective protection. *The Quarterly Journal of Economics*, 83, 415–33.

Humphrey, D. B. and Tsukahara, T. 1970: On substitution and the effective rate of protection. *International Economic Review*, 11, 488–96.

Jones, R. W. 1971: Effective protection and substitution. *Journal of International Economics*, 1, 59–81.

Leith, J. C. 1968: Substitution and supply elasticities in calculating the effective protective rate. *The Quarterly Journal of Economics*, 82, 588–601.

—— 1971: The effect of tariffs on production, consumption and trade: a revised analysis. *American Economic Review*, 61, 74–81.

Lewis, S. R. Jr. and Guisinger, S. E. 1968: Measuring protection in a developing country: the case of Pakistan. *Journal of Political Economy*, 76, 1170–98.

Ramaswami, V. K. and Srinivasan, T. N. 1968: Tariff structure and resource allocation in the presence of factor substitution. Discussion Paper No. 33, Indian Statistical Institute, Planning Unit, mimeo.

—— 1970: Tariff structure and resource allocation in the presence of factor substitution. In J. N. Bhagwati, *et al.* (eds), *Trade, Balance of Payments and Growth: Essays in Honor of Charles P. Kindleberger*. Amsterdam: North-Holland.

Soligo, R. and Stern, J. J. 1965: Tariff protection, import substitution, and investment efficiency. *Pakistan Development Review*, 5, 249–70.

Tan, A. H. H. 1970: Differential tariffs, negative value-added and the theory of effective protection. *American Economic Review*, 60, 107–16.

Travis, W. P. 1964: *The Theory of Trade and Protection*. Cambridge, Mass: Harvard University Press.
_____ 1968: The effective rate of protection and the question of labor protection in the United States. *Journal of Political Economy*, 76, 433–61.
Walker, F. V. 1968: The effective rate of protection with factor substitution. Mimeo.

10
Effective Protection Revisited

Essay 7, originally published in 1966, gave rise to a large theoretical literature and, perhaps more important, led to a great deal of empirical work. In fact, there was a boom in the calculation of effective rates of protection, following on the pioneering work of Balassa (1965) and Basevi (1966), and generally using essay 7 as the theoretical basis or take-off point. I expanded essay 7 into several chapters of a book, *The Theory of Protection* (Corden, 1971), aiming to clarify many matters, especially the essentially general equilibrium approach of the theory of tariff structure. The simple concept of the effective protective rate (a history of which is given in that book, pp. 245–9) is only one ingredient in the broader approach which I sought to stress. In particular, the broader approach represents a departure from the two-product models which used to dominate trade theory and still play a large role.

The partial equilibrium exposition of the effective protective rate should only be regarded as a first step in the broader analysis. In essay 9, therefore I follow the procedure of first showing how the effective rate with substitution fits into the partial equilibrium analysis (as represented by the supply curve *SS'* drawn in figure 9.3), and later proceed to fit it into the general equilibrium story – when *relative* effective rates become crucial. The general equilibrium role of the new concept – that is, the idea that it was meant to fit into a general equilibrium framework – should be quite clear in the discussions of the 'scale of effective rates', the 'exchange rate adjustment' and the 'four concepts of protection' in essay 7. Nevertheless, various scholars appeared to miss this. Hence I wrote essay 8, designed to present a particular general equilibrium model of a very traditional kind – that is with only two activities – where effective rates were an explicit ingredient.

I The Scale of Effective Rates, Resource Pull Effects and the Jones Model

Something more must be said about the brief but quite central discussion of the 'scale of effective rates' in essay 7. This 'scale' was designed as a concept that would embody a great deal of information about a country's trade tax-subsidy structure. There has been much discussion of my brief remarks that this scale 'tells us the *direction* in which this structure causes resources to be pulled as between activities producing traded goods. Domestic production will shift from low to high effective-protective-rate activities'. I spelt this out a little further in *The Theory of Protection* (pp. 84–5). There I stressed, what had seemed to me obvious when I wrote essay 7, that actual resource movements *also* depend on production substitution elasticities. When I talked of a resource *pull* I did not mean an *actual* resource movement. For example, if the production substitution elasticity between two activities were zero, a resource pull from one activity to another created by a difference in their effective rates would not lead to any actual resource movement. Hence in *The Theory of Protection* (p. 84), I wrote that 'domestic production will *tend* to shift from low to high-effective protective rate activities and hence the demand for those primary factors in which the high effective-rate activities are intensive will rise relative to those in the low effective-rate activities', and (p. 85), 'the effect of a tariff structure on an activity depends not just on the position in the scale of effective rates, but on the activity's position relative to those other activities which are significant substitutes on the production side'.

The picture I had in mind was of a set of bilateral production transformation curves embodying bilateral production substitution elasticities, where movements along the transformation curves are brought about by changes in relative value added or effective prices. In *The Theory of Protection* I noted the possibility of some substitution elasticities being zero. In principle they could also be negative, reflecting complementarity. In a three-activities model, if A and B are complementary, while both are substitutes relative to C (our concern always being with substitution only on the production side), a positive effective rate for A, with the others zero, would draw resources not just into A but also into B.

In spite of the careful qualifications, it needs to be stressed here that this approach is still not entirely satisfactory. Other than in the two-activity case expounded in essay 8, it is not based on an explicit underlying general equilibrium model. It does appear to contain elements of partial equilibrium. The nature of the problem is best brought out by considering the case discussed in essay 5. This essay presents a three-activities model. A tariff on manufactures reduces the output of wheat, as one might expect, but *raises* the output of wool. Thus wool and manufactures are complementary in a general equilibrium sense. A well-specified general equilibrium production structure yields this result, and other structures could also be produced which would yield unexpected results if one's expectations were based on the simple exposition of essay 7. Thus, there has to be some explicit production structure. It is not sufficient just to assume a set of bilateral production substitution elasticities, even though this may be intuitively appealing.

Effective protection revisited

It is here that Jones (1975) has come to the rescue. He has supplied the formal model which comes close to what I had in mind when writing about the resource pull effects of a scale of effective rates. It is his model which provides a formal basis for my 'common-sense' suppositions.[1] We make the assumption of fixed coefficients between traded inputs and the final product (as in the first part of essay 7) and hence assume away the 'substitution problem', to be discussed later. Hence we have a set of well-defined activities, with each activity producing one product. An 'activity' is what I have called in essay 8 a 'value-added product'. It results from the inputs of the primary factors.[2] Now we come to the key Jones assumption, which was also implicitly my assumption in essay 7.

He makes use of the specific factors model. Each activity is produced by two factors, namely one which is specific to the particular activity, and one which is mobile between all the activities (call it labour). Hence with n activities there are $(n + 1)$ factors, and the mobile factor is paid a uniform wage throughout the economy. In each activity there is substitutability between labour and the relevant specific factor.

A positive effective tariff for one activity with others zero (or a rise in one effective rate when the others are constant) will draw labour into that activity, expand its output, raise the rent of the specific factor, and reduce output elsewhere. The reductions in output elsewhere will, of course, not be uniform: they will depend on the importance of labour in that activity and on the elasticity of the marginal product of labour curve. We can then imagine a rise in the effective rate in another activity. This will draw resources out of the first industry, among others. In analysing the resource allocation effects of such a change in effective protection, Jones remarks that 'many features of the solution can be readily understood by reference to the standard partial equilibrium model in which one variable factor is combined with one fixed factor to produce output subject to the law of diminishing returns'.

Comparing the effective rate structure with free trade, let us suppose that two activities have uniform positive effective rates while others have zero rates. The argument would also apply if the others obtained a uniform rate which was less than that of the two high-protected industries. Resources – that is labour in this model – will then be drawn into both of the high-protected industries out of the others, but the two industries will not necessarily expand in the same proportion. The one where the share of

---

1. I sketched this model out verbally (but without full details or formalizing it) in *The Theory of Protection* (Corden, 1971, p. 95).
2. In the section where Jones expounds the relevant part of his model he assumes that industries have *no* produced inputs, so that he refers only to *nominal* tariffs and to *industries*, rather than activities. Later he introduces produced inputs and effective protection. But his early argument is fully applicable to the effective protection model, provided the substitution problem is assumed away, as I have assumed it away here.

labour is higher (i.e. which is more labour intensive) will expand more. These and other results are worked out in more detail by Jones (1975).

In Jones's model the free trade nominal prices of all traded goods (and there are no non-traded goods) are held constant, so that the nominal exchange rate is fixed, while the nominal wage varies to maintain equilibrium in the labour market. A rise in a tariff in one activity, with the others constant, will raise the nominal wage. This happens because the rise in the tariff increases the demand for labour by the industry concerned. This rise in the nominal wage relative to the free-trade prices of traded goods is the equivalent, in terms of essay 7, of a real appreciation. The same result could be obtained by holding the nominal wage constant and allowing the nominal exchange rate to appreciate as effective tariffs are increased.

Given this correspondence between wage adjustment in the Jones model and exchange rate adjustment in essay 7, one can see the relevance of a powerful result in his paper, a result which links resource reallocation and income distribution effects. All activities can be divided into two groups, namely those in which the rent to the specific factor rises relative to the return to the mobile factor (the wage), and those in which it falls relatively. All activities in the first group expand and those in the second group contract. Jones shows that a proportional domestic price change of an activity (i.e. a change in what I have called in essay 8 the effective price) must always be of the same sign as the proportional change in the rent of the specific factor in that activity, but the change in the rent must be greater.

It follows that, if we held the nominal wage constant, we could say that the imposition of an effective protection structure which is generally positive will lead to an appreciation of the exchange rate to maintain equilibrium in the market for the mobile factor, labour. Let us define the *net* effective protective rate in relation to the exchange rate, as in essay 7, but without reference to non-tradables. Then, those activities where the net effective rate is positive will expand, and those where it is negative, will contract. And when an activity expands the rent of the specific factor rises and when it contracts, the rent falls.

It is clear that even in the specific factors model, as soon as the number of activities exceeds two, a ranking of effective rates need not coincide with a ranking of proportional changes in outputs that are induced by the effective rate structure. When activity A receives zero effective protection, and B, C and D are ranked in ascending order of effective protection, we can say that output of A must fall and of D must rise, but cannot say whether B's and C's outputs will rise or fall, and which one will rise or fall more. Thus one cannot say whether the rents of the specific factors in B and C will rise or fall. The inability to order proportional output changes from a ranking of effective rates has been considered by some writers a serious weakness of this whole body of theory. It is obviously possible that the proportional output ranking is quite different from the ranking on a scale of effective rates.

The solution seems to be to distinguish the *possible* from the *probable*. In the absence of precise knowledge of the underlying production structure, all things are possible. But some things are more probable. Suppose that, in the Jones model, the distributive shares of the mobile factor (labour) were the same in each activity, and that, in addition, the elasticities of the various marginal product of labour curves were the same, then a ranking of effective rates would give us a ranking of proportional output changes. In the absence of detailed knowledge of the underlying production structure, this is the most probable outcome. If we have reason to believe that particular distributive shares are higher or lower than others, or particular elasticities higher or lower than others, the simple presumption would then be adjusted appropriately.

Furthermore, there is the possibility that the production structure is *not* a pure specific factors case. It is highly likely that, in the short run, there is at least one significant specific factor in each activity. But there may be more than one mobile factor – especially in the medium or long run, which is more relevant for analysis of a system of protection – and these may have different distributive shares (i.e. different factor intensities) in the various activities. Elements of the Heckscher–Ohlin model then enter, and we can get numerous possible complications, an example of which is in essay 5. My approach (as in *The Theory of Protection*) is to keep these possibilities in mind, and when there is some knowledge or likelihood of such complications, these would then be built into predictions of the effects of changes in the scale of effective rates, or of a movement to complete free trade.

All these difficulties really have nothing to do with the concept of the effective rate of protection *per se*. If there were no intermediate goods, but if there were more than two industries, the same problem would arise. This problem must not be mixed up with the substitution problem – which is of its essence to do with the presence of intermediates and the concept of effective protection. Ethier, in particular, has been at pains to stress the distinction. He wrote 'To search for a measure of effective protection that would also be free of the defects that plague nominal rates even in an ideal world of no intermediate goods is obviously a futile task' (Ethier, 1971), and 'The scale of effective rates is subject to the same qualitative limitations as is a scale of nominal rates in the absence of intermediate goods' (Ethier, 1977). This brings us, then, to one of the central theoretical issues, elaborately analysed in essay 9, namely the substitution problem.

II The Substitution Problem Once Again

Essay 7 opened up a subject which turned out to be central to the pure theory of effective protection and which gave rise to a very sophisticated literature. I analysed the effects of substitution between the tradable input and the primary factor – thought of as a single factor at this stage – and came up with the crucial answer, which subsequent analysis has found to be correct, that 'calculations of effective rates which use the data of the protection situation will always tend to *overstate* the effective rates if there is any substitution from primary inputs toward material inputs or vice versa'. Thus the usual calculations would have an upward bias. But the analysis did not pursue the general equilibrium implications, and was limited by assuming only a single primary factor input. This then led to a much more thorough investigation of the issue in essay 9.

When there are fixed coefficients there is really no doubt about the definition of the effective rate, and three definitions which I have used – namely that given at the beginning of essay 7, that given later in the discussion of substitution in that essay and that given in essay 9 – all come to the same thing. But once substitution is allowed for, essay 9 gives the correct answer. The distinction between the definition in the latter part of essay 7 and that of essay 9 is that the former argues that the correct effective rate requires use of the input coefficients of the free trade situation, while the latter argues that it requires use of coefficients which are *between* the input coefficients of the free trade and of the protection situations. With either definition, use of the free trade coefficient will lead to an overstatement, and this remains the main result. In any case, while I have reproduced in this book the 'substitution' discussion of essay 7 because it happened to be the beginning of a lively literature, this early discussion is really overtaken by essay 9.

What are the principal conclusions of essay 9? The first is that 'substitution between the traded input and the value-added product always raises the effective rate'. This conclusion presents no problems at all.[3] The second is that gross outputs no longer move necessarily to the same extent or even in the same direction as value-added products. Thus an example is given where the value-added product stays constant while gross output declines. This cannot happen in a model with fixed coefficients between the traded inputs and the value-added product. The important question is then raised whether we are really interested in value-added (products) or in gross outputs, bearing in mind that the effective rate refers to value added. The third conclusion, already mentioned, is that use of the input coefficients of the protection situation will always lead to overstatement of effective rates.[4] The general equilibrium implication is that the overstatement could well differ between activities, so that the order on the scale of effective rates could be altered. Calculation of 'true' effective rates would require knowledge of the substitution elasticities.

The fourth conclusion is that 'biased substitution effects' throw in doubt the whole concept of the 'value-added product' and thus of the effective

---

3. This conclusion also applies to substitution between different traded inputs. This was shown formally in a section of the original article not reproduced in essay 9.
4. This also applies to substitution between different traded inputs, and was also shown in the original article on which essay 9 is based.

rate. When the production function has the special form $J(V(K,L), i)$, where K and L are the two primary factors, i is the produced traded input, V is the value-added product and J is gross output, it is *separable*. This is to be distinguished from the function $J(K,L,i)$, which is *not* separable. Biased substitution effects result from absence of separability. In fact, one has to say that in the absence of separability, 'value added' ceases to be well defined, and this negative conclusion must then apply also to the concept of a change in the price of value added (the effective price), this change having been defined in essays 8 and 9 and in *The Theory of Protection* as the effective protective rate.

We have thus three problems to cope with caused by substitution. All three problems would disappear if there were fixed coefficients between gross output and the traded inputs. The fourth, and most fundamental, problem is not caused by substitution as such, but only by absence of separability.

This 'non-separability' problem is theoretically the most destructive, because if there were reason to believe that it was empirically important it would throw into question the whole concept of effective protection. But, in fact, there is no evidence of its empirical importance and, again, one needs to distinguish the possible from the probable. In the absence of clear evidence of frequent biases of sufficient size it seems sensible to presume that substitution effects are *not* biased. In particular cases, where biases are known to be large, implications can be worked out in detail, showing in which direction calculations do err.[5]

The probability approach also seems to be sensible with regard to the third problem, namely the overstatement of effective rates resulting from the usual measurements. It is probable that substitution effects *do* exist, so that, in general, one would expect measured rates to be overstatements of 'true rates'. While the empirical evidence about the extent of possible substitution is not conclusive, in the absence of more specific evidence, the first assumption should surely be that substitution effects, even though they do exist, do *not* alter the order on the scale of effective rates.[6]

---

5. As far as I am aware, the only empirical work on this issue has been done by Humphrey (1975). He presents estimates of factor (capital, labour) and intermediate input substitution for six groups of the US manufacturing sector over the period 1947–58 and tests a hypothesis of average factor-intermediate separability. The evidence seems to support the hypothesis, so that, 'Corden's use of a value-added product concept in effective protection theory is thus far supported'. See also Humphrey and Wolkowitz (1976), where there is further empirical support for separability. In addition, using other data and methods, Humphrey and Moroney (1975) find that in the USA, 'capital and labour may be analysed as functionally separable from natural resource products'.

6. Some empirical work suggests that substitution effects may not be strong enough to make a great deal of difference (quite apart from the question of separability). See the references in footnote 4 of essay 9. This also seems to be supported by the evidence given by Humphrey (1975), but, on the other hand, Humphrey (1977) did find significant substitution effects.

Finally, there is the point that gross output may move in a different direction from value added. This also seems rather unlikely (as indicated by the example in essay 9), but the possibility must at least be entertained. The effective rate, as I have always conceived it, refers to value added (even though with fixed coefficients, gross output and value added must move together). One might be interested primarily in gross outputs, perhaps because external effects are believed to be associated with gross outputs, or just for forecasting purposes. In that case – when substitution effects are believed to be large and the particular relationships of nominal rates are as indicated in essay 9 (with t_i greater than t_j but not too much greater) – one might modify the probabilistic conclusions drawn from the scale of effective rates. But changes in value-added products – on which the scale of effective rates is meant to shed light – should still be the main concern if one is interested either in resource (i.e. factor) movements or in factoral income distribution effects, that is in effects on factor rents.

Taking all this into account, my own conclusion (Corden, 1975), has been that 'clearly, one must not place too much value on the calculations or estimated figures. Theory certainly has a useful role to play in bringing out various possible paradoxes, implicit assumptions, and so on, but finally some judgement is required as to what is important or probable, and there will never be enough empirical information to give one certain answers'.

Apart from the papers that were already published when I wrote essay 9 and that are referred to in the first footnote in that essay, and the paper by Jones (1971), which was written simultaneously, attention should be drawn to six papers dealing in very sophisticated fashion with the substitution problem and related issues, namely Ethier (1971, 1972, 1977), Bruno (1973), Khang (1973) and Bhagwati and Srinivasan (1973). They all confirm the basic analysis and analytical conclusions of essay 9, especially the crucial role of unbiased substitution effects (separability) for the survival of the basic concepts.

Ethier proposes an alternative concept of 'own-value added', and prefers a focus on gross outputs, because these have natural units, unlike the value-added product. Khang (1973), while accepting the possibility of 'perverse' responses, concludes fairly positively, in line with my own thinking: 'A very general concept of value-added product is seen to possess many useful properties which facilitates the analysis of problems involving intermediate goods in the theory of international trade. . . Thus, our analysis suggests that the foundation on which the theory of effective protection rests is not entirely sound. However, not everything is lost. Within the framework of our model, we know that a perverse response cannot occur in cases in which production functions are of the separable type or of the type satisfying the regularity condition and that an index of effective protection can be found which will correctly predict resource allocational shifts resulting from certain changes in the tariff structure.' On the other hand, Bhagwati and Srinivasan (1973) are much more nihilistic, essentially because of the various complications and possibilities which I have discussed here.

III Non-traded Inputs and Other Problems

There are really two central problems in the concept and measurement of effective rates which are inherent in the effective rate, as distinct from the nominal rate, aspect, that is in a model with intermediate goods. One is the substitution problem and the other is the problem of non-traded inputs.

The latter problem was also first raised in essay 7, but has attracted relatively less attention from pure theorists – with the notable exceptions of Leith (1968), Massell (1968) and Ray (1973). On the other hand, actual calculators have had to form views on the subject since they have had to make decisions as to whether or not to include non-traded inputs in value added or to lump them with traded inputs. Frequently they resolved the matter by making calculations both with the Balassa method and the Corden method. As I have compared various methods in detail in *The Theory of Protection* (pp. 157–63), and have also summarized various possible methods (Corden, 1975, pp. 63–4), I can be brief here.

If there are no traded inputs in non-traded inputs, it seems clear that the simple method proposed in essay 7 is theoretically the correct one. It lumps non-traded inputs with value added (not with traded inputs, as in the Balassa method). It has become known as the 'Corden method'. This conclusion is endorsed in the only rigorous general equilibrium analysis of the problem by Ray (1973). But if there are traded inputs in non-traded inputs, the logic of footnote 5 in essay 7 must be followed through: the traded input content of non-traded inputs must be lumped with direct traded inputs. I spelt this out in more detail in *The Theory of Protection*, and it is endorsed by Bruno (1972), who compares the method of domestic resource cost calculation with effective protection, and finds that the same principles operate.

Here one might note some other difficulties that have been found important by researchers, which are not referred to in essay 7, and which have sometimes led to considerable differences in the figures produced by different researchers for the protective structures of the same country in similar time periods.[7] In general, these difficulties entitle one to be highly sceptical of greatly aggregated figures obtained quickly. More value can be placed on detailed calculations for particular cases, perhaps as parts of industry studies, or on thorough, comprehensive calculations drawing on considerable resources. One should not place much emphasis on small variations or differences between calculated rates.

When quotas are the principal instruments of protection, comparisons between domestic and world market prices must be made in order to obtain implicit nominal rates of protection, which must be the starting point for any calculations. This is relevant for many developing countries. The margin for error is vast here. With a given quota structure or policy,

---

7. This discussion comes from Corden (1975, pp. 62–3).

and with demand and supply curves shifting over time, implicit effective rates may vary greatly year by year.

Even when tariffs alone are used, there may be much tariff redundancy, also necessitating price comparisons. A difficulty in these comparisons is that the quality of the local product and the substitute import may differ. If the price of the local product is below the tariff-inclusive price of the import, one cannot automatically assume that there is tariff redundancy. This raises the wider issue of product differentiation. Effective rates are calculated for traded goods, that is, goods where the domestic product and the import are, in theory, perfect substitutes. In the case of manufactures, substitution is rarely perfect, though it may be high. This presents no real difficulty if there is simply a constant quality difference between the products. But a problem does arise if they are differentiated products in the true sense, the consumers' choices between them depending on relative prices. The elasticity of substitution on the demand side will then bear on the impact of the tariff on the domestic producer.

All effective-rate calculations involve tariff averaging of some kind. The choice of averaging method can be a major source of error or at least divergence between different figures, and the more aggregated they are, the greater the difficulty (Tumlir and Till, 1971). I have attempted to clarify the theory of tariff averaging by developing the concept of the 'uniform tariff equivalent' (Corden, 1966a; see also Balassa, 1965; Basevi, 1971). The uniform *ad valorem* tariff that would have the same effect on the total value of imports as the existing tariff structure is, ideally, the figure one is seeking (though, in principle, there are many other possible uniform tariff equivalents, for example the one that leads to the same amount of protected production). But this concept does not resolve the practical problems. In most calculations, it is customary to obtain the basic nominal tariffs required to calculate effective rates in a given category from import and customs revenue data, and so obtain import-weighted averages. For well-known reasons, these data lead to understatements. The effective rates themselves, once calculated, may then be averaged on some other basis, perhaps with domestic production weights, but an averaging error is built in at the source.

To conclude, two further matters should at least be mentioned. Firstly, note must be taken of the general equilibrium model-building approach to estimating the resource allocation and income distribution effects of a protective structure. If the data are available it is clearly preferable to build a complete model to provide answers to the general equilibrium questions we have posed, than to calculate a scale of figures which cannot claim to give more than indications of effects, based on probabilities and so on. Why pause half way to the complete answer?

This issue was first raised by Evans (1971) who had built a model for Australia, and the question has been asked many times since. I sought to answer it in *The Theory of Protection* (p. 241): 'The data for complete general equilibrium, programming exercises do not normally exist for those countries where the analysis of protective structures is particularly important. The desirability of the more ambitious exercises, if practicable, and bearing in mind their cost, need not be denied. But something is better than nothing.' It should also be added that effective rate calculations can usually be more disaggregated – that is allow for more products or industry sub-groups – than is normally possible in the big models.

The other matter is the normative role of effective protection figures. I discussed this in detail in *Trade Policy and Economic Welfare* (ch. 13). It was argued there that it is in second-best optimizing situations – where there are various constraints or distortions – that effective rate calculations become relevant for policy. For example, effective rates could help in an efficient process of selecting industries to protect when there is an industrialization target or when there is a uniform rate of marginal divergence between private and social costs applying to a whole category, say the whole of manufacturing value added. It should also be added that the scale of effective rates can contribute to giving an indication of where the main costs of protection might be. This would apply to a situation where free trade would actually be first best, and was discussed in the Further Notes to essay 1.

Normative analysis has been interpreted here as analysis that is concerned with aggregate welfare in the Pareto-efficiency sense. If the concern is purely with sectoral income effects, then the earlier discussion of positive effects, especially in the context of the Jones (1975) model, is relevant. Indeed, Jones has put particular stress on the usefulness of effective rates in indicating factoral distribution effects (effects on rents) of a protective structure. This is especially important if one is concerned with the political economy of protectionism – that is with the various pressures which actually explain the existence of a protective structure.

Something further must be added about the normative significance of effective rates. This matter was only touched upon in *Trade Policy and Economic Welfare*. If there are significant distortions of some kind – divergences between private and social costs or benefits – that are not included in the effective rate calculations themselves, then effective rate figures cannot have any direct normative significance *on their own*. They can only tell part of the 'distortions story'. For normative analysis it is necessary to allow for these 'other' distortions. This applies whether the aim is to provide an *ex-ante* guide to resource allocation in a small part of an economy, possibly one project, as in social cost-benefit analysis, whether it is to provide an *ex-ante* guide to broad policy reform, taking general equilibrium effects into account, as in the construction of an optimal protective system subject to specified constraints, or whether the concern is with *ex-post* cost of protection calculations. An example of a distortion not usually included in effective rate calculations would be a divergence between the private and the social cost of labour. When such distortions are allowed for, the effective rate figures can be translated into domestic resource cost figures, which *do* have normative significance. This cannot be discussed further here, but important discussions on the connection between effective protection and domestic resource cost are given by Bruno (1972) and Krueger (1972).

References

Balassa, B. 1965: Tariff protection in industrial countries: an evaluation. *Journal of Political Economy*, 73, 573–94.

Basevi, G. 1966: The United States tariff structure: estimates of effective rates of protection of United States industries and industrial labor. *Review of Economics and Statistics*, 48, 147–60.

────── 1971: Aggregation problems in the measurement of effective protection. In H. G. Grubel and H. G. Johnson (eds), *Effective Tariff Protection*. Geneva: Graduate Institute of International Studies.

Bhagwati, J. N. and Srinivasan, T. N. 1973: The general equilibrium theory of effective protection and resource allocation. *Journal of International Economics*, 3, 259–81.

Bruno, M. 1972: Domestic resource costs and effective protection: clarification and synthesis. *Journal of Political Economy*, 80, 16–33.

────── 1973: Protection and tariff change under general equilibrium. *Journal of International Economics*, 3, 205–26.

Corden, W. M. 1966a: The effective protective rate, the uniform tariff equivalent and the average tariff. *The Economic Record*, 42, 200–16.

────── 1966b: The structure of a tariff system and the effective protective rate. *Journal of Political Economy*, 74, 221–37. (Essay 7, this volume.)

────── 1971: *The Theory of Protection*, Oxford: Oxford University Press.

────── 1974: *Trade Policy and Economic Welfare*. Oxford: Oxford University Press.

────── 1975: The costs and consequences of protection: a survey of empirical work. In P. B. Kenen (ed.), *International Trade and Finance: Frontiers for Research*. Cambridge: Cambridge University Press.

Ethier, W. J. 1971: General equilibrium theory and the concept of effective protection. In H. G. Grubel and H. G. Johnson (eds), *Effective Tariff Protection*. Geneva: Graduate Institute of International Studies.

────── 1972. Input substitution and the concept of the effective rate of protection. *Journal of Political Economy*, 80, 34–47.

────── 1977: The theory of effective protection in general equilibrium: effective-rate analogues of nominal rates. *The Canadian Journal of Economics*, 10, 233–45.

Evans, H. D. 1971: The empirical specification of a general equilibrium model of protection in Australia. In H. G. Grubel and H. G. Johnson (eds), *Effective Tariff Protection*. Geneva: Graduate Institute of International Studies.

Humphrey, D. B. 1975: Estimates of factor-intermediate substitution and separability. *Southern Economic Journal*, 41, 531–14.

────── 1977: Substitution in an input–output table. *Journal of Economics and Business*, 30, 38–45.

Humphrey, D. B. and Moroney, J. R. 1975: Substitution among capital, labor, and natural resource products in American manufacturing. *Journal of Political Economy*, 83, 57–82.

Humphrey, D. B. and Wolkowitz, B. 1976: Substituting intermediates for capital and labor: with alternative functional forms: an aggregate study. *Applied Economics*, 8, 59–68.

Jones, R. W. 1971: Substitution and effective protection. *Journal of International Economics*, 1, 59–81.

―――― 1975: Income distribution and effective protection in a multicommodity trade model. *Journal of Economic Theory*, 11, 1–15.

Khang, C. 1973: Factor substitution in the theory of effective protection: a general equilibrium analysis. *Journal of International Economics*, 3, 283–90.

Krueger, A. O. 1972: Evaluating restrictionist trade regimes: theory and measurement. *Journal of Political Economy*, 80, 48–62.

Leith, J. C. 1968: Substitution and supply elasticities in calculating the effective protective rate. *The Quarterly Journal of Economics*, 82, 588–601.

Massell, B. F. 1968: The resource-allocative effects of a tariff and the effective protection of individual inputs. *The Economic Record*, 44, 369–76.

Ray, A. 1973: Non-traded inputs and effective protection: a general equilibrium analysis. *Journal of International Economics*, 3, 245–58.

Tumlir, J. and Till, L. 1971: Tariff averaging in international comparisons. In H. G. Grubel and H. G. Johnson (eds), *Effective Tariff Protection*. Geneva: Graduate Institute of International Studies.

Part III
Multinationals and Trade Theory

11
International Trade Theory and the Multinational Enterprise*

The purpose of this essay is to consider the implications of the multinational enterprise for international trade theory. The emphasis is constructive. The aim is to show that international trade theory can be adapted to analyse the location decisions of multinational firms and their welfare implications for host countries.

I What is Trade Theory?

The first problem is to define what is meant by international trade theory for the purpose of the present discussion.

It is not difficult to list the main questions, positive and normative, with which trade theory is concerned. Why do countries export and import the sorts of products they do and how are these trade flows related to the domestic characteristics of a country? How does trade affect domestic factor prices? What are the effects of trade interventions, such as tariffs, on output and demand patterns and on factor allocations and factor prices? What are the gains from trade (a closed economy compared with free trade)? What are valid arguments for trade intervention, and what are the principles of optimal trade intervention?

Trade theory could be defined narrowly to include only the central body of rigorous general equilibrium theory which is devoted to answering these questions. This central body of theory – to be called the 'orthodox theory' here – is usually (though not necessarily) presented geometrically in terms of two goods, and has the characteristic that each part fits explicitly into the main theoretical system and, hence, is clearly related to every other part. It is hardly necessary to survey or expound it since so many surveys and

---

* From John H. Dunning (ed.) 1974: *Economic Analysis and the Multinational Enterprise*, London: George Allen & Unwin. The section on the 'enclave approach' has been excluded, and appears here as essay 12.

expositions are available. Here it will only be observed that while there is some problem in precisely delimiting trade theory so defined, it is this body of theory which students are systematically taught and which is very influential. But the definition is not meant to be so narrow that it includes only the Heckscher–Ohlin–Samuelson (H–O–S) theory. Thus Meade (1952) expounded orthodox theory in its pre-H–O–S phase. This body of theory takes some account of international capital movements, but certainly not of the multinational enterprise. We will return to this point shortly.

Alternatively, one could include in trade theory the whole vast literature which is concerned in one way or another with answering the questions listed above. One would include, then, a peripheral literature that has not been integrated in the orthodox theory. In this peripheral literature there are many articles and some books that refer extensively to international capital movements and some that refer specifically to the international movement of technology and management and to the multinational firm. Some discuss these matters in relation to trade, notably articles and books by Posner (1961). Hufbauer (1965), Vernon (1966, 1971), and Dunning (1970, 1973b). Perhaps the most systematic model seeking to explain trade and investment flows together, and giving a prominent role to the multinational enterprise, is the well-known article by Vernon (1966).

This essay is concerned only with the orthodox theory. This does not mean that the peripheral literature is not important. But most of the papers concerned do not easily lend themselves to summarizing, simplicity of argument being generally sacrificed to the search for realism.[1] In addition, the essay is concerned only with *real* or *pure* trade theory. It will always be assumed that balance of payments equilibrium is maintained by appropriate exchange rate adjustments, and internal balance by appropriate monetary and fiscal policies.

II Characteristics of Trade Theory

Let us now look at five aspects of trade theory which are likely to be relevant if one wishes to allow for the multinational enterprise.

Capital Movements

The multinational enterprise is a conduit of international capital movements. It is, of course, much more than this, but this is certainly one of its aspects. Therefore it is necessary to know whether trade theory takes some account of such movements.

---

1. The papers which come closest to dealing with the issues of the present essay are Robertson (1971), Caves (1971), Johnson (1970a, 1972) and Dunning (1973a). Robertson deals specifically with trade aspects, Johnson with normative aspects and Dunning with the location problem.

The answer is that the very simplest body of theory – the *core* theory – does not. It assumes that each country has a given stock of factors of production. This does not mean that all the conclusions obtained from this simple theory turn out to be wrong when capital movements are allowed for. More important, at a more complex level, capital movements have been allowed for, and there is in fact an extensive literature within the broad framework of orthodox trade theory that takes into account capital movements both from a positive and a normative point of view. Trade theorists would, indeed, have been excessively naïve if they had failed to allow for such an obvious feature of the world. This literature will be summarized in the next section.

Transfer of Knowledge

A crucial role of the multinational enterprise is to transfer knowledge or technology – including managerial know-how – between countries. Some writers, notably Johnson (1970a), regard this as its main role. Orthodox theory has not explicitly incorporated such knowledge transfers.

Sometimes theorists have assumed that production functions for any given product are the same in all countries. This is one of the simplifying assumptions of the H–O–S model at its basic level, and is one of the assumptions required if trade is to equalize factor prices. It implies that knowledge is, in fact, costlessly and perfectly mobile between countries, but does not concern itself with the *process* of knowledge transfer. In any case, this assumption cannot be regarded as a central assumption of orthodox theory. It can be, and has been, removed within the framework of the H–O–S model, since various implications of production functions differing between countries have been explored (for example by Jones, 1970). Furthermore the H–O–S model is not the whole of orthodox trade theory.

More generally, orthodox theory assumes only that there are given production functions for each product in each country. These may differ between countries, and among the causes of international trade and the sources of the gains from trade are international differences in production functions. The original Ricardian exposition of comparative costs can be interpreted in these terms. Furthermore, production functions may be altered by exogenously-determined technical progress, and the trade theory literature has exhaustively explored the implications of various types of bias in such technical progress on countries' production structures and their terms of trade. But the important point here is that technical progress is always conceived of as exogenous to each country, with no necessary connection between progress in one country and another.

Connections Between Firms

The multinational enterprise generally involves some kind of international integration so that a good deal of international trade is intrafirm trade. This has numerous implications, to some of which we shall refer below. The main point is that the apparent international trading partners may not be independent of each other. The transfer prices they record for international transactions may not be 'arm's-length' market prices. Each partner may not be concerned with maximizing his own profits; rather, the interest may be in maximizing joint profits.

None of this is provided for by orthodox trade theory. It is always assumed that the trading firms in one country are entirely distinct from the trading firms in another country or, if there are any connections, these play no role in the analysis.

Monopoly and Oligopoly

It is generally said that the multinational firms compete in international markets as oligopolists. Furthermore, in many countries they are so large that they are also monopsonistic buyers of factors or of produced inputs.

Generally equilibrium trade theory does not allow for oligopoly or monopoly. There are, of course, piecemeal analyses of monopolistic situations, notably in connection with dumping, but these are all partial equilibrium. An important point (stressed by Johnson (1967)) is that orthodox trade theory is essentially general equilibrium, and no one – whether in or out of trade theory – has yet succeeded in adequately incorporating monopolistic or oligopolistic considerations in a general equilibrium framework. The result is that orthodox trade theory assumes perfect competition. Through the theory of the optimal tariff, it takes into account the possibility that a nation can exploit its monopoly or monopsony power in international trade; but this theory assumes that the nation will only do so if governments intervene, private enterprise being perfectly competitive.

On the face of it, the perfect competition assumption seems a crippling limitation. Yet perhaps it is not so serious. It is not necessary to have all the conditions of perfect competition for a situation to exist where, taking a longer period into account, firms cannot significantly affect the prices of the goods they sell or the factors they buy – and this is the crucial implication of the perfect competition assumption. Sometimes, an oligopolistic situation leads to much the same result. Furthermore, the assumption does not appear to be essential to some of the results of orthodox trade theory. Finally, it is sometimes possible to modify orthodox theory in a partial equilibrium way to allow for monopoly in particular markets. All of this does not, of course, resolve the problems completely.

Closely connected with the problem of monopoly is that of economies of scale. These are clearly very important in the case of the multinational corporation. Economies of scale have been discussed in trade theory over a long period, especially in connection with the infant-industry argument for protection. But internal economies of scale are not compatible with perfect competition, so that, following the method of Marshall, orthodox trade theory has allowed for economies of scale by assuming them to be external to firms and internal to the industry. There is an intricate literature exploring the implications of scale economies, so defined (Kemp 1969, ch. 8). It is possible that the conclusions derived from it would still be roughly applicable if the scale economies were internal to firms – as is more realistic – but this is not certain.

Whose Welfare Is Being Maximized?

The interests of the multinational enterprise may not coincide with the interests of the populations of the host countries in which it operates or with the interests of large sections of the population in its own home country. If one is concerned with normative questions, one cannot just focus on the maximization of gross national product produced within the geographical boundaries of a particular country nor on the total income received by the population as a whole. In the case of the host country one must, at the minimum, distinguish income received by the local population from income earned and retained after tax by the foreign enterprises, and one must really go further and distinguish the interests of different sections of the community. The latter distinction must also be made in the case of the home country.

Some simple theorems in orthodox trade theory focus on Pareto efficiency, hence ignoring income distribution. This applies, for example, to the simple but influential gains-from-trade argument. It is also true of the literature on optimal trade intervention in the presence of domestic distortions which argues that, in general, divergences between social and private costs or benefits which are domestic in nature should be dealt with by domestic and not trade interventions. Indeed it is true of a large body of the literature which assumes that government policy brings about costlessly a desired income distribution. Nevertheless, trade theory cannot really be accused of ignoring the income distribution effects of trade policies. The Stolper–Samuelson (1941) theorem shows how factor prices and hence income distribution are affected by trade and trade restrictions within the context of the H–O–S model. Meade (1955) has developed a comprehensive approach for assessing trade policies while taking into account income distribution effects by attaching 'distributional weights' to the various effects of a particular policy.

III Capital Movements in International Trade Theory

Let us now look, in somewhat more detail, at the role that international trade theory has given to international capital movements. This is certainly relevant for studying the implications of the multinational enterprise for trade theory. First of all, multinational enterprises have increased international capital mobility. It is true that sometimes a corporation may establish a subsidiary in a particular country and draw mainly on domestic capital. Nevertheless it always has the potentiality of importing capital and presumably finds domestic capital cheaper in such cases. Second, the transfer of technology and managerial know-how which is so central to the purpose of the multinational corporation is essentially the transfer of a form of capital – human capital – and hence the theory of international capital movements should be applicable in analysing it.

The problem is how international capital movements and international trade are related. We must distinguish positive from normative theory here.

Positive Theory

One approach has been to study the effects of a given factor movement from one country to another, considering the effects on the terms of trade and on factor prices, and taking both supply and demand repercussions into account (Meade, 1955, ch. 27). One can also draw out of these models rather obvious effects on trade flows. If capital flows from A to B, production in the former will fall and the latter rise; and if the comparative advantage pattern is given, there will be a relative rise in output and fall in the price of the product that is mainly produced in B, at least if one focuses only on the supply side. If owners of the transferred capital do not move out of country A, there will be an increase of exports from B to A, necessary to transfer the returns on the capital. In addition there will be demand effects, which can be quite complex. If demand patterns of people in A and B are identical but the capital movement raises aggregate world income, the relative price of the income-elastic good will tend to rise on that account, and so the terms of trade of the country that exports that product will tend to improve.

The other approach is more interesting. Capital is assumed to move internationally in response to relative returns, the tendency being for capital movements to equalize the returns to capital in different countries. There is an extensive literature, mainly continental European, which has explored the nature and consequences of such induced capital movements. This has been surveyed by Caves (1960, ch. 5).

As early as 1906, Pigou (1935) made the further and crucial point which has become a central proposition of the Heckscher–Ohlin model that factor movements are, at least to some extent, a substitute for trade, and vice versa. Ohlin (1933) developed this theme at length. The point is, by now, most familiar. A country relatively well endowed with capital (and which, in isolation, would thus have low returns to capital) will tend both to export capital-intensive goods and to export capital. Both trade and factor movement will raise the returns to capital in that country and tend to bring closer together its factor prices and the factor prices in the country that is well endowed with labour, which will be exporting labour-intensive goods and importing capital. Ohlin stressed that trade on its own would only *tend* to equalize factor prices; because of transport costs and differences in production functions, trade and factor movements are not perfect substitutes.

Modern theorists have built the H–O–S model upon Ohlin's work. Mundell (1957) has explored the special case where trade and factor movements are perfect substitutes. There are no transport costs, production functions for each good are identical in the two countries and the same product is relatively labour- or capital-intensive in each country (no factor reversals), so that free trade on its own will completely equalize factor prices. This extreme model leads him to various extreme results: starting with free trade, the imposition of a tariff, however small, will create factor price differences which will then be eliminated by a capital movement that will restore factor price equalization and equalize commodity prices. With commodity prices equalized by the capital movement, all trade will cease. If the tariff is then removed, there will still be no inducement for any trade, so a temporary tariff has become prohibitive of trade.

The virtue of Mundell's analysis is to bring out the logic of an extreme model. Its danger is that such a fantastic result makes the model look ridiculous. In fact, as soon as one introduces differences in production functions between countries or transport costs, the extreme result disappears.

A number of authors, notably Kemp (1969, ch. 9), Jones (1970) and Chipman (1971), have explored this general type of model further. They have two products, two countries and two factors, labour being immobile in each country and capital perfectly mobile, so that its reward is equalized between countries. There are no transport costs, but they allow technology to be different in the two countries. The latter assumption is necessary because otherwise, in the absence of factor reversals, they would simply have the Mundell (1957) model. They have explored such questions as whether in either or both countries production would be specialized in one product, and how changes in demand would affect capital movements and also commodity and factor prices.

In general, all things seem possible, and the refinements of these sophisticated articles cannot be spelt out here. But two results are worth noting. Chipman has shown that, over a range, a shift in demand in either country will lead to a movement of capital between countries rather than to a change in relative commodity or factor prices. Jones has explored the important question of which country will have a comparative advantage in which good. When capital is perfectly mobile, one can no longer apply the simple H–O–S factor-endowment approach, arguing that the country that is relatively well endowed with capital must export the capital-intensive good. For it may export its capital instead, to the point where it ceases to be relatively well endowed with capital. If country A is more efficient (has a more favourable production function) in product I compared with country B, and if either the two countries are equally efficient in the case of product II, or if country B is more efficient in producing that product, one would expect that A would export I and B would export II (unless demand effects were offsetting).

Jones has brought out another consideration. Suppose that country A is more efficient to the same extent in both products compared with country B. Capital will then tend to flow to country A to exploit this efficient environment, so that the capital–labour ratio finally will be higher in A than in B. Thus the more efficient country A will export the capital-intensive product and import the labour-intensive one. This will be so even if initially, before any capital movements are allowed, country B is the country relatively well endowed with capital. Of course, if the higher efficiency of country A is itself the result of investment in human capital, which is assumed here to be immobile, or imperfectly mobile, we must say that while B may be initially well endowed with potentially mobile capital, country A is well endowed with immobile (human) capital.

The models of Kemp, Chipman and Jones operate within the traditional framework by having only two factors and two products, but at least they allow for different production functions between countries. Furthermore, it would be possible to allow for economies of scale, and perhaps additional immobile factors could also be added without too much difficulty. One could also allow for factor reversals, in which case trade might widen the wedges between factor prices internationally and so actually stimulate capital movements. A general framework of analysis which lends itself to the exploration of many cases and to the addition of various complications is certainly available.

Normative Theory

The normative theory of international capital movements is a very recent development, and its integration with the normative theory of trade even more recent. At a rigorous level, the theory really began with the well-known article by McDougall (1960), who used simple neo-classical methods to show in which circumstances a capital-receiving country would gain or lose from a capital inflow. The main point that emerged was the crucial role of taxation: a gain is likely when, as is usual, the profits are taxed by the government of the capital-receiving country, and provided this is not offset by subsidies.

Subsequently Kemp (1962) extended this analysis by applying the standard optimum tariff argument to capital imports and exports. From a national point of view, and assuming no retaliation, a capital-importing country may be able to exploit its monopsony power or a capital-exporting country its monopoly power by imposing a tax on the import or export of capital respectively. These will improve the terms of foreign borrowing or lending, and along familiar lines derived from elementary monopoly theory there will be an optimum rate of tax which will depend on the foreign capital supply or demand elasticities. The object of this approach, it must be stressed, is not to maximize tax revenue but rather to arrive at a Pareto-efficient position from a national point of view.

Recently this theory of the optimum tax on capital inflow or outflow has been integrated with the theory of the optimum tariff by Kemp (1966), Jones (1967) and Gehrels (1971). The following exposition assumes that the concern is with a single country's national welfare, no foreign retaliation, and that the country can affect both its terms of trade and its terms of foreign borrowing or lending. We shall refer to the case of a capital importer, though the analysis is fully applicable to capital-exporting countries. The relevant literature is quite intricate, and it is only possible to sketch out some of the main results and arguments here.

The first-best policy must be distinguished from second-best policies. The first-best policy is to use two instruments of policy – the tariff (or export tax) and the tax on the import of capital; essentially the first is directed to optimally improving the terms of trade and the second to improving the terms of borrowing. In addition, there are two second-best situations that have been considered: the only instrument of policy might be the tariff (or export tax), or alternatively the only policy instrument might be the tax on capital imports.

Let us begin with the first-best situation. The complication here is that a tariff may not only affect the terms of trade but may also affect the terms of borrowing. What is relevant here is the effect that the tariff has on the foreign capital supply curve facing the country. Suppose that the foreign country (which is the capital-exporting country) exports its capital-intensive product. This, of course, would be so if the simple assumptions of the H–O–S model applied. A tariff by the home country will then reduce the foreign country's exports, hence will lower the price of capital there, and thus will shift its capital-export supply curve downwards, so improving the home country's terms of borrowing. In this case a tariff has more than just improved the home country's terms of trade; it has also improved its terms of borrowing. Similarly, a tax on capital imports would not only improve the home country's terms of borrowing but would also improve its terms of trade. It is quite useful to draw attention to these indirect repercussions, and the authors referred to show that the optimal rates of tariff and tax will be higher than otherwise because of them. In the anti-Heckscher–Ohlin case, where the capital-exporting country exports its labour-intensive product, the optimal rates of tariff and tax will be lower than otherwise, and indeed one of them could be negative.

Next consider the second-best cases. Since the two cases of a tariff as the only instrument of policy and the tax on the import of capital as the only instrument are completely symmetrical, we need only consider one case, and shall take the case where the only policy variable is the tariff. It could be assumed more realistically that there is some given rate of tax on profits of capital inflow, but that it cannot be changed, and is below the optimum. To simplify, let us ignore the foreign repercussion, supposing that the foreign capital supply curve is not affected by a tariff.

We can suppose that, initially, a tariff is imposed which improves the terms of trade optimally. Next we must ask whether the tariff encourages or discourages capital inflow. If the import-competing product is capital intensive and the exportable labour intensive, a tariff will raise the return to capital and so encourage capital inflow. This is undesirable. The first-best way of bringing about the appropriate restriction of capital inflow would be through the optimal tax on capital inflow, but in the absence of such a tax the tariff should then be lower than otherwise, the aim being to improve rather than worsen the terms of foreign borrowing. The extent to which the second-best optimal tariff is below the level it would be in the absence of any effect on capital inflow represents the role of the tariff in taking the place of the first-best optimal capital tax. Essentially the tariff is reduced in order to squeeze foreign capital. It is even possible that the second-best optimal tariff is negative in such a case.

There is a lot more to be drawn out of these models, even though their ingredients are very simple. One could introduce the foreign repercussion into the second-best case, and also work out the case where the tax on capital inflow or outflow is the only policy instrument.

A more comprehensive but less rigorous analysis of the relationship between optimal trade intervention and foreign investment is given by Corden (1967). The simple assumptions of the H–O–S model are dropped. Capital is assumed to be 'sector specific', externalities are allowed for, as well as monopoly and distorting taxes on domestic capital. The general argument is that tariffs can act as second-best taxes or subsidies on foreign capital. Furthermore, if there is a given non-optimal tariff system the gains or losses from foreign investment will be affected. Foreign capital that is attracted by tariffs may inflict a loss on the economy when it might have yielded a gain if it had come without protection.

This completes a brief review of how trade theorists have taken into account capital movements. It is, of course, not complete. While the literature on capital movements is very old, especially in continental Europe, the emphasis on the relationship with trade really stems from Ohlin's great work. Much formal theory has indeed assumed that factors are immobile between countries, but it can no longer be said that orthodox international trade theory in general neglects capital movements.

IV The Location Decisions of Multinational Enterprises

Can the basic methods and concepts of trade theory be used to set out a framework for analysing the location decisions of multinational corporations? A general approach will be sketched out here. It will be assumed that the corporations aim to maximize profits. From the point of view of the corporations the analysis is normative but from the point of view of individual countries it is positive. Only those considerations which trade theory can handle easily will be introduced; this means that we must ignore peculiarly oligopolistic behaviour which is discussed by Vernon (1974). The present discussion and that of Vernon might be regarded as complementary.

Essentially we are concerned with what determines costs of production and marketing in different locations, including the costs of bringing products to particular markets. When we concern ourselves with the international location of production we are also concerned, as a byproduct, with the international pattern of trade. Taking demands in various countries as given (which may not always be a justified assumption), flows of exports and imports fall naturally out of the production location decisions.[2]

We consider a firm which produces a number of different products that it expects to sell in the world's markets. In each market it faces demand curves which take into account the state of competition there, or its absence. The corporation can produce in any country. We make eight assumptions, and then remove all but the first.

1) In each country the corporation faces production functions for each of its products which allow for inputs of at least three factors. The factors are capital, knowledge and the immobile factor(s), which we can call labour. Since knowledge is a special type of capital, one could say, alternatively, that there are two types of mobile capital, namely conventional capital which finances waiting and physical capital goods, and human capital, taking the form of knowledge.
2) Capital and knowledge are perfectly mobile internationally within the corporation.
3) The production functions and the factor endowments facing the corporation do not change over time.
4) There are constant returns to scale in all production functions.
5) Government restrictions and taxes, such as tariffs and profit taxes, are absent, or at least do not affect the corporation's location decisions.
6) There are no transport costs.
7) Production functions for any given product in all locations are identical.
8) In each location, there is only one immobile factor, namely labour, which is also identical between countries.

These assumptions yield a Mundell (1957) type result. The returns to capital and knowledge will be equalized throughout the corporation's empire, and given the constant returns to scale assumption, this will also equalize the marginal products of labour. The tendency will then be for costs of production to be the same in all locations. It will not matter where

2. A recent paper by Helpman (1984) deals with this subject rigorously in the framework of a simple two-sector model of international trade in differentiated products.

any product is produced. Trade could, though need not, cease; it will be a matter of indifference.

Now remove assumption 8. Let there be at least two immobile factors, say skilled and unskilled labour, or alternatively labour and land, and let the endowment ratios vary between countries. Immediately, we are back in the familiar H–O–S world. Skilled-labour-intensive products will be produced in the countries relatively well endowed with skilled labour and unskilled-labour-intensive products in countries relatively well endowed with unskilled labour. Note that only the relative intensities of the *immobile* factors are relevant. It does not matter at this stage whether a product is capital- or knowledge-intensive.

Now remove assumption 7 and allow production functions to differ. It must be remembered that knowledge is mobile so production functions must differ for other reasons. Interpreting the concept 'production function' broadly, the physical infrastructure provided by governments, or political conditions, including security, may differ. Furthermore, there may be some types of knowledge that are immobile and can be treated as influencing production functions. In any case, we now obtain further familiar guides to location decisions with obvious consequences. The Jones point is relevant here: countries which are generally more efficient, not just in some but in most or all products, will attract more of the mobile factors, and hence will tend to produce and export the products intensive in these mobile factors. This appears to be confirmed by casual observation.

Now remove assumption 6 and allow for transport costs. If transport costs were very high there would be no trade and the corporation would have to satisfy demand in each country from local production. In the absence of such an extreme situation one can only say that there will be a tendency for production to be near markets. If tastes differ between countries the location decisions will be influenced by these differences; furthermore, production will tend to take place in the large markets. Of course, all this may be overridden by significant cost differences, owing to different factor endowments or production functions.

Now remove assumption 5. Tariffs and import restrictions as well as export taxes will have the same effects as transport costs, encouraging import substitution rather than exporting, and so being trade restricting. International trade theory has certainly laboured this effect. Furthermore, the location decisions may be affected by differences in taxation. The general point is well known, but the subject of differential taxation is too large and complex to be discussed here.

Now remove assumption 4 and allow for increasing returns to scale. If we had not removed assumptions 5 to 8 the corporation would then locate each product in one country only. If the increasing returns are to some extent external to its various products though internal to the corporation, and if locational proximity is required for the external effects to be reaped, then the corporation will locate all its activities in one country only. Once we allow for different production functions and different immobile-factor endowment ratios, cost curves will differ between countries for each product and the consideration discussed earlier will come back into the story. Because of increasing returns, the tendency will be to avoid locating production of any product in more than one or a few locations.

When we allow for transport costs and trade restrictions, the sizes of domestic markets for various products will become relevant. In the absence of economies of scale, one could say that, because of transport costs, countries will tend to produce for home markets, and so their production patterns will be biased towards goods for which there is a domestic demand up to the point where domestic demand is satisfied; the tendency will be for trade to be restricted. But when there are economies of scale, transport costs will have further effects: they will give countries with large domestic markets for particular products a comparative advantage in these goods if the latter are economy-of-scale intensive, and will cause them to export these products.

Now remove assumption 3 and allow production functions and factor endowments to change over time. For example, one country's educational system or the extent of its educational effort may change over time, or alternatively it may 'learn-by-doing' more rapidly than other countries so that its endowment of immobile human capital may change: unskilled may turn into skilled labour or the production functions facing the corporation may change. At a theoretical level it may be somewhat arbitrary whether one regards a certain change as increasing the factor endowment or improving the production function. In any case, this will then require the corporation to reallocate its resources.

Finally, remove assumption 2 and allow knowledge (techniques and managerial know-how) to be imperfectly mobile within the corporation. Knowledge may be generated as a form of investment in the corporation's home country and may spread outside at a cost and with lags. Thus over a period of time, knowledge in the outer provinces of the corporate empire improves and so, again, comparative advantage changes. This is one element in the 'product-cycle' approach of Vernon (1966).

The general conclusion is that it is possible to use various bits of analysis derived from trade theory to study the location decisions of multinational corporations and their effects on trade flows. Perhaps the main point is that models must be used which allow for some mobile and some immobile factors, and once one allows for more than one immobile factor or allows production functions to differ between countries one arrives at results generally familiar from trade theory.

V Multinational Enterprises and the Theory of Tariffs

Let us now see how tariff theory may be affected if one takes into account trade by multinational enterprises. We shall look briefly at three familiar arguments for protection or intervention of some kind: the terms of trade argument, the income distribution argument and the antimonopoly argument. Finally, we look at the problem of transfer pricing.

Terms of Trade

The familiar terms of trade argument for tariffs or export taxes rests, among other things, on two assumptions. First, it assumes that while the country has potential monopoly or monopsony power, this is not exploited by private producers or traders. If exports were already controlled by monopolists, there would be no need to induce them to restrict exports so that marginal costs would be equal to marginal revenue of the industry. Second, the concern is with maximizing total real income produced in the country (in the potential Pareto sense), normally with no regard to internal distribution effects.

The first assumption is unlikely to be valid when trade is in the hands of multinational enterprises. One might imagine a continuum of possibilities. At one end the exporting and importing firms are quite competitive, extra exports by one firm lowering the profits of other firms, and this effect not being taken into account at all in any one firm's decisions. In that case the usual optimal tariff and export tax formulae apply. At the other end there is a complete monopoly, hence no need for government intervention to induce monopolistic behaviour, and the optimal tariff or export tax is zero. In between there may be some degree of competition and some degree of collusion, and the optimal tariff or export tax will be positive but less than indicated by the usual formulae.

The second assumption is also unlikely to be valid. The concern is likely to be to maximize the real incomes of residents, perhaps excluding those managers of the multinational who are foreign in origin or permanent residence. If profits tax rates on foreign corporations are given, there are then two considerations to take into account.

First, the greater the profits of the corporations the bigger the revenue gain to the country, the taxpayers or the Treasury of the country, in effect, being shareholders in the corporation. If tariffs increase the profitability of foreign-owned import-competing industries, some part of this benefit will thus be returned to the people or government of the country.

Second, tariffs and export taxes shift real incomes away from factors intensive in export industries towards factors intensive in import-competing industries, and there will be some net redistributive effect even allowing for taxation. The familiar optimal tariff-export tax structure will maximize the combined income of residents and subsidiaries of the corporations, but not the income of residents on their own. We have here, in fact, the second-best problem which we discussed earlier. First-best policy would be to apply the optimal tariff-export tax structure (taking into account the existing degree of monopoly or collusion) and combine this with the optimal structure of taxes on foreign capital. But if taxes on

International trade theory 171

foreign capital are given, being either too low or too high, it may be necessary to vary the tariff-export tax structure so as to squeeze foreign capital appropriately.

Internal Income Distribution

Let us now consider the income distribution argument for protection. We have already referred to income distribution in our discussion of terms of trade effects; and in order to isolate income distribution considerations, let us now assume that the country concerned is small and cannot affect its terms of trade. But we assume that it can still affect the cost of capital and knowledge that it obtains through the multinational corporations. Suppose it is desired to shift income distribution towards workers in certain import-competing industries, and that foreign corporations operate in these industries. A tariff will have the desired effect of raising the wages of the relevant labour; but it will also shift income distribution towards foreign profits, which is presumably not desired.

We have here the usual complications created when inappropriate instruments are used to pursue particular targets. If it is desired to shift income distribution of residents towards particular types of labour, first-best policy is to raise taxes from the general population in a minimum-distortion way (probably by income taxes), and then subsidize or remit taxes to the sections of the population which it is desired to favour. At the same time foreign enterprises should be taxed so as to optimally exploit the country's monopsony power in relation to them, as indicated by the approach discussed earlier. Taxes on trade are second- or third-best methods of bringing about desired income redistribution effects. Not only are they likely to be imprecise in bringing about the desired income distribution effects, but they also create distortions in the production and consumption patterns which could be avoided, or at least reduced, if more direct methods were used.

Monopoly and Market Structure

Next, let us consider the role of tariffs when there is actual or potential monopoly in domestic markets, or at least when the market structure is not perfectly competitive. International trade theory is notoriously inadequate in this area, mainly – as Johnson (1967) has pointed out – because of its concern with general equilibrium. Hence one cannot really draw on any adequate existing analysis. All that will be done here is to draw attention to a few points.

First of all, consider the question of how tariffs affect market structure. Suppose that a particular product market is supplied by a number of firms, some producing domestically and some producing abroad and selling in the domestic market as well as to their own markets. The product may be differentiated. The number of firms and their behaviour may be influenced by various barriers to entry, and various kinds of oligopolistic behaviour patterns may operate. Given the market as we find it before tariffs, we want to know what effect the injection of a tariff will have primarily on the number of sellers, but also on the intensity of competition between them, determining the extent to which the group will exploit its joint monopoly power. A tariff is a discriminatory tax on producers, taxing only the products of foreign producers not domestic producers. How does such a discriminatory tax affect market structure?

One approach is to focus on the dominant firm effect. If the dominant firms are domestic while the smaller firms and potential entrants are foreign, a tariff will increase concentration and monopoly power. On the other hand, if the dominant firms are foreign while the smaller firms and potential entrants are domestic, a tariff will have the opposite effect. The same results could be brought about not by an actual tariff, but by the threat of a tariff designed in the first case to preserve a domestic dominant firm and in the second case to preserve domestic competition and protect small producers.

Now let us introduce foreign investment and the multinational enterprise into this story. The relevant point is that a firm producing abroad and handicapped by a tariff can leap the tariff wall by setting up a domestic production facility. Yet our basic argument is not affected. Suppose there is a foreign dominant supplier, and a tariff is imposed to handicap him, the aim being to increase competition. So he responds by setting up his factories behind the tariff wall. If his original success was based on low costs of production in his own country, the geographic transfer of his production may be a very imperfect substitute for producing in his own country and then exporting; but if his success was based on brand goodwill, connections with distributors, patents and know-how, these can all be carried with him.

Nevertheless any tariff imposes some handicap on him even if he can manage to stay in the market by moving his enterprise, or part of it, geographically. If in the absence of the tariff he chose to produce in his own country and export, then presumably that would be more profitable. The tariff forces him to choose a less economic location and hence to raise his prices or reduce his profits, or both.

Let us now consider another problem. A multinational firm is the only actual and potential foreign supplier of a product and is also the only potential domestic producer. Thus there is complete monopoly. This, of course, is an extreme case but is a simple way of posing an important problem. A tariff is imposed to encourage it to cease exporting the product from overseas and to establish domestic production. How would one analyse the gains or losses to the tariff-imposing country?

In the absence of the tariff, the corporation exports from abroad and there is no domestic production. This maximizes its profits. The tariff forces it to shift the location of some of its production. It may yield the corporation good profits from its new subsidiary, but its world-wide profits will fall, for otherwise it would have set up in the country without the tariff. The corporation's costs of supplying the market of the tariff-imposing country will have gone up. If this is true of marginal costs, it will then charge a higher price. Hence some of the burden of the tariff will be borne by the company itself, and part will be borne by consumers of the tariff-imposing country. This consumer cost might be described as the gross cost of protection to the country. But there may be gains to set against these, notably profits tax collected from the company. Furthermore, the establishment of its subsidiary will increase the demand for labour in the country and raise the wage rate. If the effect is more than marginal and if labour is paid its marginal product in alternative uses (and even more so, if it is paid *more* than its marginal social product, as is likely in less developed countries) there will be a further gain on this account. On balance a net gain to the country is thus possible even though consumers will lose.

Transfer Pricing

Finally we come to the problem of transfer pricing. When the subsidiary of a multinational firm imports from or exports to another part of the firm, the nominal prices at which goods are transferred may not be equal to true marginal costs or to world market ('arm's-length') prices but may be adjusted so as to minimize tax or tariff payments.

One implication of this is for the calculation of effective protective rates. A subsidiary may import components from another subsidiary, and the transfer prices may deliberately over-price these components so as to shift taxable profits away from the component-importing country which may have the relatively higher tax rates or which may restrict the remittance of profits. The components may even be priced so high that it appears that they cost more than the value of the final product when the latter is valued at world market prices. In this latter case there appears then to be negative value added at world prices, the rate of effective protection being infinite (though arithmetically negative) (Corden, 1971, pp. 50–5). In any case, even if such an extreme result does not come about, an impression is conveyed of very high protection for the activity of producing or assembling the final product. Yet this may not convey a true impression since the calculation is based on component prices that are in excess of the prices that the corporation must be using for its own resource allocation decisions.

It is well known that a vertically-integrated multinational enterprise can use transfer prices to shift profits between countries and so reduce its tax payments, at least if tax rates differ significantly between the various countries in which it operates. It can shift profits away from a country by raising transfer prices on imported components or lower transfer prices on goods that it exports. A country may thus impose a high rate of profits tax, higher than that payable by the corporation in its home country or other bases of operation, and yet the net result may be for the country to lose revenue compared to a situation with a lower profits tax. Where then do tariffs come in?

A firm can reduce the incidence of *ad valorem* tariffs by *under*valuing imported components. But it is not sufficient to look at the amount of customs revenue that the corporation avoids paying in order to assess its gains from the undervaluation. Recorded profits will be shifted away from the supplying country towards the importing country; and if the profit tax rate is higher in the latter than in the former, there will be a net loss to the corporation on this account, which must be set against the gain from saving tariff payments.

If the aim of the tariff is to protect domestic producers of the components, a government can counter such partial evasion of tariffs by fixing component prices for duty purposes which are closer to market prices, by imposing anti-dumping duties, by converting *ad valorem* into specific tariffs or by replacing tariffs with import quotas. But if the aim is to raise revenue, the tariff-imposing country is actually likely to gain from the understatement of import values induced by an *ad valorem* tariff. Its loss in customs revenue is likely to be more than offset by a gain in profits taxes. This suggests a simple remedy to profits tax evasion through overstatement of import values. Governments should impose tariffs on those imported components believed to be *over*priced through tax-evasive transfer pricing, and hence encourage the corporation to *under*price them instead.[3]

VI Conclusions

One might ask whether international trade theory should be radically reconstructed or perhaps abandoned completely because a significant part of world trade is carried on by and within multinational corporations.

Some reconstruction and development is clearly needed. In particular, the main body of the theory should allow for some internationally mobile factors as well as for immobile factors. While capital mobility has not been ignored there has, perhaps, been too much emphasis on models where all factors are internationally immobile.

In assessing the usefulness of trade theory, one needs to bear in mind its limited objective. It can hardly be expected to give a precise and detailed description of the real world; and the fact that countries produce more than two products, and industries are not generally perfectly competitive, does

---

3. A thorough analysis of the effects of tariffs on transfer pricing and the location of production of the multinational firms is given by Horst (1971). He considers both the increasing and the decreasing cost case. The method is partial equilibrium (as is some of the discussion of the present essay), but shows a useful direction in which rigorous analysis can go. He confirms some of the propositions in the present essay but also goes much beyond the argument here.

not necessarily mean that the theory as usually taught is useless. One cannot do better than quote Johnson (1970b, p. 10) here:

> In the broader context of economics as a systematic approach to the understanding of economic phenomena and as the organisation of disciplined thinking about these phenomena and about policies relating to them, however, the purpose of theory is to abstract from the complexity of the real world a simplified model of the key relationships between dependent and independent variables, and to explore the positive and normative implications of changes in the 'givens' of this hypothetical system. For this purpose, the validity of the empirical foundations of a theory is, obviously within limits, not of such crucial importance, in the sense that the principles of interrelatedness, of systematic response to change, and of optimisation remain valid in the face of wide variations in assumed economic structure.

Nevertheless, there is a deeper question that one needs to face. The multinational corporation cuts across national boundaries and makes a good deal of international trade into intrafirm trade. Financial capital is quite mobile within the corporation, as are senior managerial talent and the technical and managerial know-how which possibly provide the main rationale for the existence of the corporation. A model which assumes factor immobility between nations and which places primary importance upon national boundaries would seem to be utterly irrelevant. It could then be argued that trade theory should be abandoned altogether, at least for the analysis of the activities of the multinational corporations. The world – perhaps the non-communist world – should be treated as a single market in which large corporations compete and collude in various ways. The theory of market structure and performance elaborated for the study of the large United States market would then be appropriate. One would think of all factors of production with the exception of natural resources as mobile. There would still be questions of location to discuss, but these questions would be of interest only to landowners, property developers and those concerned with land-use planning. The central economic questions would have to do with productivity in particular industries throughout the vast market and with competitiveness and oligopolistic behaviour.

Yet this approach, in spite of a superficial appeal, is not satisfactory. The main reason is that all factors are not mobile. In general, labour is fairly immobile between countries, and this is the factor with which policy is primarily concerned. Financial capital and certain types of knowledge may be mobile, but human capital embodied in the labour force of different countries is not mobile. Furthermore, the capital embodied in the infrastructure of different countries must be regarded as more or less immobile except over a very long period. With labour somewhat immobile, governments are attached to different areas, exercising controls of various kinds, taxing and seeking to maximize the welfare of the mainly immobile population living in the area. Hence it is still important to know how individual countries (or regions) are affected by the operations of the multinational corporations, whether they locate in one area or another and whether they raise or lower the welfare of people in particular countries. As long as separate countries (or regions) matter in this sense, the basic concepts of trade theory will continue to be of some relevance.

References

Caves, R. E. 1960: *Trade and Economic Structure*. Cambridge, Mass: Harvard University Press.
―――― 1971: International corporations: the industrial economics of foreign investment. *Economica*, 38, 1–27.
Chipman, J. 1971: International trade with capital mobility: a substitution theorem. In J. N. Bhagwati et al. (eds), *Trade, Balance of Payments and Growth: Essays in Honor of Charles P. Kindleberger*. Amsterdam: North-Holland.
Corden, W. M. 1967: Protection and foreign investment. *The Economic Record*, 43, 209–32.
―――― 1971: *The Theory of Protection*. Oxford: Oxford University Press.
Dunning, J. H. 1970: *Studies in International Investments*. London: Allen & Unwin.
―――― 1973a: The determinants of international production. *Oxford Economic Papers*, 25, 289–336.
―――― 1973b: *The Multinational Enterprise*. London: Allen & Unwin.
Gehrels, F. 1971: Optimal restrictions on foreign trade and investment. *American Economic Review*, 59, 147–59.
Helpman, E. 1984: A simple theory of international trade with multinational corporations. *Journal of Political Economy*, 92, 451–71.
Horst, T. O. 1971: The theory of the multinational firm: optimal behaviour under different tariff and tax rates. *Journal of Political Economy*, 79, 1059–72.
Hufbauer, G. C. 1965: *Synthetic Materials and the Theory of International Trade*. London: Duckworth.
Johnson, H. G. 1967: International trade theory and monopolistic competition theory. In R. E. Kuenne (ed.), *Monopolistic Competition Theory: Studies in Impact*. New York: Wiley.
―――― 1970a: The efficiency and welfare implications of the international corporation. In C. P. Kindleberger (ed.), *The International Corporation*, Cambridge, Mass: M.I.T. Press.
―――― 1970b: The state of theory in relation to the empirical analysis. In R. Vernon (ed.), *The Technology Factor in International Trade*. New York: Columbia University Press.
―――― 1972: Survey of the issues. In P. Drysdale (ed.), *Direct Foreign Investment in Asia and the Pacific*. Canberra: Australian National University Press.
Jones, R. W. 1967: International capital movements and the theory of tariffs and trade. *The Quarterly Journal of Economics*, 81, 10–11.
―――― 1970: The role of technology in the theory of international trade. In R. Vernon (ed.), *The Technology Factor in International Trade*. New York: Columbia University Press.
Kemp, M. C. 1962: The benefits and costs of private investment from abroad: comment. *The Economic Record*, 38, 56–62.

―――― 1966: The gains from international trade and investment: a neo-Heckscher–Ohlin approach. *American Economic Review*, 56, 788–809.

―――― 1969: *The Pure Theory of International Trade and Investment*. Englewood Cliffs, NJ: Prentice-Hall.

MacDougall, G. D. A. 1960: The benefits and costs of private investment from abroad: a theoretical approach. *The Economic Record*, 36, 13–35.

Meade, J. E. 1952: *A Geometry of International Trade*. London: Allen & Unwin.

―――― 1955: *Trade and Welfare*. Oxford: Oxford University Press.

Mundell, R. A. 1957: International trade and factor mobility. *American Economic Review*, 47, 321–35.

Ohlin, B. 1933: *International and International Trade*. Cambridge, Mass: Harvard University Press.

Pigou, A. C. 1935: *Protective and Preferential Import Duties*. London: London School of Economics.

Posner, M. V. 1961: International trade and technical change. *Oxford Economic Papers*, 13, 323–41.

Robertson, D. 1971: The multinational enterprise: trade flows and trade policy. In J. H. Dunning (ed.), *The Multinational Enterprise*. London: Allen & Unwin.

Stolper, W. F. and Samuelson, P. A. 1941: Protection and real wages. *Review of Economic Studies*, 9, 58–73.

Vernon, R. 1966: International investment and international trade in the product cycle. *The Quarterly Journal of Economics*, 80, 190–207.

―――― 1971: *Sovereignty at Bay*. New York: Basic Books.

―――― 1974: The location of economic activity. In J. H. Dunning (ed.), *Economic Analysis and the Multinational Enterprise*. London: Allen & Unwin.

12
The Enclave Approach*

This essay presents a systematic framework for analysing the effects on host country economic welfare of multinational corporations. An approach will be sketched out here which makes use of trade theory, which focuses on the interests of the residents of the countries in which the corporations operate, but which involves a departure from the usual approach.

The Kemp–Jones–Gehrels theory of optimal trade and capital taxes summarized in essay 11 conceives of a country buying and selling both goods and factors from and to the outside world; it concerns itself only with goods and factors that pass across the country's borders, but it does not allow for the multinational corporation as an agency which is apparently both a foreign supplier and buyer and a domestic supplier and buyer of these goods and factors. Furthermore, it does not integrate into the analysis the numerous possible divergences between private and social costs and benefits – that is, domestic distortions of all kinds. The enclave approach can deal with these matters more easily.[1]

We can think of the multinational enterprise as an enclave cutting across national boundaries that is rather like an independent country. This enclave (a) buys and sells factors, (b) buys and sells goods, (c) makes and receives transfers, and (d) creates various external effects. We are interested in the effects of these four types of operations on Our country – which we should think of as any country in which the corporation operates other than its home country. There will be linkages with Our country,

---

* From John Dunning (ed.) 1974: *Economic Analysis and the Multinational Enterprise*, London: George Allen & Unwin. An expanded version of one section of the original paper.
1. The enclave concept is not new in discussions of foreign investment in the export industries of developing countries. The principal normative analysis of the multinational enterprise is given by Johnson (1970), and in certain respects the approach here is implicit in his paper. The concept of 'development enclaves' is used by Lewis (1976), though with an emphasis on income distribution effects and no use of trade theory concepts. Lewis notes the adverse effects of development enclaves on traditional sectors, a kind of Dutch disease effect (see essays 15 and 16).

The enclave approach

namely (a) the corporation raises some capital locally and employs local workers, (b) it buys raw materials locally and sells some of its final products to local consumers, (c) it pays taxes to the local Ministry of Finance, and possibly also receives some subsidies, and (d) it creates a variety of external effects – that is effects that by-pass the market – for example through labour and managerial training, through spreading modern techniques of various kinds and through pollution. The problem is to analyse each of these linkages between the corporation and Our country.

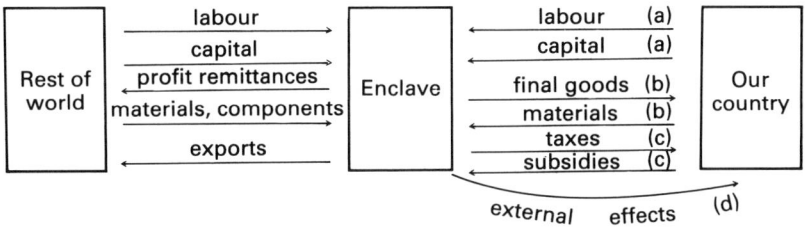

Figure 12.1

These linkages are summarized in figure 12.1. We have a model with three trading units – Our country, the Enclave and Rest of world – between which there are various linkages. The direct linkages in the form of trade, factor and other flows between the Rest of the world and Our country are not shown in the diagram as they are not of immediate interest. In fact, as noted below, the flows between the Enclave and the Rest of the world are also not of interest. The focus is on the flows between the Enclave and Our country. If one wanted to use a two-country model for welfare analysis one should group the Enclave with the Rest of the world, not with Our country, as is usual in trade theory.

Two questions can then be asked. First, does Our country gain from the presence of the corporation on our soil, the alternative being the complete absence of the corporation and of the package of factors, technology and know-how that it brings with it? Second, can taxes, subsidies or restrictions maximize Our country's gain from the presence of the corporation? The first question is the equivalent of the familiar 'gains from trade' question: does a country gain from trade compared with no-trade, and the second is the equivalent of the optimal-trade-intervention question: given various constraints and domestic distortions, what is the optimal structure of tariffs, export taxes, subsidies and so on?

We begin by considering the first question. It is important to stress that if one accepts this approach, one is only interested in trade between the corporation and Our country; thus the corporation's sales to domestic consumers of import-competing products are of interest, but its sales to foreign consumers of export products are not. This is a complete reversal of the normal approach in international trade theory. Similarly, the corporation's import of capital and knowledge from its mother country is not of interest, but its use of locally-raised capital and labour is.

I The Gains and Losses from Linkages

Consider first linkages (a) and (b) (factor and trade movements). Let us just take two of them. Our country sells labour to the corporation. If the labour supply curve is upward-sloping and the wage rate is equal to the marginal opportunity cost of labour in Our country, there will be no gain on the last man employed, but there will be an intra-marginal gain. If the wage rate exceeds the marginal opportunity cost of labour – as it may well do in many less-developed countries, especially but not only if the labour would otherwise be unemployed – there will be a gain even on the last man employed, and an even greater intra-marginal gain.

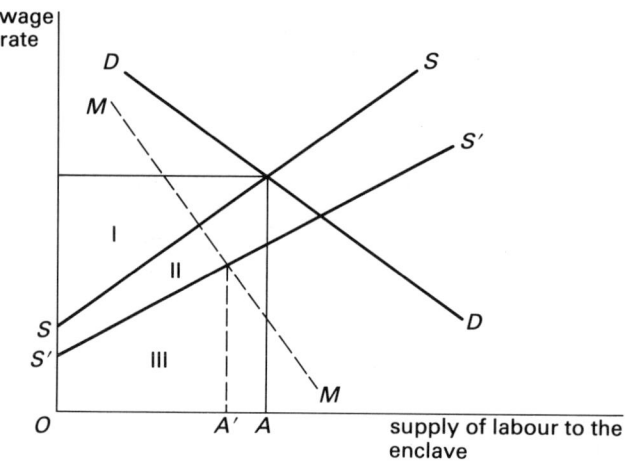

Figure 12.2

This is represented in figure 12.2. SS is the supply curve of labour to the corporation and DD is the corporation's demand curve for labour. The wage bill paid is the rectangle (I + II + III). If the wage rate was always equal to the marginal social product of labour in Our country (i.e. if it indicated the opportunity cost of labour moving into the corporation) then area (II + III) would represent output lost in Our country (excluding output of the corporation). The net gain to Our country is then area I. If the wage in Our country exceeds its marginal social product (for example if there are diminishing returns, and labour is paid its average rather than its marginal product or if some of the labour is unemployed but has a positive reservation wage) then we must draw the curve $S'S'$ tracing out the marginal social cost of labour separate from SS. The gain will then be area (I + II).

Next, Our country buys products produced by the corporation. If these are non-tradable goods, there may well be a gain: the corporation will have increased the supply of these goods, this will have brought down their prices, and this will yield an intra-marginal gain to consumers (consumers' surplus). But the corporation's products are more likely to be traded goods, replacing goods that would otherwise have been imported. If they are sold at the same price as the imports replaced, there will be no gain or loss because of this linkage. But if tariffs or import restrictions make it possible for the price to be higher, there will be a consumer loss on this account. Indeed, this may often be the main source of loss from multinational corporations in countries where high rates of protection are prevalent. This loss would have to be set against the two main sources of gain: the gain through employment of labour and the gain through tax revenue.

One could analyse in a similar way all the other linkages. When the corporation issues shares to local investors, are they paying a price which is equal to or departs from the marginal social product of capital when invested locally? Furthermore, what is the marginal cost to Our country of the demands that the corporation makes on local infrastructure, and how does this compare with the corporation's payments, if any?

The corporation may be highly efficient and make use of the latest and best technology. It may make big profits and export vast amounts of goods from its local subsidiary to other countries. But all of this is of no interest in this approach, other than as an indication of the taxable potential of the corporation and hence the opportunity it presents of being squeezed. It has to be remembered that often the linkage through taxation of multinationals is likely to be the most important one. We should not be interested in growth of geographical GNP or in the flow of trade as usually understood, especially as trade flows may be valued by transfer prices designed to minimize tax payments. We should be interested only in the taxes paid by the corporation and in the valuation of the various linkages, including those that bypass the market completely. We may also wish to take into account the income distribution effects in Our country by attaching distributional weights to the income gains and losses of different sections of the population, as suggested by the method of Meade (1955).

II Optimal Taxation

Finally, let us consider briefly our second question. What would be the optimal intervention by the government of Our country in the latter's goods and factor trade with the corporation so as to maximize Our country's benefits? This is quite an intricate subject, and it is only possible here to indicate lines of approach, ignoring necessary qualifications. We shall consider three possible cases.

First, suppose the corporation cannot be taxed directly through profits tax. This is equivalent to the situation between independent countries, where one country cannot tax another country directly. Our country might then exercise any monopsony or monopoly power it has in its purchase (or sale) of goods and factors from (to) the corporation. This is the equivalent of the usual optimal tariff-export tax argument. The corporation's elasticities of demand for or supply of goods and factors will be relevant in determining appropriate rates of tax, as well as the degree of private monopoly already existing among Our country's suppliers and buyers.

In figure 12.2 the optimal tax will be derived by drawing the marginal curve MM to the DD curve. If $S'S'$ represents the social marginal cost curve to Our country the tax would be such as to reduce labour services purchased from OA to OA'. Of course, if SS were the marginal social cost curve the tax would need to be higher. A tax would reduce the wage paid to workers but raise revenue that could be redistributed to them. Alternatively, labour supply might be restricted by regulations, in which case the wage paid would rise. Next, at the other extreme, suppose that it is possible to charge and collect any rate of profits tax desired. The previous policy, which was designed to redistribute income from the corporation to Our country by manipulating trading prices, will then be second best. First-best policy will be to aim at maximizing geographic product and then impose the optimal profits tax. If one thinks of the corporation as an indivisible operation that either stays in the country or does not, the optimal profits tax will be the highest rate of tax compatible with the corporation not going away as a result. The maximization of geographic product may involve taxes and subsidies designed to correct distortions but not designed to improve the terms of trade of Our country relative to the corporation.

A third possibility is that there is a positive rate of profits tax which cannot be varied. It may be equal to the rate of tax in the corporation's home country since a lower rate would simply cause the home country's treasury to scoop up the difference (given the usual arrangements whereby host-country tax paid by a subsidiary is deducted from tax payable in the home country), and since a higher rate would lead to evasion of Our country's tax through transfer pricing. In that case it will again be optimal for Our country to seek to improve its terms of trade through restricting or taxing the demand for (or supply of) goods and factors by (to) the corporation. But the optimal rates of tax will be lower than in the first of our three cases where the profits tax was assumed to be zero.

References

Johnson, H. G. 1970: The efficiency and welfare implications of the international corporation. In C. P. Kindleberger (ed.), *The International Corporation*. Cambridge, Mass: M.I.T. Press.

Lewis, W. A. 1976: Development and distribution. In Alec Cairncross and Mohinden Puri (eds), *Employment, Income Distribution, and Development Strategy: Problems of the Developing Countries*. London: Macmillan.

Meade, J. E. 1955: *Trade and Welfare*. Oxford: Oxford University Press.

Part IV
Growth and Trade

13
Economic Expansion and International Trade: A Geometric Approach*

A geometric technique based on Meade's *A Geometry of International Trade* (1952) can help to clarify some points made by Hicks (1953), Johnson (1955) and Mishan (1955) in connection with the effects of economic expansion on international trade and the long-run dollar problem.

Assume a two-country, two-product 'real' model where exports always equal imports and resources are always fully employed. The case will be illustrated where there is some kind of economic expansion in country A while the economy of country B – the rest of the world – is static.

In figure 13.1 measure along the axis OY the amount of country A's importable product, blankets, and along the axis OX' the amount of its exportable product, apples, consumed in country A. Then in the quadrant $X'OY$ can be drawn a map of the A-consumption indifference curves. In the right-hand quadrant XOY, measure along the OY axis the quantity of blankets imported from country B and along the OX axis the quantity of apples exported to B.

Initially country A is consuming OL of apples and OF of blankets. It is exporting OM of apples in exchange for OC imports of blankets. Hence it is producing LM of apples and FC of blankets. Assuming increasing costs in country A, no tariffs or transport costs, perfect competition and that this is an equilibrium situation, the price ratio between apples and blankets within country A must be equal to the marginal rate of substitution and the marginal rate of transformation at home, as well as to the foreign price ratio, or terms of trade. This price ratio is represented by the slope of the line OD (the terms of trade) or the line zz' (the internal price ratio).

---

* *Oxford Economic Papers*, 8, June 1956, pp. 223–8. I am indebted to James Meade in the development of these ideas, which formed part of my Ph.D. thesis.

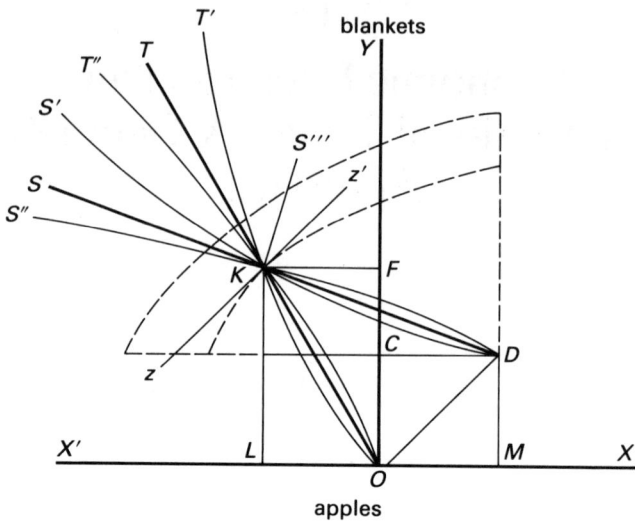

Figure 13.1

It follows that country B's offer curve – which shows the quantities of blankets B is prepared to sell in exchange for different quantities of apples – must run through D with its origin at O. It also follows that country A's transformation curve must be tangential to zz' at K. The inner dotted outline shows country A's 'production block'. With D as the origin it shows the various possible combinations of apples and blankets country A can produce.

The effect of an economic expansion, whether due to an increase in productivity, capital or population, is to enlarge the production block. For example the block may expand to the outer dotted outline. Another effect of an economic expansion *may* be to shift the community demand (or indifference curve) pattern. If tastes remain constant and the effects of the economic expansion on the distribution of income are ignored, the community indifference curve map can alter only in the case of a population increase. We shall consider first an economic expansion due to increased productivity or capital; so, assuming constant tastes and no distribution of income effect, the demand pattern remains unchanged.

From the assumption of full employment and the equality of exports and imports it follows that, as output expands, demand will expand also. If we translate one good into the other at the given price ratio, in terms of either good the proportionate increase in output and in demand must be the same. The critical question is whether – at the given price ratio – the increase in output of blankets is greater or less than the increase in demand. Since there are only two goods, and total demand equals total supply, it follows that if (for example) the demand for blankets increases more than the supply of blankets, then the demand for apples must have increased less than the supply. If demand is not equal to supply at the given price ratio, there will have to be a change in the price ratio (or terms of trade).

In figure 13.1 the straight line DKS is one particular 'output expansion line'. It traces out the points where the new transformation curves have a slope equal to the slope of zz'. Thus it shows by how much the production of apples and of blankets would expand as the economy grows, provided the price ratio remains constant. Since DKS is a straight line the output expansion is 'neutral'. The output of apples and of blankets increases in the same proportion. If the output expansion line rises at an increasing rate, such as DKS', then – to use Johnson's (1955) terminology derived from Hicks (1953) – the output expansion is 'import-biased'. The output of blankets (importables) increases proportionately more than the output of apples (exportables), and hence proportionately more than output as a whole. If the line rises at a decreasing rate, such as DKS'', then the output expansion is 'export-biased'. If it slopes negatively, such that an economic expansion at constant price actually causes the output of one of the goods to fall, then the expansion is (again, in Johnson's terminology) 'ultra-biased'. The line KS''' represents the case of ultra-import-bias.

The nature of the output expansion can depend on a large number of factors: the relative rate of productivity increase in the two industries, the relative factor intensities and which factor of production increases more, and which of the industries is subject to greater or less economies or diseconomies of scale.

Similarly the straight line OKT represents one particular 'demand expansion line'. It shows how, at constant prices, demand for the two goods expands as income rises. If there is no change in the demand pattern – that is if there is no change in population, tastes or distribution of income – this depends purely on the income elasticity of demand, and the demand expansion line corresponds to what is usually called the 'income-consumption line'. If it is a straight line through the origin, like OKT, then the demand expansion is neutral; the income elasticity of demand is unity. If it rises at an increasing rate, such as OKT', then – in Hicks's and Johnson's terminology – the demand expansion is export-biased. This means that the income elasticity of demand for exports is less than unity; the demand expansion is biased *against* exports. If it rises at a decreasing rate, such as OKT'', the demand expansion is import-biased; the income elasticity of demand for imports is less than unity. With constant population, tastes and distribution of income, only if one of the goods is inferior could the demand expansion be ultra-biased so that the demand for one of the goods actually falls as income rises.

If the demand expansion line cuts the new production block above the output expansion line then – unless prices change – the demand for blankets will have increased more than the supply and the demand for apples less than the supply. The relative price of blankets will then rise, and if the foreign exchange market is stable, equilibrium will again be restored. Similarly if the demand expansion line cuts the new production block below the output expansion line, the relative price of blankets will fall and so country A's terms of trade will improve.[1] It follows therefore that the effect of the economic expansion on the terms of trade depends on whether the demand expansion line cuts the new production block above or below the output expansion line. From the diagram some simple but important propositions become clear.

Firstly, if both the demand and the output expansion are neutral – which is perhaps the most reasonable a priori assumption in many cases – the terms of trade must worsen. Geometrically, it can be seen that this can be attributed to the demand and the output expansion lines having different origins. The greater the initial volume of trade the more these origins diverge and hence the greater at constant prices the gap between the demand and the supply of the two products caused by the economic expansion.

Secondly, if the output expansion is import-biased it becomes more probable that the terms of trade will improve; yet such an improvement is not *certain* even if the demand expansion is also import-biased. The point is that the output expansion must be sufficiently import-biased for the output expansion line to cut the block above the demand expansion line.[2]

Thirdly, provided there are no inferior goods, the terms of trade must improve if the output expansion is ultra-import-biased. Similarly the terms of trade must worsen if the output expansion is ultra-export-biased.

It is at this point that a valuable proposition developed by Rybczynski (1955) comes in useful.[3] Under certain assumptions one can say that the output expansion must have an ultra-bias; hence one can say what will happen to the terms of trade without making any particular assumption about the demand expansion other than that there are no inferior goods. Suppose that there are only two factors of production – say labour and capital – and that one of the products is consistently labour-intensive and the other consistently capital-intensive,[4] that the factors of production are perfectly mobile between the two industries, that there are constant returns to scale and that one of the factors – say capital – is then increased. Rybczynski has shown that the ratio of the factor prices and hence of the

---

1. This assumes that the foreign exchange market is stable. If it is not stable then the balance between demand and supply could be restored in this case by an exchange rate adjustment which worsens the terms of trade. Henceforth a stable exchange market will be assumed.
2. This is the point Mishan (1955) makes. This diagram may make the point clearer than his construction.
3. Rybczynski (1955) has developed a geometric proof of this proposition.
4. Blankets, for example, are consistently capital-intensive compared to apples if, at any ratio of the price of capital to the price of labour, the ratio of capital to labour employed in the blanket industry is higher than in the apple industry.

product prices can only remain constant if the output of the labour-intensive product actually falls.[5] If blankets (importables) are the capital-intensive product, an increase in capital means in these conditions an output expansion which is ultra-import-biased. Hence an increase in capital must – provided apples are not an inferior good – lead to an improvement in the terms of trade. By means of the same sort of argument

5. The proposition can be proved mathematically. Let

L = total quantity of labour
C = total quantity of capital
L_a = labour employed in the apple industry
L_b = labour employed in the blanket industry
C_a = capital employed in the apple industry
C_b = capital employed in the blanket industry
X_a = ratio of capital to labour in the apple industry at the given prices of capital and labour
X_b = ratio of capital to labour in the blanket industry, also at the given factor prices
O_a = output of the apple industry
Y_a = average product of labour in the apple industry

Then

$$L = L_a + L_b, \quad C = C_a + C_b$$

$$X_a = \frac{C_a}{L_a}, \quad X_b = \frac{C_b}{L_b}, \quad L_a = \frac{O_a}{Y_a}$$

It follows that

$$C = X_a L_a + X_b L_b$$
$$C = X_a L_a + L X_b - L_a X_b$$
$$C = L X_b + L_a (X_a - X_b)$$
$$C = L X_b + \frac{O_a}{Y_a}(X_a - X_b)$$

In the absence of economies of scale, if the ratio of the product prices is to be constant, the ratio of the factor prices – and hence the ratio of capital to labour in each industry – must also be constant. So X_a and X_b are constants. With a constant ratio of capital to labour and no economies of scale the average product of labour Y_a must also be a constant.
Taking differentials

$$dC = dL X_b + \frac{d(O_a)}{Y_a}(X_a - X_b)$$

It can be seen that if (a) capital increases, so that dC is positive, (b) labour does not increase, so that dL is zero, (c) the average product of labour in the apple industry Y_a is positive, and (d) the blanket industry is more capital intensive than the apple industry, so that X_b is greater than X_a, then dO_a must be negative, i.e. the output of apples must fall.

it can be shown that if there is an increase in productivity solely in country A's blanket industry the terms of trade must improve.

It is possible here to reconcile Hicks (1953) and Mishan (1955). Mishan is quite right in saying that for country A's (or America's) terms of trade to be certain to improve it is not sufficient that the output expansion is import-biased. But perhaps what Hicks really had in mind was an ultra-import-biased output expansion in America where practically the whole increase in productivity was concentrated on America's import-competing goods.

This type of model can have a widespread application to problems of economic development. In Corden (1955) I have found it useful in studying the effects of a population increase on a country's foreign trade. In this case the community's demand pattern is likely to change and it is necessary to distinguish between the demand expansion line and the income consumption line. For every level of population there will be a different income consumption line. If the population increase causes real income per head to fall, then the bias in the two lines will be opposite. For example, if the income elasticity of demand for imports of a given population is less than unity, so that the income consumption line is import-biased, a fall in real income per head will cause a rise in the proportion of expenditure on imports; so the demand expansion line will be export-biased. In this case an ultra-biased demand expansion becomes possible even though there are no inferior goods.

Further Notes: The Effects of Growth on Trade

The Taxonomy

Johnson (1955) produced the first systematic taxonomy of the effects of growth on trade, doing so purely verbally. The paper reproduced as essay 13 was the first to present a geometric taxonomy, focusing particularly on the relevance of ultra-bias on the production side for determining the ultimate terms of trade effect of unilateral growth. Incidentally, the whole methodology is also of interest for showing effects on the *volume* of trade even when the terms of trade are not significantly affected, as in the small country model. Subsequently Johnson (1962) produced a slightly different geometric exposition, one which did not use, as I did, Meade's geometry.

Johnson's method is represented in figure 13.2, where T_0T_0 is the initial transformation curve, the slope of NN indicates the given terms of trade, the initial production point is A, the consumption point is B and the initial trade triangle is shaded. Economic expansion shifts out the transformation curve, yielding a new production point A' and consumption point B', and a new trade triangle, also shaded. In the diagram it is assumed that the output and demand expansion paths are both neutral, so that the trade triangle expands in proportion to the growth of the economy. Biases would

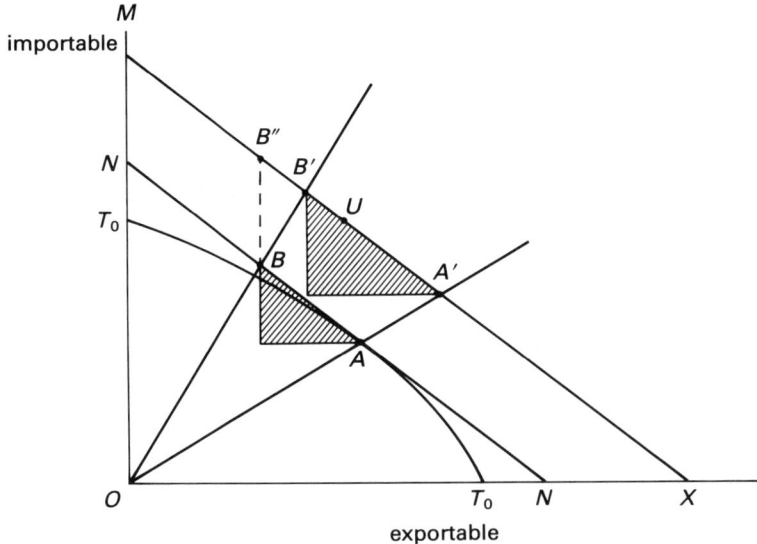

Figure 13.2

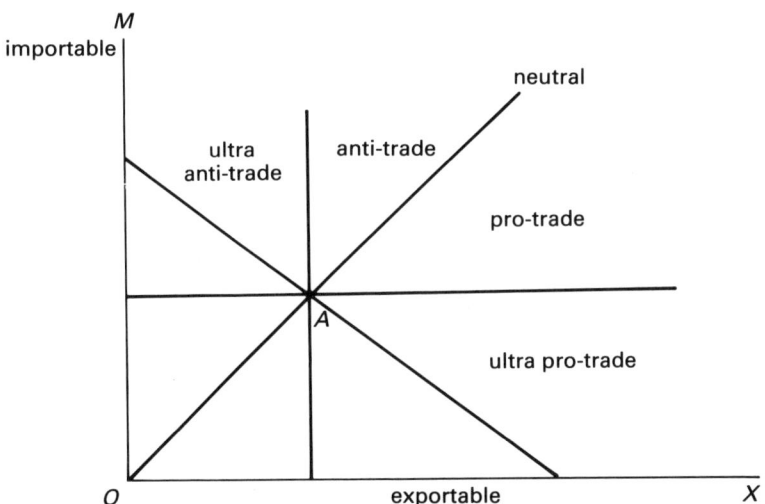

Figure 13.3 Production Expansion Biases

be reflected by the elasticities of these expansion paths, as in figure 13.1. In the large country case the terms of trade improve if the size of the trade triangle contracts (i.e. if the country's desire to trade at constant terms of trade falls). It must do so if the production expansion is ultra-biased (point U), while the demand expansion is at or to the right of B''.

Johnson also produced an improved terminology. Biases are pro-trade if they tend to increase trade (i.e. a bias towards exportables on the production side and towards importables on the consumption side), and anti-trade if they *tend* to reduce trade. The classification (on the production side) is shown in figure 13.3.

This approach of Johnson (1962) still has a limitation. It cannot show clearly the net results of the various combinations of biases on the demand and supply side. Here a diagram due to Ikema (1969) is particularly helpful, and makes an excellent supplement to the Johnson geometry.

The ingredients are E_s, the elasticity of output of M with regard to aggregate output (income), E_d, the elasticity of demand for M with respect to aggregate output (income), and E_n, the elasticity of imports with respect to aggregate output, there being biases when any of these depart from unity. They are derived as follows. Let D = domestic demand for M, S = domestic supply of M, Q = imports and Y = aggregate output (equal to income). Changes that result from the output expansion at constant prices are dD, dS, etc. and relative changes are $\hat{D}$, $\hat{S}$, etc.

$$dQ = dD - dS \tag{13.1}$$

$$E_d = \frac{\hat{D}}{\hat{Y}} \tag{13.2}$$

$$E_s = \frac{\hat{S}}{\hat{Y}} \tag{13.3}$$

$$E_n = \frac{\hat{Q}}{\hat{Y}} \tag{13.4}$$

From (13.1) to (13.4)

$$E_n = E_d \left(\frac{D}{Q}\right) - E_s \left(\frac{S}{Q}\right) \tag{13.5}$$

From (13.5)

$$E_n = E_d + \frac{S}{Q}(E_d - E_s) \tag{13.6}$$

Figure 13.4 shows how various combinations of E_s and E_n lead to particular values of E_n. When $E_n = 1$, trade expands in proportion to growth, and when $E_n < 0$ there is net ultra-anti-trade bias, that is trade contracts at constant prices, so that the terms of trade must improve. As long as $E_n > 0$ the terms of trade of a unilaterally growing country must deteriorate.

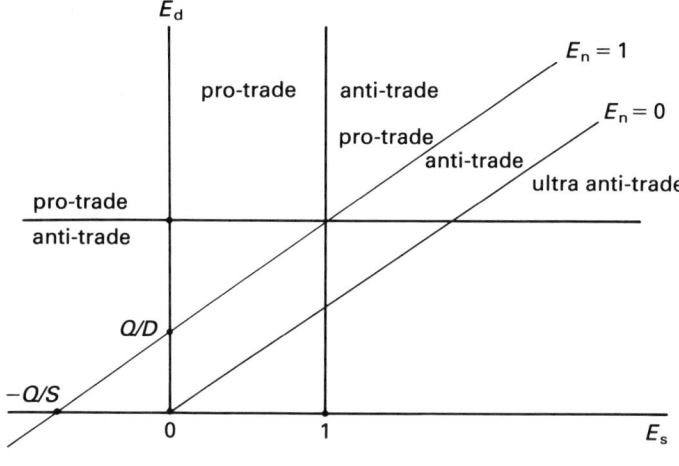

Figure 13.4

Ultra-Bias and Factor Growth

Rybczynski (1955) showed geometrically in a famous article that – given certain assumptions, notably two factors and constant returns to scale – if one factor expands while the supply of the other is unchanged, at constant prices, output of the product which is intensive in the non-expanding factor must *actually contract*. I also showed this algebraically in the paper reproduced as essay 13. As shown by Johnson and me, the significance of this result is that it produces ultra-bias on the production side, on the basis of which various further results noted above can be reached. But one should not stop at the Rybczynski (1955) proof. A generalization is given by Guha (1963), namely that a sufficient condition for ultra-bias on the production side is that the *incremental* factor ratio (ratio of the *total* increase in supply of one factor to the other) is outside the two *existing* factor ratios, the Rybczynski case being a special case of this.

Technical Progress

Essay 13 contains the sentence: 'By means of the same sort of argument it can be shown that if there is an increase in productivity solely in country A's blanket industry the terms of trade must improve' – in other words, there must be an ultra-biased production expansion. This proposition (deliberately reproduced from the original paper) was based on some remarks by Johnson (1955) and should have been qualified as referring only to a factor-neutral productivity increase, that is one that is neither labour nor capital saving. The argument can be illustrated geometrically.

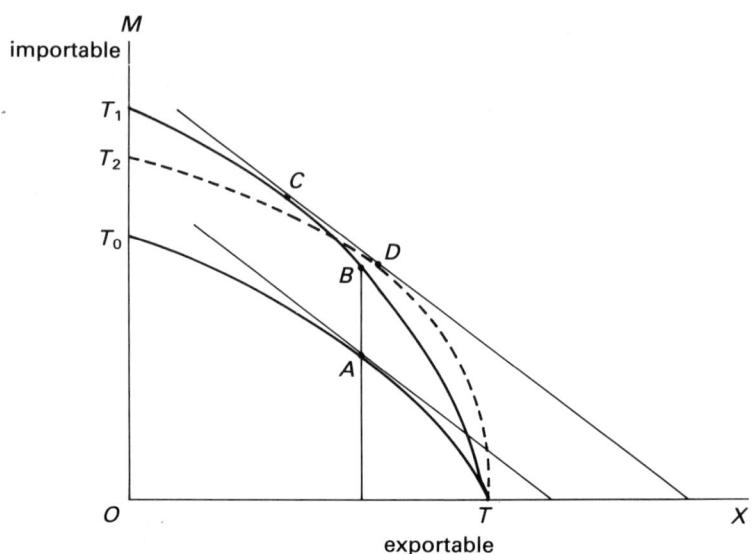

Figure 13.5

Factor neutral technical progress (with constant returns to scale) in industry M means that technical progress leaves the contract curve (the curve tracing out tangencies of production isoquants in a factor endowment box) unchanged, each point on it representing the same output of X and a higher output of M, the proportion by which output of M increases being the same at all points. This then leads to an expansion of the transformation curve in figure 13.5 from T_0T to T_1T such that the latter is a constant proportion vertically above the former. If factors did not move, output would shift from A to B. This represents the *primary* expansion of output of M as a result of the technical progress. But the relative price of M will now have fallen (the slope at B is steeper than at A), so there will have to be a movement of factors out of X into M if the relative price of M is to return to where it was at A. Output then moves to C. Thus we get the *secondary* expansion of output of M at constant prices, this leading to reduced output of the static industry, and hence an ultra-biased expansion. This is a simple way of explaining the brief sentence in my paper.

A major contribution to this field came from Findlay and Grubert (1959). They picked up my unqualified sentence, and noted correctly that if technological progress in one industry (with the other industry static) is factor-biased, ultra-bias of the production expansion is no longer certain.

Exposition of the Findlay–Grubert argument can be quite complex. Here let me explain the essential point and show geometrically the outcome of one case. Suppose that progress in M is capital saving (labour using). This factor bias has the same kind of effect as would an increase in the supply of capital relative to labour to the economy as a whole. This factor bias will therefore tend to expand the capital-intensive industry relative to the labour-intensive one. Similarly, if the factor bias had been the other way, the tendency would be for the labour-intensive industry to expand, and the capital-intensive industry to contract on this account. This 'bias' effect must then be added to the industry bias already expounded, that is to the fact that the whole of the progress is in industry M, which (on its own) creates an ultra-bias towards M (ultra-anti-trade bias).

Let us suppose then that the bias in industry M is capital saving and that M is the labour-intensive industry. This will illustrate the central Findlay–Grubert point. The effect will thus be to shift factors out of M into X, the capital-intensive industry. The difference in the factor intensities between the two industries will be increased, since the relatively labour-intensive industry M has become even more labour intensive.

All this is summed up by the movement from T_1T to T_2T in figure 13.5. Factor neutral progress solely in M would have expanded the transformation curve from T_0T to T_1T, bringing output at constant terms of trade to C. Next we introduce a factor bias in technical progress in M such that the value of output at the given price ratio does not change from its new level (being the same at D as at C), but the transformation curve becomes T_2T, with D below C because technical progress has been capital saving and X is the capital-intensive industry. T_2T is more concave than T_1T because the difference in factor intensities has increased. While the movement from T_0T to T_1T represents the effect of technical progress *per se*, the movement from T_1T to T_2T represents the pure factor bias effect. It is clear that D could be to the left of A (so that there is still ultra-bias), or it could be to the right. The key point is that ultra-bias is no longer certain even though the technical progress is wholly in M.

References

Corden, W. M. 1955: The economic limits to population increase. *The Economic Record*, 31, 242–60.

Findlay, R. and Grubert, H. 1959: Factor intensities, technological progress, and the terms of trade. *Oxford Economic Papers*, 11, 111–21.

Guha, A. 1963: Factor and commodity prices in an expanding economy. *The Quarterly Journal of Economics*, 77, 149–55.

Hicks, J. R. 1953: An inaugural lecture. *Oxford Economic Papers*, 5, 117–35.

Ikema, M. 1969: The effect of economic growth on the demand for imports: a simple diagram. *Oxford Economic Papers*, 21, 66–9.

Johnson, H. G. 1955: Economic expansion and international trade. *The Manchester School of Economic and Social Studies*, 23, 95–112.

——— 1962: *Money Trade and Economic Growth*. London: Allen & Unwin.

Meade, J. E. 1952: *A Geometry of International Trade*. London: Allen & Unwin.

Mishan, E. J. 1955: The long-run dollar problem: a comment. *Oxford Economic Papers*, 7, 215–20.

Rybczynski, T. M. 1955: Factor endowment and relative commodity prices. *Economica*, 22, 336–41.

14

The Effects of Trade on the Rate of Growth*

This essay shows how opening up an economy to trade may affect its rate of growth. One country's growth in the closed economy is compared with its growth under free trade in an open economy. Given production functions are assumed and the focus is on capital accumulation effects. The essay is an attempt to marry modern trade theory with neoclassical growth theory. If international trade theory is to be a useful aid to thought on practical issues it clearly must include a rigorous theoretical analysis of the effects of trade on growth. This is at least as necessary as the analysis of the effects of growth on trade, on which there is now a valuable body of theory.[1] The growth effects of trade to be discussed here are those that emerge most clearly from a simple neoclassical model.[2] It seems sensible to begin by rigorously exploring this type of model, though further advance on this front will clearly require departures from the neoclassical assumptions.

Most of the ingredients will be familiar to students of growth theory, but a novel effect is introduced in section V in the form of the 'factor-weight' effect. Essentially it is argued that opening up trade may affect the rate of growth through (a) the 'impact' effect (section II), (b) the effect of the gains from trade raising the rate of capital accumulation, or, in short, the 'gains from trade' effect (also section II), (c) the 'substitution' effect operating through a change in the relative price of investment goods (section III), (d) the income distribution effect (section IV), and (e) the 'factor-weight' effect (section V). The effects of the opening up of trade on the path to the steady

---

* From Jagdish Bhagwati et al. (eds) 1971: *Trade, Balance of Payments, and Growth: Papers in Honour of Charles P. Kindleberger*, Amsterdam: North-Holland. Slightly abbreviated, but figure 14.1 added. I am indebted to J. S. Flemming, S. Goldman, I. M. D. Little, R. I. McKinnon, M. D. Steuer, L. R. Webb and especially to John Black, who developed the argument further (Black, 1970). An early version of the paper was presented before the Conference of the Association of University Teachers of Economics at York, UK, in March 1968.
1. See Johnson (1955, 1962), Corden (1956) and Findlay and Grubert (1959).
2. See section IX for references to some other effects.

Effects of trade on rate of growth

state are discussed principally in 'The Simplest Model' and 'Different Factor Intensities. . .'. Up to the latter it is assumed that the country concerned is small, facing given terms of trade; terms of trade effects are considered in the penultimate section. The analysis is extended to tariff changes in the final section. I begin with a brief description of the static characteristics of the model.

I The Static Foundations: A Two Stage Production Function

The model used in this essay is slightly unusual. The aim is to take into account two separate distinctions between goods, that between consumption goods and investment goods and that between exportables and importables. This problem could be solved by having a simple two-good model where the consumption good is the exportable and the investment good the importable, or vice versa.[3] In such a model, when the price of importables relative to exportables changes, the price of investment goods relative to consumption goods changes to the same extent. This would be a special case of the more general model to be used here. The justification for using this model will be given shortly. First let us expound it.

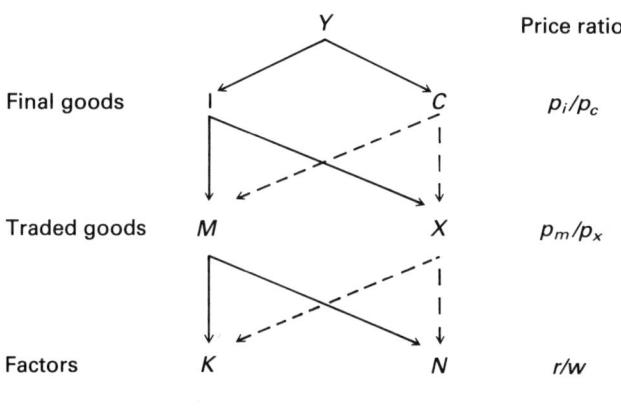

Figure 14.1

The production structure described here is represented in figure 14.1. Final usage or 'absorption' by the country under consideration consists of two goods, the investment good I and the consumption good C. The prices of these two goods are p_i and p_c. Real income, output and expenditure, denoted by Y, are always equal, namely to the sum of I and C produced and absorbed. Now I and C are each produced by two inputs, M and X,

---

3. As in Oniki and Uzawa (1965), Bardhan (1965) and Baldwin (1966).

and each has a constant-returns-to-scale production function with continuous substitution between these inputs. The prices of the two inputs are p_m and p_x. The price ratio p_i/p_c is related to the price ratio p_m/p_x. If I is M intensive relative to C (so that, at a given p_m/p_x, I would employ a higher ratio of M to X than would C) then a rise in p_m/p_x will involve a rise in p_i/p_c; and vice versa if C is the M intensive product.[4]

The two inputs, M and X, are in turn produced by two primary factors of production, capital K and labour N. Here also there is in each case (for M and for X) a constant-returns-to-scale production function with continuous substitution between the two primary inputs. It is important to note that the primary factors are inputs only into M and X, and not directly into I and C. The prices of the two factor services are the real wage w and the real rental on capital goods r, and the factor price ratio r/w is related to the p_m/p_x ratio in the same way as the p_m/p_x ratio is related to the p_i/p_c ratio. Thus, if M is capital intensive relative to X, a rise in r/w will be associated with a rise in p_m/p_x, and vice versa if M is the labour-intensive product. Hence there are three price ratios in the model and two factor-intensity conditions.

In a closed economy, we would be able to determine equilibrium prices and outputs if we knew the stocks of N and K, the four production functions and the final demand function. The latter expresses the community's demand for investment goods relative to consumption goods. When the country's propensity to save (i.e. invest) is constant this demand function has the characteristic that the income and price elasticities of demand for I and C are unity. In an open economy, we must specify also which factors and products are traded. We shall assume that only M and X are traded; there are no primary factor movements in or out of the country. This means, in particular, that the opening up of trade is *not* associated with opening up to international capital movements. All I and C are produced within the country, though from produced factors that may have been imported. Hence for the two traded goods, we also require a foreign offer curve. The elasticity of foreign reciprocal demand is assumed infinite (terms of trade given) up to section VII. Balance of payments equilibrium as well as full employment is also assumed.

In sections II and III it will be assumed that the factor intensities (labour or capital intensities) do not differ between M and X. This has two implications: First, when the economy is opened to trade and the domestic M/X price ratio falls as a result, the primary factor price ratio r/w does not alter. Second, if in the process of growth this primary factor ratio r/w alters, the M/X price ratio need not alter. Geometrically, the M/X

---

4. The two-good model, where I and C *are* X and M, gives the extreme cases for the relationship between p_m/p_x and p_i/p_c, the two changing then in the same proportion. (The signs of the changes will be the same if I is M intensive and opposite if C is M intensive.) When I and C use both X and M, then p_i/p_c will change less than proportionally with p_m/p_x.

transformation curve will be a straight line and even if N and K are growing at different rates the transformation curve will expand in an 'unbiased' way, its slope remaining constant. By contrast, in sections IV, V and VI the M/X factor intensities will be assumed to differ. Hence, when the M/X price ratio alters as a result of opening trade the income distribution will change. Geometrically, the M/X transformation curve will be concave to the origin and (if N and K are growing at different rates) will expand in a 'biased' way; if capital is growing faster than labour the bias will be towards the capital-intensive good.

In sections II, IV, V and VI it will be assumed that the factor intensities (M intensities) do not differ between I and C. Hence opening of trade, or a change in primary factor prices, will not affect the p_i/p_c ratio. By contrast, in section III the M intensities of I and C will be allowed to differ, and hence the implications will be explored of the opening of trade altering the p_i/p_c ratio through the alteration in p_m/p_x.

We therefore consider in the following pages three cases: (a) in section II there are no factor-intensity differences between M and X nor between I and C: this is the simplest model; (b) in section III there are such differences between I and C (but not between M and X), and (c) in sections IV, V and VI there are differences between M and X (but not between I and C).

What is the point of our unusual model with its two-tiered production structure? Why not just have a two-good model where one good is the investment good and the importable (or exportable) and the other the consumption good and the exportable (or importable)? This would draw too sharp a distinction between investment and consumption goods as they enter foreign trade; since there would only be two goods, each would have to double duty as an import or export and as investment or consumption good. But the multitude of goods entering foreign trade is largely intermediate inputs entering both consumption and investment without being uniquely associated with either. Hence neither consumption nor investment is likely to consist wholly of importables or exportables. Our model, limited and highly formal as it may seem, is meant to be realistic in this respect. Furthermore, the model makes it possible to analyse the effects of trade on growth in separate elements, one at a time. The opening of trade alters the domestic M/X price ratio. We can allow this to affect the primary factor price ratio while not altering the I/C price ratio, so that we can ignore complications that result from a change in the I/C price ratio. Also, we can allow it to alter the I/C price ratio without affecting the primary factor price ratio, so that other complications can be ignored. We have then a device of great analytical convenience.

II The Simplest Model

We start with a growing, closed economy with two factors of production, labour and capital, and an aggregate constant-returns-to-scale, neoclassical production function that may be thought of as being built up from the constant-returns-to-scale production functions of I, C, M and X.[5] The growth rate of labour is given exogenously, there is no technical progress, investment is brought into equality with savings by the rate of interest, and the savings propensity is given and uninfluenced by the level of income per head, income distribution or the rate of interest.[6] For exposition we shall assume that at a point in time t_0, at which our story begins, the rate of growth of capital is greater than the given rate of growth of labour.

Now in year t_0 the economy is opened up to trade. There are the familiar static gains from trade, so that real income rises. The assumption at this stage that the factor intensities do not differ between M and X means that the country will specialize in X, and that income distribution will not be affected by the change. The assumption that the M intensities do not differ between I and C means that opening-up trade has not altered the relative price of investment goods to consumption goods. The main point to be developed at this stage is that the economy will be able to absorb or use more goods and services in real terms, whether consumption or investment goods. The effect will now be the same as if there had been a once-and-for-all technical improvement. The opening of trade has shifted outwards the economy's 'absorption-possibility' frontier.[7]

What then is the effect on the rate of growth? We may distinguish two effects, (1) the impact effect, and (2) the capital accumulation effect. The latter has (a) an immediate implication, and (b) a steady-state implication. All these effects are identical with those that would result from a once-and-for-all technical improvement. If by growth, we mean not growth of output but growth of real income or absorption, then the impact effect is obviously to raise the rate of growth temporarily in year t_0 and to fall back again in the subsequent year. We assume that the economy's adjustment to trade – its reallocation of resources – is completed within the year t_0. This temporary effect will not play any significant part in our analysis. The capital accumulation effect is perhaps not so obvious. A permanent rise in real income or absorption has resulted. With a constant savings propensity, some part of the increase will then be saved and invested. Thus the absolute amount of investment in year t_0 and all subsequent years will rise above what it would have been otherwise. If one starts with a given capital stock at time t_0, a rise in the rate of growth of capital will result. And this will pull up with it the rate of growth of output. If $K =$ capital stock,

---

5. We have thus a 'two-level' production function. See Black (1969) on the derivation of such 'two-level' or derived production functions. Note that there is no index number problem because we are at this stage holding the price ratio between the two final goods, C and I, constant.
6. Hence we have an elementary form of the neoclassical growth model as described by Meade (1962), Solow (1956) and Swan (1956).
7. The term 'absorption' is used to emphasize that we are concerned not just with consumption possibilities but with possibilities of consuming or *investing*. Alternative terms might be 'situation-possibility' frontier or 'availability' frontier or envelope.

Effects of trade on rate of growth

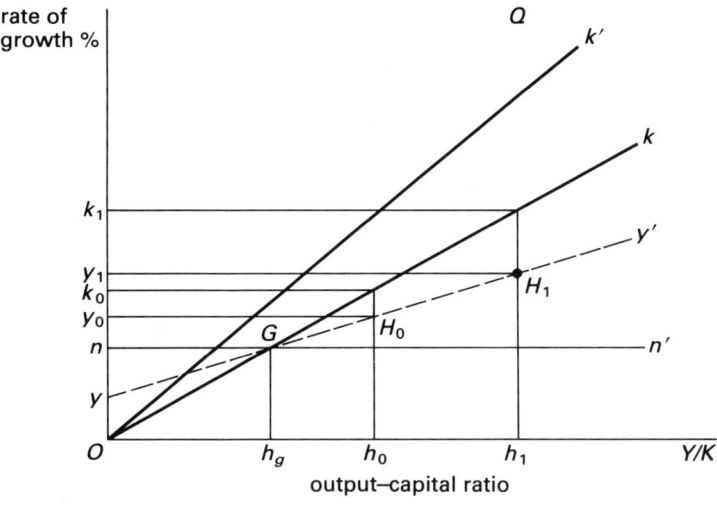

Figure 14.2

dK = increase in capital stock, s = savings propensity, Y = real income (absorption), then $dK/K = sY/K$, and the opening-up of trade has raised Y.

This capital accumulation effect of the gains from trade has an implication for the steady state and for the path toward the steady state that will be explained geometrically later. The main point is that in the closed economy, with capital growing faster than labour and hence output growing more slowly than capital, the capital–output ratio would have been steadily rising, hence, the rate of growth of capital and of output steadily falling. This is an oft-told neoclassical tale: output and capital growth approach the given labour growth rate – that is, there is a tendency towards a steady state. The effect of the opening up of trade on the movement to a steady state is simple if we assume that the international terms of trade are given to the country and do not change over time. Thus we may suppose that the rest of the world is already in its steady state. The opening up of trade has displaced K/Y downwards, and so raised dK/K. But, given our simplifying assumptions, there will still be a movement toward a steady state, the growth rate of which will still be determined by the given labour growth rate. While in non-steady-state situations the opening up of trade raises the rate of growth for more than just year t_0, it does not alter the steady-state rate of growth.

Figure 14.2 shows rates of growth of real income, capital and labour on the vertical axis and the output–capital ratio Y/K on the horizontal.[8] The horizontal line nn' shows the given labour growth rate. For a given savings propensity, the straight line through the origin Ok shows the rate of growth

---

8. The diagram comes from Swan (1956).

of capital at various levels of Y/K. The rate of growth of output (real income in the open economy) is given by the line yy'. The constant-returns-to-scale assumption means that when capital and labour are growing at the same rate, output must also grow at that rate, so that all three lines intersect at G. The yy' line would be a straight line as drawn only with a Cobb–Douglas production function (output growth being a weighted average of labour and capital growth, with the weights constant), but this assumption is not essential to our argument.

At time t_0 in the closed economy, Y/K is h_0 and hence the rate of growth of output is y_0. The system would tend towards the steady state at G where Y/K is h_g and the rate of growth is n. The opening up of trade in time t_0 displaces Y/K to the right, to h_1. Temporarily – just in that year and with a given amount of investment – it raises the rate of growth to some point, such as Q, shown in the diagram vertically above h_1. This is the impact effect, and will henceforth be ignored. We proceed to the capital accumulation effect. The rate of growth of capital will increase from k_0 to k_1 simply because Y/K has risen while the savings propensity has remained constant. And this pulls up the rate of growth of output (real income) to y_1. If there were not diminishing returns to capital because capital is growing faster than labour it would stay at that level (unlike the rise owing to the impact effect which is temporary in its very nature). But in fact, with the capital–labour ratio steadily rising, and hence the output–capital ratio Y/K steadily falling, the economy will tend to the steady state at G, moving this time not from H_0 to G, as in the closed economy, but from H_1 to G. In the steady state Y/K will be the same as in the closed economy.[9]

This is a growth-orientated diagram and can be misleading. This type of approach tends to give the impression that only growth rates matter, and expecially the growth rates in the steady state. It seems that the gains from trade eventually disappear, and for those who regard 'eventually' as more interesting than 'now' this could be a short step to saying that (in this type of model) there are no gains from trade. But this would be quite wrong, as becomes clear from figure 14.3. The vertical axis shows output or real income per head (Y/N), and the horizontal axis, time t. At time t_0, Y/N is j_0. The production function relates Y/K to Y/N, so that j_0 could be derived from h_0 in figure 14.2 and the production function. In the closed economy Y/N would rise, since, with capital growing faster than labour, output would also be growing faster than labour. It would approach the steady state Y/N, namely j_g, which is uniquely related by the production function

---

9. While H_1 will in this simple model be on the straight line GH_0 extended (so that opening-up trade does not alter, at time t_0, the relative weights attaching to the capital and labour growth rates in determining the rate of growth of output), the economy will not move from H_1 to G along yy', but rather along a curve above yy'. This follows from an argument in Footnote 18, but is a refinement that does not affect the argument so far.

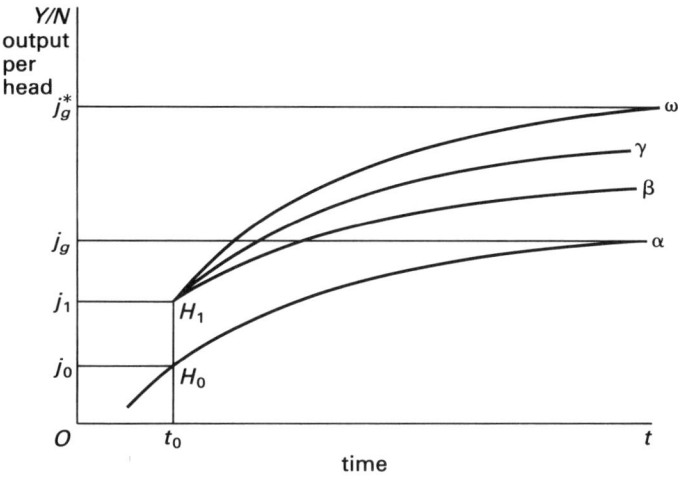

Figure 14.3

to the steady state Y/K, namely h_g. Thus the closed economy path of Y/N is given in figure 14.3 as the line $H_0\alpha$.

Now the economy is opened up in time t_0, thus raising real income or absorption per head to j_1. The vertical distance H_0H_1 represents the static gains from trade, expressed on a per-head basis. It yields the impact effect on the rate of growth. If this gain did not grow with the economy and there were no change in capital accumulation as a result of the opening up of trade it would simply be carried forward over time, Y/N in every subsequent year being greater than otherwise by the amount H_0H_1. The path of Y/N would then be $H_1\beta$. But in fact it will grow with the economy. In the present model, with the terms of trade given from outside and constant, and no 'biases' in the growth pattern because the factor intensities between M and X are assumed not to differ, the gain from trade will remain a constant proportion of income and so will grow at the same rate as income. In section VI this question of the growth in the gains from trade will be looked at again for the case where the factor intensities between M and X do differ. The present assumption makes the opening up of trade the equivalent of a Hicks-neutral technical improvement. It means that in figure 14.3 the growth path will be given by the curve $H_1\gamma$, which is a constant proportion above $H_0\alpha$.

Finally, we must allow for the effect of the opening up of trade raising the rate of capital accumulation. This, as we have seen, raises the rate of growth above what it would be otherwise, the excess of the open economy over the closed economy rate of growth declining towards zero as the steady state is approached. Hence Y/N grows faster than indicated by $H_1\gamma$ (which assumed a constant rate of growth, other than in year t_0). The path of Y/N is now given by $H_1\omega$. The steady-state real income per head will now be j_g^*. This should be compared with the steady-state income per head in the closed economy, namely j_g. Both are associated with a Y/K of h_g. But in the open economy it is possible to have a higher income per head for any given Y/K than in the closed economy since the economy has, in fact, become more productive.

The gains from opening up the economy at any time after t_0 can now be broken down into three elements.[10] The first is the static gain from trade H_0H_1. The second is the growth of the static gain over time; the gain grows (given our present assumptions) in proportion to closed economy output; its growth is measured by the vertical distance between $H_1\beta$ and $H_1\gamma$. The third results from the rise in the rate of growth caused by the increase in capital accumulation and might be described as the 'growth gain' from opening-up trade. It is measured by the vertical distance between $H_1\gamma$ and $H_1\omega$. The growth gain results when parts of the static gain are invested. It thus represents a particular allocation of the static gain – an allocation which raises real income in the future rather than consumption now – and thus is not additional in a welfare sense. Any trade policy that raises real income creates a static gain and, for any given propensity to save, also raises the rate of growth. Thus the growth effect may reinforce but does not alter policy arguments based on static effects.

The argument developed so far does not depend wholly on the precise assumptions under which it has been developed. Quite generally one can argue as follows: Opening trade or altering trade restrictions may bring about static gains or losses, the subject matter of the static theory of trade and welfare. These depend on factor endowments and intensities, on economies of scale, domestic distortions, the flexibility of factor prices, terms of trade effects, the tariff structure, and so on. The message of our capital accumulation effect is simply that if the marginal propensity to save and invest is positive, the growth rate will rise if the static gains rise and fall if the static gains fall. Further, it is not necessary to assume that the marginal propensity to save is constant or equal to the average propensity. It is necessary only that it is positive. One could make the savings propensity a positive function of real income per head or perhaps dependent on a utility function of some kind.[11] One could construct a realistic model of a closed subsistence economy with zero net savings; when it is opened up to trade, net savings begin for the first time, the gain from trade thus being the initiator of growth.

---

10. This analysis should help to clarify the discussion of these issues, involving much the same variables, by Linder (1961, pp. 60–73).
11. See, for example, Baldwin (1966), where the propensity to save depends on the marginal productivity of capital and a simple time-preference function. A steady-state tendency still emerges.

III The Relative Price of Investment Goods

We now assume that opening the economy to trade alters the price relationship between investment goods and consumption goods. Hence the importable/exportable intensities (the M intensities) must differ as between I and C. Opening-up trade lowers the domestic prices of importables relative to the prices of exportables. If then I is the M intensive good, the price of I relative to the price of C will fall while if C is the M intensive good, the relative price of I will rise.

A constant savings propensity means that the proportion of expenditure on investment is constant. When the relative price of I changes as the result of opening up trade the ratio of I to C must then change. Thus, if investment goods are M intensive, so that the relative price of I falls, the ratio of I to C must rise. This has effects on capital accumulation. For a given rise in real income at constant prices, the increase in investment will be greater if I is M intensive than if it is X intensive. The argument is illustrated in figure 14.4. Quantities of I are shown along the vertical axis and of C along the horizontal axis. The 'absorption frontier' in the closed

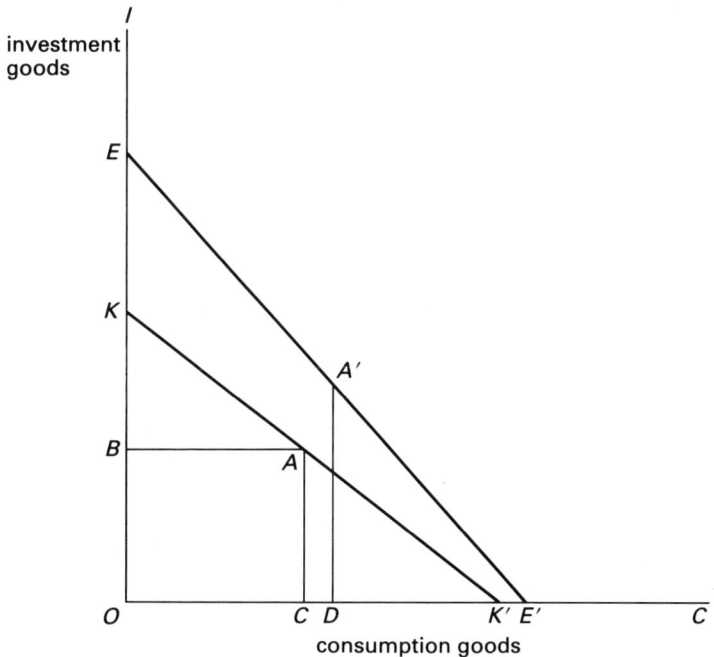

Figure 14.4

economy at time t_0 is KK'; it depends on the stocks of labour and capital, and on the production functions of M, X, I and C. We assume at this stage that the factor intensities (labour or capital intensities) of X and M do not differ so that the absorption frontier is a straight line. The given propensity to save is assumed to be CK'/OK' ($= OB/OK$) and determines the actual absorption point A, with consumption OC and investment OB. When trade is opened up the absorption frontier expands to EE', its steeper slope reflecting the fall in the relative price of I (with I being M intensive). The new absorption point is A' ($DE'/OE' = CK'/OK'$). The movement from A to A' could be decomposed into an *income* and a *substitution* effect. The first raises absorption of C and I in equal proportion; this is the static gains from trade effect discussed in the previous section. The second switches absorption from consumption to investment in this particular case. The effect is the same as that of a once-and-for-all technical improvement which is product biased towards the investment-goods industry. If the relative price of I had risen (if I were X intensive) the 'substitution' effect would have led to some fall in investment by comparison with the constant price case.

If the factor intensities (labour or capital intensities) differed between X and M the transformation curve between them would be concave to the origin rather than a straight line, and the closed economy absorption frontier derived from it in figure 14.4 would also be concave. But the basic argument would not have changed. There would still be an income and a substitution effect of opening-up trade. Furthermore, this analysis does not really require a constant savings propensity. There is a substitution effect if a fall in the relative price of investment goods causes the ratio of I to C in absorption to rise (or vice versa for a rise in the price ratio); it does not have to rise (or fall) exactly to the extent required to maintain the proportion of expenditure on investment goods constant, because this is the special case where the elasticity of substitution in the static demand or preference function implied in our savings propensity assumption is unity.

It is certainly more plausible to make the weak assumption that there is *some* substitution effect – that is, that a fall in the relative price of I has some effect in raising I/C (and vice versa) – than to make the strong assumption that the savings propensity is absolutely rigid. Indeed the implausibility of assuming an absolutely constant savings ratio emerges when one asks whether the substitution effect could exactly offset or even more than offset the income effect so that the opening-up of trade leads to no change or even a fall in either consumption or investment. It can be shown that with a constant savings propensity this is indeed possible, and, in certain limiting cases, inevitable. We shall consider this question for the two limiting cases where our model would collapse into a two-good case. The first case is where C uses only X and I only M, so that in fact $C = X$ and $I = M$. Given equal factor intensities between X and M, and so maintaining the straight line case, the points K' and E' in figure 14.4 would coincide. A constant savings propensity would place A' directly above A, so that the

Effects of trade on rate of growth

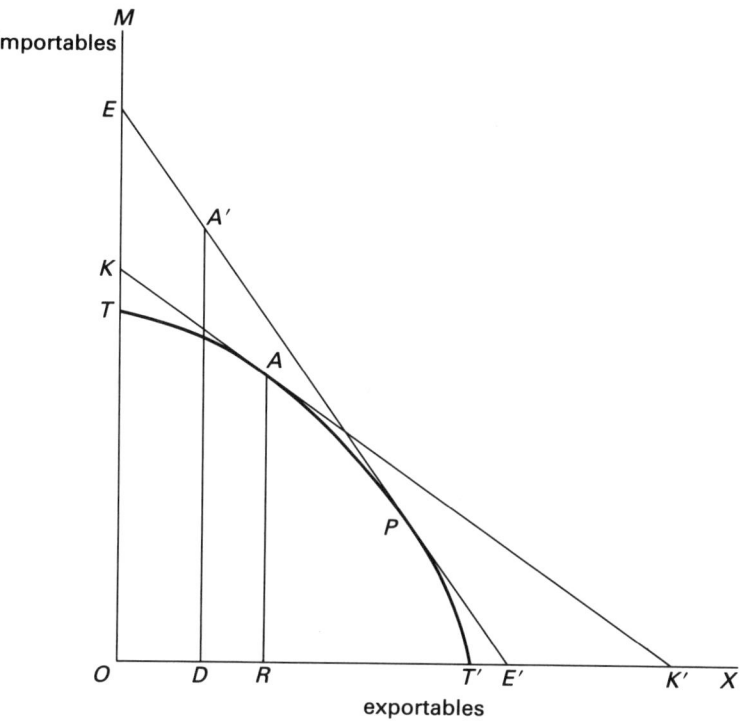

Figure 14.5

opening up of trade would lead to no immediate change in consumption; all the gains from trade would be invested. The second case is where C uses only M and I only X, so that in fact $C = M$ and $I = X$. In this case the relative price of I would rise and there would be no change in investment, the gains from trade all going into consumption. These are the limiting results which are approached as the difference between the M intensities of I and C increases. But given equal factor intensities between X and M (and hence the straight-line case) it is not possible, with a given savings propensity, for consumption or investment actually to fall.

The possibility that, with a constant savings propensity, the opening up of trade leads to an absolute fall in consumption or investment arises once we allow the factor intensities between X and M to differ. Again, we consider the limiting cases where the model collapses into a two-good case. In figure 14.5, M is shown along the vertical axis and X along the horizontal, and the closed economy absorption frontier TT' is concave to the origin. Actual output and absorption in the closed economy are given by the point A, the closed economy price ratio being indicated by the slope of KK'. Closed economy income in terms of X is OK'. If $X = C$ and $M = I$, then the propensity to save is RK'/OK' while if $X = I$ and $M = C$, then it is OR/OK'. If the world price ratio (terms of trade) is given by the slope of EE', the opening up of trade causes production to shift to P and income in terms of X to fall to OE'. The new absorption point A' must be to the left of A if the proportion of expenditure on the two goods is to stay constant. Thus, if $X = C$ and $M = I$ the propensity to save is now DE'/OE', which must be equal to RK'/OK'. It follows that in this case when $X = C$ consumption must fall absolutely as a result of the opening up of trade while when $X = I$ investment would fall absolutely. Thus the substitution effect outweighs the income effect on that good the price of which has risen relatively. This result is certain in the limiting two-good case. When the difference between the M intensities of I and C is not so extreme the result is still possible, though not certain. The greater this difference in M intensities, the more likely it is. All this depends, it must again be stressed, on the assumption of a rigidly constant savings propensity. But when this assumption leads to such extreme results one must conclude that it is hardly compatible with a plausible intertemporal utility function.

Let us now integrate the substitution effect into our growth model of section II and figure 14.2. The substitution effect means that, in addition to the various effects on the rate of growth discussed in section II, there are the effects of the change in the relative price of investment goods. If investment goods are M intensive this effect will raise the rate of growth. In figure 14.2, the Ok line swings then to the left, to Ok', so that for any given Y/K (and with a constant savings propensity) the capital growth rate is higher than before. This higher rate of growth of capital will pull up with it the rate of growth of output.[12] There are thus two capital accumulation effects when trade is opened up, both raising the rate of growth: first, the capital growth rate rises because Y/K has increased, this being the gains-from-trade effect, and second, the Ok line has swung, this being the substitution effect. The economy again moves towards the steady-state growth rate n. Comparing two cases with the same initial rise in Y/K and Y/N at constant prices, but with relative prices constant in one and the price of investment goods having fallen in the other, the steady state Y/K will be lower, and the steady state Y/N higher, for the latter. The higher steady-state income per head is explained by the higher 'growth gain' from trade explained in turn by the higher growth up to the steady state.

All these conclusions are reversed when I is X intensive. As we have seen, with a constant savings propensity there is then even the possibility

12. We now have an index number problem in defining Y, since the relative price of investment goods to consumption goods is no longer constant (as in section II, earlier). Here Y could be defined as $C + I$ added together at the closed-economy prices existing at time t_0, but this would be quite arbitrary. A better approach is to suppose that there is a social utility function with C and I as the arguments, where Y is an indicator of utility. With a constant savings propensity this function would have an elasticity of substitution of unity.

that the substitution effect completely offsets the income effect (if $I = X$ and $C = M$, and if their factor intensities do not differ), or even outweighs it, so that the rate of capital accumulation is actually reduced (if $I = X$ and $C = M$, and the absorption frontier is concave to the origin).

The conclusion that the rate of capital accumulation *may* be reduced by the opening up of trade should not be misinterpreted. It does not necessarily yield an argument for deliberately keeping the economy closed so as to avoid a fall in the growth rate. Incurring a static loss (i.e. foregoing the gains from trade) in order to raise the rate of capital accumulation would be justified only if (a) the socially desired savings propensity were higher than the private one, and (b) first-best policies for raising the savings (i.e. investment) propensity were not feasible. Trade policy affects both the absorption pattern and the production pattern, and the production effect of closing an economy (or restricting trade) would be an unwanted distortion.

IV Income Distribution and the Savings Propensity

Opening-up trade or the imposition of trade restrictions may affect income distribution, and if savings propensities differ between different sectors or factors, they may then affect the overall savings propensity and hence the rate of capital accumulation. This is well known and was pointed out by A. S. Johnson (1908)[13] 60 years ago, and is implicit in classical writings and in much modern discussion of trade and growth. We shall now assume (a) that the factor intensities differ between X and M, so that the opening up of trade shifts income distribution towards the factors intensive in the production of X, (b) that the M intensities of I and C are identical, so that the relative price of investment goods stays constant, and (c) that the propensity to save out of profits is greater than that out of wages, each of the sectional propensities being constant; the overall savings propensity is thus a weighted average of the two sectional propensities, the weights depending on the income distribution. If X is capital intensive the overall propensity will rise while if M is capital intensive it will fall. The rate of capital accumulation will then rise or fall because of this effect, which has to be added to the effects already discussed.

The point is quite general and is very relevant in a study of the growth effects of protection. The relevant income distribution effect need not be limited to the distribution between wages and profits as a whole but could concern a shift from one type of profits to another, or perhaps, as between rural rents and urban profits.

Keeping an economy closed or restricting trade may conceivably yield a higher rate of capital accumulation because of this income distribution

---

13. An earlier Johnson! See A. S. Johnson (1908), summarized by Caves (1960, ch. IX), where other discussions of the effects of trade on growth are also reviewed.

effect, but it would be a fourth-best policy, even given that the socially optimum savings propensity exceeds the private one. If it is desired to foster savings, the first-best policy is directly to supplement or subsidize savings or to subsidize the purchase of investment goods, the second-best policy is to redistribute income towards profits directly by subsidizing profits and taxing wages (yielding possibly an undesirable income distribution), the third-best policy is to subsidize directly the capital-intensive industry (shifting income distribution towards profits but creating a production distortion that reduces compensated real income), and fourth-best policy is a tariff on the capital-intensive import (which adds in addition a consumption distortion).

V The Factor-weight Effect

The next effect to be considered is not on the rate of capital accumulation but on the relative productivity of capital and labour. It arises only if (a) the factor intensities differ between X and M, and (b) the economy at time t_0 is out of its steady state, so that capital and labour are growing at different rates. In addition, we assume, as in the previous section, that I and C do not differ in their M intensities, so that the relative price of investment goods stays unchanged. As in section II we have a straightforward aggregate production function. Real income or output Y can be defined in terms of either I or C and depends on inputs of M and X, which in turn depend on inputs of capital and labour and on transformation through trade. If the M, X and I (and hence C) production functions are constant-returns-to-scale, the aggregate production function which relates output Y to inputs K and N must be also.[14]

Now the point of the factor-weight effect is simply that, with a constant-returns-to-scale aggregate production function, the rate of growth of output is a weighted average of the capital and labour growth rates, and the opening up of trade may change the weights. If y = growth rate of output, n = growth rate of labour, k = growth rate of capital, w = wage rate and r = rental on capital goods, with factor prices equal to values of their marginal products, then in our constant-returns-to-scale model

$$y = n\left(w\frac{N}{Y}\right) + k\left(r\frac{K}{Y}\right) \tag{14.1}$$

where the expressions in parentheses (the weights) are the factor shares. Now opening-up trade alters Y/N and Y/K in the same proportion. But it may alter the weights by altering the ratio w/r. If X is capital intensive, the opening up of trade will lead to a shift in output toward the capital-

---

14. See Black (1969) on 'two-level' production functions.

intensive product, substitution of labour for capital in both X and M, and a higher marginal product of capital (and so higher r) and lower marginal product of labour (lower w). If capital is initially growing faster than labour the growth rate then rises. Of course, if M were capital intensive, the growth rate would fall because of this consideration (though on balance it may still increase owing to a rise in the rate of capital accumulation). The main point is that opening the economy to trade alters the relative importance of the two factors of production if X and M have different factor intensities. If it raises the importance of the faster-growing factor, the rate of growth will rise, while if the importance of the faster-growing factor is lowered, the growth rate will fall owing to this effect. If there were a single industry in a closed economy, the same effect would result from a factor-biased, once-and-for-all technical improvement. In figure 14.2 when Y/K rises to h_1, the growth rate thus moves to somewhere above or below y_1.

There appears to be no systematic discussion of this effect in the international trade (or the growth) literature.[15] It has been outlined only briefly here and the discussion should be regarded as tentative.[16]

The more general message of the factor-weight effect is that trade or trade restrictions may alter the relative importance of different industries and so indirectly of different factors. If factors are growing at different rates, the overall growth rate may then alter. Since land (natural resources) is usually the slowest growing factor, it follows, for example, that if trade is expanded between a land-scarce country and a land-plentiful one, the rate of growth in the former may well rise and in the latter fall, if other effects are excluded.

However, it would be a fallacy to leap to the conclusion that the land-plentiful country should then restrict its trade. Similarly, if capital is growing faster than labour and importables are capital intensive, an economy might indeed grow faster if it were closed than if it were open, but nevertheless it would not gain from staying closed. At every point in time, real income in the closed economy would be below what it would be in the open economy (except in the special case where the closed and open economy price ratios are identical). It could never pay to close an economy or restrict its trade, and thus to reduce its current income, unless this results in a transfer of real income from present to future, that is, an act of saving and investment. The gain from opening the economy may indeed grow more slowly than closed economy income so that the rate of growth of the two combined – the income of the open economy – would be lower than the rate of growth of closed economy income alone, but this does not

---

15. The exceptions are Meade (1962, ch. 3), where there is a discussion of the effects of changing factor weights owing to biased technical progress on the rate of growth in the closed economy; and Brown (1966, pp. 23–34, 57–8), where this is also briefly referred to.
16. See Black (1970) for further development of this subject.

214 Growth and trade

alter the fact that at every point in time, other than when closed and open economy price ratios are identical, there is a positive gain from trade. As will emerge more clearly in the next section, the essence of the factor-weight effect is that, with the M/X factor intensities differing, the gain from trade no longer grows in proportion with the economy unless the primary factors of production happen to be growing at the same rate – that is, unless the economy is in a steady state.

VI Different Factor Intensities and the Movement Toward the Steady State

In section II the movement toward the steady state and the growth in the gains from trade was discussed subject to the assumption that the factor intensities in M and X were the same. In section V we have just shown how the rate of growth in year t_0 is affected when the factor intensities in M and X are allowed to differ. Now we shall combine the two analyses and consider the movement from year t_0 toward the steady state and the growth in the gains from trade when the factor intensities between M and X differ. We shall assume away earlier complications by holding the relative price of investment goods constant (the M intensities of I and C are the same) and supposing that the overall savings propensity is not affected by income distribution. We continue to assume that the world terms of trade are given to the country and constant over time, and, as usual, start with capital growing faster than labour.

Now the first point to note is that, both in the closed and the open economy, the system will again move toward the steady state Y/K and rate of growth determined by the given rate of growth of labour. In this model, where there is only one factor that is growing at a given rate, the introduction of the factor-weight effect of trade does not affect the steady-state rate of growth.[17] The explanation of the movement toward the steady state is just as before: the capital accumulation rate declines because the capital–output ratio is rising and keeps on declining until capital is growing at the same rate as labour.

Nevertheless, the factor-weight effect does play a role on the way to the steady state. Consider equation (14.1). Once trade is opened up and w and r have attained their new values, they will remain unchanged as long as the country remains unspecialized and the terms of trade are constant. The product price ratio given by the world market will fix the factor prices. But

---

17. Black (1970) shows that if there is *more than one* 'natural' factor – that is, a factor with a given rate of growth – the steady-state growth rate may be affected by opening up trade. It will be the weighted average of the growth rates of the various 'natural' factors; trade may alter the weights. This is an important development of the argument here. It could also be shown that trade may alter the steady-state growth rate if there is technical progress.

in the movement to the steady state, Y/N rises, and Y/K falls. So the weight attached to k rises while that attached to n falls. Thus, as the overall capital–labour ratio rises the weight attached to capital growth relative to labour growth in determining the output growth rate rises. So, for this reason, the rate of growth will decline more slowly than it would otherwise.[18]

Next consider the changes over time in the gains from trade. In the model of section II the static gains from trade grew in the same proportion as the growth of the economy. This depended on the assumption that the factor intensities of M and X were identical. When they are not, then as the capital–labour ratio in the economy rises, the production transformation curve between M and X will acquire an increasing bias towards the capital-intensive good, whichever one it is. With the product price given from outside, this will then lead to an increasing shift in the production pattern towards this good. If M is capital intensive, the output pattern in the open economy will shift increasingly toward M and away from X, growth being thus anti-trade biased. The gain from trade as a proportion of national income will fall, and if biased growth continues, the gain will eventually fall absolutely until imports cease completely and there is no gain from trade at all because there is no trade. Another way of stating this fact is to say that the closed economy price ratio between M and X moves continually closer to the world terms of trade, until the two price ratios are equal, when the gains from trade disappear. But continued growth of capital relative to labour will then turn M into the exportable, so that trade reversal will lead now to the gains from trade growing more rapidly than the size of the economy. If X were capital intensive – so that the country has even initially a comparative advantage in that product which is intensive in its faster-growing factor – there would, right from year t_0, be proportionately growing gains from trade. But this proportionate growth in the gains from trade cannot go on indefinitely. In the movement toward the steady state, the bias in the output expansion will gradually decline and thus modify the growth in the gain. In the steady state itself, there will be no output expansion bias towards X or M, and hence the gains from trade will grow only at the same rate as the economy. Finally, if the factor intensities of M and X were identical there would be no bias in the output

---

18. Meade (1962, ch. 3) shows that in a closed economy the direction in which the factor weights move in the process of growth depends on whether the elasticity of substitution is greater or less than unity. The open economy case here considered is the equivalent of an elasticity of substitution that is infinite. See also Brown (1966). This discussion relates to the point made in footnote 9. If the factor weights change in the movement toward the steady state, the yy' line will not be a straight line. The argument in the text means geometrically that the open-economy yy' line (not drawn in figure 14.2) will be concave from below and will generally lie above the closed-economy yy' line.

expansion in the first place, and hence the gains from trade would always grow proportionally with the size of the economy.[19]

VII The Case in Which Terms of Trade are Not Constant

The assumption that the world terms of trade are constant will now be removed. The terms of trade may change either as a result of the changing trade offers of the country under consideration, country A, or may change exogenously, that is, the elasticity of the foreign reciprocal demand curve at any point in time may be less than perfectly elastic, or may be infinitely elastic but shifting over time. Of course the terms of trade may change as the combined result of both effects, but this more complex case will not be considered here.[20]

If the foreign reciprocal demand in year t_0 when trade is opened up is less than perfectly elastic, a movement from no trade to free trade will involve a static gain as before. While the gain would be greater if the economy had moved not to free trade but to the optimum level of restricted trade, as indicated by optimum tariff theory, nevertheless there must be some gain.[21] So there will be a gains-from-trade effect raising the rate of growth, and substitution, income distribution and factor-weight effects that may go either way. The previous analysis stands completely.

Next assume that country A faces a perfectly elastic foreign reciprocal demand but the terms of trade are exogenously changing over time. To isolate the main effect, assume that the factor intensities of M and X are identical so that we have the simple model of section II where, with constant terms of trade, the rise in the growth rate was explained solely by the increase in capital accumulation (apart from the impact effect). But if the terms of trade change, the static gains will grow faster or slower than

19. In section II the main analysis assumed a marginal propensity to save equal to the average. But it was pointed out that provided the marginal propensity to save is positive the gains from trade effect will lead to some rise in the rate of capital accumulation. It might be thought that a positive marginal savings propensity, though it has not rested in this essay on an explicit intertemporal utility function, is a sufficiently weak assumption to be reasonable. Yet, taking into account the discussion in the present section, an absolute fall in savings when trade is opened up might be compatible with a plausible intertemporal utility function. All one needs to assume is that the gains from trade are expected to grow over time so that the country is justified in making reduced provisions for what looks like a rosy future, rosier compared to the present than when the economy was closed and expected to stay closed. I owe this point to John Black.

20. One could analyse this case essentially as an amalgam of the two simpler cases. For complete two-country, two-product, neoclassical growth models in which the terms of trade are endogenous, see Oniki and Uzawa (1965), Bardhan (1965) and also Baldwin (1966). None of these compare closed- and open-economy growth, and in Baldwin (1966) the special assumption is made that investment goods are capital intensive.

21. For a formal proof of this see Kemp (1964, ch. 11).

closed economy output, so that there is an additional (positive or negative) growth effect. An improvement in the terms of trade would shift outwards the absorption-possibility frontier; when the improvement is continuous, we can say that the productivity of transformation through trade is steadily rising. Hence the effect is the same as that of a positive rate of technical progress. The opening up of trade would then lead to a rise in the growth rate of national income even if there were no increase in the rate of capital accumulation, though (with a positive marginal propensity to save) the rate of capital accumulation will in fact rise over time in relation to its constant terms of trade movement and on balance may no longer decline towards the given labour growth rate.

Now consider the relationship between terms of trade changes and the movement to the steady state. The rest of the world, to be called here country B, may be in or out of its steady state. If it is in its steady state, then its relative prices will be constant. Given the assumption that country A is a very small country that cannot affect prices in country B it follows that country A's terms of trade are then constant. This is the special case considered in earlier sections of this paper. If country A was in its steady state before its economy was opened, it will be jolted out of it by the opening up of trade and, as has been described earlier, will then begin a movement to a new steady state with a different level of income per head and perhaps output–capital ratio.

If country B is not in its steady state and factor-intensities between its traded products differ, the terms of trade will be changing. And as long as the terms of trade are changing country A cannot, with an open economy, reach its steady state. Momentarily in country A, all factors and outputs may come to grow at the same rate; but if the terms of trade continue changing because country B is not yet in its steady state this cannot last. In other words, in the open economy the small country cannot be in its steady state before the large country is, but the large country does not depend on the small country. If neither country were so small as to be unable to affect the terms of trade, it would be impossible for either country to be in its steady state while the other was not.[22]

22. Mr. Renshaw of Warwick University has pointed out to me the following implication of the factor-weight effect in a two-country world where neither country is small. Suppose that (a) neither country is in its steady state when trade is opened up, (b) capital is growing faster than labour in both, (c) their savings propensities are the same, and (d) there are no factor reversals. Assume that A has the higher capital–labour ratio, so that (1) A will export the capital-intensive and B the labour-intensive product, and (2) A will have the higher income per head. The factor-weight effect will then cause opening-up trade to raise the rate of growth in the richer country A, and to lower it in the poorer country B – though there will also be other effects on the growth rate. But this yields of course no argument from B's point of view for restricting trade to raise its growth rate. It may be more plausible to assume that the richer countries are the land-intensive countries, in which case the factor-weight effect will tend to lower growth rates in the richer and raise them in the poorer countries.

VIII The Effects of Tariffs on the Rate of Growth

An analysis of the effects of opening-up trade on the rate of growth is clearly not of the same practical interest as an analysis of the effects of tariff changes. But the conclusions can readily be adapted to tariff theory.[23] Indeed, this essay was stimulated by an interest in the effects of tariffs and other forms of protection on growth in the belief that it may indirectly shed light on issues of current controversy. It is assumed now that all tariff revenue is automatically redistributed in a non-distorting manner.

First assume that the terms of trade are given. A reduction in tariff barriers has then the same type of effect on the rate of growth as a movement from a closed economy to free trade. It increases the gains from trade and so raises the rate of growth. If I is M intensive, it lowers the relative price of investment goods and so raises the rate of growth further (and lowers the rate of growth if C is M intensive). If X is capital intensive, it shifts income distribution towards profits and so may raise the rate of growth (vice versa if X is labour intensive). Finally, if X is capital intensive and capital is growing faster than labour then a tariff reduction probably raises the rate of growth by raising the weight of capital in determining output growth (and lowers it if X is labour intensive).[24] All this applies in reverse for an increase in tariffs and is just a revision of our earlier conclusions.

The matter is a little more complicated if the terms of trade are not given, the elasticity of foreign reciprocal demand being less than perfectly elastic. Consider first the gains from trade effect in isolation. There is now an *optimal* tariff at which the gains from trade, defined as including the gains from improved terms of trade, are maximized. Whether a tariff change raises or lowers the gains from trade, and hence the rate of growth, now depends on whether the movement is toward or away from the optimal tariff level. When the tariff is below the optimum an increase raises the rate of growth.

Next consider the substitution, income distribution, and factor-weight effects. These all depend on the direction of the relative price change within the domestic economy brought about by a tariff change. Normally one would expect a tariff reduction to reduce protection of importables, so that, as with the opening up of trade, it lowers the relative price of M

---

23. No attempt is made here to spell out the effects of a tariff on the path to, and the characteristics of, the steady state. These can be easily derived by combining the earlier models in the essay with the analysis in this section.
24. The word 'probably' appears because I have not been able to prove rigorously that the factor-weight effect applies in a simple manner to tariff changes, and there is indeed some doubt whether it does so. This qualification applies to all references to this effect in this section. (See further discussion of this issue at the end of the Further Notes).

domestically. The substitution, income distribution, and factor-weight effects are then as for the constant terms of trade case, depending on whether I or C is M intensive and X or M is capital intensive. But there is also the paradoxical Metzler (1949) possibility that a tariff reduction raises the relative price of M domestically, because the effect of a reduced tariff margin over the external (duty-free) price of M has been more than offset by the rise in its external price (the deterioration in the terms of trade). This paradox results when the sum of the foreign elasticity of demand for exports in terms of imports and country A's marginal propensity to import is less than one. In that case, a tariff reduction has substitution, income distribution and factor-weight effects opposite to those of the constant terms of trade case. The basic analysis required is identical.

IX Final Remarks

One might wonder whether the parts of this essay that have been concerned with the steady state have dealt with anything important. Yet this concern – inherited from the literature of growth theory – can be given a broader interpretation. It may be uninteresting to describe a state which is many years ahead and which may indeed never be reached, since on the way to it parameters are likely to change. But it is of interest to know in which direction growth rates may move and what consequences for real income per head and the growth rate can be expected some years after a particular alteration in trade policy. Focusing on a theoretical ultimate state is thus purely an expositional device. At the same time, a concern *only* with steady states would have obscured significant aspects of the trade and growth process. Notably it would have obscured the factor-weight effect.

The essay has been concerned with only a few effects of trade on growth, and in a highly simplified model. There are obviously many possible relationships between trade and growth.[25] The relationships that have been discussed here happen to follow naturally from models of trade and of growth that are already familiar. A more complex model might allow the impact effect to be spread over a longer period than just the year when trade is opened up, and more sophisticated assumptions about saving and investment behaviour might be introduced; perhaps a plausible intertemporal utility function might be built explicitly into the model. Economies of scale could be introduced. One could allow the shift either in the production pattern or in the consumption pattern that results from opening

---

25. Various relationships between trade and growth not embraced in the formal model of this essay are discussed by Kindleberger (1962). The growth-and-trade theme runs consistently through Charles Kindleberger's writings, especially his historical contributions. Various relationships between protection and growth not dealt with here are also discussed by Corden (1974, chs. 10 and 11).

up trade to lead to growth-promoting or growth-inhibiting effects through raising or lowering the 'learning rate' of the economy. Furthermore, other effects, concerned with technical progress or adaptation, with the inflow of foreign capital in response to trading opportunities, and with the inducement to invest by domestic entrepreneurs, may be at least as important or more important.

One might also have framed the question differently. Instead of asking how opening up trade or a change in trade restrictions affects the rate of growth, one might have assumed an open and possibly unrestricted economy to begin with and might have considered how trade and balance of payments effects either fostered or retarded growth. This is the more realistic approach that Kindleberger (1962, ch. 12) takes in his discussion of the impact of trade on the rate of growth. He distinguishes between trade as a leading, a balancing, or a lagging sector. The models of export-led growth to which he gives prominence tend to be demand-motored models which assume that increased demand for exports can lead to extra output from existing resources and can induce extra investment; such models can be contrasted with the neoclassical model in the present essay which is essentially supply motored, assuming full employment and full capacity utilization at all times and that investment at any point in time is limited by available savings that do not depend on expected rates of return. Growth in this model is explained by growth in the supply of the factors of production and their productivity, whether internal or through foreign trade. There is clearly scope for the construction of rigorous demand-motored models on the lines sketched out by Kindleberger and the authors he cites, and for combining them with supply-motored models of the type expounded in this essay.

Further Notes: The Effects of Trade on the Rate of Growth

Essay 14 has managed to obtain some fairly clear results by making three crucial simplifying assumptions. Something should be said about each.

Introducing Non-tradables

While the factors are non-traded, the goods at the base level – that is the products directly produced by the factors (M and X in the model) – are fully traded. This has meant that – as long as there is non-specialization – the domestic base level product price ratio has been completely determined by the world market. This product price ratio, in turn, has then determined both the factor price ratio and the relative price of consumption goods to investment goods. The latter, of course, *have* been non-traded, being both produced wholly by what can be called the base level goods.

A necessary complication would be to introduce non-tradables at the base level. The domestic product price ratio would then be *influenced* by world prices when trade is opened up, but it would not be wholly determined by these prices; it would also depend on the domestic factor ratio and on the final demand pattern. In fact, we would get a compromise result between the open-economy-tradables-only case of essay 14 and the closed-economy outcome. Non-tradables represent an element of 'closedness'.

Findlay (1973, ch. 6) has, in fact, analysed in detail a model very similar to the one presented in essay 14 – with growth through capital formation and a constant saving ratio, and with a two-level production structure where consumption and investment goods are, in turn, produced by two base goods (my term). But the crucial feature of his model is that the two base goods are a tradable and a non-tradable. It is clear that marrying the Findlay paper with the model of essay 14 could yield a more comprehensive story.

Introducing International Capital Mobility

It may seem a little odd to open up trade but not factor markets. One might ask what would happen if the capital market were opened up at the same time. In discussing this we will continue to assume zero labour mobility here.

We then encounter the crucial Mundell (1957) result. In the simple two-factor two-good Samuelson–Heckscher–Ohlin model trade and factor mobility are perfect substitutes. The point can be made by supposing, for the moment, that the capital market were opened up but trade remained closed. If the opening up were complete and the domestic return to capital had to be equalized to the foreign return, the domestic r/w ratio would then be determined by the world capital market. With r/w determined, p_m/p_x would then be determined; and with p_m/p_x determined, p_i/p_c would be determined. The higher the rate of return on the world capital market relative to that which ruled in the closed economy, the more would the opening up of the capital market raise the relative price of the capital-intensive good, shift income distribution towards capital and raise or lower the relative price of the investment good, depending on whether the latter is capital or labour intensive. The growth rate would then be affected through the usual channels. If trade were opened up as well, there would be a problem – the Mundell (1957) problem – if the p_m/p_x ratio that was determined in the world market did not happen to be the same one that emerged as a result of the opening up of the capital market.

This 'Mundell' problem only arises in a very simple model. It has been helpful in the model of essay 14 to have just two products and two factors of production. It has avoided many complications. But when we open up both trade and the capital market the simplicity of the assumptions *creates* complications. Since in the real world there are certainly more goods and more factors, it hardly seems necessary to pursue the difficulties of a two-factor two-good model too deeply.

The matter can be resolved as follows. First, if all factors were and remained non-traded, the simple story of essay 14 would give some indication of the direction of effects that are likely to result from opening-up trade. But the results are extreme. They must be qualified by allowing for at least one non-tradable good (bringing in results from Findlay (1973)) and, in addition, by bringing in at least one sector-specific factor (which generally tends to moderate results, as shown by Neary (1978)). Secondly, if all goods were non-tradable, the story sketched out above would give an indication of results when the capital market is opened up. Here, also, results would be moderated if capital mobility were not perfect and if some non-tradable bonds or equities were introduced. One can then put the two stories together, bearing in mind that, with some non-tradable goods and some non-tradable capital (strictly rights to capital), the Mundell (1957) problem will be avoided.

Two-Country Model

Apart from a brief discussion in section VII the world price ratio has been regarded as given, or as changing exogenously. Thus, while some note has been taken of growth in the rest of the world, a complete two-country growth model has not been presented. There is a literature, pioneered by Oniki and Uzawa (1965), which allows explicitly for growth in two countries that trade with each other. As noted in essay 14, Oniki and Uzawa assumed that the consumption good is identical with the exportable and the investment good with the importable, or vice versa. To that extent the model of essay 14 is more general. In any case, it permits a clear exposition of various ingredients that are more obscure in the various complex two-country models. One might also argue that the small country case is of interest for its own sake.

Further Literature

Attention should be drawn to various papers in this field published since essay 14 was written which are along further or similar lines.

In the main, the literature is surveyed by Findlay (1984) and Smith (1984). See also Smith (1977) for a consolidation of various results in a framework similar to the present paper (mainly the single country approach). Particularly to be noted is Johnson (1971), which appeared in the same book as the original version of essay 14 and dealt with some of the same issues but used different geometry, and Findlay (1973, chs. 6 and 7). Deardorff (1973) and Bertrand (1975) both deal with the gains from trade issue, while Stiglitz (1970) and Fischer and Frenkel (1974) appear to be the two principal two-country neoclassical growth model contributions since Oniki and Uzawa (1965) and Bardhan (1965).

Coming to the central methodological aspect of essay 14, the device of the two-level production structure has been used, as mentioned, by Findlay (1973, ch. 6), and also by Sanyal and Jones (1982). The latter propose a two-tier approach to the whole of trade theory, with an input tier that combines local resources to produce middle products for the world market, while an output tier makes use of traded middle products to produce final consumption goods.

Finally, in section VIII of essay 14 it was suggested that the factor-weight analysis could be applied not only to the effects of the opening up of trade but also to tariff changes, though some doubts about that were expressed in a footnote. Here it must be observed that, after the paper was written, Johnson (1970) showed that a tariff may raise or lower the rate of growth, unless both factors are accumulating at the same rate, the outcome depending in a complex way on the two production functions and the magnitude of the tariff. Thus the factor-weight effect does *not* apply in a simple way to tariff changes, although it is an element in the analysis.

This matter was finally sorted out by Cassing (1983), who has shown that the relative substitution elasticities in production are crucial. For example, if capital is growing faster than labour and the import-competing industry is labour-intensive, a rise in the tariff will lower the rate of growth (the expectation from the factor-weight effect) provided the elasticity of substitution in the import-competing industry is very low relative to that in the export industry. But if the relationship goes the other way, the growth rate could rise as the result of a increase in the tariff.

References

Baldwin, R. E. 1966: The role of capital-goods trade in the theory of international trade. *American Economic Review*, 56, 841–8.

Bardhan, P. K. 1965: Equilibrium growth in the international economy. *The Quarterly Journal of Economics*, 79, 454–64.

Bertrand, T. J. 1975: The gains from trade: an analysis of steady state solutions in an open economy. *The Quarterly Journal of Economics*, 89, 556–68.

Black, J. 1969: Two-level production functions. *Economica*, 36, 310–13.

─── 1970: Trade and the natural growth rate. *Oxford Economic Papers*, 22, 13–23.

Brown, M. 1966: *On the Theory and Measurement of Technological Change.* Cambridge, UK: Cambridge University Press.

Cassing, J. H. 1983: A note on growth in the presence of tariffs. *Journal of International Economics*, 14, 115–21.

Caves, R. E. 1960: *Trade and Economic Structure.* Cambridge, Mass: Harvard University Press.

Corden, W. M. 1956: Economic expansion and international trade: a geometric approach. *Oxford Economic Papers*, 8, 223–8. (Essay 13, this volume.)

─── 1974: *Trade Policy and Economic Welfare.* Oxford: Oxford University Press.

Deardorff, A. V. 1973: The gains from trade in and out of steady-state growth. *Oxford Economic Papers*, 25, 173–91.

Findlay, R. 1973: *International Trade and Development Theory.* New York: Columbia University Press.

―――― 1984: Growth and development in trade models. In R. W. Jones and P. B. Kenen (eds), *Handbook of International Economics: Volume 1*. Amsterdam: North-Holland.

Findlay, R. and Grubert, H. 1959: Factor intensities, technological progress and the terms of trade. *Oxford Economic Papers*, 11, 111–21.

Fischer, S. and Frenkel, J. A. 1974: Interest rate equalization and patterns of production, trade and consumption in a two-country growth model. *The Economic Record*, 50, 555–80.

Johnson, A. S. 1908: Protection and the formation of capital. *Political Science Quarterly*, 23, 220–41.

Johnson, H. G. 1955: Economic expansion and international trade. *The Manchester School of Economic and Social Studies*, 23, 95–112.

―――― 1962: *Money Trade and Economic Growth*. London: Allen & Unwin.

―――― 1970: A note on distortions and the rate of growth of an open economy. *The Economic Journal*, 80, 990–2.

―――― 1971: The theory of trade and growth: a diagrammatic analysis. In J. N. Bhagwati et al. (eds), *Trade, Balance of Payments, and Growth: Papers in International Economics in Honor of Charles P. Kindleberger*. Amsterdam: North-Holland.

Kemp, M. C. 1964: *The Pure Theory of International Trade*. Englewood Cliffs, NJ: Prentice-Hall.

Kindleberger, C. P. 1962: *Foreign Trade and the National Economy*. New Haven: Yale University Press.

Linder, S. B. 1961: *An Essay on Trade and Transformation*. New York: Wiley.

Meade, J. E. 1962: *A Neo-Classical Theory of Economic Growth*. London: Allen & Unwin.

Metzler, L. A. 1949: Tariffs, the terms of trade and the distribution of national income. *Journal of Political Economy*, 57, 1–29.

Mundell, R. A. 1957: International trade and factor mobility. *American Economic Review*, 47, 321–37.

Neary, J. P. 1978: Short-run capital specificity and the pure theory of international trade. *The Economic Journal*, 88, 488–510.

Oniki, H. and Uzawa, H. 1965: Patterns of trade and investment in a dynamic model of international trade. *Review of Economic Studies*, 32, 15–38.

Sanyal, K. K. and Jones, R. W. 1982: The theory of trade in middle products. *American Economic Review*, 72, 16–31.

Smith, A. 1977: Capital accumulation in the open two-sector economy. *The Economic Journal*, 74, 273–82.

―――― 1984: Capital theroy and trade theory. In R. W. Jones and P. B. Kenen (eds), *Handbook of International Economics: Volume I*. Amsterdam: North-Holland.

Solow, R. M. 1956. A contribution to the theory of economic growth. *The Quarterly Journal of Economics*, 70, 65–94.

Stiglitz, J. E. 1970: Factor price equalization in a dynamic economy. *Journal of Political Economy*, 78, 456–88.

Swan, T. W. 1956: Economic growth and capital accumulation. *The Economic Record*, 32, 334–61.

15
Booming Sector and De-industrialization in a Small Open Economy*

This essay attempts to provide a systematic analysis of some aspects of structural change in an open economy. In particular, we are concerned with an increasingly common phenomenon in both developed and developing countries, sometimes referred to as the 'Dutch disease': the coexistence within the traded goods sector of progressing and declining, or booming and lagging, subsectors. In many cases – minerals in Australia, natural gas in the Netherlands, or oil in the United Kingdom, Norway and some members of OPEC – the booming sector is of an extractive kind, and it is the traditional manufacturing sector which is placed under pressure. Hence a major aim of the essay is to explore the nature of the resulting pressures towards 'de-industrialization'.[1] However, our analysis is equally applicable to cases where the booming sector is not extractive (such as the displacement of older industry by technologically more advanced activities in Ireland, Japan or Switzerland). This is so because we are primarily

---

* *The Economic Journal*, 92, Dec. 1982, pp. 825–48. Written jointly with J. Peter Neary. The discussion in the original article of the case where capital is mobile between all three sectors has been excluded. We are indebted to the Institute for International Economic Studies, Stockholm, and the Committee for Social Science Research in Ireland for supporting this research, also to Ronald Jones, two anonymous referees, and participants in seminars at Geneva, Oxford, Renvyle (IAUTE), Sheffield, Stockholm, Vienna (IIASA) and the SSRC Summer Workshop on International Economics (University of Warwick, 1980) for helpful comments.

1. Of course, in many countries, including the United Kingdom, the effects of the booming sector are superimposed on a downward trend in the share of manufacturing in national output due to other reasons. Indeed, prior to the recent appreciation of sterling many British economists saw North Sea oil primarily as a potential source of tax revenue which might be used to cure de-industrialization rather than as a factor contributing to it (see the discussion by Blackaby (1978)). More recently, however, commentators such as Forsyth and Kay (1980) have adopted a general-equilibrium viewpoint closer to ours. See also various papers in Eltis and Sinclair (1981).

concerned with the medium-run effects of asymmetric growth on resource allocation and income distribution, rather than with the longer-run issue of optimal depletion rates which has been the focus of recent work on the economics of exhaustible resources (Dasgupta and Heal, 1979). Moreover, in order to highlight the structural aspects of a boom we ignore monetary considerations and focus on its implications for real rather than nominal variables. We are thus able to draw on and extend the standard tools of international trade theory in order to throw light on the specific problem of a sectoral boom.

The plan of the essay is as follows. Section I introduces the basic framework, which is essentially a variant of the 'dependent economy' model of Salter (1959), producing two traded goods and one non-traded good.[2] This section outlines the various models to be examined and introduces an important distinction between the two principal effects of a boom. The next two sections consider the effects of a boom in one of the traded goods sectors under different assumptions about the factor-market underpinnings of the model. The penultimate section discusses some extensions of the basic model, showing that the tools developed may also be applied to the effects of booms which arise from a variety of exogenous shocks in a small open economy, including a change in world prices. Finally the last section summarizes the essay's principal conclusions, while the appendix sets out the model in algebraic form and gives the derivation of the principal results.

I The Effects of a Boom: An Overview

In this section we set out the main assumptions underlying the analysis and introduce a basic decomposition of the effects of a boom. The framework we adopt is one of a small open economy producing two goods which are traded at exogenously given world prices, and a third non-traded good, the price of which moves flexibly to equalize domestic supply and demand. We label the two traded goods 'energy' X_E and 'manufactures' X_M and the non-traded good 'services' X_S, although in terms of formal structure the models are consistent with many alternative interpretations. For the present we assume that all goods are used for final consumption only, postponing until page 238 a consideration of the case where energy is used as an intermediate input by other sectors.

The questions we address concern the effects of a boom in the energy sector on the functional distribution of income, and on the size and

---

2. In using this model to analyse the effects of a boom in one sector, we draw on and extend the analysis of the Australian case by Gregory (1976), Snape (1977) and Porter (1978), whose general applicability has been noted by Corden (1981b). In particular we build on the contribution of Snape, who presents the same model as that in section II below and anticipates some of our results.

profitability of the manufacturing sector. Although there are many reasons why a boom might occur, we concentrate for much of the essay on the case of a once-and-for-all Hicks-neutral improvement in technology. As we shall see from p. 237 other sources of a boom will have different effects, but the analysis we develop for the simple case is readily applicable to more complicated cases.³

We make two other simplifying assumptions. First, as already noted, the models are purely real ones, and ignore monetary considerations: only relative prices (expressed in terms of the given prices of traded goods) are determined, and national output and expenditure are always equal, so that trade is always balanced overall. (Of course, trade in either one of the two traded goods need not balance, and indeed until p. 238 it is immaterial which of X_E or X_M is imported in the initial equilibrium.) Secondly, we assume that there are no distortions in commodity or factor markets: in particular, real wages are perfectly flexible, ensuring that full employment is maintained at all times. This assumption (which, as noted later, is easily relaxed) rules out the possibility of 'immiserizing growth' for the economy as a whole. Hence the boom must raise potential national welfare and we can focus on the distribution of the gains between different factors.

Our approach in the essay is to consider two real models characterized by different degrees of intersectoral factor mobility. We begin, following Jones (1971) and Snape (1977), by assuming that each of the three sectors uses a single specific factor as well as a factor which is perfectly mobile between sectors. Following traditional usage we refer to the mobile factor as labour and the specific factors as capital, but other interpretations are of course possible: for example, some skill categories of labour may be quite immobile, especially in the short run, while the specific factor in the energy sector can be thought of as including natural resources as well as specific capital. This model has been implicit in much discussion of these issues and yields results which are intuitively plausible.

Later we assume instead that more than one factor is intersectorally mobile, thus introducing a production structure more akin to that of the standard Heckscher–Ohlin model. Even confining attention to the Heckscher–Ohlin categories of capital and labour, there are a number of possible combinations of assumptions which might be considered, and we have chosen to concentrate on one which appears in our view to throw light on particular real-world cases. We examine the case where the energy sector stands on its own, using a specific factor and sharing only labour with the other two sectors, while both capital and labour are mobile between

---

3. Of course, the discovery of new natural resources, typically as a result of previous investment in surveying and exploration activities, is not the same as a costless improvement in technology. Nevertheless, as noted in the introduction, the special issues raised by a natural resource discovery are not necessarily crucial from the point of view of medium-run allocation and distribution problems.

manufacturing and services.[4] This model gives rise to some unexpected results.

Until 'Other Sources of a Boom' (p. 236) the terms of trade are assumed to be given, so that the relative price of the two traded goods, energy and manufactures, does not change. However, the real exchange rate, which we define as the relative price of non-traded to traded goods, can change, a rise in the relative price of the non-traded good (services) corresponding to a real appreciation. Throughout the essay we take manufacturing output as *numéraire* so that factor prices are measured in terms of manufactured goods. However, we are also concerned with changes in the real wage from the point of view of wage-earners, which depend on how the wage rate varies relative to the price of services as well as to the prices of traded goods.

A central feature of the analysis of both models is a distinction between two effects of the boom, namely the resource movement effect and the spending effect. The boom in the energy sector raises the marginal products of the mobile factors employed there and so draws resources out of other sectors, giving rise to various adjustments in the rest of the economy, one mechanism of adjustment being the real exchange rate. This is the resource movement effect. If the energy sector uses relatively few resources that can be drawn from elsewhere in the economy this effect is negligible and the major impact of the boom comes instead (as it has in Britain) through the spending effect. The higher real income resulting from the boom leads to extra spending on services which raises their price (i.e. causes a real appreciation) and thus leads to further adjustments. Clearly the importance of this effect is positively related to the marginal propensity to consume services. In the model used below, with only labour mobile between all three sectors, both effects lead, as expected, to de-industrialization, but this is not inevitable in the more Heckscher–Ohlin-type model used later.

II The Effects of the Boom when Labour is the Only Mobile Factor

Pre-Boom Equilibrium

We begin by describing the pre-boom equilibrium, which corresponds to points A and a in figures 15.1 and 15.2 respectively. Figure 15.1 illustrates the labour market, with the wage rate (in terms of manufactures) measured on the vertical axis and the economy's total labour supply given by the

---

4. Logically there are three possible cases, in each of which one sector has a specific factor and shares only labour with the other two sectors, while both capital and labour are mobile between the remaining two sectors. The sector that stands on its own can be the booming sector itself, as in the present essay, it can be the non-traded good sector, so that traded goods are grouped together; or it can be manufacturing. Long (1983) explores the second case.

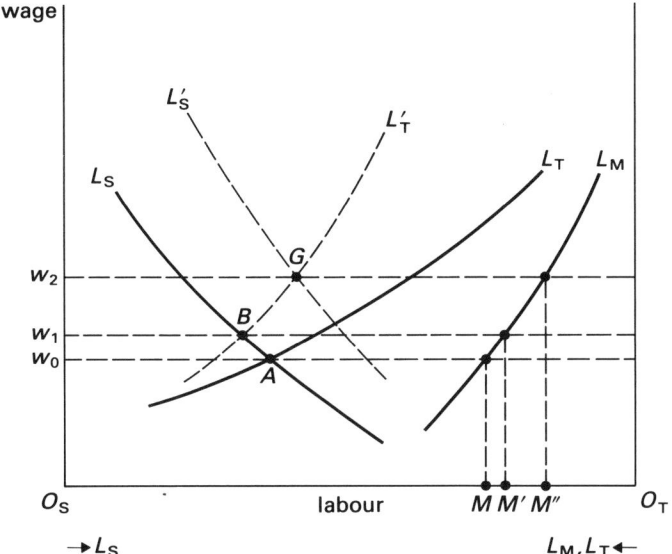

Figure 15.1   Effect of the boom on the labour market.

horizontal axis $O_S O_T$. Labour input into services is measured by the distance from O_S while distances from O_T measure labour input into the two traded-goods sectors. Given the assumptions of the model, the demand for labour in each sector is a decreasing function of the wage rate relative to the price of that sector's output. Thus L_M is the labour demand schedule for the manufacturing sector, and by laterally adding to this the initial labour demand schedule for the energy sector we obtain L_T, the pre-boom labour demand schedule for the two traded-goods sectors combined. Similarly, L_S is the initial labour demand schedule for the services sector, drawn for the initial price of services. Initial full-employment equilibrium is at A, where L_T intersects L_S, and so the initial wage rate is w_0. However, figure 15.1 does not provide a complete illustration of the initial equilibrium, since the profitability of producing services and hence the location of the L_S schedule depend on the initial price of services, which is not exogenous but is determined as part of the complete general equilibrium of the model.

To illustrate how the initial equilibrium price of services is determined, we turn to figure 15.2, which is the familiar Salter diagram with traded goods on the vertical axis and services on the horizontal. Since the terms of trade are fixed, energy and manufacturing output can be aggregated into a single Hicksian composite traded good X_T. The pre-boom production possibilities curve is TS and, in the absence of commodity or factor-market distortions, the initial equilibrium is at point a, where the production possibilities curve is tangential to the highest attainable indifference curve

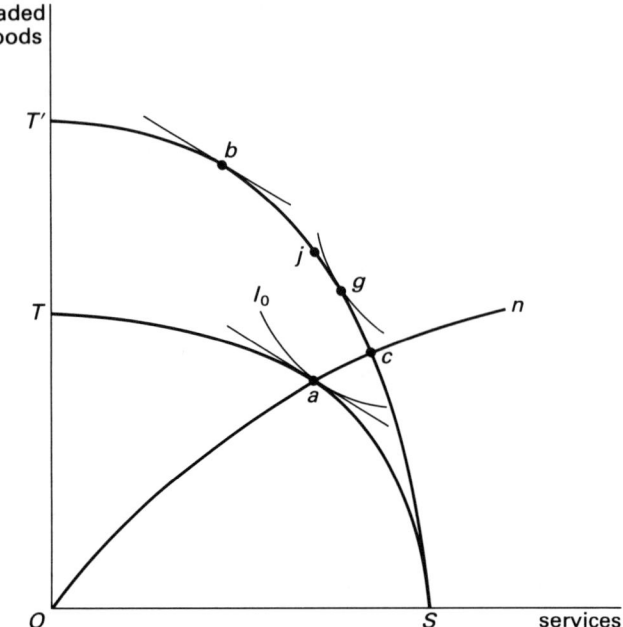

Figure 15.2 Effect of the boom on the commodity market.

I_0. (We use indifference curves as a shorthand way of summarizing aggregate demands, and ignore the well-known fact that changes in income distribution cause them to shift, except under highly restrictive assumptions.) The initial price of services, that is the initial real exchange rate, is thus given by the slope of the common tangent to the two curves at a.

Effects of the Boom on Outputs

Consider now the effects of a boom in the form of Hicks-neutral technological progress in the energy sector. Following the distinction introduced in the last section, we look separately at the resource movement effect and the spending effect in turn. In the case of the resource movement effect we conduct a two-stage analysis: first the real exchange rate (the relative price of services) is held constant, and then it is allowed to vary to restore equilibrium in the market for services. Thus, at the first stage, the curve L_S in figure 15.1 and the price ratio in figure 15.2 are unchanged.

Beginning then with the resource movement effect, the energy sector's labour demand schedule shifts upwards by an amount proportional to the extent of the technological progress: the latter acts in exactly the same way as a price increase, raising profitability and the demand for labour in the energy sector at a given wage rate. This in turn causes the composite labour demand schedule L_T to shift upwards to L'_T, and so a new equilibrium at B is attained. This effect, which raises the wage rate to w_1 at a constant real exchange rate, thus causes labour to move out of both the manufacturing and services sectors. Since employment in manufacturing therefore falls from $O_T M$ to $O_T M'$, we may say that the resource movement effect gives rise to direct de-industrialization. Turning to figure 15.2 the boom does not change the economy's maximum output of services OS, but it raises the maximum output of traded goods from OT to OT'. The production possibilities curve therefore shifts out asymmetrically to $T'S$ and the resource movement effect at a constant real exchance rate is represented by the movement of the production point from a to b. The movement of labour out of the services sector leads to a fall in the output of services and so point b lies to the left of point a.[5]

For the present we wish to abstract from the spending effect, so we assume that the income-elasticity of demand for services is zero, which implies that the income-consumption curve in figure 15.2 is a vertical line through a, intersecting $T'S$ at j. Hence at the initial real exchange rate the resource movement effect leads to excess demand for services. There must therefore be a real appreciation to restore equilibrium: the price of services must rise to eliminate the excess demand, switching demand away from services and dampening the fall in that sector's output induced by the resource movement effect. However, the fall in the services sector's output cannot be reversed: in figure 15.2 the equilibrium following this adjustment must be at some point on $T'S$ between b and j, implying that the output of services is lower than in the initial equilibrium as a result of the resource movement effect.

Next, consider the spending effect on its own. In order to abstract from the resource movement effect we now assume that the energy sector does not use any labour. Hence at the initial real exchange rate the boom has no effect in figure 15.1 (since the curves L_T and L_M coincide) while in figure 15.2 the boom displaces the production possibilities curve vertically upwards, point b lying vertically above point a. Provided the demand for services rises with income (i.e. services are normal in the aggregate), demand at the initial real exchange rate moves along an income-consumption curve such as On, which intersects $T'S$ at point c. Once again, there is excess demand for services at the initial real exchange rate and so a real appreciation must occur. But this time the new equilibrium must lie somewhere between j and c, so that the output of services rises compared with the initial situation.

When the two effects are combined we see that both contribute to a real appreciation: the final equilibrium at point g in figure 15.2 has a higher

---

5. The boom has thus given rise to 'ultra-biased' growth, in the sense that it reduces the output of both other sectors at given commodity prices. Conditions under which this takes place have been explored in different models by Johnson (1955), Corden (1956), Findlay and Grubert (1959) and Neary (1981) among others.

relative price of services than the initial equilibrium at a. However, the resource movement effect tends to lower the output of services whereas the spending effect tends to raise it, and there is no presumption as to which will dominate. (The exact condition is given by equation (15.A.18) in the appendix.)[6] Figure 15.2 illustrates the case where the spending effect is stronger and so point g lies to the right of j.

The same ambiguity of output response does not apply to manufacturing however, as may be seen by returning to figure 15.1. The services sector's labour demand schedule shifts upwards to L'_S because of the rise in the price of services and so the final equilibrium is at point G. As a result the wage rises further to w_2, which reduces manufacturing employment from $O_T M'$ to $O_T M''$. Thus the boom gives rise to both direct de-industrialization, reflected in the fall in manufacturing output from $O_T M$ to $O_T M'$, and now indirect de-industrialization, reflected in the additional fall to $O_T M''$. The former is caused by the resource movement effect alone, while the latter is caused by the real appreciation which results both from the reduced output of services (at the initial real exchange rate) due to the resource movement effect, and from the increased demand for services due to the spending effect. Clearly, since manufacturing employment unambiguously falls, the same must also be true of that sector's output.

Effects of the Boom on Factor Incomes

Consider first the impact of the boom on the real wage. The resource movement effect on its own leads to a fall in the output of services, which is associated with a rise in the wage measured in terms of services. Since, as shown in figure 15.1, the wage measured in terms of traded goods must rise as a result of the resource movement effect, the real wage – which takes account of changes in the prices of all goods consumed by wage-earners – must rise because of the resource movement effect. On the other hand, the spending effect on its own leads to a rise in the output of services and hence to a fall in the wage measured in terms of services. Since the wage in terms of traded goods must rise because of the spending effect (through the mechanism of a real appreciation, as shown in figure 15.1), the real wage may rise or fall because of the spending effect. Thus, when both effects are taken into account, the effect of the boom on the real wage is uncertain. A fall in the real wage is more likely, the stronger is the spending effect relative to the resource movement effect and the greater the share of services in wage-earner's consumption (see equation (15.A.19) in the appendix).

Turning next to the returns to the specific factors in the three sectors, the changes in each of these may be interpreted as measures of the impact of the boom on the profitability of each sector. It is clear that profitability in

---

6. Snape (1977) first showed that the output of non-traded goods may fall even though there must be a real appreciation.

manufacturing must unambiguously fall. Profitability in the services sector would rise if there were only a spending effect, but once the resource movement effect is allowed for, profitability in this sector could fall. This is because the rise in the wage rate relative to the price of services brought about by the resource movement effect squeezes profitability in that sector, and may do so sufficiently to reduce it in terms of traded goods. Of course, if the output of services rises, profitability in services measured in terms of all goods must rise. Finally, in the energy sector, profitability must rise because of the resource movement effect, but it must fall because of the spending effect. The factor specific to the energy sector fails to benefit from the spending effect, because the price of energy is fixed at the world level. It is thus possible for the benefits of the boom to be spread to other factors to such an extent that the owners of the factor specific to the booming sector actually lose.[7] This outcome requires a rather implausible set of parameter values, but is more likely the greater the rise in the wage rate, which means in turn the smaller is the compensated price-elasticity of demand for services and the larger is its income-elasticity of demand (see equation (15.A.20) in the appendix).

Finally, while it is clear that the return to the specific factor in manufacturing must fall in absolute terms, it is not necessarily the case that it must fall relative to the returns obtainable in other sectors. A key issue here is that of factor intensities in terms of value shares, for, if the share of labour in the value of manufacturing output is smaller than that in either of the other sectors, then a given rise in the wage rate reduces its profitability by less than it reduces that in the other sector. For example, if manufacturing is capital intensive relative to services, and if the resource movement effect dominates the spending effect, the boom may raise profitability in manufacturing relative to services. While, if manufacturing is more capital intensive than the energy sector and the spending effect dominates, it is actually possible that profitability in manufacturing could fall by less than in the booming sector (though, as noted already, this outcome requires an implausible combination of parameter values: see equation (15.A.25) in the appendix).

These observations are relevant to the issue of whether the boom necessarily gives rise to de-industrialization. As already pointed out, when this is defined as a fall in output and employment in manufacturing, there must be de-industrialization in this model provided there is any spending or

---

7. This apparent paradox may be understood by noting that it is a case of 'immiserizing growth' accruing to the energy sector. The latter may be viewed (for this purpose only) as a 'mini-economy' exporting energy and importing labour. This mini-economy faces a fixed price of energy but an upward-sloping supply schedule for labour, and since no 'optimal tariff' is imposed on imports of labour we know from standard theory that immiserizing growth (which means in this context a fall in r_E) is possible. Of course, as already noted, immiserizing growth for the economy as a whole cannot take place in this model.

resource movement effect. Furthermore, profitability in manufacturing must fall when measured in terms of traded goods and (when there is any real appreciation) even more when measured in terms of services. In addition, the balance of trade in manufacturing must deteriorate since output falls while home demand necessarily rises (provided manufactures are normal goods). However, as we have just seen, de-industrialization in the sense of a decline in relative profitability need not take place if manufacturing is capital intensive in value share terms so that it is less vulnerable than other sectors to the squeeze on profits induced by the rise in wages. Since it is relative rather than absolute levels of profitability which drive medium-run resource reallocation, we would therefore expect that the impact of the boom in reducing manufacturing output may in some cases be reversed rather than enhanced when capital begins to move between sectors in response to intersectoral differences in returns, and this indeed turns out to be a possibility in the models of the next two sections.

III Effects of the Boom when Capital is Mobile between Two Sectors

In assuming that only one factor was mobile between sectors, the analysis of the previous section was firmly wedded to the short run. In the present section we turn to consider the effects of the boom over a somewhat longer time horizon, assuming that the manufacturing and services sectors draw on a common pool of mobile capital. However, we continue to assume as before that the energy sector uses a specific factor and shares labour only with the other two sectors.

In order to analyse this model, it is helpful to view the manufacturing and services sectors as comprising a miniature Heckscher–Ohlin economy which faces a variable supply of labour equal to the total endowment of labour in the economy less the amount employed in the energy sector. Since this miniature economy exhibits all the conditions for the Stolper–Samuelson theorem, including constant returns to scale and non-specialization, there is a unique relationship between the equilibrium wage rate and the price of services (both, as always, measured in terms of traded goods), which depends only on the technology in the two mobile-capital sectors and so is unaffected by the boom. This relationship is drawn in the left-hand panel of figure 15.3 as an upward-sloping curve, reflecting the assumption that manufacturing is capital intensive relative to services. In the right-hand panel are drawn the supply and demand schedules for services, but these are to be interpreted as general – rather than partial-equilibrium curves. Thus the supply curve X_S (which can be derived from a production possibilities curve such as $T'S$ in figure 15.2) is the outcome of both the reallocation of resources between manufacturing and services and the movement of labour between these two sectors and the energy sector in response to a change in the relative price of services. This curve is

Booming sector and de-industrialization

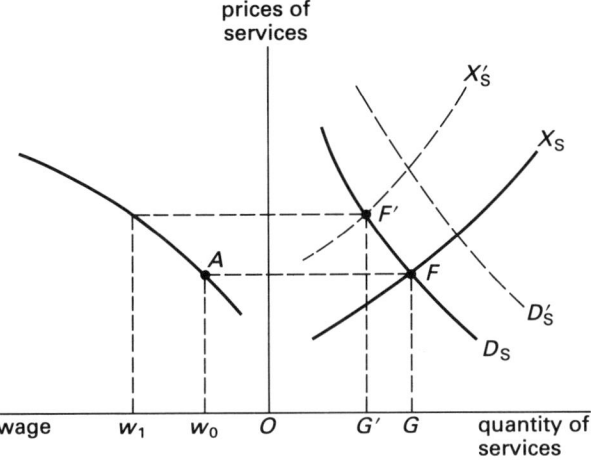

Figure 15.3 *Effects of the boom when capital is mobile between manufacturing and services.*

upward-sloping, reflecting the fact that the supply response of the economy is normal. Similarly, the demand curve D_S is drawn on the assumption that expenditure is always equal to income, where the latter is determined by the production possibilities curve for any given price. The pre-boom equilibrium is represented in figure 15.3 by points A and F.

As in the last section, we begin by considering the resource movement effect of the boom separately. Initially, therefore, we assume a zero income elasticity of demand for services, which eliminates the spending effect and so ensures that the demand curve in figure 15.3 does not shift. At the initial wage rate, the boom raises the energy sector's demand for labour and so reduces the amount available to the two mobile-capital sectors. The effects of this follow from a straightforward application of the Rybczynski theorem: at constant prices the output of the capital-intensive good rises and that of the labour-intensive good falls, as shown by the leftward shift of the services supply schedule in figure 15.3 from X_S to X'_S. The services sector equilibrium moves from F to F'. Output falls from OG to OG', the wage rises from w_0 to w_1 and the price of services rises. However in this model a fall in the output of services must be associated with an *increase* in the output of manufacturing. Hence in this case the resource movement effect gives rise to pro-industrialization![8]

---

8. This result follows from the fact, noted in section II, that if services are labour intensive (in terms of value shares) relative to manufacturing, the resource movement effect raises the return to the specific factor in manufacturing relative to that in services. This generates an incentive for capital to move into manufacturing which leads, in the model of the present section, to a rise in the output of manufacturing. The 'short-run capital specificity' hypothesis assumed here is surveyed by Neary (1978).

Suppose alternatively that manufacturing is labour intensive relative to services. In this case the schedule in the left-hand panel of figure 15.3 is downward-sloping, since a higher relative price of services is now associated with a lower real wage, while in the right-hand panel the boom shifts the supply curve to the right. As before the wage rate rises as a result of the resource movement effect, but this time the output of services rises and the price of services falls. Manufacturing output, which must change as before in the opposite direction to that of services, now falls, a 'normal' case of de-industrialization. The unexpected outcome in this case is that the real exchange rate falls: there is a real depreciation.

Consider next the spending effect of the boom. It gives rise to an outward shift of the demand schedule in figure 15.3 from D_S to D'_S, which unambiguously raises the output and price of services and thus squeezes manufacturing output, irrespective of the relative factor intensities of the two sectors. However, the higher price of services is associated with a higher wage only if services are relatively labour intensive, as in figure 15.3.

TABLE 15.1 RESOURCE MOVEMENT AND SPENDING EFFECTS WHEN CAPITAL IS MOBILE BETWEEN MANUFACTURING AND SERVICES

	Resource movement effect		Spending effect	
$k_M > k_S$	$X_S \downarrow, X_M \uparrow, p_S \uparrow$	$w \uparrow, r_{MS} \downarrow$	$X_S \uparrow, X_M \downarrow, p_S \uparrow$	$w \uparrow, r_{MS} \downarrow$
$k_M < k_S$	$X_S \uparrow, X_M \downarrow, p_S \downarrow$			$w \downarrow, r_{MS} \uparrow$

k_i, Capital–labour ratio in sector i.
r_{MS}, Rental on capital used in manufacturing and services.

All these conclusions are summarized in Table 15.1. In general the results are quite similar to those reached in the previous section. In particular, when manufacturing is relatively capital intensive the changes in prices are unambiguous and in the 'expected' directions, and the same is true of the changes in outputs when manufacturing is relatively labour intensive. However, in certain cases the two effects work in opposite directions, giving rise to the possibility of the three counter-intuitive results just mentioned.

IV Other Sources of a Boom

We have concentrated so far on one particular source of a boom in the energy sector, an exogenous Hicks-neutral technological improvement, but the analysis, and especially the distinction between spending and resource movement effects, may fruitfully be applied to other sources of structural change. To illustrate this, we begin by considering two relatively straightforward applications. First, if the source of the boom is not technological change but an exogenous inflow of foreign capital into the energy sector, then the resource movement effects are qualitatively identical to those considered earlier. However, to the extent that the additional rental income accruing to the energy sector is repatriated the spending effect of the boom is diluted. Secondly, if the boom is due to technological improvement as before, but there is initial unemployment due to downward rigidity of real wages, the manufacturing sector is effectively insulated from the effects of the boom, since the expanding energy sector can draw on the pool of unemployed labour without bidding resources away from other sectors. (Of course, this conclusion would have to be modified if we introduced monetary considerations, since de-industrialization could still come about in this case as a result of a nominal appreciation: see Neary (1984).)

In the remainder of this section we consider three other applications which raise slightly more complex issues.

Non-neutral Technological Progress

Whether or not technological progress is unbiased in the Hicks-neutral sense, it unambiguously raises real national income, and so the spending effect operates in a manner similar to that examined in earlier sections. However, the same is not true of the resource movement effect. When capital is assumed to be specific to the energy sector, it is possible for technological progress to be sufficiently labour-saving that it could reduce rather than increase that sector's demand for labour at the initial wage.[9] The various resource movement effects then go into reverse.

A Rise in Energy Prices

As noted earlier, Hicks-neutral technological progress has exactly the same effects on the level of profitability and the factor demands of the energy sector as an equivalent increase in energy prices. Hence the resource movement effects of the latter are exactly as considered in earlier sections. However, the same is not true of the spending effect, since a change in energy prices affects national income differently from an improvement in technology, and also has a substitution effect on the demand for services. The substitution effect works in the expected direction (tending to raise demand for services) provided energy and services are net substitutes in

---

9. As shown by Neary (1981), a necessary condition for this outcome is that the price elasticity of supply in the energy sector be less than one.

consumption (i.e. provided their compensated cross-price elasticity of demand is positive); while the sign of the spending effect depends on whether energy is an export or an import good. For example, if energy is a net import, a rise in its world price amounts to a worsening of the home country's terms of trade, so reversing the spending effect examined in earlier sections. For the prospective British situation, with oil likely to remain a net export for some time, the spending effect is on balance probably positive and so (assuming plausibly that energy and services are net substitutes) the effects of a world oil price rise are similar to those of an oil discovery.

A Rise in Energy Prices when Energy is an Intermediate Input[10]

The analysis just given of the effects of a rise in energy prices applied to the case where there is a domestic energy-producing sector and energy is used for final consumption only. However, if energy is also used as an intermediate input, a rise in its price will have additional effects. Fortunately, these effects may easily be studied using the tools developed earlier, once it is recognized that, by reducing profitability in energy-using sectors, a rise in energy prices is exactly analogous in its effects to an exogenous deterioration in technology, that is to technological regress.[11] In particular, the reduction in profitability reduces the demand for factors of production by energy-using sectors, giving rise to a negative resource movement effect. It is clear that the effects of this exogenous shock raise no new analytic issues, although the combined outcome of the expansionary effects of the energy boom itself and the contractionary effects resulting from its impact on energy-using sectors depends to an even greater extent than before on the relative magnitudes of different parameters. As far as the central issue of de-industrialization is concerned, however, there is no ambiguity provided manufacturing is intensive in its use of energy: the reduced profitability brought about by the rise in input prices reinforces the effects already considered in tending to depress manufacturing output and employment.

V Summary and Conclusion

This essay has analysed the effects on resource allocation, factoral income distribution and the real exchange rate of a boom in one part of a country's

10. Bruno and Sachs (1979) present an analysis of an energy price rise which resembles ours in a number of respects.
11. The analogy between technological regress and an input price increase has been drawn by Malinvaud (1977). If more than one factor is mobile, the analogy becomes strained unless energy is separable in production from labour and capital. However, the analytic problems to which non-separability gives rise are well known from the literature on effective protection and need not detain us here.

traded goods sector. In the simplest of the models considered, which assumed that only labour was mobile between sectors, de-industrialization (a decline in the non-booming part of the traded goods sector, assumed here to be manufacturing) was shown to follow in most of the usual senses of the term, including a fall in manufacturing output and employment, a worsening of the balance of trade in manufacturing and a fall in the real return to factors specific to the manufacturing sector (though not necessarily in their return relative to those of factors specific to other sectors). Furthermore, it was shown in this model that the boom gives rise to a real appreciation, that is a rise in the relative price of non-traded relative to traded goods. (This outcome is sometimes blamed as an independent cause of de-industrialization though, as our analysis shows, it should more properly be seen as a symptom of the economy's adjustment towards the new post-boom equilibrium.) However, in the later model, which allowed for intersectoral mobility of more than one factor, it was shown that some of these outcomes could be reversed.

The analysis of the essay has been conducted subject to many limiting assumptions, including a concern with real and not nominal magnitudes, absence of international capital mobility and (except in the previous section) continual full employment. However, the analysis we have presented, and in particular the key distinction between the resource movement effect and the spending effect of the boom, would remain important ingredients in a more complete analysis of the issues arising from the 'Dutch disease', or of the policy implications of natural resource development. Among other omissions from our analysis, we note particularly that we have assumed that the income gains from the boom are spent by the factors that directly gain real incomes. In reality, however, since a large part of the rents accruing to specific factors in the booming sector are typically paid in taxes, the manner in which the government spends its extra revenues is a crucial element in determining the magnitude and direction of the spending effect. We have also not touched on the issue of whether a deliberate policy of preventing a real appreciation – that is a policy of exchange-rate protection designed to protect the traded goods sectors – should be pursued.[12] In addition, it should be noted that the manufacturing sector of a country may include some non-traded as well as traded goods sectors, so that the decline of the sector as a whole because of a resource boom is by no means inevitable.[13] Finally, the various effects we have considered must be superimposed on a background of general

12. Such a policy would have to be accompanied by an appropriate monetary or fiscal accommodation. See Corden (1981a, 1981b) and Neary (1984). Corden (1981a) explores the relationship between real wage rigidity and exchange-rate protection. Furthermore, the spending effect of a sectoral boom in the presence of nominal wage and money supply rigidities is analysed. Naturally, it becomes possible for total employment to vary, and the nominal exchange rate becomes determinate.
13. The same outcome follows if manufacturing is assumed to be a traded good but it faces a downward-sloping world demand schedule. This is the assumption made by

Appendix

Preliminaries: The Markets for Labour and Services

In both models labour is assumed to be fully employed at all times. Following Jones (1965), this may be written as follows, where a_{ij} denotes the quantity of factor i used per unit of output in sector j

$$a_{LE}X_E + a_{LM}X_M + a_{LS}X_S = L \qquad (15.A.1)$$

In addition, it is assumed that the market for services always clears. The demand for services may be written in differential form as a function of changes in the price of services and in the level of real income y

$$\hat{C}_S = -\epsilon_S \hat{p}_S + \eta \hat{y} \qquad (15.A.2)$$

We use a circumflex to denote a proportional rate of change (e.g. $\hat{y} \equiv d\ln y$); ϵ_S and η are the compensated own-price elasticity and the income elasticity of demand respectively. Except in the penultimate section of this essay, the only source of a change in real income is the technological improvement in the energy sector. Hence

$$\hat{y} = \theta_E \pi \qquad (15.A.3)$$

where θ_E is the share of the energy sector in national income and π is the Hicksian measure of the extent of technological improvement (and so measures the proportional increase in energy output holding constant the employment of all factors in that sector). Substituting (15.A.3) into (15.A.2), the demand for services may thus be written as

$$\hat{C}_S = -\epsilon_S \hat{p}_S + \eta \theta_E \pi \qquad (15.A.4)$$

The Model with Labour as the Only Mobile Factor

In the model of the second section of the text, (15.A.1) is supplemented by full-employment equations for each of the three sector-specific stocks of 'capital'

Buiter and Purvis (1982), although since their model does not have a resource movement effect and they consider only two sectors, the real appreciation following a domestic resource discovery does not affect the steady-state output of the manufacturing sector in their model.

Booming sector and de-industrialization

$$a_{Kj}X_j = K_j \quad (j = E, M, S) \tag{15.A.5}$$

Using (15.A.5) to eliminate output levels from (15.A.1) and totally differentiating the latter (keeping in mind that the endowments of all factors are fixed) yields

$$\lambda_{LE}(\hat{a}_{LE} - \hat{a}_{KE}) + \lambda_{LM}(\hat{a}_{LM} - \hat{a}_{KM}) + \lambda_{LS}(\hat{a}_{LS} - \hat{a}_{KS}) = 0 \tag{15.A.6}$$

where λ_{ij} is the proportion of factor i used in sector j. The expressions in parentheses in (15.A.6) may be related to the change in the real wage facing each sector by invoking the definition of the elasticity of substitution between labour and capital

$$\hat{a}_{Lj} - \hat{a}_{Kj} = -\sigma_j(\hat{w} - \hat{r}_j) \quad (j = E, M, S) \tag{15.A.7}$$

and the price-equal-to-unit-cost equations

$$\hat{p}_E = \theta_{LE}\hat{w} + \theta_{KE}\hat{r}_E - \pi \tag{15.A.8}$$

$$0 = \theta_{LM}\hat{w} + \theta_{KM}\hat{r}_M \tag{15.A.9}$$

$$\hat{p}_S = \theta_{LS}\hat{w} + \theta_{KS}\hat{r}_S \tag{15.A.10}$$

where θ_{ij} is the share of factor i in the value of output in sector j and $\hat{p}_M$ is zero by choice of *numéraire*. Substituting all these equations into (15.A.6) with p_E assumed constant until section IV, and simplifying yields

$$\hat{w} = \xi_E \pi + \xi_S \hat{p}_S \tag{15.A.11}$$

where ξ_j is the proportional contribution of sector j to Δ, the wage elasticity of the aggregate demand for labour

$$\xi_j \equiv \frac{1}{\Delta} \lambda_{Lj} \frac{\sigma_j}{\theta_{Kj}} \quad (j = E, M, S) \tag{15.A.12}$$

$$\Delta \equiv \lambda_{LE} \frac{\sigma_E}{\theta_{KE}} + \lambda_{LM} \frac{\sigma_M}{\theta_{KM}} + \lambda_{LS} \frac{\sigma_S}{\theta_{KS}}$$

Turning to the market for services, their supply in this model depends only on the real wage facing entrepreneurs in that sector

$$\hat{X}_S = \phi_S(\hat{p}_S - \hat{w}) \tag{15.A.13}$$

where ϕ_S, the price elasticity of supply, equals $\sigma_S \theta_{LS}/\theta_{KS}$. Equating demand and supply of services, (15.A.4) and (15.A.13), therefore yields

$$(\phi_S + \epsilon_S)\hat{p}_S = \phi_S\hat{w} + \eta\theta_E\pi \qquad (15.A.14)$$

Equations (15.A.11) and (15.A.14) may now be solved jointly for the effects of the boom on p_S and w

$$A\hat{p}_S = (\eta\theta_E + \phi_S\xi_E)\pi > 0 \qquad (15.A.15)$$

$$A\hat{w} = [\eta\xi_S\theta_E + (\phi_S + \epsilon_S)\xi_E]\pi > 0 \qquad (15.A.16)$$

where

$$A \equiv \phi_S(1 - \xi_S) + \epsilon_S > 0 \qquad (15.A.17)$$

The expression $(\phi_S + \epsilon_S)$ is the compensated elasticity of excess supply of services at a given wage rate, while A is the same elasticity when the change in w induced by a change in p_S is taken into account. Clearly, both of these elasticities of excess supply must be positive.

Some other comparative-static effects may now be derived. First, the change in the real (product) wage in the services sector (which determines the change in that sector's output and employment levels) is given by

$$A(\hat{w} - \hat{p}_S) = [-\eta\theta_E(1 - \xi_S) + \xi_E\epsilon_S]\pi \qquad (15.A.18)$$

Next, if α_S is the share of services in the consumption basket of wage-earners, then the change in the real wage from their standpoint is

$$A(\hat{w} - \alpha_S\hat{p}_S) = \{\eta\theta_E(\xi_S - \alpha_S) + \xi_E[\phi_S(1 - \alpha_S) + \epsilon_S]\}\pi \qquad (15.A.19)$$

Finally, (15.A.15) and (15.A.16) may be combined with (15.A.8), (15.A.9) and (15.A.10) to determine the changes in the rentals on specific capital in each sector

$$\theta_{KE}A\hat{r}_E = [-\eta\xi_S\theta_{LE}\theta_E + \phi_S(1 - \theta_{LE}\xi_E - \xi_S) + \epsilon_S(1 - \theta_{LE}\xi_E)]\pi \qquad (15.A.20)$$

$$\theta_{KM}A\hat{r}_M = -\theta_{LM}[\eta\xi_S\theta_E + \xi_E(\phi_S + \epsilon_S)]\pi < 0 \qquad (15.A.21)$$

$$\theta_{KS}A\hat{r}_S = [\eta(1 - \theta_{LS}\xi_S)\theta_E + \xi_E(\theta_{KS}\phi_S - \theta_{LS}\epsilon_S)]\pi \qquad (15.A.22)$$

Also of interest are the change in the rental in the energy sector relative to the price of services

$$\theta_{KE}A(\hat{r}_E - \hat{p}_S) = [-\eta\theta_E(\xi_S\theta_{LE} + \theta_{KE}) + \phi_S\xi_M + \epsilon_S(1 - \theta_{LE}\xi_E)]\pi \qquad (15.A.23)$$

and the change in the rental differential between the manufacturing and energy sectors

$$\theta_{KE}\theta_{KM}(\hat{r}_E - \hat{r}_M) = \theta_{KM}\pi + (\theta_{LM} - \theta_{LE})\hat{w} \quad (15.A.24)$$

Substituting from (15.A.16) for $\hat{w}$ this becomes

$$\theta_{KE}\theta_{KM}A(\hat{r}_E - \hat{r}_M) = \{\eta\xi_S\theta_E(\theta_{LM} - \theta_{LE}) + \phi_S(\theta_{KE}\xi_E + \theta_{KM}\xi_M) \\ + \epsilon_S[\theta_{KE}\xi_E + \theta_{KM}(1 - \xi_E)]\}\pi \quad (15.A.25)$$

All these results may be related to the discussion in the text by noting that η determines the magnitude of the spending effect and ξ_E that of the resource movement effect. If both of these parameters are zero then the increase in r_E is proportional to π and no other domestic variables are affected by the boom.

The Model with Capital Mobile between Two Sectors

In the model of the third section, with capital mobile between the manufacturing and service sectors, the rentals in these two sectors (r_M and r_S) must be equal. Writing r_{MS} for the common value of the rentals, equations (15.A.9) and (15.A.10) may be manipulated to obtain a relationship between the wage rate and the price of services (both, it will be recalled, measured in terms of manufactures)

$$|\theta|\hat{w} = -\theta_{KM}\hat{p}_S \quad (15.A.26)$$

where $|\theta|$ is the determinant of the matrix of factor shares in the manufacturing and services sectors, and is positive if and only if manufacturing is more labour intensive than services

$$|\theta| \equiv \theta_{LM} - \theta_{LS} = \theta_{KS} - \theta_{KM} \quad (15.A.27)$$

Equation (15.A.26) is illustrated in the left-hand panel of figure 15.3. Note that, from the Stolper–Samuelson theorem, the change in p_S determines the direction of change in the real wage, however defined

$$|\theta|(\hat{w} - \hat{p}_S) = -\theta_{KS}\hat{p}_S \quad (15.A.28)$$

Turning to factor allocations and output levels, in this model equation (15.A.5) continues to hold for the energy sector but for the other two sectors it is replaced by

$$a_{KM}X_M + a_{KS}X_S = K_{MS} \quad (15.A.29)$$

The total stock of capital available to the two sectors K_{MS} is given, but the amount of labour available is not, since it equals the economy's endowment of labour less the amount in use in the energy sector. To reflect this it is convenient to rewrite (15.A.1) as

$$a_{LM}X_M + a_{LS}X_S = L_{MS} \tag{15.A.30}$$

where

$$L_{MS} = L - L_E \tag{15.A.31}$$

But L_E in turn depends only on the wage rate and on the level of technology in the energy sector (since p_E is held constant)

$$\hat{L}_E = \frac{\sigma_E}{\theta_{KE}}(\pi - \hat{w}) \tag{15.A.32}$$

(This result may be obtained by combining (15.A.8) with equations (15.A.5) and (15.A.7) for the energy sector.) Differentiating (15.A.31) and substituting from (15.A.32) therefore yields the labour supply function facing the two mobile-capital sectors

$$\hat{L}_{MS} = E_{Lw}(\hat{w} - \pi) \tag{15.A.33}$$

where the labour supply elasticity is non-negative and is defined as

$$E_{Lw} = \frac{\lambda_{LE}}{1 - \lambda_{LE}} \frac{\sigma_E}{\theta_{KE}} \tag{15.A.34}$$

We may note that when this elasticity is zero there is no resource movement effect in this model.

Equations (15.A.29) and (15.A.30) combined with (15.A.33) define a standard Heckscher–Ohlin economy facing a variable supply of labour. Using the approach of Jones (1965) and Martin and Neary (1980) the model may be solved for the general-equilibrium services sector supply function (which is illustrated in the right-hand panel of figure 15.3)

$$\hat{X}_S = \bar{E}_S \hat{p}_S + \frac{\lambda_{KM}}{|\lambda|} E_{Lw} \pi \tag{15.A.35}$$

where $|\lambda|$ is the determinant of the matrix of factor allocations to the manufacturing and service sectors, and is positive if and only if manufacturing is relatively labour intensive

$$|\lambda| \equiv \lambda_{LM} - \lambda_{LS} \tag{15.A.36}$$

(Since there are no factor–market distortions by assumption, $|\lambda|$ and $|\theta|$ must have the same sign.) The term $\bar{E}_S$ is the general-equilibrium price elasticity of supply of services taking account of the variability of labour supply. It is related to (and, by the Le Chatelier–Samuelson principle, larger than) the corresponding fixed labour supply elasticity E_S as follows

$$\bar{E}_S = E_S + \frac{\lambda_{KM}\theta_{KM}}{|\lambda||\theta|} E_{Lw} \qquad (15.A.37)$$

where E_S itself is a complicated function of the elasticities of substitution and other parameters of the manufacturing and service sectors.

Equating demand and supply of services, (15.A.4) and (15.A.35), we may solve for the effect of the boom on the price of services

$$B\hat{p}_S = \left(\eta\theta_E - \frac{\lambda_{KM}}{|\lambda|} E_{Lw}\right)\pi \qquad (15.A.38)$$

where

$$B \equiv \bar{E}_S + \epsilon_S \qquad (15.A.39)$$

is the general-equilibrium elasticity of excess supply of services and is necessarily positive. Equation (15.A.38) may be substituted in (15.A.35) to find the change in the output of services. However, we are more interested in the change in the output of manufacturing, which by a series of derivations similar to those which led to (15.A.35) may be shown to equal

$$\hat{X}_M = -\bar{E}_M\hat{p}_S - \frac{\lambda_{KS}}{|\lambda|} E_{Lw}\pi \qquad (15.A.40)$$

where $\bar{E}_M$ is defined analogously to $\bar{E}_S$ and is positive. Substituting from (15.A.38) for $\hat{p}_S$ (and making use of the fact that $\lambda_{KM}\bar{E}_M = \lambda_{KS}\bar{E}_S$) yields the required result

$$B\hat{X}_M = -\left(\eta\theta_E\bar{E}_M + \epsilon_S\frac{\lambda_{KS}}{|\lambda|} E_{Lw}\right)\pi \qquad (15.A.41)$$

References

See p. 266.

16
Booming Sector and Dutch Disease Economics: Survey and Consolidation*

This essay aims to consolidate the growing literature on booming sector economics and the Dutch disease. The term Dutch disease refers to the adverse effects on Dutch manufacturing of the natural gas discoveries of the 1960s, essentially through the subsequent appreciation of the Dutch real exchange rate.[1] The essay also aims to fill some theoretical gaps, notably in the sections dealing with immigration (p. 252); endogenous terms of trade effects (p. 254); domestic absorption (p. 255); and dynamics (p. 259). The issues have been widely discussed in many countries, especially the oil exporters. The key article in the British discussion on the effects of North Sea oil is that of Forsyth and Kay (1980).[2]

Booming sector models can also illuminate many historical episodes where there have been sectoral booms, with adverse general equilibrium effects on other sectors. Thus there is wide scope for application in economic history. For example, Forsyth and Nicholas (1981) have interpreted the consequences on Spanish industry of the inflow of American

---

* *Oxford Economic Papers*, 35, Nov. 1984, pp. 359–80, slightly abbreviated.
1. The first printed reference to the term, I have found, is in the article 'The Dutch Disease' in *The Economist*, 26 November 1977, pp. 82–3. A fuller account of the Dutch case, including Dutch policy discussion, is given by Ellman (1981). Incidentally, it might be argued that the true Dutch disease in the Netherlands was not the adverse effects on manufacturing of real appreciation but rather the use of booming sector revenues for social service levels which are not sustainable, but which it has been politically difficult to reduce.
2. Early papers are McKinnon (1976) on Kuwait, and Gregory (1976) and Snape (1977) on Australia. Enders and Herberg (1983) draw attention to an early paper on Norway – Eide (1973), in Norwegian – and the issues have been discussed, for example, in OECD reports on Norway. Several articles in the *Bulletin of Indonesian Economic Studies* have dealt with the issues. The international literature in this field is extensive, and a fairly comprehensive list is given in the references. A general book referring to the 'oil or industry' issue with respect to Canada, Mexico, the Netherlands, Norway and Britain, is that of Barker and Brailovsky (1981).

Booming sector and Dutch disease   247

treasure in the sixteenth century in Dutch disease terms. Cairnes (1859) recognized that the gold discoveries in Australia in the 1850s had Dutch disease effects on some Australian industries, and this episode has been studied by Maddock and McLean (1984).

I The Core Model: Spending Effect and Resource Movement Effect

The starting point here is the core model, presented in the first two sections of essay 15. There are three sectors, the booming sector B, the lagging sector L and the non-tradable sector N. The first two produce tradables facing given world prices. Output in each sector is produced by a factor specific to that sector, and by labour, which is mobile between all three sectors and moves between sectors so as to equalize its wage in all three employments. Measured in terms of L the wage is W and the three rents are R_b, R_l and R_n. All factor prices are flexible and all factors are internationally immobile.

A boom in B has the initial effect of raising aggregate incomes of the factors initially employed there. This boom can be thought of as happening in one of three ways: (1) There has been a once-for-all exogenous technical improvement in B, represented by a favourable shift in the production function, this improvement being confined to the country concerned; (2) there has been a windfall discovery of new resources (i.e. increase in supply of the specific factor); (3) B produces only for export, with no sales at home, and there has been an exogenous rise in the price of its product on the world market relative to the price of imports. Unless indicated otherwise, we shall have case (1) in mind below.

Spending Effect

If some part of the extra income in B is spent, whether directly by factor owners or indirectly through being collected in taxes and then spent by the government, and provided the income elasticity of demand for N is positive, the price of N relative to the prices of tradables must rise. This is a real appreciation. It will draw resources out of B and L into N, as well as shifting demand away from N towards B and L.

In figure 16.1 the vertical axis shows P_n, namely the price of N relative to that of L. The supply curve is derived from the transformation curve between N and the two tradables. The demand curve shows the demand for N at various prices of N when expenditure is always equal to income.[3]

---

3. Since income depends on output, the demand curve is not independent of the supply curve. For a particular price ratio we draw the budget line tangent to the transformation curve, this determining supply of N. This also fixes income in terms of tradables or in terms of N at that price. Demand for N is then determined by the chosen consumption point at that price ratio and income level.

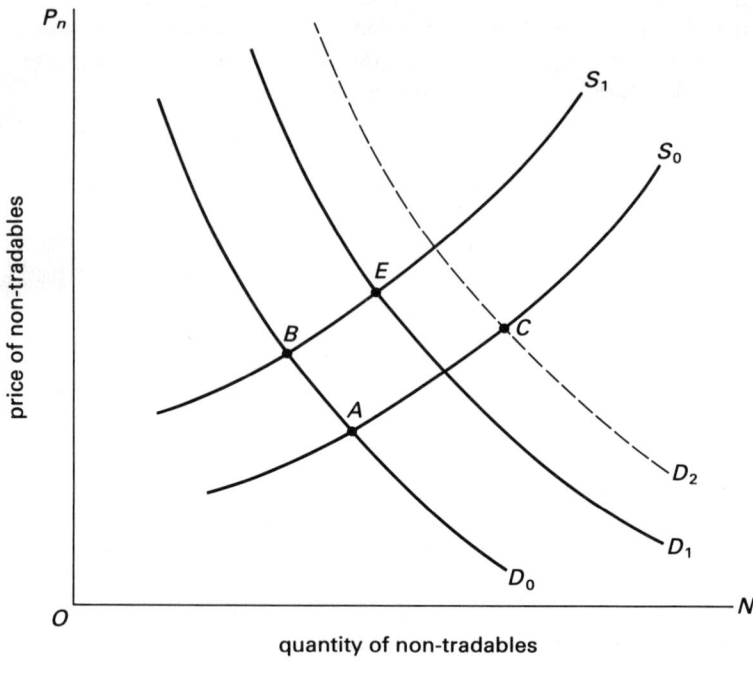

Figure 16.1

The spending effect has shifted the demand curve from D_0 to D_1 and thus has raised P_n, drawing resources out of L into N.

Resource Movement Effect

In addition, the marginal product of labour rises in B as a result of the boom so that, at a constant wage in terms of tradables, the demand for labour in B rises, and this induces a movement of labour out of L and out of N. This effect has two parts.

1) The movement of labour out of L into B lowers output in L. This can be called direct de-industrialization because it does not involve the market for N and thus does not require an appreciation of the real exchange rate.

2) There is a movement of labour out of N into B at a constant real exchange rate. This is represented in figure 16.1. The resource movement effect has shifted the supply curve from S_0 to S_1, and thus creates excess demand for N additional to that created by the spending effect, and so brings about additional real appreciation. Thus it brings about an additional movement of labour out of L into N, reinforcing the de-industrialization resulting from the spending effect. The two effects combined, leading to a movement of labour from L to N, bring about indirect de-industrialization,

which supplements the direct de-industrialization that resulted from the movement of labour from L to B. As is evident from figure 16.1, the output of N could finally be higher or lower than initially. The spending effect tends to make it higher and the resource movement effect to make it lower.[4]

There is a complication concerning the relationship between the spending effect and the resource movement effect. This was not discussed in essay 15. It concerns the effects that a changed income distribution at a constant price of N has on spending on N.

The spending effect on its own is unambiguous, since (to isolate it) it is assumed that no labour is employed in B (or any labour is specific): hence, before P_n rises, the income of only one factor changes, all extra spending thus coming out of R_b. But the resource movement effect, before P_n changes, raises W, and lowers R_l and R_n. Spending on N out of R_b and W will rise and out of R_l and R_n will fall. Only in the special case where the marginal propensities to spend on N are the same and positive for all factors will the spending effect be independent of the resource movement effect, and must it always be positive. This was the assumption implicit in essay 15.

In the general case, with marginal propensities differing, the spending effect will depend on the resource movement effect via income distribution. When the marginal propensities to spend on N of initial losers are sufficiently higher than of gainers, the spending effect could actually be negative.

As noted in essay 15, there are various factoral income distribution consequences of a boom in this core model. Both spending and resource movement effects lower the real rents of the specific factor in L, this being the essential problem of the Dutch disease, at least as seen from the point of view of this factor. In addition, both effects raise the wage W defined in terms of L, because both increase the demand for labour. But P_n rises, so – bearing in mind that wage-earners also consume N – there is a question whether the 'true' real wage W^* (the real wage defined in terms of a consumption basket of tradables and N) rises or falls. The answer is unambiguous in the case of the resource movement effect: since output of N falls as a result of that effect, the real wage in terms of N – that is W/P_n – must rise, and since W also rises, W^* must then rise. On the other hand the spending effect causes N to rise, and hence W/P_n to fall, so that, with W having risen, W^* could have risen or fallen. Finally, the real rent in N could rise or fall.

4. The various model-building papers listed in the bibliography can be classified by whether they have a spending effect only, or whether they also have a resource movement effect. Spending effect only: Gregory (1976), McKinnon (1976), Forsyth and Kay (1980), Buiter and Purvis (1982), Bruno and Sachs (1982), Corden (1981a), van Wijnbergen (1982, 1984a, 1984b), Eastwood and Venables (1982), Enders and Herberg (1983). Both effects: Snape (1977), Stoeckel (1979), Long (1983), Corden and Neary (1982), Neary and Purvis (1981, 1982), Cassing and Warr (1985).

It has to be underlined that the lagging sector can be producing both non-boom exportables and importables, and it need not consist only of manufacturing industry. In Australia and Nigeria, for example, a significant component would be producing tradable agricultural products. The term 'de-industrialization' can thus be misleading (with a major effect possibly being de-agriculturalization), and should be regarded as no more than shorthand. Furthermore, if products are subject to binding quantitative restrictions, so that their domestic prices are not determined by world market prices, but rather by domestic demand and supply conditions, they should be treated as non-tradables even though they are potentially tradable. It might also be noted that locally-produced manufactures are often close but not perfect substitutes for imports. They might be thought of as containing both a tradable and a non-tradable element so that they could, on balance, be beneficiaries from the spending effect.

The core model can be varied in numerous ways, so that none of the outcomes can be regarded as inevitable. We now introduce a number of complications.

II The Paradox Model: More than One Factor Intersectorally Mobile

Let us now suppose that more than one factor is mobile between at least two of our three main sectors. Of the various possibilities, one case was presented in detail in essay 15 and will be called here the paradox model. As in the core model, B has its own specific factor and labour is mobile between all three industries. But this time capital is mobile between the two non-boom industries, L and N. Thus these two industries both employ labour and capital in varying proportions, making up a mini-Heckscher–Ohlin economy, one industry being capital intensive and the other labour intensive.

As was shown in essay 15, within this particular structure the resource movement effect can have some paradoxical results. At a constant real exchange rate it will cause the output of the capital-intensive industry to expand, this being the result of the movement of labour out of the mini-Heckscher–Ohlin economy into B because of the boom. If L happens to be the capital-intensive industry there will then be a tendency to pro-industrialization because of the resource movement effect. Of course this can be offset by the spending effect which, through the mechanism of real appreciation, will move both capital and labour from L into N. But, on balance, output of L could expand. It was also shown that, if N happened to be the relatively capital-intensive industry in the paradox model, the boom could cause a real depreciation.

III Decomposition of the Lagging Sector

Similar factors operate when the lagging sector is decomposed into several industries and, in addition, more than one factor is allowed to be mobile between its component industries. It is then perfectly possible that some of the non-boom tradable industries actually expand even though the sector as a whole contracts.

Consider the following case from Snape (1977) and Cassing and Warr (1985). The sector consists of M and X, both of which employ labour and capital, both these factors being mobile between the two industries but employed in different proportions to each other. (Thus the lagging sector makes up a mini-Heckscher–Ohlin economy). In addition labour is used in B and N, as in our core model, and B and N each have a specific factor. The boom brings about the usual movement of labour out of the lagging sector as a whole. But this time there will be a rearrangement within the lagging sector. With the stock of capital for the sector as a whole fixed and the amount of labour reduced, it follows from Rybczynski (1955) that the labour-intensive industry will contract output but the capital-intensive industry will expand.

IV International Capital Mobility

A move in the direction of realism is to allow for some degree of international capital mobility. Consider the simple case where each sector employs sector-specific capital but each of the three kinds of capital is internationally mobile to some extent. Thus capital does *not* move between industries, but there is some degree of *international* mobility for each type of capital.

First it is necessary to note what happens to rents in the core model – that is when the supply of the specific factor (the capital stock) is fixed in each sector. Rents in L fall, rents in B are likely to rise (and must rise when measured in terms of tradables), while rents in N could go either way, but would rise if output of N rose. Assume now that, before international capital mobility, rents in L fall and in B and N rise, output moving in the same direction as rents.

International capital mobility will then lead to a flow of capital *out of L* but into B and N. This will reinforce the output effects but moderate the effects on returns to capital. De-industrialization will be greater but the adverse effects of the boom on profitability in the lagging sector will be less because of the capital outflow. In the case of N capital mobility will make the supply curve more elastic and so lead to a further rise in output as well as moderating the real appreciation required for restoration of equilibrium.

The extreme case of a perfectly elastic supply of capital from the rest of the world is worth noting as a limiting case. Consider first L. In this case the rate of return on capital in L will not fall at all, the whole adjustment to the boom being through a fall in output. Given our assumption that there are only two factors in L – internationally mobile capital and intersectorally mobile labour – and if, in addition, there are constant returns to scale, the wage in terms of L – that is W – must then also stay unchanged. Coming to N, perfect capital mobility would actually fix the price of N in terms of tradables, at least (again) if there are only two factors employed in N and there are constant returns to scale. In other words, the supply curve for N is horizontal, all changes in demand being absorbed by output changes. There is then no possibility of a real exchange rate change.

V Immigration

Some degree of migration in response to booms is very common, especially when there are regional booms and the migrants come from other parts of the country – as can be found in the history of Brazil, Canada and the United States. But the following analysis was inspired by the issues raised by Maddock and McLean (1984), which deal with the effects of the Australian gold rushes in the middle of the nineteenth century, when massive immigration resulted.

It was shown in section I that in the core model the boom may raise the 'true' real wage W^*. Both the spending effect and the resource movement effect must raise W (the wage in terms of tradables); bearing in mind that P_n rises, the spending effect could raise or lower W^*, while the resource movement effect must raise it. Let us now assume that W^* does rise and that this attracts migrants until W^* is again restored to where it was before the boom. The subsequent analysis is, of course, relevant for the case where W^* is not fully restored as a result of migration.

First, let us consider the effects of immigration on its own, working within the assumptions of the core model. At constant P_n migration will increase both demand for and supply of N. In general one cannot say which will increase more, and thus whether immigration will lead to real appreciation or depreciation. Finally output of both L and of N will be greater than before migration, and R_b and R_n will thus be higher.[5]

This raises the interesting question whether migration could fully offset the de-industrialization effects of the boom by fully restoring the output of L. In fact, could there be an overshooting effect, with L finally being higher than originally? A related question is whether P_n must be fully restored, or could even fall relative to the pre-boom situation.

The change in output of L depends on what happens to W (an increase in W leading to a fall in L), so the principal question is whether the

---

5. This is not necessarily so in the paradox model. If L is labour intensive relative to N, output of N at a constant P_n will fall as a result of immigration.

Booming sector and Dutch disease

restoration of W^* to its pre-boom level implies a rise, fall or constancy of W. The simple answer – to be expounded below – is that if there were no extra demand for N either as a result of the spending effect (i.e. if this effect were zero) or as a result of migration – that is there were no migrants' spending effect – then restoration of W^* would also lead to restoration of W and of P_n. But provided there is some spending effect, or migrants' spending effect, the restoration of W and of P_n will not be complete even when sufficient migrants have come in to restore W^*. Thus some de-industrialization remains, essentially because of the extra demand for non-tradables. Overshooting is not possible.

First it should be noted that a constant W^* requires the fulfilment of one of three conditions as follows:

$$\hat{P}_n = \hat{W} = 0, \quad \hat{N} = 0 \tag{16.1}$$

$$\hat{P}_n > \hat{W} > 0, \quad \hat{N} > 0 \tag{16.2}$$

$$\hat{P}_n < \hat{W} < 0, \quad \hat{N} < 0 \tag{16.3}$$

where the hats indicate the proportional change from the pre-boom to the post-boom post-migration situation. This says that a rise in the real wage in terms of tradables, that is $\hat{W} > 0$, must be associated with a fall in terms of non-tradables, that is $\hat{P}_n > \hat{W}$, and vice versa. Furthermore, when the real wage in terms of non-tradables falls, output of N must rise, and vice versa.

Let us first assume that there is a resource movement effect, but neither kind of spending effect – that is, there is no extra demand for N at a given P_n either as a result of the boom or of the migration. Thus in figure 16.1 the demand curve stays at D_0. The resource movement effect of the boom shifts the supply curve from S_0 to S_1, bringing equilibrium from A to B. Migration then shifts the supply curve back again, so that, as the migrants come in, equilibrium moves along D_0, and P_n falls. The movement will stop when W^* is back where it was. It can be readily shown that only at A will this condition be fulfilled. Before A is reached, $\hat{P}_n > 0$ but $\hat{N} < 0$, while beyond A, $\hat{P}_n < 0$ but $\hat{N} > 0$, so conditions (16.2) and (16.3) cannot be fulfilled. Thus the resource movement effect will exactly restore the product and factor prices of the pre-boom situation provided migration restored the real wage W^*. It might be noted that this would also be the result of capital inflow if the mobile factor were capital, rather than labour.

Now let us introduce the two spending effects. The spending effect of the boom shifts the demand curve to D_1, while the migrants' spending effect shifts it further, say to D_2. At C output of N and P_n must be higher than at A, even though P_n need not be higher than at E (i.e. migration on its own could raise or lower P_n). Comparing C with A we note that the real wage in terms of N must have fallen, since output of N has risen; hence W, the real wage in terms of tradables, must have risen. Thus condition (16.2) is fulfilled. With W higher, L must be lower at C than at A, so that some de-industrialization must remain.

Before leaving the subject of migration, one might also note the 'Alberta case', described by Helliwell (1981). The rents from the booming sector may go primarily to the government, then being redistributed to the population in the form of tax reductions, improved public facilities and so on. This attracts migrants seeking to share in the rents. These migrants will tend to go into both N and L, so that output of L (and rents in that sector) could recover, as well as a real appreciation being moderated or even avoided. This effect operates even when the pre-tax (and constant public facilities) real wage W^* stays constant before migration. In various historic episodes of regional or even national booms one might expect that migration was induced both by the rise in W^* – the gold rush effect – as well as by the Alberta effect.

VI Endogenous Terms of Trade Effects

The small country assumption can now be removed, even though we return to the assumption of a fixed national factor stock. As mentioned earlier, the boom may have been caused by an exogenous terms of trade improvement, that is rise in the price of B. Now we want to allow for an endogenous terms of trade change. This will have two parts to it.

Firstly, extra exports of B owing to technical progress in B or any other reason may lower the world price of B. This is an obvious effect, and we can suppose that it has already been incorporated in the calculation of the size of the boom. We now assume that the country is small in the world market for the booming sector product, say oil, so that P_b is given.

The second part of the terms of trade effect is concerned with what happens within the lagging sector. It is now necessary to distinguish exportables from importables. The lagging sector is assumed to produce both importables M (which are perfect substitutes for imports) and exportables X. The term 'exportables' is used here only for lagging sector products; in addition there are, of course, exports of the booming sector product. We use P_m as the *numéraire*, and the question is what happens to P_x. It will be shown that it is likely to rise, at least in an extended core model, so that there will be an endogenous terms of trade improvement.

At constant prices the demand for X will rise owing to the spending effect. This refers to spending on X, rather than on N, as elsewhere in this essay. Staying within an extended core model (with X and M *each* now having a specific factor, and labour mobile to all four industries), output of X will fall owing to the resource movement effect; this is direct de-industrialization. There will thus be excess demand not only for N (as in the core model) but also for X, and both prices will rise. The fact that P_n has to rise – that is that there will be a real appreciation expressed in terms of P_m – strengthens the rise in P_x. This is another way of saying that the real appreciation raises demand for, and reduces supply of, X in the way shown in the simple version of the core model with respect to the effect on L.

The presumption of an endogenous terms of trade improvement is somewhat reduced in an extended version of the model discussed in section III where the lagging sector was decomposed. The lagging sector as a whole becomes more capital intensive as labour moves into the booming sector and (after P_n has risen) into N. If, within the lagging sector, X is capital intensive relative to M, then at constant P_x output of X would *rise*, and output of M fall even more, an example of the Rybczynski (1955) effect. The net result of higher output of X, even with increased demand for X, as before, could be excess supply of X and thus a fall in P_x.[6]

VII Domestic Absorption Effect

So far we have assumed that the booming sector product is wholly exported. Let us now allow for the case where part of it is consumed at home and where the source of the boom is an exogenous rise in the world price. We return to the small country model. Thus we are now considering the effects of an oil price rise on an exporting country. The procedure is to superimpose on the core model a domestic absorption effect – namely the effect of the price rise of a product that is produced and sold at home, even though the actual price may be determined in the world market. There will only be such an effect if the price to domestic consumers is actually allowed to rise, whether partly or wholly, in line with the world price.

It is useful to keep the domestic absorption effect separate from our main analysis for two reasons. Firstly, the basic booming sector analysis is more general, also applying to products where there is no significant home consumption and to booms that do not originate in a price rise. Secondly, even in the case of the oil price rise – to which the domestic absorption effect is particularly relevant – many exporting countries have detached domestic from world price changes, sometimes not raising the price of oil to domestic consumers at all, and sometimes raising it after a lag or to a lesser extent than the world price rise. An analysis which assumes that domestic prices always move with world prices would not allow for such cases.

Booming Sector product as a final consumption good

Initially we assume that the product is a final consumption good, not an

---

6. There is also the possibility of a fall in the demand for X at constant P_n if the marginal propensities to consume X out of R_b and out of W are less than that out of returns to capital. At this point the standard theory of the effects of biased growth on the terms of trade is relevant. See essay 13 and the Further Notes to that essay.

input. We are now looking *only* at the effects of a higher price for home sales, not of exports.

First we consider the spending effect. The booming sector is taxing consumption of product B by the rest of the economy. There will be a positive spending effect out of R_b and a negative spending effect out of the other factors. If the marginal propensities to spend on N were the same out of R_b as out of R_l, R_n and W combined, there would be no net spending effect as a result of the domestic absorption effect. But if the marginal propensities to spend on N differed, the net spending effect could go either way, leading finally to real appreciation or depreciation. To these income effects must be added a substitution effect: the higher price of B faced by domestic consumers may lead to substitution in favour of L and N, this increasing the likelihood of appreciation.

Finally, the resource movement effect will be exactly the same as in the core model: the marginal product of labour in B will initially rise relative to that in L and N. The resource movement effect of the home price rise must then be added to the resource movement effect of the export price rise, so that the various source allocation and income distribution effects will be greater than in the core model.

Oil as intermediate good

The matter is more complicated once we allow the booming sector product to be an input into L and N, rather than a final consumption good. B will now be called oil. This time consumers are not directly affected, even though they will be indirectly affected through a change in P_n. As before, there is a positive spending effect out of R_b. With a higher price of oil, values added per unit (the effective prices, as distinct from the nominal prices) in L and N are squeezed at a constant price of P_n, so that R_l, R_n and W fall, leading to a negative spending effect from these sources. As earlier, the positive and negative spending effects may or may not cancel out.

The resource movement effect will be greater than when oil was a final consumption good. Not only does the marginal productivity of labour in B rise, but it falls in L and N owing to the declines in the two effective prices.

In addition there are two substitution effects. Firstly, there may be a resource movement effect between L and N if one is more oil intensive than the other. Thus output of N at constant P_n will tend to rise if N is relatively less oil intensive, and in that case the real appreciation will finally be less. Secondly, L and N will tend to be substituted for oil, this adding to the rise in demand for N and thus the tendency to real appreciation.

VIII Classical Unemployment

In the models presented so far all factor prices have been flexible, so involuntary unemployment has been ruled out. We now allow for 'classical' unemployment resulting from real wage resistance. There are plausible cases where the boom would increase unemployment, and others where it would reduce it. The general principle is the same in all cases. If the boom would have raised the real wage in the flexible-factor price model, then with a rigid real wage it would reduce unemployment instead, while if it would have reduced the real wage in the flex-price model, it would generate unemployment in the fix-price case. Two interesting cases will now be considered.

Unemployment in the Lagging Sector

Suppose that some types of labour are specific to the lagging sector in the medium run at least, and practise real wage resistance. This case has been in the forefront of Dutch disease discussion. If the real wage were flexible it would fall, both because of the movement of mobile factors into other sectors and because of the rise in P_n even with no intersectoral factor movements. With real wage resistance of the specific factors the Dutch disease then manifests itself, partly at least, in extra unemployment of such factors. Unemployment would be intensified if workers in the lagging sector actually sought real wage *increases* so as to maintain their wage relative to those of workers specific to the booming sector, where market forces will have raised real wages.[7]

Unemployment in Non-Tradables: Foreign Exchange Constraint

A very interesting case yields a result that is the opposite of the previous one. Suppose that N is produced mainly by labour specific to non-tradables. We focus on the spending effect. In the flex-price case the boom will raise the real wage of such labour (i.e. raise R_n in the core model) because the demand for non-tradables has gone up. Now introduce real wage resistance and initial unemployment. The spending effect will then increase employment in that sector. Combining this with real wage resistance of labour specific to the lagging sector, there is then a *positive* employment effect in the non-tradable sector and a *negative* employment effect in the lagging sector.

This result can be related to the popular 'foreign exchange constraint' model.[8] Suppose that there are simply two sectors, an exporting booming

---

7. Nankani (1979) has noted this problem for a number of developing mineral-exporting countries: high real wages in their minerals sectors tended to spread to the rest of the economy (in spite of some wage dualism and low employment levels in minerals) and then generate unemployment.
8. Various papers by Thirlwall contain or imply such a model. See, for example, Thirlwall (1980). This approach is applied to the Australian case by Shann (1982), where further references are given. I am indebted to this paper for making me aware of the relevance of this approach.

sector distinct from the rest of the economy (so that there is no potential resource movement effect), and a domestic output sector which produces for the home market and within which there are no relative price changes. We can imagine the non-tradable sector to have expanded at the expense of the lagging sector until the latter has disappeared. The nominal price of domestic output is fixed, perhaps as a result of a fixed nominal wage combined with a fixed percentage profit margin and constant returns. There is initially unemployment and a fixed nominal exchange rate. If the real wage were flexible downwards, full employment combined with continuous balance of payments equilibrium could be obtained with nominal demand expansion combined with appropriate devaluation (or a floating exchange rate that would depreciate as a result of the expansion). But real wage resistance prevents this: the expectation that nominal wages would increase to compensate for the devaluation-induced rise in import prices in domestic-currency terms rules out an exchange rate change and lies behind a fixed exchange rate policy.

Demand expansion to increase employment is thus prevented by adverse balance of payments effects – that is the 'foreign exchange constraint'. Additional export income resulting from the boom, if spent on non-tradables, will then expand this constraint and allow extra demand expansion.

While this sort of model is usually presented in 'foreign exchange constraint' terms (implying that the problem could be solved with import controls) the key assumption, often only implicit, is real wage resistance. Furthermore, because of its assumption of rigid prices it is sometimes thought of as being 'Keynesian', though real wage resistance is, of course, a thoroughly non-Keynesian assumption.

IX Keynesian Unemployment

The experience of Britain in 1980 and 1981 generated interest in a case where a money supply rigidity (because of the pursuit of money growth targets) is associated with a boom or the expectation of it. Combining this with *nominal* wage rigidity downwards (and thus having two nominal rigidities) it is then possible to get Keynesian unemployment through a number of channels. In all cases the unemployment could be remedied by increasing the money supply. The boom can thus give rise to short-term unemployment caused essentially by a failure of monetary policy.[9]

---

9. See Corden (1981a), Eastwood and Venables (1982), Neary and van Wijnbergen (1984) and Neary (1984), all concerned with employment effects when the money supply is fixed. Short-run monetary aspects ('transitional dynamics') of a boom are also analysed by Turnovsky (1983).

X Dynamics: Spending, Saving and Investment

So far the analysis has been static. The rise in the value of output and hence income of the booming sector, the spending effect, the resource movement effect, and hence the real appreciation, have all happened at the same time. The balance of payments on current account (strictly the balance of trade) has stayed constant, at zero. Of course this was not so during the process of capital inflow, but our analysis in section IV was, in fact, timeless, the outcome, rather than the process of capital inflow being described.

In fact, output, expenditure, resource movements, the exchange rate and the current account may follow particular time paths, the paths differing with the source of the boom and the expectations about it. Before going into details, a general picture can be given.

Changes in Spending and the Current Account

The spending effect may anticipate, or alternatively follow with a lag, the rise in the value of output of B. This spending effect will bring about real appreciation and Dutch disease effects as indicated in our static analysis. The resource movement effect could also anticipate, but is more likely to follow with a lag, the initial rise in output; it will, of course, raise output further, and will bring about further real appreciation and Dutch disease consequences. The current account outcome is the net result of the spending and the value of output changes.

Changes in the current account need not coincide with changes in the real exchange rate. For example, in period 1 (the announcement period) spending may rise to a new, higher, level owing to the expectation of a boom, in period 2 (the boom period) output (or its value in foreign currency terms) may rise, surpassing the new spending level, and in period 3 output may fall again – the boom having been temporary – while spending may continue at its higher level. In periods 1 and 3 there will thus be a current account deficit – with decumulation of financial assets – and in period 2 a surplus, with financial asset accumulation. There will be a once-for-all real appreciation in period 1 owing to the spending effect, a further real appreciation in period 2, and a depreciation in period 3, the last two changes attributable to the resource movement effect.

Spending reflects both consumption spending and domestic investment. For the moment let us assume that domestic investment does *not* change, and just concentrate on changes in consumption and in the value of output, assuming rational behaviour by public and private decision makers.

The outline just presented applies to a temporary oil price rise in the case of an oil exporting country ('oil' representing any booming sector product that is exported). In period 1 (the announcement period) the price rise is expected, so consumption rises, in period 2 (the boom period) the price actually rises, and in period 3 the price falls back again. It will be rational to run current account deficits (relative to what would have happened otherwise) in periods 1 and 3, and a surplus in period 2. The precise pattern of consumption over time will depend on the world rate of interest and intertemporal time-preferences along Fisherian lines. The rise in spending may take place with a lag, and may vary with expectations about the future price pattern. Mistakes can be, and have been, made, and one can also imagine overshooting tendencies while the learning process is still going on.

If the price rise is expected to be permanent there is no case for running so large a surplus in period 2, nor a deficit in period 3; rather consumption should rise more initially, with a greater deficit in period 1, and there should be surpluses to offset this in later periods. A once-for-all technical improvement that is expected to retain its value permanently, or the discovery of a new resource that is believed to be inexhaustible, will have the same sort of effect as an oil price rise expected to be permanent.

Exhaustible Resource

Consider now the discovery of an exhaustible resource. A rational response to the discovery in the announcement period would be a rise in consumption, even before any of the resource is extracted. But there is likely to be uncertainty about the size of the resource, not to speak of the price at which it can be sold. This uncertainty will be reduced or will disappear once actual output takes place; hence risk-averse behaviour is likely to involve some positive response of consumption to actual output, so that the whole of the rise in spending may not take place in the announcement period.

Optimal output decisions will depend on the considerations familiar, in the optimal depletion literature.[10] Essentially it is a matter of optimally converting assets under the ground or the sea into foreign financial assets (or reduced foreign liabilities), achieving at any point in time an optimal portfolio taking into account current and expected prices of the two assets. At the same time the rise in consumption will be financed by reducing foreign assets. The resource movement effect will, again, tend to depend on the actual rise in output (i.e. exhaustion of the resource).

Domestic Investment: Productivity Effect and Portfolio Effect

Finally, let us allow for changes in domestic investment. There are two

---

10. See Dasgupta and Heal (1979) and literature cited therein. Dasgupta, Eastwood and Heal (1978) specifically consider the optimal depletion issue in the open economy. They find that if the rate of return on foreign assets is exogenous (essentially a small country assumption, since the country faces a given asset price) the depletion rate should be independent both of the discount rate and of the elasticity of marginal utility.

distinct effects to be considered here, the productivity effect and the portfolio effect.

In the core model rents of specific capital have risen in the booming sector, fallen in the lagging sector, and may have risen in the non-tradables sector. The expected productivity of new investment in the three sectors will change commensurately, so that appropriate investment responses result. With a world capital market, freedom of capital movements and a given world rate of interest, such investment or disinvestment will manifest itself in the current account.

Let us assume now that the favourable booming sector effects on total investment dominate. There will thus be a rise in investment in the announcement period, hence bringing about a greater rise in output in later periods. In fact, no rise in physical output is likely to be possible as a result of technical progress, and no extraction of resources, without such prior investment. In the case of an oil price rise the boom need not await prior investment; in that case the extent of investment will depend, among other things, on how temporary the price rise is expected to be. This increase in domestic investment thus adds to the spending effect, and hence the real appreciation and the current account deficit, in period 1.[11]

Next we come to the portfolio effect. So far we have assumed that savings are invested on a world capital market where foreign and domestic financial assets are perfect substitutes and their prices are given to the small country. Extra savings are invested in foreign financial assets, while borrowing to finance investment comes from this same capital market, the two types of transactions being quite independent. The net result is reflected in the current account. We now allow realistically for the case where foreign and domestic assets are not perfect substitutes and the small country concerned wishes to maintain a balanced portfolio. For given productivity of domestic investment and a given world rate of interest it will wish to invest some of its increased savings abroad and some at home. A complication is that accumulations and decumulations of foreign financial assets can take place quickly, while domestic investment in real assets requires lead time and cannot be varied so readily.

This consideration suggests that in period 2, when foreign financial assets are being accumulated, there will also be extra domestic investment to maintain a portfolio balance; the spending effect will then be higher and the current account surplus less. In period 3 there would be domestic disinvestment, along with decumulation of foreign assets (relative to the non-boom path). In parallel, one might expect that there would also be

---

11. The distinction between the investment boom and the later export boom has been important in Australian discussion. See Corden (1982). In addition, an expected export boom, and hence an expected appreciation, is likely to generate speculative capital inflows. This effect was probably operative in both Britain and Australia. It has not been incorporated in the analysis in this paper, but has been noted in the various analyses of the British case, and is analysed in detail by Turnovsky (1983).

domestic disinvestment in the announcement period 1, so reducing the current account deficit. But the 'lead-time' consideration suggests otherwise: the expectation of the boom may lead to such portfolio-balancing investment beginning already in period 1. All this is very relevant for public investment. As Gelb (1981) shows, the capital-importing oil exporters plunged into public investment in periods 1 and 2. This led to large rises in the demand for non-tradables. In retrospect, at least, there was overshooting in public spending, leading eventually to budget deficits.

XI Protection of the Lagging Sector

It is natural that governments will be urged to protect the lagging sector, or parts of it, from the adverse effects of a boom. We now assume that resource depletion and spending decisions have been made, taking into account optimal saving and investment considerations as perceived by the private sector and policy makers, and that these decisions have not been influenced by considering the adverse effects on the lagging sector. The question is whether policies should be further adjusted to reduce the adverse impact on the lagging sector, that is actually to *protect* it. Three arguments for protection appear relevant.

1) The 'conservative social welfare function' argument (Corden, 1974) is that real income or rent losses to particular factors resulting from an unexpected shock should be avoided. The case against is that such a redistribution objective is better pursued directly, by taxing the booming sector factor and using the revenue to subsidize losing factors of production, and that, in any case, conservatism is a doubtful basis for a social welfare function.

2) The employment argument can be made when there is real wage resistance in the lagging sector. The case against is that it would be better to subsidize employment directly, and that short-term unemployment may be needed as a signal to induce a desirable resource reallocation.

3) A version of the infant industry argument might apply when the boom is expected to be temporary and the decline and later recovery of the lagging sector are thought to lead to non-optimal decumulation of physical and human capital during the boom period. The qualifications to this argument are the same as those that apply to the infant industry argument in general: the validity of the argument requires externalities, lack of information or foresight on the part of factors in the lagging sector, or imperfection of the capital market.

If it is nevertheless desired to protect the lagging sector to some extent, the first-best method would be to subsidize output of the sector directly, perhaps financing the subsidy from the taxes levied on the specific factor in the booming sector. Two popular protectionist approaches are thus plainly inferior.

The first is exchange rate protection, (discussed more fully in essay 17), namely a policy of avoiding real appreciation, and hence protecting tradables at the expense of non-tradables. The objections, compared to direct subsidization of the lagging sector, are that it would lead to excessive accumulation of foreign assets and that it would protect not only the lagging sector but also the booming sector.

The other widely advocated policy is to increase ordinary protection by raising tariffs or tightening import quotas. The avoidance of a loss to import-competing industries will then be at the expense of lagging sector exportables as well as of the booming sector. The lagging sector exportables will then be hit twice; first by the real appreciation (which will now be greater than before) and then by the direct resource loss to importables. The adverse effect on importables will have been moderated only by intensifying the adverse effect on lagging sector exportables. If the main concern is with conserving real incomes or rents then it is clearly not a logical policy.

Appendix

Trade Reversal and Britain's North Sea Oil

If the preceding analysis is applied to an oil boom it could be interpreted as referring either to the effects of an oil discovery at a given world price of oil, to a rise in the price of oil when oil is an exportable, or to a combination of the two. But when oil is and stays an importable an actual or expected rise in the price of oil would have a negative wealth and hence spending effect. Let us now consider the more complex and much-discussed British case: first there was the discovery of oil reserves implying various potential levels of profitable output at various price levels for a limited period. Then there were the oil price rises. The combined effect was to turn oil from an importable into an exportable.[12]

Let P_0 be the original oil price relative to the general price-level – that is the level ruling before 1973 – while P_1 is the higher price now, assumed to stay at the new level. While there was actually a limited period when oil

---

12. I follow here the main argument of Bank of England (1982) and Byatt et al. (1982). See also Flemming (1982). These papers – as well as Forsyth and Kay (1981) – also discuss the indirect effects on the British real exchange rate of a redistribution of world income away from countries that compete with the UK as exporters. See also Bond and Krobl (1982) on the UK case.

    The central argument that the simple Dutch disease model does *not* apply to the UK seems quite convincing, in spite of Forsyth and Kay (1980) and others, including the present writer in earlier incarnations. One should also note Niehans (1981) who seems to have shown that the severe UK real appreciations of 1979 and 1980 can be explained mainly by a monetary squeeze, not Dutch disease effects.

    It is also possible that some part of the real appreciation was explained by over-optimistic expectations about oil exports.

had been discovered and yet the price had not risen, to simplify here we suppose that there are three periods, namely period I before the discovery and the price rise, period II beginning with the discovery and the price rise and ending when the oil runs out, and the oil-less period III.[13]

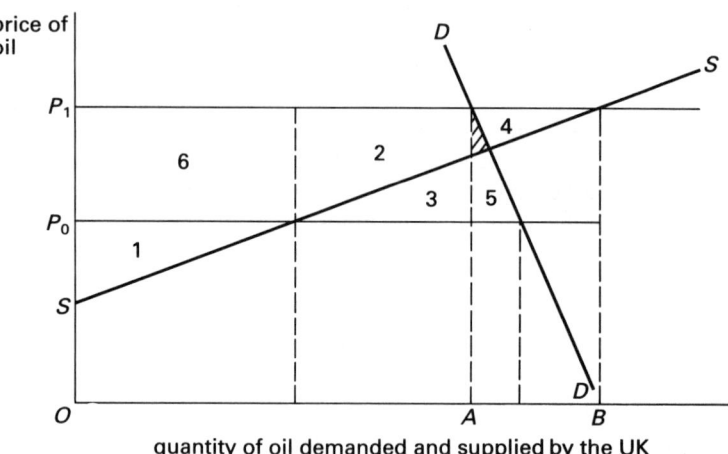

Figure 16.2 (Note that the shaded triangle is included both in area 4 and in area 5.)

Figure 16.2 represents period II for Britain. The oil demand curve DD is drawn for the aggregate expenditure level appropriate for that period. The supply curve SS indicates the marginal cost of North Sea oil at various levels of output. Before the oil discovery this curve did not exist (or was infinitely high). While in period I oil was wholly imported, in period II there are exports of AB. On the oil which replaces imports there is a gain of area 1, less area 3, while there is a loss of area 5 owing to reduced consumption of oil (including the higher costs of alternative energy sources). On exports the gain is area 4. Thus there could be a gain or loss compared to period I. The usual estimates now being made suggest that there would be a clear loss, essentially because North Sea oil is substantially dearer to produce than the pre-1973 imports it replaced (i.e. area 3 is greater than area 1 and area 1 may, in fact, be non-existent), while exports are not expected to be high.

It follows that the net result has been to reduce UK real income in period II relative to period I. This is so even though most of the surplus (areas

---

13. At the beginning of period 2 expectations change both with respect to potential output at various prices and with respect to future prices. It is not just the actual current price rise that is relevant, but the expectations regarding all prices for the future.

1 + 6 + 2 + 4) will end up as tax revenue. In period III, of course, real income will fall further, namely by the whole of this surplus. With wealth (i.e. expected future income) suddenly reduced at the end of period I, spending should fall to a lower level. Spending would be below income in period II and above it in period III if the aim is to even out the path of spending (though it might stay above it transitionally at the beginning of period II). Hence a current account surplus should be expected in period II and a deficit in period III. Some of the savings of period II would go to finance domestic investment so that the spending level would not fall as much as would be the case if all savings were in foreign financial assets.

The surprising result has thus emerged that equilibrium in Britain required a fall in spending and hence a real depreciation, implying *pro*-industrialization in terms of our simple model. There is no Dutch disease problem for Britain! It should be added that the resource movement effect can probably be ignored in the case of oil, since the use by the oil industry of domestic inputs, including labour, would be low in relation to their use by the rest of the economy. Directly imported inputs – including capital – do not, of course, have any resource movement effect. On the other hand, there is a resource movement effect through the expansion of substitutes.

Can one take an alternative view? One approach is to suppose that the economy has adjusted to the oil price rise (or the expectation of a price rise) in period I, this adjustment presumably including a fall in spending and a real depreciation; and then the effects of the emergence of North Sea oil at the beginning of period II are analysed. This second stage is a normal 'boom' situation, leading to higher spending, real appreciation and the Dutch disease, always compared to period I. The more period III (when the boom is at an end) is discounted, the greater the increase in spending and hence the appreciation in period II will be. The objection to this approach in the case of Britain is that the expectation of the price rise did not clearly come before the oil discoveries.

Another approach is based on the expectation that Britain will become a substantial net exporter so that, in due course, period II will yield an income gain relative to period I. Provided period III is sufficiently discounted the combined effects of the price rise and the development of North Sea oil could then lead to a *rise* in spending in period II and hence to real appreciation and the Dutch disease.[14]

---

14. When I discussed the UK North Sea oil issue in Corden (1981b), a paper first written in 1978, I took for granted that the UK would become a large exporter, so that Dutch disease problems should be expected. The same view lay behind the approach of Corden (1981a). These papers were written under the influence of optimistic assessments of North Sea oil prospects current in 1978 and 1979. Of course, the widely shared optimism at the time may help to explain the actual sterling real appreciation, which turned out to be excessive in retrospect.

References

Bank of England 1982: North Sea oil and gas: costs and benefits. *Quarterly Bulletin* March, 56–73.
Barker, T. and Brailovsky, V. (eds) 1981: *Oil or industry? Energy, industrialisation and economic policy in Canada, Mexico, the Netherlands, Norway and the United Kingdom*. London: Academic Press.
Blackaby, F. (ed.) 1978: *De-industrialisation*. London: Heinemann.
Bond, M. E. and Krobl, A. 1982: Some implications of North Sea oil for the U.K. economy. *IMF Staff Papers*, 29, 363–97.
Bruno, M. and Sachs, J. 1979: Macroeconomic adjustment with import price shocks: real and monetary aspects. Institute for International Economic Studies, University of Stockholm, Seminar Paper No. 118.
―――― 1982: Energy and resource allocation: a dynamic model of the Dutch disease. *Review of Economic Studies*, 49, 845–59.
Buiter, W. H. and Purvis, D. D. 1982: Oil, disinflation and export competitiveness: a model of the Dutch disease. In J. Bhandari and B. Putnam (eds), *Economic Interdependence and Flexible Exchange Rates*. Cambridge, Mass: M.I.T. Press.
Byatt, I. et al. 1982: North Sea oil and structural adjustment. Government Economic Service Working Paper No. 54 (March), London: HM Treasury.
Cairnes, J. E. 1859: The Australian episode. *Frazer's Magazine*. Reprinted in F. W. Taussig (ed.) 1921: *Selected Readings in International Trade and Tariff Problems*. New York: Ginn and Company.
Cassing, J. H. and Warr, P. G. 1985: The distributional impact of a resource boom. *Journal of International Economics*, 15.
Corden, W. M. 1956: Economic expansion and international trade: a geometric approach. *Oxford Economic Papers*, 8, 223–8. (Essay 13, this volume.)
―――― 1974: *Trade Policy and Economic Welfare*. Oxford: Oxford University Press.
―――― 1981a: The exchange rate, monetary policy and North Sea oil: the economic theory of the squeeze on tradeables. Oxford Economic Papers, 33, 23–46.
―――― 1981b: Exchange rate protection. In R. N. Cooper et al. (eds), *The International Monetary System under Flexible Exchange Rates*. Cambridge, Mass: Ballinger Publishing Company. (Essay 17, this volume.)
―――― 1982: Exchange rate policy and the resources boom. *The Economic Record*, 58, 18–31.
Corden, W. M. and Neary, J. P. 1982: Booming sector and de-industrialisation in a small open economy. *The Economic Journal*, 92, 825–48. (Essay 15, this volume.)
Dasgupta, P. and Heal, G. 1979: *Economic Theory and Exhaustible Resources*. Welwyn, Herts: James Nisbet and Co. and Cambridge: Cambridge University Press.
Dasgupta, P., Eastwood, R. and Heal, G. 1978: Resource management in a trading economy. *The Quarterly Journal of Economics*, 92, 297–306.
Eastwood, R. K. and Venables, A. J. 1982: The macroeconomic implications of a resource discovery in an open economy. *The Economic Journal*, 92, 285–99.
Eide, E. 1973: Virkninger av Statens Oljeinntekter pa Norsk Okonomi. *Sosialokonomen*, No. 10, 12–21; see also Institute of Economics Reprint Series No. 106, University of Oslo.
Ellman, M. 1981: Natural gas, restructuring and re-industrialisation: the Dutch experience of industrial policy. In T. Barker and V. Brailovsky (eds), *Oil or Industry?* London: Academic Press.
Eltis, W. A. and Sinclair, P. J. N. (eds) 1981: *The Money Supply and the Exchange Rate*. Oxford: Oxford University Press.

Enders, K. and Herberg, H. 1983: The Dutch disease: causes, consequences, cure and calmatives. *Welwirtschaftliches Archiv*, 119, 473–97.

Findlay, R. and Grubert, H. 1959: Factor intensities, technological progress and the terms of trade. *Oxford Economic Papers*, 11, 111–21.

Flemming, J. S. 1982: U.K. macro-policy response to oil price shocks of 1974–75 and 1979–80. *European Economic Review*, 18, 223–4.

Forsyth, P. J. and Kay, J. A. 1980: The economic implications of North Sea oil revenues. *Fiscal Studies*, 1, 1–28.

―――― 1981: Oil revenues and manufacturing output. *Fiscal Studies*, 2, 9–17.

Forsyth, P. J. and Nicholas, S. J. 1981: The decline of Spanish industry and the price revolution: a neoclassical analysis. *Journal of European Economic History*, 12, 601–9.

Gelb, A. H. 1981: *Capital Importing Oil Exporters: Adjustment Issues and Policy Choices*. World Bank Staff Working Paper No. 475 (August), Washington, DC: The World Bank.

Gregory, R. G. 1976: Some implications of the growth of the mineral sector. *Australian Journal of Agricultural Economics*, 20, 71–91.

Helliwell, J. F. 1981: Using Canadian oil and gas revenues in the 1980s: provincial and federal perspectives. In T. Barker and V. Brailovsky (eds), *Oil or Industry?* London: Academic Press.

Johnson, H. G. 1955: Economic expansion and international trade. *Manchester School of Economic and Social Studies*, 23, 95–112.

Jones, R. W. 1965: The structure of simple general equilibrium models. *Journal of Political Economy*, 73, 557–72.

―――― 1971: A three-factor model in theory, trade and history. In J. N. Bhagwati *et al.* (eds), *Trade, Balance of Payments and Growth: Essays in Honor of C. P. Kindleberger*. Amsterdam: North-Holland, 3–21.

Long, N. V. 1983: The effects of a booming export industry on the rest of the economy. *The Economic Record*, 59, 57–60.

McKinnon, R. I. 1976: International transfers and non-traded commodities: the adjustment problem. In D. M. Leipziger (ed.), *The International Monetary System and the Developing Nations*. Washington, DC: Agency for International Development.

Maddock, R. and McLean, I. 1984: Supply shocks: the case of Australian gold. *The Journal of Economic History*, 44, 1047–68.

Malinvaud, E. 1977: *The Theory of Unemployment Reconsidered*. Oxford: Basil Blackwell.

Martin, J. P. and Neary, J. P. 1980: Variable labour supply and the pure theory of international trade: an empirical note. *Journal of International Economics*, 10, 549–59.

Nankani, G. 1979: *Development Problems of Mineral-Exporting Countries*. World Bank Staff Working Paper No. 354 (August). Washington, DC: The World Bank.

Neary, J. P. 1978: Short-run capital specificity and the pure theory of international trade. *The Economic Journal*, 88, 488–510.

―――― 1981: On the short-run effects of technological progress. *Oxford Economic Papers*, 33, 224–33.

―――― 1984: Real and monetary aspects of the Dutch disease. In K. Jungenfeld (ed.), *Structural Adjustment in Developed Open Economies*. London: Macmillan.

Neary, J. P. and Purvis, P. D. 1981: Real adjustment and exchange rate dynamics. Discussion Paper No. 203, University of Warwick, mimeo.

―――― 1982: Sectoral shocks in a dependent economy: long-run adjustment and short-run accommodation. *Scandinavian Journal of Economics*, 84, 229–53.

Neary, J. P. and Wijnbergen, S. van 1984: Can higher oil revenues lead to a recession? A comment on Eastwood and Venables. *The Economic Journal*, 94, 390–5.

Niehans, J. 1981: The appreciation of sterling – causes, effects, policies. SSRC Money Study Group Discussion Paper (February).

Porter, M. G. 1978: External shocks and stabilization policy in a small open economy: the Australian experience. *Weltwirtschaftsliches Archiv*, 114, 709–35.

Rybczynski, T. M. 1955: Factor endowment and relative commodity prices. *Economica*, 22, 336–41.

Salter, W. E. G. 1959: Internal and external balance: the role of price and expenditure effects. *The Economic Record*, 35, 226–38.

Shann, E. W. 1982: *Policy Issues in Mineral Sector Growth: A Keynesian Model*. Discussion Paper No. 60 (December), Centre for Economic Policy Research. Canberra: Australian National University.

Snape, R. H. 1977: Effects of mineral development on the economy. *Australian Journal of Agricultural Economics*, 21, 147–56.

Stoeckel, A. 1979: Some equilibrium effects of mining growth on the economy. *Australian Journal of Agricultural Economics*, 23, 1–22.

Thirlwall, A. 1980: *Balance of Payments Theory and the U.K. Experience*. London: Macmillan.

Turnovsky, S. J. 1983: Expanding exports and the structure of the domestic economy: a monetary analysis. *The Economic Record*, 59, 245–59.

Wijnbergen, S. van 1982: Optimal capital accumulation and investment allocation over traded and non-traded sectors in oil producing countries. Development Research Center, (April). Washington, DC: World Bank. Mimeo.

Wijnbergen, S. van 1984a: Inflation, employment and the Dutch disease in oil exporting countries: a short run disequilibrium analysis. *The Quarterly Journal of Economics*, 99, 233–50.

Wijnbergen, S. van, 1984b: The 'Dutch disease': a disease after all? *The Economic Journal*, 94, 41–5.

Part V
Protection, The Exchange Rate and
Macroeconomic Policy

17

Exchange Rate Protection*

This essay develops the concept of exchange rate protection. The concept is familiar from popular discussion and casual references in the literature of international monetary economics, but it has not been brought explicitly into theoretical work. The essay has been inspired by the discussion of two recent issues – namely, the Japanese current account surpluses of 1977 and 1978 and the implications of North Sea oil revenues for British industrial structure and the balance of payments.

I The Simple Concept and Two Examples

There is exchange rate protection when a country protects its tradable goods sector (export and import-competing industries) relative to its non-tradable sector by devaluing its exchange rate, allowing the exchange rate to depreciate more than it would otherwise, or preventing an appreciation that would otherwise take place. This is a simple definition. It implies that a devaluation can indeed bring about the required domestic relative price change. A nominal devaluation leads to a real devaluation. It also leaves open the definition of the 'otherwise' exchange rate. We shall come to both points later.

The basic idea can be represented geometrically. Figure 17.1 represents the familiar Salter (1959) diagram. We make the small country assumption, so that exportables and importables can be amalgamated into the composite good 'tradables', shown on the vertical axis. The transformation curve between tradables and non-tradables is HH', and if the current account is initially in balance, the initial point of equilibrium is P, with a domestic

---

* From R. N. Cooper et al. (eds) 1981: *The International Monetary System under Flexible Exchange Rates: Global, Regional and National. Essays in Honour of Robert Triffin*, Cambridge, Mass: Ballinger Publishing Company. Reprinted with minor changes. I am indebted to John Black, Herbert Grubel, Anne Krueger, Peter Lloyd, Peter McCawley, John Martin, Richard Snape, and John Williamson. An earlier version was presented to a seminar of the International Economics Study Group, London, April 1978.

relative price ratio represented by the slope of KK'. This is the 'otherwise' position. The assumption of initial current account balance is made for simplicity, but is not crucial to the argument.

It is desired to protect the tradable goods industry so as to bring output to P'. We now make the simple assumption (reviewed later) that the nominal price of non-tradables is given. This could be the result of an exogenously determined money wage combined with a constant percentage profit margin in the non-tradable sector. We also assume, for simplicity, that foreign prices are constant. This assumption is not critical for the analysis. The desired relative price change can then be brought about by an appropriate nominal devaluation that raises the domestic price of tradables and hence alters the relative price ratio to that represented by the slope of GG'. This brings output to P', but it will also shift the pattern of absorption away from tradables, moving it from the expenditure curve OZ to OZ'. At a constant price of non-tradables there will now be excess demand for non-tradables, which is not a sustainable position, given that the nominal price of non-tradables is to stay constant. To avoid this, aggregate demand (absorption) must be reduced appropriately – namely to OL' (in terms of non-tradables) – so that we end up with absorption at C and a current account surplus of $P'C$.

If there is to be a continuing current account surplus and there are no offsetting private capital outflows (as we are assuming), the monetary inflows have to be sterilized. In terms of figure 17.1, the level of absorption has to be kept down to OL'. In the absence of sterilization, the money supply and hence the absorption level would steadily increase until the surplus disappeared. The difficulties of sterilization in the absence of a fiscal surplus are well known. In the presence of capital mobility, sterilization would lead to offsetting capital inflows as the domestic interest rate steadily rose, and in any case, a continuous surplus and continuous sterilization would not be compatible with stock equilibrium of the private sector. Thus, it has to be assumed that the current account surplus is matched by a budget surplus, this continuing budget surplus being the way in which the lower level of absorption is maintained. The government steadily redeems its debt, and when there is no more left to redeem, it builds up liquid balances with the central bank. This is, of course, not a situation of public stock equilibrium. Furthermore, at some time in the future there must be budget and current account deficits – which antiprotect the tradables sector – as the foreign exchange reserves accumulated during the period of exchange rate protection are used up. But we are concerned here only with the first period. Thus, this essay is strictly limited to a short-term analysis.[1]

The objective of exchange rate protection is often to maintain employment in the tradables sector in response to some exogenous shock that

---

1. A two-period analysis broadly in the same framework as the present essay (i.e. using the Salter model as a starting point) is given by Razin (1980).

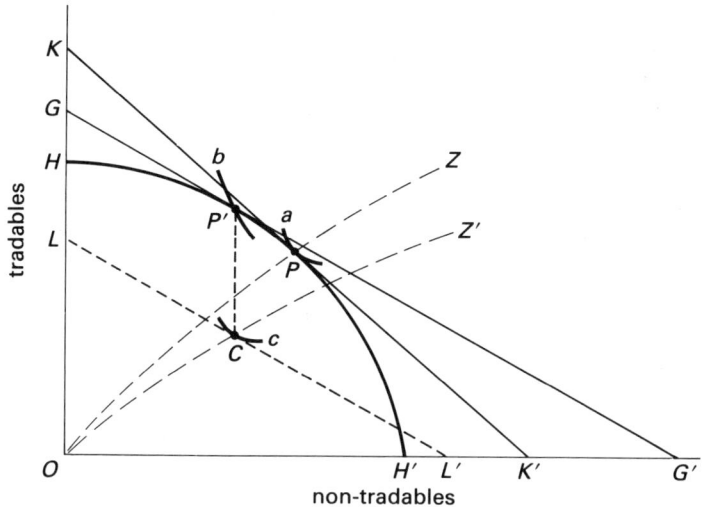

Figure 17.1 Exchange rate protection of output in the tradable sector.

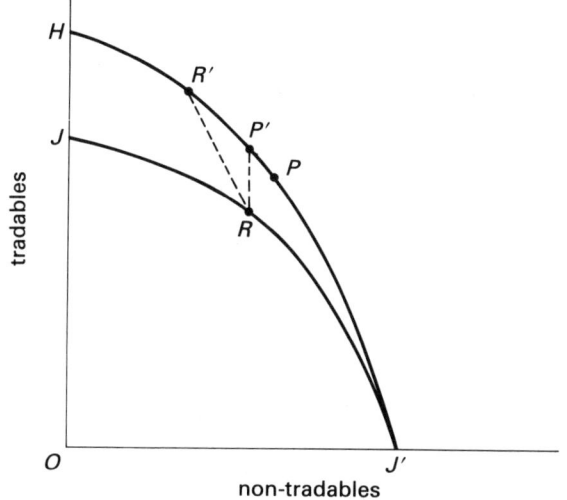

Figure 17.2 Protection of employment after a productivity improvement.

would otherwise have caused employment in that sector to fall. The motive may be short term, the object being to maintain employment temporarily. Such a case is represented in figure 17.2. Initially the transformation curve is JJ', and equilibrium is at R. A productivity improvement in the tradables sector causes the curve to rise vertically to HJ'. If there were to be no net resource shift between the two sectors, output would have to move to P', vertically above R. In the movement from R to P' there is no change in output of non-tradables. Now the question is where output would settle if the exchange rate (or the money price of non-tradables) were flexible and full employment were maintained. Suppose this 'otherwise' position were at P. Exchange rate protection would ensure that output moves to P' so as to prevent a decrease in employment in tradables.[2] To explore the position of P relative to P' further, let us consider two special cases.

1) There is a windfall oil discovery requiring no significant extra resource use. The output of tradables rises by a uniform amount independent of the resources in the tradable industries.[3] The slope at P' will be equal to the slope at R, and with the nominal price of non-tradables given, the exchange rate will be the same at P' as at R. The 'otherwise' position P will be to the right of P' (as in figure 17.2), provided the marginal propensity to absorb non-tradables is positive. Exchange rate protection – which is designed to move the production point from P to P' – keeps the exchange rate constant when it would otherwise have appreciated. It will ensure that the absorption point remains at R and that the whole of the oil windfall finances a payments surplus.

2) There is a factor-neutral and scale-neutral proportional productivity increase in the tradables industry. This is the case represented in figure 17.2. The slope at P' will be steeper than that at R, and if the nominal price of non-tradables is given, the exchange rate at P' will be appreciated relative to that at R. Hence some appreciation is required if employment in tradables is to remain constant. A constant exchange rate would actually mean an increase in employment in tradables.[4]

This time the 'otherwise' point P could be to the right or to the left of P'. Two opposing factors are at work in determining its position relative to P'. A positive marginal propensity to absorb non-tradables would tend to draw resources out of tradables (and so push P to the right of P'); on the other hand, the fact that resources in tradables are now more productive is likely to draw resources into them (and so push P to the left of P'). If the first effect is stronger, P will be to the right of P', and a need for exchange rate

---

2. This sentence assumes that constancy of output of non-tradables also means constancy of employment in that sector, and hence also constancy of employment in tradables. It assumes that output and employment always move in the same direction (apart from the effects of the productivity improvement itself).

    This would be so either (a) in a two-mobile-factors model where the productivity improvement is Hicks neutral, or (b) in a model where labour is the only mobile factor. In the more general two-factor case, with the productivity improvement factor biased, constancy of output of non-tradables can be associated with one factor moving into that sector and the other out. This is described tautologically here as zero net resource shift. Thus the complication to note is that in the general case, constant employment in tradables could mean a position to the left or right of P'.

3. The curve HJ' would be vertically displaced above JJ' by a uniform amount and would have a kink vertically above J'.

4. It would bring output to R' on the Rybczynski line RR', the slope of HJ' at R' being the same as the slope of JJ' at R'.

protection in favour of tradables will arise. The earlier 'oil' case was an extreme case where resources in tradables were no more productive than before at the margin because the whole of the output gain was a windfall.

II Three-good Model: Booming Sector and Lagging Sector

The tradable–non-tradable model used so far does not fully capture the most common reason for exchange rate protection – to protect one part of the tradables sector when there is a productivity improvement or windfall gain in another part. Hence, there is need for a model with three sectors.

We divide the tradables sector into two parts – a booming sector and a lagging sector. The booming sector is where there is a large productivity improvement or a minerals windfall. The productivity improvement may be in value terms and not in physical terms, the world price of the booming sector's output having risen even though physical productivity is constant (the oil price case). In Japan the booming sector is the progressive, dynamic part of export-oriented manufacturing. In Britain, Norway, and all the OPEC countries it is the oil sector. In the case of the Netherlands it is the natural gas sector, and in Australia it is the minerals sector. The lagging sector in these countries consists of all other export industries as well as import-competing industries. The objective of actual or proposed exchange rate protection is to protect the lagging sector. There has been discussion of this issue in all these countries (McKinnon, 1976; Gregory, 1976; Snape, 1977; Forsyth and Kay, 1980; Corden, 1982).

This model can also be adapted for the Swiss case, where a real appreciation has been generated by exogenous (or speculative) private capital inflows rather than by a boom in some export industries. Exchange rate protection would avoid the appreciation and keep the current account balance unchanged, the exogenous private capital inflow being matched by an increase in official reserves or by private capital outflow induced by monetary policy (fall in the interest rate). In this case, the private sector exporting money or short-term bonds is the booming sector.

Let us now consider how a productivity improvement in the booming sector affects the lagging sector adversely (in the absence of exchange rate protection). As before, the nominal price of non-tradables is held constant. The conclusions below follow from the formal model of essay 15 where there is a specific factor in each industry and one mobile factor used in all three industries. An adverse effect for the lagging sector means that its output and, with it, the real rent of its specific factor fall.

III Spending and Resource Movement Effects

The extra income from the productivity increase will be spent partly on non-tradables, so that at constant relative prices, excess demand for non-tradables and a balance of payments surplus (domestic excess supply of tradables) would result. In the absence of intervention, the exchange rate would then appreciate to restore equilibrium, and this appreciation will lower the output of the lagging sector, employment in that sector and the income of the specific factor there. This is the spending effect.

It should be noted that the extra income resulting from the productivity improvement will be spent in part directly by the factors of production in the booming sector and in part indirectly through extra tax revenues from the booming sector allowing increased government expenditures or reductions in other taxes. The indirect spending effect dominates in the case of British North Sea oil. When tax remissions and the benefits of extra government services are taken into account, there may finally be a net gain to the specific factor in the lagging sector even though its pretax income from employment will fall.

In so far as the productivity improvement raises the marginal product of the mobile factor in the booming sector, it will lead to resource movements of this factor out of the lagging sector, and lower the rent received by the specific factor in that sector. It should be noted that this effect does not operate through the exchange rate. It leads to direct de-industrialization.

In addition, a rise in the marginal product of the mobile factor in the booming sector will lead to a movement of the mobile factor out of the non-tradables sector, which will create excess demand for non-tradables, hence reinforcing the spending effect by giving rise to further appreciation that has an adverse effect on the specific factor in the lagging sector. The adverse effect on the lagging sector of the appreciation that results from both the spending effect and the resource movement effect can be called indirect de-industrializaion.

These results can be summarized as follows. The rent of the specific factor in the lagging sector must fall as a result of the productivity improvement in the booming sector unless (a) all the extra income from the productivity improvement is spent on tradables and (b) the marginal product of the mobile factor in the booming sector is not raised by the productivity improvement. If either some of the extra income is spent on non-tradables or the marginal product of a given quantity of the mobile factor is raised by the improvement (or if both conditions apply), the real rent of the specific factor in the lagging sector will fall. These results can be generalized in a more imprecise form to a model with more than three factors – for example, where there are several mobile factors employed in different proportions to each other (different factor intensities) in the three industries.

Exchange rate protection in its extreme form would completely prevent the appreciation that would otherwise take place. It would be associated with a reduction in absorption that completely offset the spending effect and, in addition, offset the indirect resource movement effect on the demand for non-tradables. The resultant balance of payments surplus would be equal to the reduction in absorption. Some adverse effect on specific factors in the lagging sector through the direct resource movement

The Cost of Exchange Rate Protection

It can be clearly established that exchange rate protection is not first best. Assume to begin with that it is desired to protect the whole tradables sector relative to non-tradables, and take this as given. Thus, the basic protection motive is not queried at this stage. The first-best policy is then to subsidize the purchase of tradables, financing this by a tax on the purchase of non-tradables, or alternatively, to subsidize the production of tradables, financing this by a tax on the production of non-tradables. In figure 17.1 this would bring the economy to P'. The inevitable cost of protection in this case is represented by the movement from indifference curve a to curve b. Note that with a given nominal price of non-tradables, a purchase subsidy cum tax would have to be associated with a depreciation of the exchange rate to induce production to shift appropriately and maintain equilibrium in the market for non-tradables, while a production subsidy cum tax would require an appreciation for the same reason.

The use of the exchange rate as the method of protection brings the economy to the current absorption point C and to a welfare level below that of curve b but above that of curve c. The additional cost resulting from the balance of payments surplus can be termed the absorption contraction cost. There is such an additional cost because we are assuming that the level of official reserves (and of private holdings of foreign bonds and equities) was initially optimal; in other words, if there were no exchange rate protection motive, it would be optimal for the current account to be in balance. The welfare level will thus be below b, but it will be down to curve c only if (improbably) an increase in official reserves or in private holdings of foreign bonds or equities yielded no benefits at all (in the case of the reserves, yielding no interest receipts and no increased sense of security, and being eventually confiscated by the reserve currency country or completely devalued by inflation).

Let us next turn to the more relevant three-sector model and assume that the given objective is to protect not all tradables but only the lagging sector. The first-best policy is then to subsidize directly production of lagging industries. While this will yield an inevitable cost of protection, the use of the alternative device of exchange rate protection would impose two additional costs or by-product distortions. First, by protecting all tradable industries, whether booming or lagging, it would unduly increase the size of the booming sector (above the increase that would take place in any case). Second, by generating a surplus, it would impose the absorption contraction cost.

With regard to the direct subsidy for lagging industries, one might visualize it being financed primarily out of the revenue raised from the booming industries (a case of British industrial policy being financed by

North Sea oil). But it must be stressed that the availability of extra revenue does not alter the fact that a cost of protection in the Pareto-efficiency sense is likely to be imposed when industries are subsidized for income maintenance or similar reasons.

IV The Identification Problem and Britain's North Sea Oil

Can one determine empirically when there is exchange rate protection? Let us first consider this question in the absence of interest-rate-responsive private capital movements, so that exchange rate protection will manifest itself in official exchange rate intervention policies.

The identification problem arises because one is concerned with assessing the motivation of such intervention policies. If there were no reason for a country ever to accumulate official reserves other than to depreciate the exchange rate for the sake of protecting part or all of the tradables sector, the fact of reserves accumulation would be the indicator of protection. We would at least have a quantitative indicator, which might provide a basis for estimates of the extent of depreciation brought about by this protection. But the accumulation of official reserves may have other purposes. In any particular case, one needs to estimate how much of the reserves accumulation reflects an official view that the absolute size of the reserves stock is too low in relation to the level of trade or of the GNP and in relation to other assets (or other criteria affecting judgements of reserves adequacy) and how much is the by-product only of maintaining or attaining a desired exchange rate. The 'otherwise' situation referred to earlier would be the result of pursuing a reserves accumulation policy motivated by the first set of considerations – that is, one that is concerned with the optimal accumulation of reserves irrespective of the exchange rate result.[5]

It has to be noted that a clear distinction between exchange rate protection and the optimal accumulation of reserves cannot always be made. Reserves may be accumulated optimally at a given time not only to achieve a long-term stock target but also to smooth out fluctuations in absorption and generally to avoid instability. This relates to the discussion in the next section. Awkwardly, this motive cannot be entirely distinguished from exchange rate protection because, as mentioned later, exchange rate protection may be designed to avoid a temporary fall in prices facing lagging industries, a fall that would generate misleading resource allocation signals.

---

5. The vast literature on the demand for official reserves is relevant here. See the surveys by Grubel (1971), Williamson (1973), and de Beaufort Wijnholds (1977). The present essay is not concerned with the many issues raised there but only with one additional reason that is not dealt with in this literature – why reserves may be accumulated (or reduced) by a country.

The identification of motive is even more difficult once we allow for private capital movements. A government that wishes to extend exchange rate protection to its industries need not intervene in the foreign exchange market at all. It can run a fiscal surplus and redeem some of its debt. While the resulting reduced expenditure will tend to appreciate the exchange rate, the actual or incipient fall in the interest rate will have the opposite effect, tending to depreciate the rate. If the capital flow effect outweighs the goods market effect (as is assumed in most simple models with capital mobility), the fiscal surplus will have brought about exchange rate protection without intervention in the foreign exchange market. One must then assess the motive for the fiscal surplus.

The identification problem arises in a case such as Britain's where the North Sea oil windfall is expected to be fairly short term. An optimal savings policy may call for most of the gains to be saved. If the savings are invested in domestic real assets, there will still be the spending effect and the associated appreciation (in the absence of exchange rate protection). But if it is thought optimal to invest in liquid assets, the reserves will be built up even without any exchange rate protection motivation. If the whole of the windfall were invested in liquid assets (and hence yielded a current account surplus to that extent), the spending effect would be zero and the exchange rate would appreciate only if there were any indirect resource movement effect. The lagging sector would lose because of this and any direct resource movement effect. In Britain's case, these two effects are likely to be small.

One might conclude that in Britain's case the much-discussed issue of exchange rate policy in response to North Sea oil divides up into three issues: (1) How much of the windfall is to be saved and how much consumed, supposing that there is no particular concern with adverse effects on lagging industries? (2) How much of the savings is to be invested in real assets domestically and how much in liquid assets, again disregarding effects on lagging industries? (3) What concern is there for possible adverse effects on lagging industries (the exchange rate protection issue)?

In considering issues 1 and 2, a possible ratchet effect must be allowed for. First, suppose that the windfall is consumed, in the form of either public or private consumption – in the latter case, perhaps, because of tax remissions that raise after tax real personal incomes. Later consumption may have to fall back again. If there is a downward rigidity of public consumption and of after tax real wages (a ratchet effect), a problem will be stored up for later. It may lead later to an inevitable balance of payments deficit and to unemployment. It may be wiser not to allow consumption to rise so far that it will later have to be reversed. This is an argument for investing, rather than consuming, the windfall. It is not necessarily an argument for investing the windfall in liquid assets, as distinct from domestic real assets, and so avoiding an appreciation.

Next, suppose it is decided to increase spending domestically, for either consumption or real investment. The exchange rate will appreciate, which will raise real incomes of factors specific to or intensive in non-tradable industries, notably labour. If the real wage is flexible upwards but rigid downwards, again, trouble will be stored up for the future, when the exchange rate moves back again. This consideration may be an argument for avoiding or moderating an appreciation and investing instead in liquid assets. It must be distinguished from the exchange rate protection motive. It is concerned with avoiding a temporarily favourable effect for non-tradables, as distinct from avoiding an unfavourable effect for lagging industries.

V Exchange Rate Protection and the Theory of Protection

How does exchange rate protection fit into the existing theory of protection? Exchange rate protection uniformly raises the domestic prices of all tradables relative to the prices of all non-tradables. This relative price change has effects not only on the output pattern and on income distribution, but also (when combined with the appropriate change in absorption) on the balance of payments.

By contrast, much of standard protection theory does not include non-tradables at all. It is concerned with shifts in the pattern of output within the tradable goods sector, usually between importables and exportables. More recently, non-tradables have been introduced into the theory of protection. But it is always assumed that the balance of payments is kept unchanged as a result of protection (Corden, 1971, chs. 4 and 5). This is normally thought of as happening through exchange rate adjustment. The assumption is part of the familiar dichotomy between the real theory of international trade and the monetary or balance of payments theory, with variations in the balance of payments being permitted only in the latter. Thus, in the existing theory of protection, the instrument of protection policy is the tariff or some similar device, while the exchange rate adjusts to attain a constant balance of payments. By contrast, with exchange rate protection, the exchange rate is the instrument of protection policy, and the balance of payments effect becomes a residual. In both approaches, it must be emphasized, a nominal exchange rate change is assumed to lead to a real exchange rate change. It is the change in the *real* exchange rate that affects resource allocation, the demand pattern and income distribution.

It has been shown in the theory of protection that in a model with an importable, an exportable, and a non-tradable, a tariff will protect the importable not only relative to the exportable, but also relative to the non-tradable. One can calculate a net protective rate that represents the rate of protection of the importable relative to the non-tradable (Corden 1971, ch. 5). But this does not represent general protection of tradables relative to the non-tradable, since, when the exchange rate adjustment takes place, the exportable is antiprotected relative to the non-tradable by the tariff. Hence, in spite of the concept of the net protective rate, exchange rate protection is not part of the existing theory of protection.[6]

Reasons for Exchange Rate Protection

Let us now turn to reasons for exchange rate protection. These are similar to those for 'ordinary' protection and need to be analysed in the same way. The fact that there are reasons does not mean that they are good reasons.

Probably the most common explanation for exchange rate protection is sectional real income maintenance, the sections concerned being factors specific to or intensive in the lagging industries. This motive is usually short term, a response to sudden shocks that, in the absence of protection, would reduce real incomes of particular sections of the community markedly. This might be described as the expression of a 'conservative social welfare function' by policymakers.[7] Alternatively, one might see such income maintenance policies not as the fruits of a coherent 'social welfare function' that is concerned to shelter losers in an economy but as a response to sectional pressures intensified by the prospect of, or actual, real income losses.

Real wages in the lagging industries may be rigid downwards and labour may be immobile. An argument for protection designed to maintain total employment can then be made. It would also apply if labour were mobile and the lagging industries were labour intensive.[8]

The windfall in the booming industries may be known to be temporary by the government and by 'informed' observers, so that there ought not to be any long-term resource shifts out of the temporarily lagging industries. It has been argued (for example, in Britain) that an appreciation would set up signals that would induce such undesirable resource shifts. Exchange rate protection is needed to produce the right signals. This argument implies that private decision makers are influenced by current rather than expected profitability or that their expectations are based on inferior information.

All of these arguments apply to the protection of lagging industries within the tradables sector, rather than to the protection of tradables as a

6. Essay 19 seeks to clarify the distinction between ordinary protection and exchange rate protection further.
7. The argument that a principal motive for protectionist policies is the pursuit of a 'conservative social welfare function' is set out by Corden (1974, pp. 88–90, 107–9).
8. It was argued above that if the windfall were temporary, it might be undesirable to allow an appreciation because it would raise real incomes in non-tradables, which would lead to unemployment in that sector later, when the exchange rate movement has to be reversed. This should be combined with the present argument. If there is downward real wage rigidity (and other things are equal), an appreciation will cause unemployment now in the lagging industries and unemployment later in non-tradable industries. This is the familiar argument for preventing price fluctuations because of ratchet effects.

whole. It is more difficult to think of arguments for protecting all tradables relative to non-tradables. A neophysiocratic tendency in Britain to glorify manufacturing relative to services on account of supposed differential growth effects has at times been transformed into an argument for protecting tradables relative to non-tradables.

Possibly an infant-industry argument for protection of manufacturing might be used. It may apply particularly to exports of manufactures in the form of a 'long-term market development argument'. Sometimes the German surplus has been justified, from Germany's point of view, in these terms. When the infant-industry argument refers to the protection of manufacturing relative to services it is subject to the same sorts of qualifications that apply when, as is more usual, it refers to manufacturing relative to agriculture (Corden, 1974, ch. 9).

Incidentally, one can also envisage a situation of reverse exchange rate protection: The non-tradables sector is protected at the expense of the tradables sector through the avoidance of a devaluation and thus the prolongation of a balance of payments deficit. The motive might be to maintain incomes of persons employed in non-tradables (e.g. in the public sector). If labour is mobile between the sectors and non-tradables are relatively labour intensive, protection of non-tradables will raise real wages above the level they would otherwise be. In that case, devaluation may be avoided because it would either lower real wages or, with real wage rigidity, create unemployment.

The Choice between Exchange Rate Protection and Ordinary Protection

To return to the protection of the lagging tradables sector, given that such protection is desired, how does exchange rate protection compare with tariffs and export subsidies for these industries? First, tariffs and export subsidies for the lagging industries ('ordinary' protection) shift the pattern of consumption away from lagging toward booming industries when it is only desired to affect prices facing producers. They thus impose a consumption distortion cost within the tradables sector as a whole that exchange rate protection avoids. Second, exchange rate protection creates two by-product distortions that ordinary protection avoids: (a) The booming sector is protected relative to non-tradables when protection of the booming sector is certainly not desired, and (b) there is the absorption contraction cost because of the balance of payments surplus. Thus, at the a priori level, one cannot choose between the two devices, though one might wish to give a heavy weight to the absorption contraction cost, in which case exchange rate protection would be inferior.

Other considerations are also relevant in choosing between these policies. Protection may be intended to be temporary. The chances of exchange rate protection being temporary may be greater than the chances of tariffs and export subsidies being removed in due course. Administratively, exchange rate manipulation and tariffs are both easier than various kinds of subsidies. Furthermore, there are strong international rules against export subsidies. In comparing tariffs with exchange rate adjustment, three considerations may possibly favour use of the latter from the point of view of the government, at least in the short term. First, tariffs need generally to be legislated, while the exchange rate can be freely manipulated by the monetary authorities. Second, international commitments may prevent increases in tariffs. Third, tariff increases and the imposition of import quotas are more obviously protective than exchange rate depreciation and hence are more likely to provoke international retaliation.

VI Upward Flexibility of Nominal Wages: The Story Retold

Instead of assuming the nominal price of non-tradables constant one could have assumed a constant nominal wage. The general argument would still stand: a devaluation would raise the relative price of tradables.[9]

Alternatively, one might prefer to assume that the nominal wage is rigid downwards but flexible upwards. If one starts in an equilibrium sitiuation and then aims to protect tradables, it would still be necessary to devalue if one desired to maintain the level of employment. A reduction of absorption on its own would create unemployment without bringing down the price of non-tradables. But the matter is quite different for the case on which we have been focusing, where a productivity improvement in the booming sector would, in the absence of exchange rate protection, lead to an appreciation. Let us retell this story with the assumption of a firmly fixed exchange rate and with upward flexibility of nominal wages and prices.

Again, we start with a productivity improvement in the booming sector and initially assume no policy designed to shelter the lagging sector. The extra demand for non-tradables generated by the spending effect and the indirect resource movement effect will raise nominal wages and prices of non-tradables. The higher wages will raise the costs of the lagging sector and hence affect profits in that sector adversely. In our earlier story, this adverse result was brought about by appreciation combined with constant wages. A policy designed to avoid this adverse cost effect (a policy equivalent to exchange rate protection) would consist of an offsetting policy of reducing absorption that ensured that demand for non-tradables and labour did not rise in the first instance. There would then be no rise in nominal wages. If the initial source of the extra demand in the absence of

---

9. This would be so if labour and capital were mobile between the sectors and non-tradables were relatively labour intensive, or if only labour were mobile while capital is specific to each sector. It would not be so in the improbable case where non-tradables are relatively capital intensive (see Jones and Corden, 1976).

such a policy had been wholly the spending effect, the aim would be to keep absorption constant, with extra private spending by the booming industry possibly being offset by reduced public spending. Alternatively, the higher income of the booming sector may be largely siphoned off by taxes (as in the case of Britain's North Sea oil), while government expenditure is held constant.

It is certainly a significant point that the basic analysis of this chapter applies even when the nominal exchange rate is fixed, provided nominal wages are flexible upwards. Exchange rate protection consists in this case not of preventing appreciation but of preventing a rise in nominal wages. As noted earlier, the crucial variable is the real exchange rate and not the nominal exchange rate.

One might also consider the case where the nominal exchange rate is an instrument of policy but where nominal wages and prices of non-tradables are flexible upwards. As explained above, with a fixed exchange rate, the extra spending resulting from the booming sector's boom would have led to an inflationary rise in wages. The question is whether this would have been allowed or whether it would have been deliberately avoided by appreciation. In our earlier account, with rigid nominal wages or prices of non-tradables, the appreciation was needed to avoid excess demand for non-tradables. Now it is needed to avoid an inflationary adjustment. In both cases the spending effect of the boom leads to appreciation and to an adverse effect on the lagging sector, and exchange rate protection is the policy of avoiding this.

VII Large Country Model: How Exchange Rate Targets can become Compatible

The analysis needs to be extended to the large country case. The small country assumption has allowed the analysis to focus on the protectionist country itself, with the rest of the world being a sponge that absorbs any surplus or deficit that this country wishes to generate. Since exchange rate protection appears to have been practised to some extent by the capitalist world's largest economies – notably, Germany and Japan – this is clearly not an adequate approach, though it is a beginning. The following discussion is particularly relevant to the issues that were debated in relation to the large Japanese current account surpluses of 1977 and 1978.

A two-country model, where neither country is small, brings out the essential issues. The two countries could be thought of as Japan and the United States. In such a model it would not be possible for each country to fix independently a target real exchange rate for itself. Given its own real exchange rate, a particular balance of payments surplus or deficit will be generated. But one country's deficit must be the other's surplus. The implicit idea that countries have real exchange rate or current account targets gives rise to the popular view that the international monetary system requires policy co-ordination.

The non-coordinated system can be rescued by departing from the fixed target approach. It can be shown that it is possible to have a two-country equilibrium without policy co-ordination. Instead of having a fixed real exchange rate or current account target for each country, each country can be assumed to take the interest rate into account when it formulates its exchange rate or balance of payments policy. Thus, the size of the current account target becomes a positive function of the interest rate. A country will seek to accumulate less foreign exchange reserves the lower the interest rate it expects to obtain on these reserves. Similarly, a country planning a deficit will bear in mind that the lower the foreign interest rate, the less the cost of this deficit – that is, the less the gain foregone in running down foreign exchange reserves or the lower the cost of foreign borrowing. If a country's current account target is achieved not by intervention in the foreign exchange market but by fiscal policy (an increased fiscal surplus generating a higher current account surplus and an increased fiscal deficit similarly increasing a current account deficit), the idea is that fiscal policy would take into account the interest rate.

Applying this interest rate consideration to the exchange rate protection concept, it can be said that exchange rate protection has a cost to a country and that this cost varies with the interest rate. The cost of this form of protection is the cost of excess lending abroad for the sake of protecting the tradables sector. The lower the interest rate obtainable, the greater the cost of exchange rate protection for the surplus country and thus the less exchange rate protection it will seek. Similarly, as pointed out above, the lower the interest rate, the more the deficit country will wish to borrow.

A world equilibrium model can then be built where the interest rate becomes endogenous – as it must be in a two-country model. Suppose that at the existing interest rate, Japan's target current account surplus is greater than the US target current account deficit. In other words, at the existing interest rate, Japan wishes to buy more financial assets than the United States wishes to sell. Each target, and especially that of Japan, may be influenced by the exchange rate protection consideration. In this particular case there will be an excess demand for financial assets, and hence the interest rate – a single world interest rate – will fall. This will raise Japan's cost of exchange rate protection and hence reduce her target current account surplus. Similarly, the US target deficit will increase since borrowing will be cheaper. In this way, the decline of the interest rate will bring the two current account targets together and hence make their exchange rate policies compatible.

VIII Summary

The purpose of this essay has been to discuss various aspects of exchange rate protection – defined as a policy designed to protect tradables relative to non-tradables. It has been stressed that the concern is with the real exchange rate, that exchange rate protection requires an appropriate reduction in absorption, and that it will yield a balance of payments surplus (or lesser deficit than otherwise). A common reason for exchange rate protection is to maintain employment, output or profitability in 'lagging' tradables industries when there is a boom in one part of the tradables sector. This is the case of British North Sea oil, and effects of a sectional boom on the lagging industries are detailed in the section on the three-good model.

It has been noted that the first-best way of protecting a lagging sector is by direct subsidies. The use of exchange rate protection imposes the absorption contraction cost (excessive lending abroad) and also unduly increases the size of the booming sector.

There is some difficulty in identifying exchange rate protection in practice. It is a matter of uncovering the motives for intervention in the foreign exchange market or of a fiscal surplus that lowers the domestic interest rate and depreciates the exchange rate: Is it to build up foreign exchange reserves to an optimal level, or is it to protect producers of tradables? This matter is discussed with respect to Britain's North Sea oil. There may be some argument in favour of the accumulation by Britain of foreign financial assets – and hence not allowing as much real appreciation as otherwise – because of the temporariness of the oil income. If British absorption is raised now, it may be difficult to get it down again later. Furthermore, optimal savings policy may justify some extra accumulation of assets.

The relation between exchange rate protection and the concept of 'ordinary' protection has also been spelled out. The main point is that ordinary protection is concerned with resource (and income distribution) shifts within the tradables sector, while exchange rate protection is concerned with protection of the whole tradables sector relative to non-tradables. The reasons for protection are similar in both cases, and particular weight has been given in this essay to the 'conservative social welfare function' motive. A comparison has also been made between the method of ordinary protection (tariffs or export subsidies) and exchange rate protection to achieve given protection of a lagging tradables sector. Each method imposes particular distortion costs, and in general it cannot be said that one method must be preferable, though the likely importance of the absorption contraction cost suggests that exchange rate protection may, in total, have a greater cost.

It has been noted that exchange rate protection can apply even in a fixed exchange rate system, bearing in mind that the concern is with the real exchange rate. This is so when a rise in nominal wages and prices of non-tradables that would otherwise have taken place in response to a sectional export boom is avoided by a policy of preventing an increase in absorption. The object is to prevent a rise in costs and hence a fall in profits and employment in lagging tradables industries. Finally, a two-country model, where both countries have exchange rate protection or current account targets and the problem of incompatibility of targets arises, is briefly discussed. The main point is that an international equilibrium (in which the targets become compatible) would be achieved if the world interest rate – which is endogenous in the model – affects the target levels.

References

Beaufort Wijnholds, J. A. H. de, 1977: *The Need for International Reserves and Credit Facilities*. Leiden: Martinus Nijhoff.
Corden, W. M. 1971: *The Theory of Protection*. Oxford: Oxford University Press.
―――― 1974: *Trade Policies and Economic Welfare*. Oxford: Oxford University Press.
―――― 1982: Exchange rate policy and the resources boom. *The Economic Record*, 58, 18–31.
Forsyth, P. J. and Kay, J. A. 1980: The economic implications of North Sea oil revenues. *Fiscal Studies*, 1, 1–28.
Gregory, R. G. 1976: Some implications of the growth of the mineral sector. *Australian Journal of Agricultural Economics*, 20, 71–91.
Grubel, H. G. 1971: The demand for international reserves: a critical review of the literature. *Journal of Economic Literature*, 9, 1148–66.
Jones, R. W. and Corden, W. M. 1976: Devaluation, non-flexible prices, and the trade balance for a small country. *The Canadian Journal of Economics*, 9, 150–61.
McKinnon, R. I. 1976: International transfers and non-traded commodities: the adjustment problem. In D. M. Leipziger (ed.), *The International Monetary System and the Developing Nations*. Washington, DC: Agency for International Development.
Razin, A. 1980: Capital movements, intersectoral resource shifts and the trade balance. Seminar Paper No. 159, (October), Institute for International Economic Studies. Stockholm: University of Stockholm.
Salter, W. E. G. 1959: Internal and external balance: the role of price and expenditure effects. *The Economic Record*, 35, 226–38.
Snape, R. H. 1977: Effects of mineral development on the economy. *Australian Journal of Agricultural Economics*, 21, 147–56.
Williamson, J. 1973: Surveys in applied economics: international liquidity. *The Economic Journal*, 38, 685–746.

18
Relationships between Macroeconomic and Industrial Policies*

The central question of this essay is: How do the policies for which the ministry of finance and the central bank are responsible relate to the policies that fall within the spheres of the ministries for industries and for regional development?

Thus the essay aims to sort out the relationship between what are broadly called macroeconomic policies and industrial policies. Macroeconomic policies are monetary policy, fiscal policy (determination of the general levels of taxation and government expenditure) and exchange-rate policy. Industrial policies will be understood to refer to 'industry-specific' or 'sectoral' policies, notably to direct and indirect subsidies to particular industries or to parts of industries located in particular regions, to voluntary export restraints negotiated with suppliers of imports, import quotas and tariffs, and to export subsidies and taxes. Of course, industrial policy is usually interpreted to have many other aspects – such as indicative planning of industrial structure and competition policy – but these are not so relevant for the present essay.[1]

I A Simple Approach

It might be argued that the distinction between macroeconomic policies and industrial policies is really very simple and that the two types of

---

* *The World Economy*, 3, Sept. 1980, pp. 167–84, (slightly abbreviated). The essay is a revised version of a paper presented to the International Symposium on Industrial Policies for the 1980s organized by the Spanish Ministry of Industry and Energy, in co-operation with and under the patronage of the Organisation for Economic Cooperation and Development, in Madrid on 5–9 May 1980. I am indebted to Ross Garnaut, Ephraim Kleiman and Peter Oppenheimer.

1. One of the best surveys of recent industrial policy issues is by Pinder, Hosomi and Diebold (1979). See also OECD Secretariat (1975, 1978). Industrial policy has even become an issue in the United States, on which see Lawrence (1984).

policies can be pursued independently from each other. Macroeconomic policies are concerned with the economy as a whole, making no distinctions among industries. They are aimed at macroeconomic targets. The aim is to manipulate the level of real activity and of inflation in terms of a Phillips curve trade-off. It is nowadays widely accepted that the effects of macroeconomic policies on the real level of activity are only or almost wholly short term while long-term effects are primarily on the rate of inflation. On the other hand, industrial-policy instruments are concerned with sectoral effects, with differentiating between industries or regions, and the effects can certainly be both short and long term.

The comparison between macroeconomic policies and industrial policies can be taken rather further if we focus on what is clearly a common concern of both policies, namely employment. Consider first industrial policy.

Defensive and Positive Industrial Policies

When it is 'defensive' in nature, industrial policy is concerned with preserving employment in a particular industry or region or, at least, preventing too sharp a decline that might otherwise take place. The causes of the potential decline may be shifts in domestic or world demand, technological changes or increased foreign competition. In all cases adverse employment effects could be moderated or even avoided if the real cost of labour fell sufficiently. There is usually some real wage level that would ensure the survival of an industry. When industrial policy takes the form of protection, direct or indirect, the approach is, in effect, to take the real labour costs as given and artificially – at the cost of consumers or taxpayers – shift up the private value of the marginal product of labour above where it would be in a free market.

The alternative to 'defensive' industrial policy is 'positive adjustment'.[2] This may take three forms. First, it may take the form of adjustment measures designed to improve the efficiency of the industry. The real wage rate is, again, taken as given, but this time the aim is to maintain employment in the industry by pushing up the marginal private and social products of labour, possibly by raising the marginal physical product. Secondly, the aim may be to try and get real wage rates down, at least temporarily, while adjustment measures work themselves out. But, because of the downward rigidity of nominal wages, industrial policy rarely aims at or succeeds in bringing this about. Thirdly, the aim may be not to preserve employment – whether in defensive or positive ways – but to reduce the labour force in the industry concerned in an orderly way, to minimize dislocations, hence bringing about structural relocations designed to fit the new demand patterns or technological developments.

---

2. This is a term invented by OECD. See OECD Secretariat (1979). A comprehensive general reference on adjustment, positive and defensive, is given by Wolf (1979).

Macroeconomic Demand Expansion and Real Wages

Let us now turn to macroeconomic policy. What is the mechanism by which a demand expansion increases employment? One view – which originated in Keynes's *General Theory* – is that it does so through a process which involves a fall in real wages. This approach assumes that the product market *is*, and stays, in equilibrium, but there is initially excess supply of labour at the ruling real wage, so that the labour market is *not* in equilibrium. Nominal wages tend to be either rigid or, if not completely rigid, not as flexible as prices. A demand expansion raises prices relative to nominal wages, hence real wages fall, and thus the increase in employment which results from the demand expansion is associated with a decline in real wages – at least relative to trend productivity. Alternatively, one could argue that it is the fall in real wages which has brought about the rise in employment, and this fall in real wages has, in turn, been brought about by the demand expansion. Because of a downward rigidity of nominal wages, the fall in real wages required for extra employment will not come about through nominal wages falling with prices given; prices have to rise. There are institutional rigidities, or money illusion, which allow real wages to fall through price rises, but not through nominal wages falling.

For a single economy the process is strengthened when a flexible exchange rate is allowed for. Demand expansion with given nominal wages in the first instance worsens the current account of the balance of payments and, provided offsetting capital inflows are not encouraged by a higher interest rate, this brings about depreciation of the exchange rate. In turn, the depreciation raises domestic prices of imports and exportables, and this tends to reduce real wages.

It has to be said that this is just one model of the macroeconomic employment-increasing mechanism. Prices do not always rise relative to wages when demand is expanded, and nevertheless output and employment increase because there was initially excess capacity, so that the product market was not initially in equilibrium. In other words, diminishing returns to increased employment do not set in immediately. Real wages may even rise if nominal wages respond more rapidly to extra demand for labour than prices do to extra product demand. Nevertheless, in time it is likely that a substantial employment expansion would have to be associated with declines in real wages, at least of some categories in the labour force and, of course, relative to trend increases in productivity.

Another qualification is that there may be a tendency to downward rigidity of *real* wages (rather than just nominal wages) through the indexation, formal or implicit, of nominal wages. In that case, an initial employment boost which required a fall in real wages may be quickly reversed as nominal wages catch up with prices. In fact, monetary policy then becomes ineffective other than in the very short run when lags in the wage-adjustment process allow some fall in real wages and there is an element of surprise in the monetary expansion. Essentially, demand expansion and exchange-rate depreciation are effective through what is almost a trick, a trick which brings about indirectly, through price rises, falls in real wages even though direct and obvious falls through reductions in nominal wages are not possible. The difficulty is that tricks do not work forever. The effectiveness of such policies in other than the very short term has tended to be reduced owing to the tendency for nominal wages to react rapidly to price increases.

Demand Expansion and Industrial Policy Compared

Let us now suppose that the *General Theory* process does apply and demand expansion does lead to a fall in real wages. How does this compare with industrial-policy measures designed to maintain employment? The obvious distinction is that macroeconomic policy affects the general level of real wages while industrial policy – in so far as it affects labour costs at all – acts only in particular industries. But the key difference is that industrial policy in its defensive aspect involves keeping the sectoral real labour costs constant and providing protection or subsidies to make the industries concerned privately, though not socially, economic. By contrast, demand expansion, like exchange-rate depreciation, lowers real wages and is thus – in this respect – a form of positive adjustment. In addition, as already mentioned, industrial policy may also involve positive adjustment measures, whether through improving efficiency in the industry concerned or facilitating a movement of labour out of the industry.

II The Relationships between the Two Types of Policies

We may distinguish macroeconomic instruments from industrial-policy instruments; and macroeconomic targets from industrial-policy targets. The policies meet when (a) there are mixed instruments, with macroeconomic and industrial-policy ingredients, when (b) a macroeconomic-policy instrument affects an industrial-policy target and when (c) an industrial-policy instrument affects a macroeconomic target. I shall now consider examples of each of these.

Industrial Policy Ingredients in Macroeconomic Policies

A distinction must first of all be made between industry-differentiated effects of a macroeconomic policy and an industry-discriminatory macroeconomic policy.

Suppose that credit restrictions lead to a general rise in interest rates and that there is no explicit discrimination between industries. But various industries will certainly be affected differently. Some firms will be closer to the margin than others, some will be more dependent on bank credit, and so on. Thus the effects will not be uniform, in the sense that the proportional fall in profits or in employment will not be uniform throughout the economy. Hence there are certainly effects which differentiate between firms and perhaps between industries. Such differential effects are inevitable. Another example can be given in the area of taxation. Suppose the general level of income tax is raised, while government expenditure is held constant. The lower disposable income of the public will lead to a proportionally greater decline in spending on income-elastic goods than on income-inelastic ones and thus have industry-differentiated effects. In all these cases there is no deliberate discrimination, but there are firm-differentiated or industry-differentiated effects of a macroeconomic-policy measure.

This must be contrasted with macroeconomic-policy measures which contain deliberate elements of industry discrimination. For example, when total credit is restricted, there may be a deliberate policy to focus the restrictions on particular industries or regions and to spare others. It is even possible that differential interest rates are charged to firms of equal credit-worthiness. In the field of taxation, indirect tax rates may be raised more on certain products than on others. In all cases macroeconomic policy is industry discriminatory and thus contains an industrial-policy element.

The distinction between a macroeconomic policy that has only industry-differentiated effects and one that is also industry discriminatory is not always easy to make. Most macroeconomic-policy changes are likely to involve some element of industry discrimination. To that extent it can be said that there is an industrial-policy ingredient in the macroeconomic policy, so that the instruments are mixed. The policy must then be assessed both in relation to the macroeconomic target and the industrial-policy target.

Macroeconomic Policy Affects Industrial Target

I shall now assume that macroeconomic policies are not obviously industry discriminatory even though they have industry-differentiated effects. The question is how a macroeconomic policy affects an industrial target. This depends, in turn, on how the industrial target is defined.

The industrial target may be to attain an optimal inter-industry allocation of resources subject to the correction of various externalities or market imperfections. Industrial policies, labour-market policies, environmental policies, etc. are concerned with the correction of these externalities. This is the way in which many economists would be inclined to give some role to industrial policies, although in most cases industrial policies – meaning usually subsidies or trade protection – would not be first-best methods of intervention.[3] If one then assumes that industrial policies are

---

3. See Johnson (1965) and Corden (1974).

set at 'externality-correcting' levels, there is no reason why a change in macroeconomic policy should alter the situation – that is, lead to some departure from the desired target or require a change in the industrial-policy setting.

Alternatively, an industrial-policy target with respect to a particular industry may be defined in quantitative terms. For example, the target may be to achieve a defined growth of the industry within a certain time period, to prevent any decline in employment or profits of the industry or, perhaps most commonly, to prevent an 'excessive' decline in employment or profits. In that case macroeconomic policy may affect the attainment of the target unless industrial policy is deliberately offsetting. The relationship between, on the one hand, a macroeconomic policy which reduces the general level of employment and profits in order to curb inflation and, on the other hand, an industrial policy which is designed to avoid any excessive declines in employment and profits in particular industries is sufficiently important to be discussed more fully below, when I come to the 'short-term cyclical issue'.

Macroeconomic policy may also affect an industrial target favourably. The industrial target may be to raise the productivity of particular industries. Productivity throughout industry may be affected favourably by a macroeconomic policy which is stable and predictable. Furthermore, a policy which gradually reduces the rate of inflation may favourably affect productivity, if only because inflation usually generates uncertainty. At the same time the short-term effects of an anti-inflationary policy normally reduce output and may also reduce labour productivity.

Industrial Policy Affects Macroeconomic Target

Having briefly considered the effect of macroeconomic policy on industrial targets, let me now turn to the effects of industrial policy on macroeconomic targets.

It seems convenient to think about short-term macroeconomic policy in terms of a negatively-sloped Phillips curve – a curve which indicates the short-run trade-off between unemployment and inflation. It is true that the curve shifts both exogenously and endogenously and hence, since 1973, can hardly be measured satisfactorily for most or all countries. But governments certainly act as if there were such curves and policy makers make implicit judgements about them. Policy makers act in the belief that aggregate demand expansion cannot go too far because it would stimulate inflation. At the same time, they do not regard it practicable to cease increasing the money supply altogether over a longer period – which eventually must put an end to inflation – because of the adverse effects on employment and output. They find it necessary to keep on expanding the money supply to some extent in spite of an avowed dislike of inflation. Thus their demand-management policies can, to some extent, be conceptualized as representing social or political choices along their Phillips curves. All this is compatible with the view that in the long run aggregate demand policy determines the rate of inflation, but has no effect on employment; that is, that the Phillips curve tends to be vertical.

This brief introduction is obviously an inadequate statement of the complexities of macroeconomic theory and policy. But it provides a basis for relating industrial policy to macroeconomic policy. In the short run various microeconomic policies – in particular labour-market policies but also some industrial policies – may shift the Phillips curve. When such a shift is brought about the choices open to the macroeconomic policy makers are altered. A given rate of inflation will be associated with a different rate of unemployment than before. The makers of industrial policy thus influence the decisions of the makers of macroeconomic policy. If we define the macroeconomic target as being the attainment of 'an optimal point' on a given Phillips curve then the characteristics of this optimal point will change. Alternatively, the target could be defined in terms of inflation or unemployment. It remains true that the desired target of the macroeconomic policy makers is likely to change.

An industrial policy may, for example, succeed in reducing unemployment in a particular depressed region or industry through either defensive or positive adjustment policies. In the short run at least this may reduce the overall level of unemployment for a given rate of inflation and thus modify the pressures on the monetary authorities to expand demand in order to bring down the rate of unemployment. Perhaps there is a maximum level of unemployment that is acceptable to the policy makers. It follows that industrial or labour-market policies that succeed in shifting the Phillips curve in a favourable direction will lead to an adjustment of the inflation target. It will be possible to aim for a lower rate of inflation.

All this has been concerned with the short run. If the Phillips curve is vertical in the long run it becomes possible for long-run analysis to separate macro and micro policies very neatly. Macroeconomic demand-management policies – primarily money-supply policy – determine the rate of inflation, while other policies – notably labour-market policies but also industrial policies – help to determine the rate on unemployment. But this neat dichotomy disappears once account is taken of the effects of macro-policies on real variables, notably the rate of investment.

Can anything be said in general about the way in which industrial policies can affect the short-run Phillips curve trade-off and the long-run rate of unemployment? I can think of only two generalizations, though the matter may repay further study. First, in the short run defensive industrial policy may succeed in shifting the Phillips curve in a favourable direction by reducing unemployment in industries with structural problems. This possibility has to be admitted even though defensive policies are likely to affect the economy's efficiency adversely in the long run. Secondly, in the long run industrial and labour-market policies that make labour more mobile and the economy more flexible – that is, *positive* adjustment policies, rather than defensive policies – will reduce the rate of unemployment. This will happen for two reasons. First, frictional unemployment, associated with inevitable and continuous structural changes, will be reduced. Seondly, the productivity of labour is likely to increase (that is, the marginal productivity curves are likely to shift upwards faster) if the economy becomes more efficient, and this will tend to reduce unemployment if there is some downward rigidity of real wages or in their rates of increase.

III The Short-term Cyclical Issue

How does a cyclical downturn affect actual or desirable industrial policies? This issue has been very relevant since 1974. It is well known that there has been a revivial of protectionism, partly induced by the adverse macroeconomic situation.[4] Even when actual protectionist measures have been moderate, pressures for increased protectionism have been severe. The basic question is whether there is a special role for industrial policies in mitigating the adverse effects of a cyclical downturn. While some people might immediately argue that industrial policy has no role – macroeconomic policy should deal with overall cyclical disturbances, with industrial policy confined to long-term considerations – one cannot dismiss the question so easily because of the differential industrial effects of downturns which are often substantial and generate strong pressures for intervention.

Complementary Policies

Some case can be made that industrial policy and macroeconomic policy can be complementary in dealing with a cyclical disturbance. I shall consider two cases here, first where the disturbance originates from the private sector or outside the country and, secondly, where it is itself the result of macroeconomic policy.

1) The adverse effects of a cyclical downturn originating in the domestic private sector or from overseas may be felt mainly sectionally; for example, in the investment goods or the export industries. If there is to be any offsetting intervention at all, it may then seem more appropriate to direct it narrowly. Yet macroeconomic policy, by its very nature, is overall. This is obviously so with a policy that is concerned with regulating a monetary aggregate or the general structure of interest rates. Once the principle of an intertemporal fine-tuning policy designed to moderate the effects of business cycles is accepted, there seems to be some case for fine tuning also in a given time period by having 'made-to-measure' intervention rather than using a very general device.

---

4. See International Monetary Fund (1978), Blackhurst, Marian and Tumlir (1978), and Corden (1984).

2) The downturn may be generated by public policy either through misjudgement or through a political cycle. We may imagine a situation where originally a boom was generated, by accident or by deliberate policy, perhaps to win an election.[5] Subsequently there is a danger that the boom becomes explosive, possibly through the generation of excessive expectations about the real economy, which create an excess demand situation, or through the generation of accelerating inflationary expectations. Hence a restraining monetary policy creates a short-term recession. It might have been in the power of macroeconomic policy to avoid this, but the downturn in the business cycle may be a deliberate act of policy. The intention may be to keep real demand within the limits of potential supply and to moderate wage and price increases. The more credible the policy, the quicker the responses of wages and prices, and the less unemployment, or the shorter the period of the downturn. Usually a squeeze is imposed on the private sector, and this squeeze will – it is hoped – encourage unions to moderate their wage demands and firms to resist excessive demands. But there is an almost inevitable period of pain unless the significance of the monetary restraint policy is clearly and widely understood and credibility attaches to the intention to maintain such restraint.

In this case an industrial policy which subsidizes or protects particular industries that are particularly severely affected by the squeeze might be regarded as moderating the adverse effects of macroeconomic policy without negating its effects. The aim is to spread the burden somewhat. But there is also a danger here.

Policies at Cross Purposes

When the monetary authorities impose a squeeze there will be inevitable demands for industrial policy to come to the rescue. This will be so particularly if the monetary authorities convey the impression that the pain generated was not intended, and that they can do nothing about it. At the micro-level the effects of monetary and overall fiscal policies are sometimes seen as 'acts of God' – quite beyond any power of direct remedy. But if subsidies or protection are used to help out industries in trouble – so allowing them to raise prices and give way to wage pressures – industrial policy will be at cross purposes with macroeconomic policy. Sometimes, as noted above, macroeconomic policy may be designed to impose a general squeeze, while industrial policy moderates the adverse effects in the most severe cases. But care has to be taken that industrial policy does not negate the effects in all marginal cases – since it is always in marginal cases that the necessary effects will be felt. As pointed out earlier, macroeconomic policies have inevitable industry-differentiated effects.

If differential effects were to be completely offset by industrial policies nothing would be left of the macroeconomic impact. In practice, of course,

---

5. See Nordhaus (1975, pp. 169–90).

complete offsetting is not possible, because the makers of industrial policy do not control the money supply and, essentially, can only benefit one industry at the expense of other industries. Only if money-supply growth were endogenous – depending on the fiscal deficit, which may in turn be boosted by industrial subsidies, direct and indirect – would this not be true.

The general conclusion is that industrial policy which is designed to moderate the short-term effects of the business cycle has to work in harmony with macroeconomic policy. While it may sometimes moderate the worst effects of macroeconomic policy it must not negate the latter's main thrust. It is always important to ask whether the supposed short-term task of industrial policy is not better performed by modifying macroeconomic policy directly.

Some Doubts about Short-term Industrial Policies

In theory there may be a finely constructed made-to-measure system of subsidies, direct and indirect, that would moderate or minimize the adverse effects of a business cycle, whether generated externally by the domestic private sector or through public policy. Technically it is perfectly possible to devise a policy that assists an industry temporarily, possibly with an automatically declining rate of protection built into the initial arrangements. But in practice it is possible to think of many examples where protection was originally imposed because of a short-term decline and where the protection stayed on even when the urgent need had disappeared. For example, in Western Europe (other than Britain) agricultural protectionism was given its first big boost in the agricultural depression of the 1870s, and the consequences are still with us.

Apart from the question as to whether the possibly favourable effects of short-term protection would not be outweighed by the long-term adverse effects when the protection is inevitably not temporary, there is also the more fundamental issue as to whether 'made-to-measure intervention' involving many detailed micro-decisions is desirable. The argument against such detailed intervention must rest on the mistrust of fine tuning which, in the field of macroeconomic policy, is one of the elements underlying monetarist prescriptions. It is a mistrust both of the ability of governments to make quick and fine judgements and, more important, of the motives of those that operate in the political process. Given sufficient information, there may exist in theory an 'optimal' system of intervention, but will the political process produce it? May it not produce a socially non-optimal set of interventions, responsive to pressure groups and imposing extra costs through its complexity?

In practice most governments cannot resist pressures for at least some industrial-policy intervention to moderate the adverse effects of cyclical downturns, and all such interventions need not be undesirable. The crucial need is to ensure the temporariness of these measures. It is also important for the macroeconomic policy makers to bear in mind that, if their policies are too severe, they will be countered in a piecemeal way by industrial policies which may not only negate part of the macroeconomic impact but also create distortions of their own.

IV Exchange-rate Policy and Trade Protection

There is clearly a relationship between macroeconomic policy and industrial policy on the foreign trade side. This has not been discussed so far in this essay but is very relevant to all the issues raised earlier. The nominal exchange rate is an instrument of macroeconomic policy, while tariffs, import quotas, export subsidies and taxes and voluntary export restraints can all be regarded as instruments of industrial policy. Yet an exchange-rate change can have 'industrial' effects. It therefore seems useful here to clarify the relationship between exchange-rate policy and the various micro or industrial-policy instruments.

Exchange-rate Protection

The first step is to distinguish a nominal from a real exchange-rate change and to introduce the concept of 'exchange-rate protection' of essay 17. If the exchange rate depreciates to the same extent as all costs and prices are rising (relative to costs and prices in other countries) there may be no real change at all. The nominal exchange rate is a monetary phenomenon, and it is possible that it is no more than that. A monetary authority may engineer a nominal devaluation designed to raise the domestic currency prices of exports and import-competing goods, and hence to benefit these industries. But if nominal wages quickly rise to compensate for the higher tradable-goods prices, no real effects – no rises in the absolute and relative profitability of tradable-goods industries – will remain. Monetary policy can influence the nominal exchange rate, and possibly can even maintain it at a fixed value, but it cannot necessarily affect the real exchange rate. The real exchange rate refers to the relative price of tradable and non-tradable goods. While its absolute value is difficult to measure because of the ambiguity of the distinction between tradable and non-tradable goods, changes in it are usually – and reasonably – measured or indicated by relating changes in the nominal exchange rate to changes in some index of domestic prices or costs, or possibly to the average nominal wage level. This is sometimes called an index of competitiveness.

A nominal devaluation will devalue the *real* exchange rate if there is some rigidity or sluggishness either in the prices of non-tradables or in nominal wages. The nominal devaluation will then raise the prices of tradables relative to wage costs and to labour-intensive non-tradables. Thus it protects tradables. This is 'exchange-rate protection'. It protects the whole group of tradables relative to non-tradables. It will tend to shift resources into tradables out of non-tradables and domestic demand in the opposite direction. If at the same time macroeconomic policy ensures a demand-supply balance for non-tradables – hence decreasing aggregate demand (absorption) in real terms appropriately – a balance-of-payments surplus (or a lesser deficit than before) will result. This refers to the balance of payments on current account since the concurrent fiscal and monetary policies can have varying effects on private capital inflow.

If the motive for the real devaluation was to protect tradables, then the current-account surplus will be only a by-product, leading to more accumulation of foreign-exchange reserves than the country's monetary authorities really wanted. Alternatively, if the motive for the real devaluation was to build up the foreign-exchange reserves – or to stop their decline – then the protection of tradables will be the by-product.

The main point to make is that a real exchange-rate change has effects on the relative and absolute profitability of different industries, a real devaluation favouring tradables relative to non-tradables, and a real appreciation the opposite. A nominal exchange-rate change can thus serve an industrial-policy purpose, provided it can be turned into a real exchange-rate change and that the incidental effects on the balance of payments are accepted.

This does not mean that it is an optimal form of industrial policy. As noted in essay 17, protection policy could be directed more precisely to the industries to be protected, avoiding the by-product effect of an undesired balance-of-payments surplus; and in any case it can be argued that defensive protection policy is unlikely to be optimal, positive adjustment policy being preferable. Nevertheless, it is not difficult to find examples of countries that have practised exchange-rate protection, if implicitly. They have intervened in the foreign-exchange market to prevent an appreciation of the exchange rate that might otherwise have taken place – or at least, they have 'leaned against the wind' – not because they really wanted to build up foreign-exchange reserves, but because they wanted to protect their tradable goods industries – usually mainly their export industries.

Protection Policy as Usually Understood: Policy Package

Let me now turn to the relationship between the usual instruments of protection policy – tariffs, quotas and so on – and exchange-rate policy. The usual instruments are normally regarded as affecting relative profitability and resource allocation *within* the tradable sector. Tariffs and quotas favour import-competing relative to export industries, or perhaps particular import-competing industries relative to export industries and to other less-protected import-competing industries. Export subsidies favour export industries. In the standard theory of protection which governs thinking in this field it is usually assumed that changes in these microeconomic or industrial-policy devices are automatically accompanied by changes in macroeconomic policy – including exchange-rate policy – that ensure 'internal balance' and 'external balance'; that is, in the latter case, an appropriate balance-of-payments target, which is constant for this purpose. The latter depends on many considerations, notably interest-rate policy, but the main point to make here is that normally one supposes that macroeconomic objectives are kept separate from protection objectives, the latter being defined as protection of one tradable, or group of tradables, relative to others. A change in protection as usually understood does not affect the balance of payments. Rather, it involves a policy package. At the same time as tariffs are reduced, for example, there would be a real depreciation designed to keep the relative price of tradables to non-tradables at whatever level is appropriate from a macroeconomic point of view, the principal consideration being the level of foreign-exchange reserves. It follows that exchange-rate protection is *not* included in the usual concept of protection.[6]

To summarize, it is convenient to think about protection in two stages. First, there is protection and anti-protection within the tradable sector as a whole. This is one of the main spheres of industrial policy. In some countries, such as Australia and Canada, tariffs and quotas are the principal instruments of industrial policy. To isolate the effect of this 'orthodox' form of protection one supposes that the current-account balance is kept constant by real exchange-rate adjustment when the levels of protectionist devices, such as tariffs, change. Secondly, there is protection of tradables as a whole relative to non-tradables (or vice versa) and this is brought about by changes in the real exchange rate for given levels of tariffs, quotas etc. This is exchange-rate protection, and it affects the current-account balance if, at the same time, fiscal policy maintains equilibrium in the market for non-tradables. If there is some degree of rigidity or sluggishness in nominal wages or prices of non-tradables, nominal exchange-rate policy can affect the real exchange rate and can thus have some 'industrial' effects.

Piecemeal Trade Policy may be at Cross Purposes with Macroeconomic Policy

It was stressed above that industrial policy might work at cross purposes with macroeconomic policy. A monetary squeeze may be designed to moderate price and wage increases. If industrial-policy intervention takes place so as to help out particular industries that are being squeezed, this intervention may defeat the original macroeconomic purpose.

The same type of story can be told with regard to the exchange-rate implications of such a squeeze. One effect of the monetary squeeze will be to improve the balance of payments at a given exchange rate, and hence (if the exchange rate is flexible) to lead to a nominal appreciation. Until the rate of increase of nominal wages moderates, there will be a real squeeze

---

6. See essay 19 for further development of this argument.

on tradable goods industries – in other words, there will be not just a nominal but also a real appreciation. This was an element in the British situation in 1980. If the wage-moderation effect comes with a lag, eventually the real appreciation may be reversed. In the meantime, however, industrial-policy intervention, in the form of tariffs, quotas, export subsidies and other forms of assistance, may be sought, essentially to offset the adverse effects of the real appreciation. This is a case where piecemeal trade policy may be acting at cross purposes with macroeconomic policy. If the short-term adverse effects on tradable industries are not desired it may be better to reverse the macroeconomic squeeze than to allow the growth or increase of micro-distortions within the tradable sector.

References

Blackhurst, R., Marian, N. and Tumlir, J. 1978: *Adjustment, trade and growth in developed and developing countries*. Studies in International Trade No. 6. Geneva: GATT Secretariat.

Corden, W. M. 1974: *Trade Policy and Economic Welfare*. Oxford: Oxford University Press.

―――― 1984: *The Revival of Protectionism*. Occasional Papers No. 14. New York: The Group of Thirty.

International Monetary Fund 1978: *The Rise in Protectionism*. Pamphlet Series No. 24. Washington, DC: International Monetary Fund.

Johnson, H. G. 1965: Optimal trade intervention in the presence of domestic distortions. In R. E. Caves *et al.*, *Trade, Growth and the Balance of Payments*. Amsterdam: North-Holland.

Lawrence, R. Z. 1984: *Can America Compete?* Washington, DC: The Brookings Institution.

Nordhaus, W. D. 1975: The political business cycle. *Review of Economic Studies*, 42, 169–90.

OECD Secretariat 1975: *The Aims and Instruments of Industrial Policy: A Comparative Study*. Paris: OECD Secretariat.

―――― 1978: *Report on Selected Industrial Policy Instruments*. Paris: OECD Secretariat.

―――― 1979: *The Case for Positive Adjustment Policies: Compendium of OECD Documents*. Paris: OECD Secretariat.

Pinder, J., Hosomi, T. and Diebold, W. 1979: *Industrial Policy and the International Economy*. New York, Tokyo and Paris: Trilateral Commission.

Wolf, M. 1979: *Adjustment Policies and Problems in Developed Countries*. World Bank Staff Working Paper No. 349. Washington, DC: World Bank.

19
Protection and the Real Exchange Rate*

This essay presents a geometric exposition of the relationship between protection and the real exchange rate in the 'orthodox' model, and then it compares this orthodox approach with exchange rate protection. Thus, it expounds in more detail themes already touched upon in the previous two essays. Finally, it outlines two other ways in which the exchange rate, protection and the current account may be related. Right through this essay the small country assumption (given terms of trade) will be maintained.

I The Orthodox Approach: Protection and the Exchange-rate Adjustment

Let us begin then with an exposition of the orthodox approach.[1] The macroeconomic assumptions underlying it will be discussed more fully later. Here they can be put briefly as follows. (1) Macroeconomic policy keeps income consistently equal to expenditure. (2) The nominal price of non-tradables is fixed. This means that a nominal exchange rate alteration leads to an equivalent real exchange rate change, where the real exchange rate refers to the relative price of tradables to non-tradables, the price of tradables for this purpose being the price *excluding* any tariff. It will be shown later that assumption (2) is not crucial: a real exchange rate change can also be brought about when the nominal exchange rate is fixed and the nominal price of non-tradables changes appropriately.

There are three goods in the model, exportables X, importables M and non-tradables N, and both domestic consumption and production of all three are positive. To start with, consumption exceeds production of M (the excess demand being imported), production exceeds consumption of X (the excess supply being exported), and consumption equals production

---

* This essay was specially written for this book.
1. The principal references on the 'orthodox approach' are Corden (1971, pp. 105–14) and Dornbusch (1974).

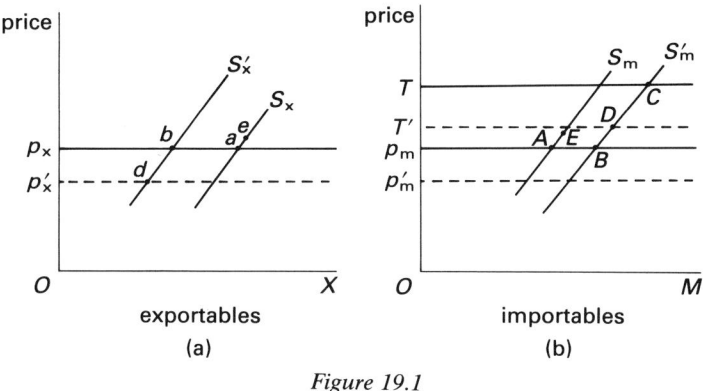

Figure 19.1

of N. Since income equals expenditure and there is zero excess demand for N, imports must be equal to exports. We describe this as current account balance, since exports and imports can refer to invisibles as well as visibles.

In figure 19.1(a) Op_x is the initial domestic price of X and in figure 19.1(b) Op_m is the initial domestic price of M, there being initially no tariff. Units of X and M are chosen so that $Op_m = Op_x$. Initial domestic production of X is $p_x a$ and of M is $p_m A$. A tariff is then imposed which raises the domestic tariff-inclusive price of M to OT, the tariff rate being $p_m T/Op_m$. This has two effects on resource allocation and hence production.

1) It shifts resources out of X into M, this being the direct protection effect. It represents a resource reallocation within the tradables sector. Hence output of X falls by ab (with the new output point at b) and output of M rises by AB. If there is a production cost of protection as a result of this reallocation, the value of output at world prices must fall, so that $AB < ab$.

2) With the exchange rate still constant, the tariff shifts resources out of N into M, the reason being that the price of N is constant while the tariff-inclusive price of M has risen. Hence output of M rises further, namely to C.

In addition to the production effects shown in the diagrams, the pattern of demand will have been affected. Demand will have shifted (or tried to shift) from M to both X and N. The net result is that, at this stage, there is excess demand for N, which is equal to a current account surplus. This is really an intermediate stage, excess demand for N being *ex-ante*, and equilibrium has yet to be re-established.[2]

Equilibrium is re-established with an appreciation of the exchange rate that lowers the domestic currency prices of X and M to Op'_x and Op'_m

---

2. We can assume that the excess demand is saved involuntarily, so that expenditure falls temporarily below income. Corden (1971, p. 105) assumes that expenditure is reduced by policy, for example a budget surplus.

respectively. The tariff-inclusive price of M falls to OT', where $p'_m T'/Op'_m = p_m T/Op_m$ (the tariff being *ad valorem*). Thus the exchange-rate adjustment does not affect the price of X relative to M, and therefore does not lead to resource reallocation or consumption shifts between them. But it does lower the prices of both M and X relative to the given price of N, and hence leads to reductions of output of both X and M. It is these output shifts towards N combined with demand shifts away from N, all resulting from the real appreciation, that eliminate the *ex-ante* excess demand for N. Hence, as a result of the appreciation, output of X falls from b to d and output of M falls from C to D. Comparing this final outcome with the initial situation, there has been a fall in the price of X from Op_x to Op'_x and a rise in the tariff-inclusive price of M from Op_m to OT'. Relative to the price of N, one of the other prices has thus fallen and the other risen, so that the market for N stays in equilibrium.

The rise in output of M and the fall in output of X have each two elements, first the *direct* protection effect, and then the *indirect* effect, which operates through the real exchange rate. In the case of M, the direct effect has raised output from A to B and the indirect effect has raised it from B to D. One can also distinguish two protection rates.

1) The ordinary rate is the tariff rate, namely $p_m T/Op_m$ (which is equal to $p'_m T'/Op'_m$); it indicates the proportional rise in the price of M relative to the price of X.
2) The *net* protective rate takes into account the exchange rate adjustment, and is $p_m T'/Op_m$; it is the rise in the price of M relative to the price of N. Both rates are relevant. It would be wrong to focus on just one or the other, as some models have done.[3]

Something must also be said about the four supply curves in the diagram. Each curve is drawn on the assumption that the cross elasticity of supply between X and M is zero (i.e. that there is no direct resource movement between X and M whatever the relative price ratio). This, of course, is not the assumption of the model. Hence a change in the relative price owing to the tariff will shift the two supply curves. The tariff shifts the supply curve of X to the left, from S_x to S'_x, and the supply curve of M to the right, from S_m to S'_m. The shifts in the supply curves thus represent the direct protection effect, and the movements along S'_x and S'_m the indirect effects.

---

3. The concept of the net protective rate was first introduced by Corden (1966). Corden (1971, pp. 105–9) takes into account both rates and both effects, but the explicitly partial-equilibrium analysis on pp. 110–14 suppresses the first (direct) effect in order to focus on the exchange-rate adjustment. It has to be stressed that finally N may not lose any resources, since it gains resources from X. Taking this into account, the protection of M is thus primarily, and possibly wholly, relative to X.

Exchange-rate Protection

Exchange-rate protection can be represented quite simply. A devaluation raises the prices of X and M uniformly, say to e (exportables) and E (importables). The movement is along the two initial supply curves S_x and S_m. There are two differences from ordinary protection, namely (a) exportables are positively protected, instead of being anti-protected, the protection being at the expense of non-tradables, and (b) if a new equilibrium is to result for more than a very short time (it is *not* suggested that it can be forever), macroeconomic policy must reduce expenditure below income so that a current-account surplus can be sustained. This has already been stressed in essay 17.

II The Dornbusch Diagram

The two diagrams show both price and output effects of the various measures and adjustments. Furthermore, they show how the partial equilibrium approach that has been used in the past is a special case. These are the advantages. The disadvantage is that they do not explicitly show demand effects, even though these are implicit in the exchange-rate adjustment, and a different, but more complicated pair of diagrams could be drawn, showing both demand and supply effects. In any case, an alternative diagram has been devised by Dornbusch (1974), which does not show output effects, but which neatly highlights the price effects, and brings out more clearly the situation in the non-tradables market.

Figure 19.2 is drawn in p_m, p_x space, initial free-trade equilibrium being at A. NN shows all the combinations of p_x and p_m that maintain equilibrium in the market for N when income is equal to expenditure. The initial domestic price ratio is represented by the ray OR, so that initial equilibrium is at A. A tariff raises the ratio facing domestic producers and consumers to OR'. At a constant real exchange rate, temporary equilibrium would move to C. Points to the right of NN represent excess demand for N and current account surplus. The real appreciation required to eliminate the surplus brings equilibrium from C to D. The proportional rise in the price of M resulting from the movement from A to D has been $p_m T'/Op_m$, which is the net protective rate, and is less than the tariff rate $p'_m T'/Op'_m$. Exchange-rate protection would be represented by a movement from A to, say, E.

III The Macroeconomic Assumptions: The Price of Non-tradables

The macroeconomic assumptions implied in both the orthodox story and the exchange-rate protection story are very special, though not unreasonable, at least as starting points for analysis.

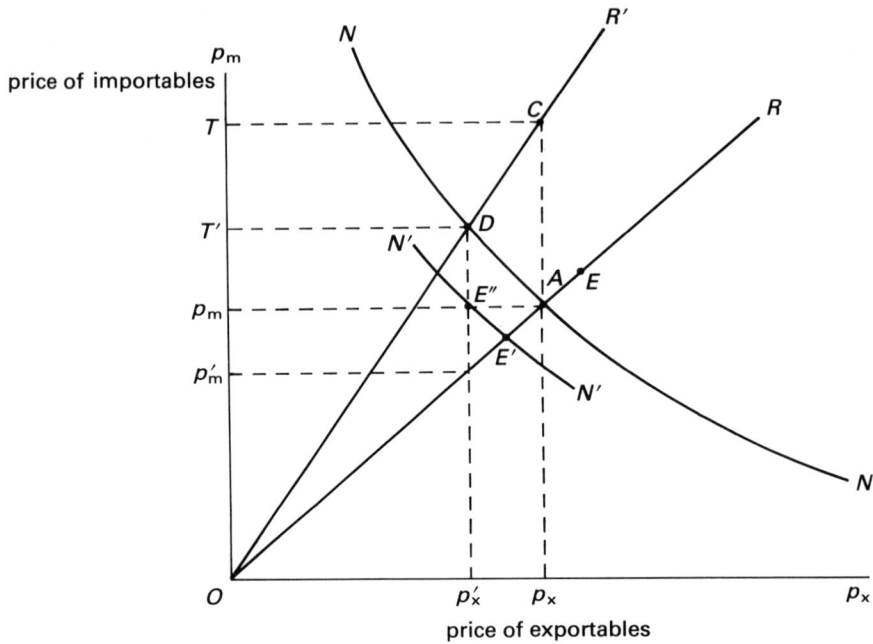

Figure 19.2

There is, first of all, the assumption that the nominal price of tradables is rigid. This is an extreme assumption that allows direct translation of a nominal exchange-rate change into a real exchange-rate change. As stressed in essay 17 with respect to exchange-rate protection, it is the real exchange rate that matters, and a real appreciation could be brought about by a rise in the price of N resulting from excess demand for N, combined with a fixed nominal exchange-rate policy. This point also needs stressing for the orthodox story.

Suppose that monetary policy keeps the nominal exchange rate fixed and a tariff is imposed. Before the price of N rises, excess demand for N results, as highlighted in our exposition. This might then lead to a rise in the price of N until equilibrium has been restored. With the price of N rising relative to the price of X, which is fixed, there has then been a real appreciation. The *real* story – that is the quantity changes and the *relative* price changes – will be identical to those presented above.

There are also various intermediate assumptions one might make. For example, one might hold the nominal wage constant and suppose that the price of non-tradables is market determined, subject to the fixed nominal wage, which is the principal element in the cost of production of non-tradables. There may then be *some* rise in the price of N, but not sufficient to restore equilibrium in the labour market. Another possibility is to

Protection and real exchange rate

assume sluggish adjustment of the price of N, so that it rises somewhat in response to excess demand for N, but a supplementary appreciation is still needed to restore market equilibrium.

IV The Macroeconomic Assumptions: The Current Account

Consider now the macroeconomic policy implications of the current account outcomes of our two stories. In the orthodox model, current account balance is maintained, except in a temporary intermediate stage, before the exchange rate appreciates, when there is a surplus. Let us now focus on the initial and final equilibria. We must start with national savings equal to national investment. The implication is that this equality is maintained in the final equilibrium.

One can think of various reasons why private savings or investment might alter. For example, the redistribution of income towards producers of importables might lead to more (or less) savings. The higher expected profitability of import-competing industries might lead to increased investment and the lower expected profitability of export industries to lower investment. On balance, investment might rise or fall. Consumers who lose from the tariff might save less if they expect the tariff to be temporary. On the other hand, some consumers will gain from the appreciation. Here we are assuming that the budget stays in balance, so that the extra tariff revenue is disbursed. But there may be endogenous budgetary effects, with all the extra revenue not being spent or compensated by tax reductions. A budget surplus might then lead to a current account surplus.

In addition, there may be a real balance effect. The average price level may rise or fall (since the price of exportables falls but the tariff-inclusive price of importables rises), and so the real money supply may fall, leading possibly to temporary savings to restore real balances, or may rise, leading possibly to dissaving. Incidentally it should be noted that the refunding of the tariff revenue, if it takes place, may reduce the price level if the refunding takes place through reduction of indirect taxes.

The implication of the model has been that monetary or fiscal policy, or both, offset the net effects of the various factors just discussed on the current account. If the 'natural' tendency, taking account of all these considerations, is for a current account surplus to emerge, monetary expansion can raise investment as required, or fiscal expansion (budget deficit) can reduce national savings. In this way monetary and fiscal policies maintain current-account balance ('external balance') while it is assumed that the exchange rate, or alternatively flexibility of the price of non-tradables, maintains equilibrium in the market for non-tradables ('internal balance'). But it should be noted that the same results would ensue – more traditionally – if monetary and fiscal policies were targeted on internal balance while the exchange rate was targeted on external balance.[4]

4. This was assumed in the discussion of protection and the exchange rate by Corden (1971, pp. 105–19).

Very little need be added on the macroeconomic assumptions behind the exchange-rate protection story, since they have already been discussed in essay 17. If the country starts in 'internal balance', so that employment is not to change, then a depreciation has to be associated with a reduction in real expenditure. This could be brought about with either fiscal or monetary contraction, or with some combination of both. Of course expenditure reduction might not be necessary if employment and income could increase owing to initial Keynesian unemployment: savings may then rise, with income rising more than expenditure.

V Alternative Links between Protection, the Exchange Rate and the Current Account

There are numerous other ways in which protection, the exchange rate and the current account can be related. Here two other cases will be noted.

Fixed Exchange Rate: Tariff Leads to Surplus

In a model with three potential variables, namely the tariff level T, the real exchange rate RE and the current account CA we have considered the orthodox model, where CA is held constant, with T and RE varying, and the exchange rate protection model, where T is held constant, with RE and CA varying. Logically there is a third case, where RE is constant, while T and CA vary. When specified in a particular way, this third case becomes very familiar.

The imposition of a tariff improves the current account, which is what many people would expect. It is described by the 'temporary' stage in the orthodox model: the tariff is imposed, the nominal exchange rate has not yet appreciated, and there is potential excess demand for non-tradables, reflected in temporary savings, yielding a current-account surplus. If this is to be more than temporary one can suppose that monetary contraction reduces investment, or a budget surplus raises public sector savings, so that equilibrium in the market for non-tradables is restored. It has to be stressed that if absorption had not been reduced below output a current account surplus could not have come about. It is the combination of expenditure reduction and 'switching' through the tariff that yields a current-account surplus combined with the maintenance of 'internal balance'.

Endogenous Protection in Response to Real Appreciation

The following case describes the situation and prospects of the United States, as seen in 1983 and 1984. A combination of fiscal expansion and monetary contraction causes the real interest rate to rise, capital to flow in, a current-account deficit to develop and the real exchange rate to appreciate. The real appreciation is part of the mechanism by which a current-account deficit is generated. In a sense it is a by-product of the particular macroeconomic policy mix.

We have here the mirror image of the exchange-rate protection story. Instead of the primary objective being to depreciate the real exchange rate so as to achieve favourable effects for tradable producers, the appropriate fiscal and monetary policies come first, the real exchange-rate appreciation being a by-product. In both cases one would expect policymakers to take 'by-products' into account, so that these cases come to much the same thing, exchange rate protection being defined by motive. If the United States budget deficit is moderated, for example, because of the adverse effect that the consequent real appreciation would have on tradables producers, then there is an exchange-rate-protection element in the fiscal policy.

Here we are concerned with an additional complication. Protectionist pressures tend to increase when a real exchange rate appreciates. The reason is that a rise in ordinary protection can moderate, or even prevent completely, the adverse effects of real appreciation on particular tradables producers. But it will do so by bringing about even greater real appreciation for a given current account surplus to be generated. Hence the effect on other tradable producers, for whom protection has not increased, will be even more adverse. Nevertheless, such protectionist pressures do take place and tend to have some success.[5]

This case can be simply represented in figure 19.2. Initially the real appreciation moves equilibrium from A to E', with both p_x and p_m falling. E' is on $N'N'$, which represents the current-account deficit that results from the macroeconomic policy. Then a tariff is imposed, yielding a domestic price ratio represented by a ray through E'' (not drawn). Thus the new equilibrium becomes E'', where this ray intersects $N'N'$. The net result is to lower p_x further, hence intensifying the adverse effect on export producers (because of the further real appreciation which a reduction in p_x represents), and restoring p_m to its original level. In this particular example the tariff fully offsets the adverse domestic price effects on import-competing producers of both the initial appreciation and the further appreciation that goes with the rise in the tariff. Of course import restrictions, voluntary export restraints imposed on suppliers, and so on, would have similar effects.

---

5. See Bergsten and Williamson (1983) and Corden (1984).

References

Bergsten, C. F. and Williamson, J. 1983: Exchange rates and trade policies. In William R. Cline (ed.), *Trade Policy in the 1980s*. Cambridge, Mass: Institute for International Economics and MIT Press.

Corden, W. M. 1966: The structure of a tariff system and the effective protective rate. *Journal of Political Economy*, 74, 221–37. (Essay 7, this volume.)

—— 1971: *The Theory of Protection*. Oxford: Oxford University Press.

—— 1984: *The Revival of Protectionism*. Occasional Papers No. 14. New York: The Group of Thirty.

Dornbusch R. 1974: Tariffs and non-traded goods. *Journal of International Economics*, 4, 177–85.

20
Real Wage Rigidity, Devaluation and Import Restrictions*

In 1975, in the depth of a recession, a group of Cambridge economists known as the Cambridge Economic Policy Group proposed that Britain should impose wide-ranging restrictions on imports of manufactured goods to accompany a demand expansion that would increase employment. The basic idea was that a demand expansion on its own would worsen the balance of payments, so that import restrictions were needed to divert the whole of the extra demand on to British goods. If expenditure rises then some imports, notably of raw materials, are bound to rise. To keep the total import bill stable, some other imports must fall, presumably of manufactures, where UK goods are substitutes for imports. They argued that total imports would not decline so that other countries would have no reason to retaliate. They were not concerned with the implications for Britain's membership of the European Community. The obvious alternative measure to accompany demand expansion would be devaluation of sterling. But they ruled this out on the grounds that it would raise import prices, hence lead to a rise in nominal wages to compensate, and so would increase inflation as well as finally negating the effects of the initial devaluation. A tendency to *real* wage rigidity was an essential element in their implicit model.[1]

---

* This essay was written especially for this book. It is based on work begun in 1975, and carried on intermittently since, in an effort to analyse rigorously the protectionist arguments that have come out of Cambridge.

,1. The Cambridge Economic Policy Group (CEPG) first put its case for wide-ranging import controls in Britain in 'Review of Britain's Economic Prospects 1975–78', *Economic Policy Review*, Cambridge, No. 1, February 1975. This attracted great attention. The CEPG repeated its arguments in *Economic Policy Review*, No. 2, March 1976, and in many other places in various forms, shifting at some stage from advocacy of quantitative import restrictions to advocacy of tariffs. Particularly relevant for the broader framework and for the search for their assumptions is the paper by Cripps and Godley (1976).

A critical analysis was produced by Corden, Little and Scott (1975), later reprinted in Scott *et al.* (1980). This latter volume also contained a detailed further analysis of the CEPG case by Maurice Scott. In addition the CEPG case and the general issues were analysed in detail by Brian Hindley, Hugh Corbet and others (Corbet *et al.*,

The purpose of this essay is to examine the issues involved in detail. When there is a tendency to real wage rigidity, is there a case for quantitative import restrictions or tariffs, in preference to devaluation? Furthermore, is it possible to bring about an increase in employment through demand expansion without real wages falling, whether or not the demand expansion is accompanied by measures to maintain a constant balance of payments? We begin with a simple three-good model designed to show the effects on real wages and output patterns of a demand expansion either on its own or accompanied by a 'switching policy', that is a policy that switches demand from extra imports on to home-produced goods.

I Assumptions

The model has three goods, namely imports M, which are wholly produced abroad, home-produced goods H, wholly produced and consumed at home, and exports X, produced at home and wholly sold abroad. Thus two goods are produced in the country concerned and two are consumed. To start with we make the small country assumption.

The model is a 'specific factors model': each of the two production sectors has a constant stock of immobile factors, and then there are one or more mobile factors that move between the two sectors in response to relative price changes. Formally we can assume that H and X are each produced by capital that is constant and immobile in the short run, and by labour N, which is mobile between the two sectors, subject in each case to a constant-returns-to-scale production function. Thus there are diminishing returns to labour in each sector.[2] In addition, we assume that none of the factors are mobile internationally. If capital were internationally mobile the stock of capital would respond to changes in profits, an important consideration to be introduced at the end of this essay.

To begin with we assume that the *nominal* wage is given. We then ask how the price-level would be affected by various policies. This tells us what will happen to *real* wages *if* nominal wages do stay constant. The next step is to point out the implications of a tendency to real wage rigidity – that is the implications of nominal wages adjusting so as to offset the effects of price level changes on the real wage.

II Effects of Demand Expansion on its Own

The three panels of figure 20.1 represent the three goods. The given foreign price of imports at the initial exchange rate is p_m, while the price of

---

1977). Some of the ideas of the present paper are foreshadowed in the present author's contribution to that publication. Many other critiques of the CEPG case have been published, one of the most thorough ones being by Collyns (1982).

2. The appendix analyses briefly some of the issues in the two-sector two-mobile-factors Stolper–Samuelson small-country model.

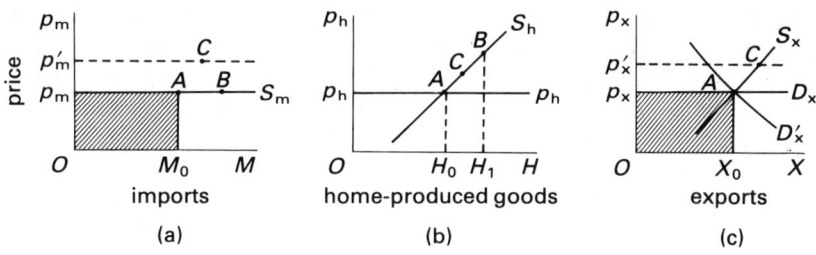

Figure 20.1

exports is p_x. The two supply curves of domestic production, S_h and S_x, are drawn on the assumption that the nominal wage is given and the supply of labour is unlimited. Points A represent the initial positions, the values of imports and exports being the two shaded areas. We shall assume that they are initially equal.

The initial position is also represented in figure 20.2. Here the vertical axis shows H and the horizontal axis both X and M, units of these two goods being so chosen that they have the same values at the given world prices. $T_0 T_0$ is the initial production transformation curve representing the initial level of employment, while the slope of RR indicates the initial price ratio between X and H (and hence M and H). With exports equal to imports at OJ, and demand and supply of H equal, the initial point of both production and consumption is A.

Suppose that there is a demand expansion while the exchange rate stays constant. We can suppose that there is a monetary or a fiscal expansion designed to increase employment, while the monetary effects of the resultant trade deficit are sterilized. Demand rises for both M and H, the points B being attained in figures 20.1(a) and 20.1(b). Output of H rises by $H_0 H_1$ so that employment rises in that industry. At this stage the export sector is unaffected. Since imports rise, there is a trade deficit. Since p_h has risen, the real wage must have fallen. In figure 20.2, demand has moved to B_d while output is at B_p, $B_p B_d$ being the trade deficit that has emerged at this stage. The new level of employment is represented by the transformation curve $T_1 T_1$.

III Introducing Devaluation

The next step is to associate the demand expansion with a devaluation such that the same increase in employment is attained while trade balance is restored. The new equilibria are represented by points C in all four diagrams. The devaluation raises the domestic currency prices of M and X uniformly to p'_m and p'_x respectively. With output of X higher, output of H

must be somewhat lower than it was before the devaluation. Comparing the final outcome at C with the initial situation at A, both imports and exports must be higher. In addition, output of H must be higher, that is C must be above A in figure 20.1(b). If it were not higher (output stayed at A) p_h would be constant, but with p_m having risen owing to the devaluation there would then be switching towards H. This would have to raise output of H, even if the demand expansion itself had not done so. While the absolute prices of M and H must rise, the *relative* price could go either way, so that net switching could be towards or away from H. The diagrams represent the case where p_m rises more (C being to the left of the demand expansion line OAZ in figure 20.2).

We have already seen that the demand expansion on its own, before the devaluation, must lower the real wage, at least as long as S_h is upward sloping, the reason being that extra demand for H raises its price. Next we consider the effect of the devaluation on its own. It raises the domestic currency price of M (from p_m to p_m') and lowers the price of H (as indicated by the move from B to C). Thus the real wage could rise or fall as a result of devaluation. Finally we note the effect on the real wage of the combination of demand expansion and devaluation, such that the increase in M equals that of X. Since both p_h and p_m rise, the real wage must fall.

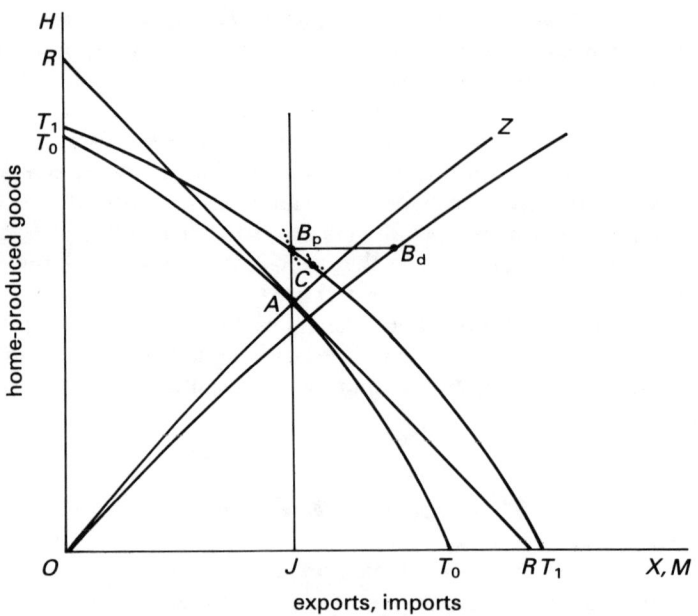

Figure 20.2

IV Import Restrictions and Tariffs

Let us now consider the two protectionist devices. We begin with quantitative import restrictions. Suppose that import quotas managed to keep imports at the initial level of OM_0 in figure 20.1(a). In addition, suppose that price control on imports prevents any rise in their domestic prices even when there are shortages. This, of course, is a very strong assumption. The import price facing domestic consumers thus stays at p_m. At the same time there is a demand expansion which raises demand for H. It also raises demand for M, but this cannot be satisfied and so is diverted towards H. Given a demand expansion designed to raise employment to the same level as in our earlier example, the point B will be attained in figure 20.1(b), while both production and consumption will be at B_p in figure 20.2. The real wage must fall because p_h has risen. Compared with a demand expansion that is associated with a devaluation the real wage could be higher or lower, since import quotas yield a higher p_h and lower p_m.

If import quotas are *not* associated with price control, the import prices facing domestic consumers would rise and quota profits would be made. To the extent that these profits are not taxed away and then refunded to wage earners, the real wage will then fall more.

Comparing import quotas with devaluation, an efficiency loss – the familiar cost of protection – is imposed. In figure 20.2 it is represented by the fact that while at C the marginal rate of transformation is equal to the marginal rate of substitution, at B_p (the import quota equilibrium) they diverge.[3] This loss is borne partly by wage-earners (in their capacity as consumers), so that the *effective* real wage decline resulting from the combination of quota and demand expansion is greater than indicated by the rise in p_h.

Similar issues arise in the case of a tariff. Let us suppose now that the demand expansion is associated with a tariff so as to keep imports at OM_0. If the tariff revenue were *not* redistributed to wage-earners, the real wage would clearly have to fall: the price of imports inclusive of the tariff would rise, and in addition p_h rises because output has moved to B in figure 20.1(b). The real wage fall could be greater or less than in the case of devaluation. If the revenue is fully redistributed to wage-earners, the decline in the disposable real wage will naturally be less. Nevertheless, it remains true that the real wage fall could be either greater or less than in the case of devaluation.

---

3. To highlight this point, social indifference curves have been drawn through B_p and tangent to C, with the curve at C being higher. Such curves can only be drawn for constant income distributions, or on the assumption that the overall demand pattern is not affected by any change in income distribution that results from a switch from devaluation to import restrictions, so that the curves should be regarded as purely illustrative.

V The Cambridge Case

One special case is of interest for later discussion. This will be called the Cambridge case. In this case the supply curve of H is assumed to be horizontal. The demand expansion on its own would then leave the real wage unchanged because p_h would not rise. On the other hand, a devaluation on its own would unambiguously lower the real wage. As in the general case it would lead to a rise in the domestic currency price of M, but this time there would be no fall in p_h. It follows that the two policies combined would lead to a lower real wage.

Turning now to quantitative import restrictions in the Cambridge case, if there is price control the measured real wage would stay unchanged, since both p_m and p_h would be unchanged. This is a crucial element in the Cambridge argument to be discussed below: the use of import restrictions instead of devaluation would avoid a fall in the real wage. But there are two qualifications, even given the Cambridge assumption. First, the *effective* real wage may fall with import restrictions because of the efficiency loss mentioned above. In effect, wage-earners are not able to buy the preferred set of goods at the given prices. Secondly, import quotas may *not* be associated with price control, surely a more realistic presumption. There will then be quota profits, and if these are not taxed away and refunded to wage-earners, the measured real wage will fall even in the Cambridge case and could fall more than with devaluation.

The same sort of analysis applies to the effects of a tariff. If the tariff revenue is not refunded, the real wage has to fall, since p_m will be higher even though p_h will stay constant. On the other hand, if there is full refunding of the tariff revenue to wage-earners the tariff will leave the measured real wage unchanged, and then a shift from devaluation to tariff would improve the measured real wage. But this leaves out of account the adverse effect of the efficiency loss, which is of the same kind for tariff as for quota.

The Cambridge case involves the extreme assumption that the S_h curve is horizontal. Alternatively it might be interpreted as implying that p_h is rigid over a range and that there is initially potential excess supply of H, with an upward-sloping S_h curve in figure 20.1(b) intersecting $p_h p_h$ to the right of the initial demand-determined equilibrium A. An increase in demand for H will then leave p_h unchanged just as it does when S_h is horizontal.

One might also consider the 'soft-Cambridge' case where p_h does rise when output of H rises, but not very much, with the result that a shift from devaluation to tariff (with revenue refunded) or to quota (with price control) would unambiguously raise the measured real wage. Demand expansion combined with devaluation would lower the real wage, while a tariff or quotas would also lower it, but unambiguously less. This 'soft-Cambridge' case will be referred to again below.

VI Terms of Trade Effects

Let us now introduce terms of trade effects. We suppose that the world price of imports continues to be given, but that the demand curve for exports is downward sloping, like D'_x in figure 20.1(c). Let us also assume that the conditions are fulfilled for a devaluation to improve the balance of trade, a sufficient condition being that the elasticity of demand for X is greater than unity. A given devaluation will now raise the value of exports by less than before; thus the devaluation has to be greater than if p_x in foreign currency terms were fixed. The rise in imports must thus be less and the rise in output of H greater.

Unambiguously, a demand expansion associated with devaluation will lower the real wage more, for a given rise in employment, than if there were no adverse terms of trade effect. In this simple model neither a tariff nor import restrictions affect exports and hence the terms of trade. By introducing terms of trade effects we thus obtain the result that a shift from devaluation to tariffs or to quotas is more likely to raise the real wage.

VII The Real Wage Target and the Determination of Employment

We shall now embody some of these results in a larger picture. In figure 20.3 the MM curve shows how the real wage has to fall as employment expands on the assumption that there are no quotas, that the tariff level is constant, possibly at zero, and that trade equilibrium is consistently maintained. A movement from A to C is brought about by demand

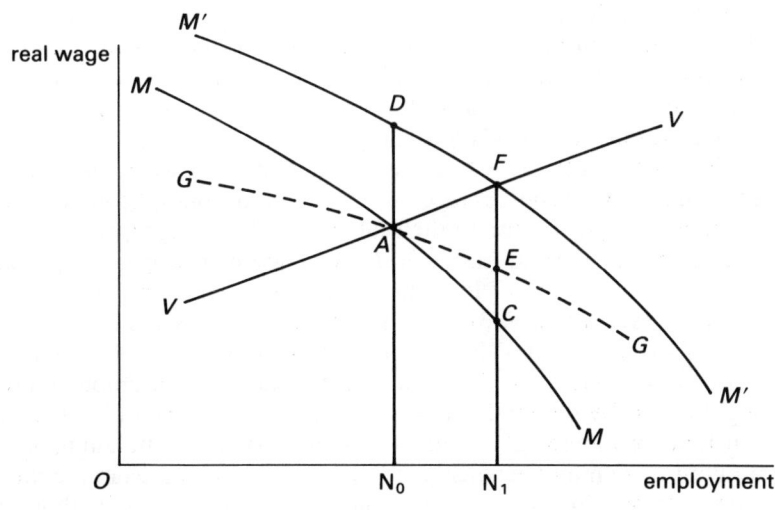

Figure 20.3

expansion associated with devaluation, the nominal wage being constant. Of course the nominal wage may rise, in which case the devaluation and the nominal demand expansion have to be greater. The curve can incorporate any terms of trade effects.

Next we draw the real wage target curve VV. We suppose that the trade unions' real wage target is not attained instantaneously, but that they adjust nominal wages after a lag so as to stay on that curve. It is possible for macroeconomic policy measures to bring the system temporarily away from this curve (because of wage contracts, the unions being surprised by prices rises, and so on); but any point off VV is a disequilibrium situation. Points below VV lead to nominal wage increases that are designed to raise the real wage, requiring accelerating demand expansion, and continued devaluation and inflation if a return to VV is to be prevented. If the unions are swift in their responses and not easily surprised, and perhaps have managed to obtain institutionalized indexation, they may be able to make any departures from VV quite temporary. The VV curve is upward sloping on the assumption that higher employment raises the real wage target. Alternatively the real wage target might be independent of employment, so that VV would be horizontal, though it might rise or fall for other reasons.

Let us now introduce protection as a policy variable. We assume that a possible policy instrument is a tariff, that no other fiscal policy variables are available, and that the tariff revenue is refunded to wage-earners. The VV curve is assumed to trace out *disposable* real wage targets. In addition we make the 'soft-Cambridge' assumptions that (a) demand expansion associated with a rise in the tariff would lower the effective disposable real wage somewhat, but that (b) this would be less than if devaluation were used, so that a switch from devaluation to tariff raises the real wage. It has to be stressed most strongly that 'soft-Cambridge' is just one possible assumption; our earlier discussion has certainly shown that a shift from devaluation to tariff does *not* have to raise the real wage. The aim here is to draw out the implications of 'soft-Cambridge'.

Given these assumptions, a tariff increase combined with appreciation designed to maintain trade balance, while demand policy keeps employment constant, will yield a rise in the real wage. This is represented by the movements from A to D and from C to F, both involving appreciation. The curve $M'M'$, on which both D and F lie, represents a constant level of tariff higher than the level along MM (which could be zero). Movements to the right along $M'M'$ involve devaluation, just as movements to the right along MM do. Such movements to the right – that is increases in employment – are brought about by demand expansion. Finally, the curve GG is drawn for a constant exchange rate, and movements to the right along it are brought about by demand expansion combined with increases in the tariff.

A given increase in employment from N_0, to N_1, brought about by demand expansion, can then have various real wage outcomes, depending on the associated switching policies. Three cases are represented in figure

Real wage rigidity, devaluation, import restrictions   319

20.3. If the tariff stays constant, possibly at zero, the real wage falls, and point C is attained. If the exchange rate stays constant and the tariff is increased (or imposed for the first time), the real wage still falls, but less so, and point E is attained. Finally, if the tariff is increased more, and the exchange rate is appreciated sufficiently, there will be a real-wage rise sufficient to attain the target real wage at the new level of employment, and so point F will be attained.

VIII The CEPG Model: No Resource Allocation Effects

The model implicit in the Cambridge Economic Policy Group (CEPG) proposals was even more special than what has been called the Cambridge case here. It certainly included the key assumption of a constant price of H. But it also assumed, at least implicitly, that S_x was vertical. This assumption meant that the whole resource allocation issue disappeared: extra employment could only be in H, and there could thus be no production cost of protection (other than through distortions *within* the H sector). In figure 20.2, C and B_p would coincide.

A subsidiary implication was that the nature of a possible terms of trade effect would be different. In our model the export price in foreign currency terms falls only because the quantity of exports put on the world market rises, the extent of the fall depending on the elasticity of demand. In the implicit CEPG model this quantity cannot rise; rather, a non-market clearing situation is envisaged where the foreign currency price falls just because there is a devaluation. In the extreme case the domestic currency price is rigid (so that export pricing is cost determined) and the foreign currency price falls to the extent of the devaluation. In the more general case there is *some* fall in the foreign currency price and some rise in the domestic price, the gains on the export side being thus split up between increased profits of exporters and reduced prices payable by foreign buyers.

Let us grant the highly implausible CEPG assumptions provisionally and analyse the implications. The principal reason why 'orthodox' economists oppose protection is because of the adverse resource allocation effects, that is, the cost of protection. But these effects disappear in this model. Different issues, which the CEPG proposals failed to highlight, then arise. The key assumption is that trade unions aim to maintain a constant post-tax real wage, and that – unless taxes on wage-earners fall – nominal wages will chase after prices, hence negating the initial effects of price rises. The central problem is then either to minimize the price rises resulting from the switching devices that need to be associated with demand expansion, or to generate revenue that can finance a sufficient reduction in taxes on wage-earners.

The desired result can be obtained in the following ways, or various mixes of them. (a) Impose quantitative import restrictions combined with rigid price control on imports. (b) Impose a tariff (presumably uniform), and use the revenue to finance a reduction of existing taxes on wage-earners – whether income tax or indirect taxes – so that their post-tax real wage does not fall. (c) Impose quantitative restrictions without price control and then tax away the rents received by quota holders, using the revenue as in the case of the tariff. (d) Devalue and tax exports so that the gains to foreign buyers as well as increases in profits of exporters are fully taxed away. Again, the tax revenue can then be used to reduce taxes on wage-earners. One special approach might be to subsidize imports, hence offsetting directly the price-raising effect of the devaluation. The export tax will, of course, avoid the terms of trade deterioration.

The choice between the various devices with the associated fiscal arrangements must depend on such matters as the practicality of price control, and the administrative costs of quotas, tariffs and export taxes. Leaving aside collection costs and administrative aspects, there is little to choose between tariffs and export taxes. As is well known from a theorem owed to Lerner, in a simple model with one import and one export, they are symmetrical.

IX The Cambridge Case for Protection Analysed

Let us now come closer to the real world and give up the key Cambridge assumptions of a horizontal S_h and a vertical S_x curve, returning to our original, more general, model. Is there then any case for protection in order to allow an employment-increasing demand expansion while maintaining trade balance and avoiding or minimizing a fall in real disposable real wages? We consider first the small country case, hence assuming that a devaluation does *not* deteriorate the terms of trade. We will ignore the idea of comprehensive price controls on imports (a proposal never made explicitly by the CEPG) and rule out as unrealistic the suggestion that prices of imports to consumers (or industrial purchasers) would not rise behind the shelter of quotas. Thus quotas must lead to quota rents. The following propositions can now be stated.

1) Demand expansion combined with quotas or tariffs must still lead to declines in post-tax real wage rates. Of course, with higher employment the wage bill may rise. The effect of the higher wage income on tax revenue is relevant, but this has nothing to do directly with the protection issue. Post-tax real wage rates must still fall, first because the price of H will rise, secondly because it is unlikely that the whole of the quota rents could be taxed away, and thirdly because it is also unlikely that the whole of the extra revenue from tariffs or the taxing of quota rents could be channelled back to wage-earners.

2) The disposable real wage could always be maintained if profits in the H and X sectors were taxed sufficiently, and the revenue were then used to subsidize wage-earners in some way, such as reducing income tax or

reducing general or particular indirect taxes. This conclusion applies as much to demand expansion associated with devaluation as to one associated with protection. In the case of quotas, the profits of quota holders should also, of course, be included in the tax net. The essential point is that profits would be taxed to subsidize wages.

3) In the CEPG argument the use of protection in place of devaluation is a way of taxing profits of exporters only in order to subsidize wages. Thus it is a discriminatory profits tax, which then gives rise to the cost of protection through inducing a misallocation of resources. There is no logical reason (in the absence of terms of trade effects) why there should be such discrimination. It reduces the rise in real national income resulting from the rise in employment, and if the real disposable effective wage rate is to be kept constant, the whole of this loss will be borne by profits. The implicit CEPG proposal to tax profits in order to subsidize wages would be achieved more efficiently by a non-discriminatory profits tax than by one that is focused wholly on exports.

4) Once we depart from the Cambridge case (ie. allow S_h to slope upwards), the use of protection (with revenue refunded) will also raise profits in the H sector: profits of exporters are taxed and of H-producers subsidized. Naturally this will induce a resource shift out of X into H, which is a misallocation of resources. The 'soft-Cambridge' assumption was that, on balance, in the shift from devaluation to protection real wages would still rise as a result of the combination of higher p_h and lower p_m, so that there would at least be some benefits from protection to set against the resource misallocation loss. But, of course, there is no general presumption that the 'soft-Cambridge' assumption is the realistic one. Protection, even though associated with the refunding of revenue, could finally lead to lower disposable real wage rates than devaluation (with the same demand expansion).

To sum up, the Cambridge proposals really come down to two separate issues. The first is: should profits be taxed in order to increase employment in the presence of wage rigidity? We shall come back to this issue below. Secondly, should the profits tax discriminate against exporting? In the absence of terms of trade effects, the answer to the second question is clearly negative, this being the argument against Cambridge protectionism.

X *The Terms of Trade Argument for Protection*

Let us now re-introduce terms of trade effects. A demand expansion associated with appropriate devaluation may well worsen the terms of trade. If one assumes a constant downward-sloping D_x curve and that exporters behave like perfect competitors, and if one considers only the national welfare (and also rules out retaliation), then there is a case for an optimal export tax – or a structure of export taxes when many products are being exported – on the basis of optimal tariff-export tax theory. In a model with only one export and one import, a tariff (associated with appropriate exchange rate adjustment) could have the same effect as an export tax. The optimal export tax would be positive even before demand had been expanded.

If the elasticity of the D_x curve were constant over the relevant range, the optimal tax rate would not change as a result of demand expansion, and so the rate of export tax should *not* increase. It would be optimal to allow some deterioration of the terms of trade. On the other hand it is plausible that the elasticity falls with movements down the curve, in which case the demand expansion would cause the optimal tax rate to rise. It would then be optimal to increase the tax rate (or a symmetrical tariff) with demand expansion, though not sufficiently to prevent any decline in the terms of trade.

All this has nothing to do with real wages. The concern is to maximize the real national product (wages and profits included) for any given level of employment.

Several qualifications must now be noted. These suggest that no Cambridge protectionist argument relevant for Britain can be built on the optimal export tax-tariff argument. Firstly, in the longer run Britain is hardly a large country in the world markets for her exports, so the elasticity is likely to be high, if not infinite, for many products. If protection were thought of solely as a short-run policy, proposals would have to include mechanisms for reducing or eliminating protection later. Secondly, in so far as elasticities are not infinite, they are likely to differ between export products; hence the optimal export tax structure would not be uniform, and no structure of tariffs or import quotas could obtain the same result. Hence an argument for an optimal export tax structure would not be an argument for import restrictions. Thirdly, many if not most manufactured products exported by Britain are differentiated products where individual firms face, at least in the short run, downward-sloping demand curves. The firms can be expected to exploit any perceived monopoly situation in world markets, and do not need taxes to restrict exports for such monopoly power to be exploited.

XI *Taxing Profits to Subsidize Employment*

Let us now examine further the implications of taxing profits to subsidize wages, so as to increase employment. Figure 20.4 brings out some of the issues. The *MM* curve should be interpreted now as the marginal private and social product of labour curve on the assumption that optimal export taxes to allow for terms of trade effects are being applied. Alternatively the curve could be regarded as applying to the small country case. We disregard existing taxes to finance public goods and redistribution and

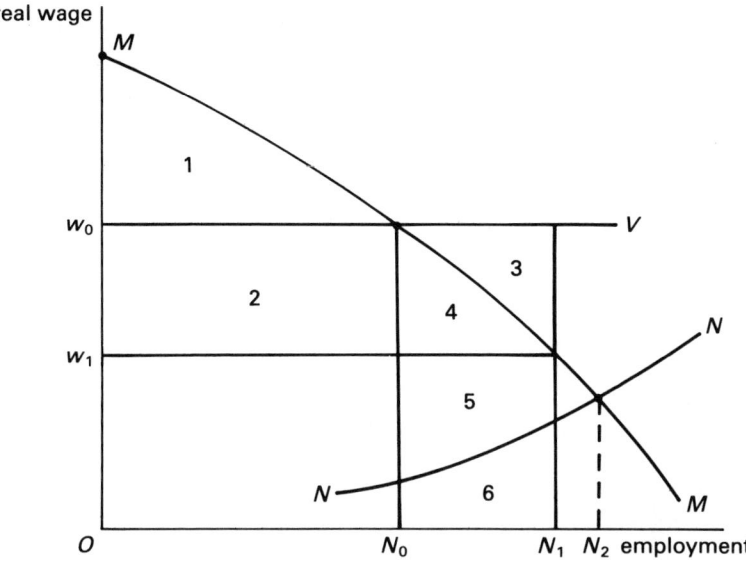

Figure 20.4

assume, as before, that demand expansion is associated with devaluation so as to maintain trade balance.[4]

We start with employment ON_0 and a real wage rate w_0. We assume that the VV curve of figure 20.3 is horizontal, so that unions simply require the post-tax real wage to stay constant at w_0 as employment rises. If employment is to increase to ON_1, the pre-tax real wage must fall to w_1, and the total cost of the wage subsidy must be the area $2 + 3 + 4$. Initially profits were the area 1, and the increase in employment causes pre-tax profits to rise by $2 + 4$. The whole of the subsidy is financed by taxes on profits, so that after-tax profits fall by the area 3. The wage bill paid to the newly employed is $3 + 4 + 5 + 6$. The labour supply curve NN indicates the social opportunity cost of labour, so that the social gain from the extra employ-

---

4. If we wished to introduce existing taxes we would have to assume that the existing tax rates are not so high that reductions would actually increase revenue. In other words, 'free lunch' opportunities have been exploited. There is a 'free lunch' if revenue raised from increasing employment or output resulting from tax cuts (which allow the pre-tax real wage to be lower and so stimulate employment) is greater than the revenue lost from taxes on existing output. Once 'free lunch' opportunities have been exploited and if fiscal balance is to be maintained, some tax rates somewhere must be increased if employment is to be raised through the mechanisms discussed here. See Corden (1981) for a detailed analysis of the 'free lunch'.

ment is 4 + 5, while area 6 represents the value of non-market output (including leisure) lost.

The significance of area 3 should be noted. It is the excess of the extra wage bill over the value of the extra market output produced by the newly employed. It is positive only because the *MM* curve slopes downwards. To go back to our original three-product model, if extra demand is directed to both *M* and *H*, and extra *M* can only be obtained with extra exports of *X*, then as long as one or both of the supply curves S_h and S_x slope upwards, extra employment must involve a fall in the real wage in the absence of subsidization. In other words, the downward slope of the *MM* curve in figure 20.4 results from upward-sloping supply curves in figures 20.1(b) and 20.1(c), at least in the small country model. In addition *MM* may slope downwards because of adverse terms of trade effects. In the presence of real wage rigidity this gives rise to the need not only for taxing away any gains in pre-tax profits resulting from the extra demand, but for taxing further so that post-tax profits finally fall.

If figure 20.4 told the whole story, the profits-tax financed subsidy to employment should be increased until employment ON_2 were reached. Of course, it does not tell the whole story.

Firstly, the process of taxing and subsidizing imposes distortion, collection and subsidy disbursement costs. The more distorting the structure of the taxes and subsidies, the greater the costs. If the taxation of capital to subsidize employment is brought about by means of protection, then the cost of protection will be included in these costs. These costs then shift the *MM* curve downwards. As a result the after-tax profits remaining for a given amount of subsidy, and hence for a given tax on profits, will fall, and in addition, the rate and amount of subsidy will have to increase. Furthermore, it will no longer be optimal to go as far as employment ON_2.

Secondly, it has been assumed most unrealistically that profits are purely rents on capital, and that the supply of capital is completely inelastic. The possibility of international capital mobility, or of domestic savings responding to profitability, has been ignored. Once there is some elasticity in the supply of capital, the simplicity of the whole approach disappears. This matter will not be pursued further here, since it gets us far away from the protection-versus-devaluation issue. Here it need only be noted that a reduction in the supply of capital will normally tend to shift the *MM* curve to the left and reduce employment for a given pre-tax real wage. A tax on profits which finances an employment subsidy may thus raise or lower employment. The more elastic is the supply of capital, the more likely it is that a tax on profits to subsidize wages would lower employment.

Appendix

Let us now consider briefly the matters discussed in this essay in the framework of the orthodox two-sector two-mobile-factors trade theory model. It is a model that seems rather less appropriate than the specific factors model used so far. There are two factors, capital and labour, both mobile between the two sectors, and the factor-intensities differ. The model is a small country one, so that the terms of trade are exogenously given.

It follows from Stolper and Samuelson (1941) that, as long as there is non-specialization and in the absence of a tariff, the real wage in terms of each product must be determined by the two production functions and by the externally-given product price ratio. An economic expansion which increased employment while trade balance was maintained would then *not* lower the real wage provided only that both goods continued to be produced. This, then, would be the outcome of a demand expansion with constant nominal wages and an associated devaluation to maintain external equilibrium. In the specific factors model, by contrast, the real wage would fall.

Continued employment expansion would eventually lead to specialization in the labour-intensive product, and from then on, further expansion *would* lower the real wage. Furthermore, it follows from Rybczynski (1955) that increased employment would lead to increased output of the labour-intensive product and *reduced* output of the capital-intensive product – that is there would be an ultra-biased expansion. This is to be contrasted with the outcome in the specific factors model, where output of both products would increase. If the employment expansion continued, eventually the economy would be specialized in the labour-intensive product, and if this is the importable, there will be a switch in the trade pattern – that is trade reversal – before specialization has been attained. In other words, as output of the 'importable' expands and of the 'exportable' contracts, while demand for both increases, the first product will begin to be exported and the latter to be imported.[5]

Let us now turn to the effects of a tariff on the assumption that the revenue is refunded. It was seen that in the specific factors model, a movement from devaluation to tariff (that is a rise in the tariff associated with appreciation) may raise or lower the real wage. In other words, with employment and external balance constant, protection could cause the real wage to go either way. This is also true in this model. As originally shown by Stolper and Samuelson (1941), as long as there is non-specialization, protection will raise the real wage if the importable is the labour-intensive product and lower it if the exportable is the labour-intensive product. The outcome does not depend on demand conditions.

Finally, let us look at the earlier discussion in section VII built around figure 20.3. In that diagram the *MM* curve shows how the real wage has to fall as employment is increased when the tariff level is constant, possibly at

5. On economic expansion with one factor growing and the other static in this kind of model, see essay 13, including the Further Notes attached, and Johnson (1962), and on the comparison of the outcome of such expansion in this model with that in the specific factors model, of the kind used in this essay, see Neary (1978).

zero, and there are no quotas. The *MM* curve would be downward sloping even when there are no terms of trade effects (small country model), while terms of trade effects would steepen its slope – that is bring about a greater real wage fall for any given rise in employment brought about by demand expansion combined with appropriate devaluation.

In the present Stolper–Samuelson small-country model, as we have seen, the real wage would stay constant with employment expansion as long as there is non-specialization. This means that the *MM* curve would be horizontal over a central stretch, but would have the normal slope at either end, in the specialization ranges. But when terms of trade effects are added the curve will be consistently downward sloping, just like the *MM* curve drawn in figure 20.3. A movement to the right (increased employment) will involve a fall in the real wage, a fall in the relative price of the labour-intensive product and, if the importable happens to be the labour-intensive product, actually an *improvement* in the terms of trade. As this is also the case in which a tariff will raise the real wage in this kind of model it is a relevant case.

References

Collyns, C. 1982: *Can Protection Cure Unemployment?* Thames Essay No. 31. London: Trade Policy Research Centre.

Corbet, H. *et al.* 1977: *On How to Cope with Britain's Trade Position*. Thames Essay No. 8. London: Trade Policy Research Centre.

Corden, W. M. 1981: Taxation, real wage rigidity and employment. *The Economic Journal*, 91, 309–30.

Corden, W. M., Little, I. M. D. and Scott, M. Fg. 1975: *Import Controls Versus Devaluation and Britain's Economic Prospects*. Guest Paper No. 2. London: Trade Policy Research Centre.

Cripps, F. and Godley, W. 1976: A formal analysis of the Cambridge economic policy group model. *Economica*, 43, 335–48.

Johnson, H. G. 1962: *Money, Trade and Economic Growth*. London: Allen & Unwin.

Neary, J. P. 1978: Short-run capital specificity and the pure theory of international trade. *The Economic Journal*, 88, 488–510.

Rybczynski, T. M. 1955: Factor endowment and relative commodity prices. *Economica*, 22, 336–41.

Scott, M. Fg. *et al.* 1980: *The Case Against General Import Restrictions*. Thames Essay No. 24. London: Trade Policy Research Centre.

Stolper, W. and Samuelson, P. A. 1941: Protection and real wages. *Review of Economic Studies*, 9, 58–73.

Author Index

Anderson, J. 125
Arndt, H. W. 53

Balassa, B. 97, 104, 106, 115, 125, 136, 150
Baldwin, R. E. 34, 199, 206, 216
Barber, C. L. 97
Bardhan, P. K. 199, 216, 222
Barker, T. 247
Barone, E. 19
Basevi, G. 56, 97, 99, 104, 106, 110, 133, 141, 150
Bergsten, C. F. 309
Berry, D. 37
Bertrand, T. J. 222
Bhagwati, J. N. 73, 86, 88, 89, 148
Black J. 202, 212–14, 216
Blackaby, F. 225
Blackhurst, R. 295
Blagburn, C. H. 4
Bond, M. E. 263
Brailowski, V. 247
Brander, J. A. 55
Brigden, J. B. 3, 37
Brown, M. 213, 215
Browne, G. W. B. 37
Bruno, M. 22, 148–9, 152, 238, 249
Buiter, W. H. 240, 249
Byatt, I. 263

Cairnes, J. E. 247
Carmody, A. H. 4
Cassing, J. H. 223, 249, 251
Caves, R. E. 158, 162, 211
Chipman, J. 163–4
Collyns, C. 312
Corbet, H. 311
Corlett, W. J. 38
Crawford, J. G. 4
Cripps, F. 311

Dasgupta, P. 226, 260
Deardorff, A. V. 222
Diebold, W. 288
Dixit, A. 55
Dornbusch, R. 302, 305
Dunning, J. H. 158

Eastwood, R. K. 249, 258, 260
Eide, E. 246
Ellman, M. 246
Enders, K. 246, 249
Ethier, W. 125, 145, 148
Evans, H. D. 19, 150

Findlay, R. x, 73, 196, 198, 221–3, 231
Finger, J. M. 125
Fischer, S. 222
Flemming, J. S. 263
Forsyth, P. J. 225, 246, 249, 263, 275
Frank, C. R. 73
Frenkel, J. A. 222

Gehrels, F. 165
Gelb, A. H. 262
Gifford, C. H. P. 4
Godley, W. 311
Graaff, J. de V. 33, 37
Gregory, R. G. 226, 246, 249, 275
Grossman, G. M. 55
Grubel, H. G. 125, 136, 278
Grubert, H. 196, 198, 231
Gruen, F. x, 69
Guha, A. 195
Guisinger, S. E. 125, 133

Haberler, G. 19
Hagen, E. 73
Hague, D. C. 38
Harberger, A. C. 73
Harris, J. R. 73, 86, 89, 90

Author Index

Harris, R. 21
Heal, G. 226, 260
Helliwell, J. F. 254
Helpman, E. 56, 167
Herberg, H. 246, 249
Hicks, J. R. xi, 187, 189, 192
Hindley, B. 311
Horst, T. O. 174
Hosomi, T. 288
Hufbauer, G. C. 158
Humphrey, D. B. 125, 147
Humphrey, D. D. 97

Ikema, M. 194

Johnson, A. S. 211
Johnson, H. G. ix, xi, 17, 19–21, 24, 26, 33, 39, 58, 60, 97, 99, 106, 158, 160, 171, 175, 178, 187, 189, 192–5, 198, 231, 233, 292, 325
Jones, R. W. xi, 125, 138, 143–5, 151, 163–5, 223, 227, 244, 283
Joseph, M. F. W. 30

Kaldor, N. 17, 33
Kay, J. A. 225, 246, 249, 263, 275
Kemp, M. C. 161, 163–5, 216
Khang, C. 148
Kierzkowski, H. 56
Kindleberger, C. P. 219–20
Krobl, A. 263
Krueger, A. O. 19, 22, 152

Lal, D. 74
Lawrence, R. Z. 288
Leamer, E. E. 21
Leith, J. C. 125, 149
Lewis, S. R. 133
Lewis, W. A. 178
Liepmann, H. 4
Linder, S. B. 206
Little, I. M. D. 37, 47, 311
Lloyd, P. J. 125, 136
Long, N. V. 228, 249
Loveday, A. 4

McDougall, G. D. A. 164
McKinnon, R. I. 246, 249, 275
McLean, I. 247, 252
Maddock, R. 247, 252
Magee, S. P. 19
Malinvaud, E. 238
Marian, W. 295
Markusen, J. 56
Marris, R. L. 4
Martin, J. P. 244
Massell, B. F. 149
Meade, J. E. 30, 37, 51, 97, 158, 161–2, 181, 187, 202, 213, 215

Melo, J. A. P. de 19
Melvin, J. 56
Metzler, L. A. 219
Mishan, E. J. 187, 190, 192
Moroney, J. R. 147
Mundell, R. A. 163, 167, 221–2

Nankani, G. 257
Naya, S. 125
Neary, J. P. xii, 222, 225, 231, 235, 237, 239, 244, 249, 258, 325
Nicholas, S. J. 246
Niehans, J. 263
Nordhaus, W. D. 296

Ohlin, B. 162, 166
Oniki, H. 199, 216, 222

Pigou, A. C. 162
Pinder, J. 288
Porter, M. G. 226
Posner, M. V. 158
Pursell, G. 56
Purvis, D. D. 240, 249

Ramaswami, V. K. 73, 89, 125, 138
Ray, A. 149
Razin, A. 272
Reddaway, W. B. 4
Richardson, J. D. 55
Robertson, D. 158
Robinson, E. A. G. 4
Rodrik, D. 44
Rybczynski, T. M. xi, 70, 82, 190, 195, 235, 251, 255, 325

Sachs, J. 238, 249
Salter, W. E. G. 226, 271
Samuelson, P. A. 4, 15, 120, 161, 325
Sanyal, K. K. 223
Schydlowsky, D. 125
Scitovsky, T. 17, 33
Scott, M. F. 311
Shann, E. W. 257
Smith, A. 222
Snape, R. H. 55–6, 226–7, 232, 246, 249, 251, 275
Soligo, R. 133
Solow, R. M. 202
Spencer, B. J. 55
Srinivasan, T. N. 86, 88, 89, 125, 138, 148
Stern, J. J. 133
Stern, R. M. 21
Stiglitz, J. E. 73, 74, 90, 222
Stoeckel, A. 249
Stolper, W. F. 4, 120, 161, 325
Suzuki, K. 72
Swan, T. W. 202–3

Tan, A. H. H. 125
Thirlwall, A. 257
Threlfell, R. L. 37
Till, L. 150
Todaro, M. P. 73, 86, 89, 90
Travis, W. P. 106, 125, 136
Tsukahara, T. 125
Tumlir, J. 150, 295
Turnovsky, S. J. 258, 261

Uzawa, H. 199, 216, 222

Venables, A. J. 249, 258
Vernon, J. 97, 114

Vernon, R. 158, 169
Viner, J. 4, 58, 60–1

Walker, F. V. 125
Warr, P. G. 249, 251
Wellisz, S. 73
Wijnbergen, S. van 249, 258
Wijnholds, J. A. H. de B. 278
Williamson, J. 278, 309
Wolf, M. 289
Wolkowitz, B. 147

Young, J. H. 109

Subject Index

Biases in economic growth
   resulting from booming sector   231
   resulting from technical
      progress   195–7
   when supply of factors
      increases   189–97, 214–16
Brigden Report   3–7, 9, 11, 16–17

Cambridge argument for
   protection   312–24
Capital movements,
   international   161–6, 221–2, 251–2, 261
Consumption cost of protection   9–10, 13–16
Cost reduction effect   60–3, 68
Customs union theory   58–68

De-industrialization   225–40
Domestic resource cost   22
Dutch disease   178, 225, 246–63

Economies of scale   20–1, 46–56, 58–68, 160–1
Effective protection
   calculation problems   115–16, 147–52
   formulae   98–100
   to labour or capital   109–12

Enclave approach   178–82
Endogenous protection   308–09
Exchange rate adjustment (associated with tariff change)   10–12, 65–6, 102–03, 300, 302–07
Exchange rate protection   263, 271–87, 298–300, 305, 308

Factor-weight effect on growth rate
   of opening-up trade   212–17
   of tariffs   218–19, 223
Foreign exchange constraint   257–8

General equilibrium
   cost of protection in   12–19, 24–6
   customs union analysis in   64–6
   effective production analysis
      in   101–04, 118–24, 135–9, 141–5
   model-building approach   150–1
Growth rate effects of opening trade
   capital accumulation effect   202–06
   impact effect   202
   relative price effect   207–11
   savings propensity effect   211–12

Harris–Todaro model   73–92

Import quotas   20, 41, 315–16, 320–1
Industrial policies   288–98
Intersectoral capital mobility
   booming sector model with   234–6, 243–5, 250
   Harris–Todaro model with   77–85
   real wage rigidity model with   324–6

Linkages   178–81
Lobbying   44

Macroeconomic policies   290–8
Made-to-measure tariffs   59, 61–3, 297
Manufacturing elasticity   76, 79–80
Monopoly and oligopoly   50–2, 54–6, 63–4, 171–3
Multinationals
   locations decisions of   166–9
   relationship to trade theory   157–76
Multiple exchange rates   108

Net effective protective rate   102–04, 144, 304–05
Non-traded inputs and effective
   protection   104–06, 149
North sea oil   263–5, 278–80

Subject Index

Paradox
  of effect of economic expansion on unemployment   82–3
  of effect of minimum wage on manufacturing output   81–2
  of effect of tariffs with biased substitution   138–9
  of effects of boom on resource movement   253–6, 250
  of optimal subsidy with monopoly   52–4
  of protection with terms of trade effects   34–6, 41–2
  of tariff that worsens terms of trade   69–72
Production cost of protection   9–10, 13–16, 315, 319

Real exchange rate   271–7, 302–09
Real wage rigidity   4, 257–8, 290, 311–25
Resource movement effect   228–37, 248–9, 276
Rybczynski theorem   70, 82–3, 190–2, 195, 325

Scale of effective rates   101–02, 141–5
Sectoral boom, effects of
  on current account   259–60
  on investment   260–2
  with international capital mobility   251–2
  with migration   252–4
  with one factor specific   228–34, 240–3, 247–50
  with terms of trade effects   254–5
  with two mobile factors   234–6, 243–5, 250
Specific factors model   74–7, 143–5, 227–35, 312
Spending effect   228, 231–7, 247–8, 275–6
Subsidies
  compared with tariffs   29–44, 89–90
  and effective protection   100–01
  with monopoly and scale economies   52–6
  transparency of   43–4
Substitution problem   112–15, 125–39, 145–8

Terms of trade, effects of tariff on   17–18, 32–7, 40–1, 71, 165–6, 170, 218–19, 321–2
Trade suppression effect   60–3
Transfer pricing   173–4
Two-stage production function   118, 136–7, 199–200, 223

Unemployment
  classical   256–8
  industrial and macroeconomic policy effects on   288–98
  Keynesian   258–9
  urban, with wage differential   73–92

Wage subsidies, effects on employment   85–9